Miracle Road

publication supported by a grant from

The Community Foundation for Greater New Haven

as part of the

URBAN HAVEN PROJECT

Miracle Road

The Story of Research Triangle Park

ALLEN PAUL + MACK PAUL

Duke University Press *Durham and London* 2026

Printed in the United States of America on acid-free paper ∞
Project Editor: Jessica Ryan
Designed by Courtney Leigh Richardson
Typeset in Garamond Premier Pro by Westchester Publishing Services

Library of Congress Cataloging-in-Publication Data
Names: Paul, Allen (M. Allen), [date] author | Paul, Mack, [date] author
Title: Miracle road : the story of Research Triangle Park / Allen Paul and Mack Paul.
Other titles: Story of Research Triangle Park
Description: Durham : Duke University Press, 2026. | Includes index.
Identifiers: LCCN 2026013457 (print)
LCCN 2026013458 (ebook)
ISBN 9781478034728 hardcover
ISBN 9781478063292 ebook
Subjects: LCSH: Research Triangle Park (N.C.)—History | Research parks—North Carolina—Research Triangle—History | Research—North Carolina—Research Triangle—History | Technology—Research—North Carolina—Research Triangle—History | Industries—North Carolina—Research Triangle—History | High technology industries—North Carolina—Research Triangle—History | Research Triangle (N.C.)—History
Classification: LCC F262.R27 P38 2026 (print)
LCC F262.R27 (ebook)
DDC 975.6/563—dc23/eng/20260409
LC record available at https://lccn.loc.gov/2026013457
LC ebook record available at https://lccn.loc.gov/2026013458

Cover art: Gertrude Elion and Dr. George Hitchings; the NC Biotech Center; the IBM 360; Bill Campbell, the first black child to integrate the Raleigh public school system; Boxyard at Research Triangle Park. Background art is a map of RTP.

In loving memory, Allen Paul (1939–2026)

CONTENTS

Preface xi

Acknowledgments xiii

Introduction 1

PART I.

A Park Is Born

(1952–1965)

1. Brain-Drain Blues 9

2. Early Collaborations 19

3. Inventing a New Place for a New Worker 25

4. New Institutions Define RTP 30

5. Bridges to Success 40

6. IBM and Validation at Last 55

PART II.

Big Dreams Come True

(1966–1999)

7. Creating a Viable Public School Option 65

8. The Birth of Life Science 73

9. A First Mover in Biotech 80

10. Case Studies of Two Superstar Scientists 89

11. Big Bets on Information Technology 97

12. Avatars of University Dynamism 108

13. The Emergence of a Start-Up Culture 118

14. RTP Shapes a Region 127

PART III.

Recalibration and Resurgence

(2000–2020)

15. Setbacks of the Early 2000s 141

16. Epiphany on a Plane 152

17. AgTech Adds Depth to the Biotech Revolution 160

18. Advanced Manufacturing Comes to the Triangle 169

19. Gene Therapy Gains Acceptance: The AskBio Story 176

20. Big Tech and Its Progeny 185

PART IV.

RTP into the Future

(2021–)

21. New Leaps in University Commercialization 197

22. Big Pharma Embraces North Carolina 205

23. RTP 3.0 214

24. "A Full Life in the Research Triangle" 220

25. Assessing RTP's Record 231

Appendix. The Highlight Reel 239

Notes 251

Index 275

PREFACE

Our lives began together in the long-gone Arbor Villa Apartments on Academy Street in downtown Cary, North Carolina. My parents took me there from Rex Hospital. At the time, my father reported for the Associated Press. Cary's population was about 3,500 souls while Raleigh's would not reach 100,000 for several more years. We entertained ourselves with trips to playgrounds and local swimming holes. My father honed his golf game on days when he was working the night shift.

Several years later, Dad jumped at the chance to work as a speechwriter in Washington, DC. At that time, Washington represented everything Raleigh was not: urban, sophisticated, and worldly. During a Cold War where the United States played global cop, Washington had a new, elevated role far beyond its roots as a swampy and sleepy government town. Conversations centered on jobs at the Pentagon or in the federal government and on Capitol Hill. My father felt at home there and constantly touted its merits—from "the *Post*" to "the 'Skins" (now the Washington Commanders) to Luigi's Pizza on 19th Street. He loved every bit of it. Other family members soon migrated from North Carolina to the DC area.

The fact we left North Carolina so long ago made an idea during my third year of law school all the more implausible. While reading case law involving Duke Power, a strange question came to me. What about the Research Triangle? I had interned for a law firm in New York City, where I went to law school, and interviewed for jobs in Los Angeles and San Francisco. I planned to move to the West Coast upon graduation along with my new bride from Los Angeles. In the early 1990s, "Big Law" handed out job offers like candy. The choices were plentiful. While nearly all my classmates sorted through offers from large firms in tier-one cities, I booked a flight to Raleigh-Durham International (RDU) Airport to explore.

I had only a hazy notion of Research Triangle Park (RTP). Based on the press, it was a place where scientists spun out technologies in a sunny, affordable, and congenial environment. At the time, pundits heralded a New Economy based on technology and innovation. Future growth would center on regions able to harness research for commercial applications. As a future service provider, I perceived RTP as a relatively safe long-term bet, offering a chance to be part of a place still unformed but promising. After returning from my visit to Raleigh, I had a vision while standing in line at a grungy market on Broadway. I could see Julie and me driving from a house along tree-lined streets to a beautifully stocked grocer with ample parking. The absence of decay and cantankerous customers was overpowering.

So, within a few months, we pivoted from our future life on the West Coast to the upper floor of a historic apartment near downtown Raleigh. It was not an easy adjustment. The lack of a vibrant and eclectic urban environment periodically stirred thoughts of a move. But each new friend, each new job, and the daily routines of a growing family deepened our ties to the area. The fundamental belief that RTP offered limitless opportunity persisted and proved true. Years later, my parents joined us, migrating back from DC. The area then had ample cultural offerings and superior health care. Not long after, my sister and her family joined us in Raleigh. And then my wife's parents arrived from Los Angeles. All of them saw the area as livable, attractive, and relatively affordable. Now our daughter, who benefited from an excellent education in the Wake County magnet system, has returned with her husband from Ireland. Both have found good job opportunities.

So goes the innumerable, individual decisions that bring roughly eighty new residents to the Triangle region each day. A seismic shift occurred in migration patterns after World War II. Moves now reflect the conscientious desire for place rather than the decision of a corporate boss. Workers seek areas with a dense labor market that allows them to move from employer to employer within the area when an opportunity arises.

That so many now choose the Triangle is all the more remarkable when reflecting on RTP's genesis as a strategy to reverse the migration of homegrown talent who left out of economic necessity. The record of decline experienced by industrial cities in the Midwest and Northeast simply demonstrates the immutable forces that ultimately determine the fate of any place. Whether a child born in Cary or Durham will choose to settle there is an intensely personal choice but, in the aggregate determines the fate of the region and affects us all.

—MACK PAUL

ACKNOWLEDGMENTS

Miracle Road: The Story of Research Triangle Park is first and foremost a collaboration. Many people from many professions have expended much time, talent, and energy to get it produced. None are more noteworthy than the nearly 170 people who were interviewed, each of them a primary source and each a leading citizen of the Park.

Indeed, their contributions are what set this book apart because embedded within what they told the authors is the powerful story of human struggles to create something new, something that changed the trajectory of an entire state. Although there are several excellent books on the Research Triangle Park, none of them has the same foundation as *Miracle Road.*

At the outset, a special word of thanks must go to Doug Edgeton, president/CEO of the North Carolina Biotechnology Center. The project would never have gotten off the ground without Doug's leadership. He and his talented staff took the lead in organizing the project and in securing the resources to underwrite it. To that end, we owe a debt of gratitude to all who provided gifts and sponsorships for the completion, publishing, and distribution of this work.

On Doug's initiative, a high-profile Oversight Committee was formed to evaluate book chapters as they were written and to open doors to high-level sources. Most recently, the Oversight Committee has been chaired by John Atkins, founder of O'Brien Atkins Associates, a leading RTP architectural firm. Other members of the Oversight Committee include Christy Shaffer, partner at Hatteras Venture Partners; Luther Hodges Jr., former US deputy secretary of Commerce and son of Gov. Luther H. Hodges; Fred Hutchison, founder of Hutch Law; Robb Teer, president, Teer Associates; and Smedes York, chairman, York Properties and former chairman of the Research Triangle Foundation. The Oversight Committee played an indispensable role in all aspects of the RTP book project.

Sadly, the Oversight Committee lost two towering figures during its tenure: Its first chairman, Bob Ingram, died in March 2023. Bob was chairman/CEO of GSK, a leading international biopharmaceutical firm. He collaborated closely with Jim Goodmon, chairman of Capitol Broadcasting Company, in the revitalization of downtown Durham. We also lost Charles Hamner on July 4, 2025. Charles was widely considered to be the father of North Carolina's dynamic biotech industry, having recruited top scientists to the state during its formative period. He also worked tirelessly to recruit European firms to North Carolina alongside Gov. Jim Hunt, who died on December 18, 2025.

Enthusiastic kudos also should go to Preston Linn, who spent his career in RTP and who offered many useful ideas for the book. He participated in all Oversight Committee meetings. We are also indebted to Tom White of the Centennial Campus at North Carolina State University and former president of the Durham Chamber of Commerce. Tom was the first person—that the authors know of—to propose that a book be written on the history, importance, and future of Research Triangle Park. Tom continued to offer suggestions and make connections through completion of the book.

In a sense, the glue that held all the moving parts together over the life of the project was our project associate, Hannah Nicholson. She had just earned her master's degree in library science from UNC-Chapel Hill and quickly earned her spurs by assessing RTP holdings at every archive in the Triangle. She found transcripts, photos, and an assortment of other valuable items that are included in the book. Best of all, with the help of the authors and the Oversight Committee, she assembled a section describing the greatest technological accomplishments in RTP history. In doing so, Hannah proved herself to be an adept writer. Along with Hannah, we could not have completed this project without the hours of review, editing, feedback, and support of Mary Paul, a sister and aunt to the authors as well as an astute critic.

Last, but certainly not least, we want to thank Duke University Press, which dedicated so many talented people to this project. They included the insightful editorial input of Alejandra Mejia and Jessica Ryan; the enthusiastic marketing support of Cameron Ludwick and Laura Sell (along with the team at Pellien Public Relations); and the design talents of Courtney Richardson. We're deeply grateful to Dean Smith, director of the Press, who attended oversight committee meetings, provided encouragement, and kept us on track.

In light of the significant lifetime accomplishments of Bob Ingram and Charles Hamner, their service to RTP, and assistance in development of this book, we hereby dedicate this book in their honor.

INTRODUCTION

Not since 1903 and the Wright brothers' gift of wings had such a consequential takeoff occurred in North Carolina. On January 9, 1959, more than six hundred leaders from business, government, and academia packed into a ballroom at the Sir Walter Hotel in Raleigh. Governor Luther Hartwell Hodges addressed the audience. He announced successful efforts to raise private funding to establish a Research Triangle Park (RTP) in an area just south of Durham. (The esteemed Sir Walter Hotel—named for an audacious gambler whose Lost Colony simply disappeared in 1590—was often called the "Third House" of state government because so many legislators stayed there during sessions of the General Assembly.) Like the Lost Colony, RTP could have disappeared into the forest. But in just one generation, RTP proved to be a successful gamble, a new innovation center that sent stunning discoveries all around the world. In so doing, it became one of the largest and most successful research parks in the world.

And its unique character—best expressed in the Tar Heel state motto, "esse quam videri," or "to be rather than to seem"—had much to do with that achievement. The "being" part was an inspired and resolute commitment by a leadership elite representing state government, business, and three tier-one research universities that made RTP an icon of a new approach to economic development, imbued with the core character traits of inventiveness and collaboration.

The scene at the Sir Walter feeds a myth about RTP—the notion that it sprang effortlessly from a forest of "possums and pines" to become an economic juggernaut that transformed a region and gained worldwide recognition for its discoveries. But great struggles to unify its founding constituencies had preceded Hodges's January 1959 announcement. And challenges in countless forms continue to this day.

This book tells the RTP story in four parts. Part I traces RTP's rocky origins from first stirrings to life through IBM's momentous decision in 1965 to site a major facility in the Park, thus validating the still embryonic endeavor to the Fortune 500 and countless others. Part II follows the trajectory of RTP to its establishment as a global brand by the end of the twentieth century. Part III examines RTP since 2000, as it faced seismic changes in the tech sector and threats to its suburban design. It shows how RTP and its constituencies recalibrated to promote new industries and bring life-saving treatments to market. Part IV considers how RTP and its key partners in government, universities, and business prepare for new challenges and opportunities in the post-pandemic era.

Other major tech centers, such as Silicon Valley south of San Francisco and Route 128 in Boston, took off during World War II through massive federal spending on military research at universities such as MIT and Stanford, and those institutions were eager to embrace commercialization. Lenders and investors on the East and West Coasts backed risky tech ventures in those locales, producing a virtuous cycle of innovation that continues to this day. Unlike Silicon Valley and Route 128, RTP reflected a state's deliberate economic strategy.

Certainly, RTP benefited from a confluence of trends. Federal spending on research exploded after World War II. Further, locations in the South such as Huntsville, Alabama, and RTP would benefit from expansive new federal facilities sited in locations, in part, to solve political calculations in Washington, DC. A slow, steady stream of migrants began moving to the Sun Belt from other parts of the United States. The invention of air conditioning helped those transplants acclimate to the hot summers.

RTP's viability and success, however, rested on the persistent engagement and support from its partners in state and local government, businesses, and universities. State government provided leadership for the initiative, recruited companies to the state, provided needed infrastructure, and created a world-renowned workforce training program. The business community formed new institutions to acquire the land for RTP, encouraged start-up companies, and financed them. The cooperation between state government and business has continued to evolve policies to provide an attractive environment for the growth and relocation of technology companies.

While business and government readily embraced the vision for RTP, university leaders held back due to concerns that research for commercial purposes posed risks to academic integrity. To ensure the enthusiastic participation of university partners, leaders collaborated to establish the Research Triangle Institute (RTI) as a contract research entity under university control. RTI would go on to become one of the largest and most successful research institutes in the world and provide an effective buffer between universities and commercial interests. As RTP grew in the 1970s and 1980s, academics began to see the advantages of consulting, research grants, and other benefits from their proximity to RTI and RTP more generally. Eventually, some academics became entrepreneurs, and a few created the largest homegrown companies in the region, employing thousands. Government support for university research labs produced Nobel Prize laureates and placed RTP on the map as a leader in life sciences. Legal changes have only made it easier for academics to take products, based on innovative research, to the marketplace.

Another important collaboration centered on RTP's relationship with surrounding communities. Its designers understood that RTP could not operate as an island. RTP's success depended on a region that put a high priority on housing for workers, transportation networks to access jobs, and quality schools for children. Workers demanded a high level of amenities in the form of outdoor recreation and cultural life to complement the area's mild climate and bucolic setting. Since its inception, RTP has led efforts to engage local governments, business, and civic leaders to think about the region and prepare for the growth generated by RTP by investing in infrastructure. Despite such planning efforts, regional growth has far exceeded that contemplated by the architects of RTP. That growth has presented some of the greatest challenges to the success of RTP. The Research Triangle area now comprises multiple counties, encompassing Alamance and Chatham Counties to the west, Granville and Franklin Counties to the north, and Johnston, Lee, and Harnett Counties to the east and south.

One other critical collaboration related to racial integration and desegregation. RTP's existence rests in large part on the ability of its leaders to navigate the South's legacy of slavery, war, and Jim Crow. When RTP got started, the South had a bad brand in the eyes of the nation. The 1954 decision in *Brown v. Board of Education of Topeka* would test whether the South could overcome its reputation and adapt to integration. Companies would not risk investments in facilities, equipment, and payrolls in areas with unstable race relations. North Carolina's ability to navigate desegregation became an advantage for RTP compared to neighboring Southern states. Black leaders counseled patience despite anger from decades of oppression. White leaders tamped down violence arising from fear over social change. By managing to mitigate unrest and build on the state's commitment to public education, leaders found a common ground that allowed RTP to flourish.

RTP now finds itself in the midst of wrenching changes. Urban planners criticize the validity of RTP's autocentric, office-park model. Do tech workers want to continue working in such an environment? A global pandemic and growing demand for "work from home" have raised even more fundamental questions about the future of the office generally. Artificial intelligence threatens to displace broad categories of work, particularly in the field of technology. What sort of demand for physical space will exist in ten years? In response, RTP leaders are revising the rules that govern the development of its property. In the future, owners will have greater flexibility to create vibrant "innovation centers" to attract workers. Beyond these regulatory reforms, RTP's success will depend on the continued engagement of government, universities, and businesses to adapt strategies to a rapidly changing world.

Given the period of its creation, growth, and recalibration, RTP reflects the story of many tech regions in the United States. Following World War II, these job centers transformed the American economy and society. In *The New Geography of Jobs*, economist Enrico Moretti argues that while comprising about one-third of the economy, the tech sector has an inordinate impact on prosperity in the United States for two reasons. First, it produces goods and services that compete in national and global markets. That fierce competition creates most of the nation's productivity gains—the fundamental basis for raising living standards. Second, tech jobs have a profound effect on the local nontech economy. Moretti calculates that one tech job generates five nontech jobs (in both professional and nonprofessional services) compared to only 1.6 jobs with traditional manufacturing jobs. Why? High-wage tech workers have more disposable income; tech companies require more sophisticated business services; and such companies tend to locate near other tech companies to poach talent.[1] This explains the tremendous growth in jobs and wages in places like Austin, Texas; Boston; Seattle; Silicon Valley; and RTP. Nearly every state wants to attract tech companies as a path to economic growth.

Therefore, the story of RTP offers a case study of how one place pursued an inspired growth strategy. In 1952, when this story begins, North Carolina had certain advantages: three major research universities, a favorable business climate, and a relatively pristine environment. But it had even greater disadvantages: limited infrastructure, anemic industrial capacity, and a poorly educated workforce. That RTP helped to transform the region and state offers certain invaluable lessons—first among them that while timing has played a major role in its success, nothing mattered more than a cultivated commitment to improve on RTP's model to succeed.

Before embarking on this story, a word about definitions. The book uses "RTP" or "the Park" when referring to the geographic footprint owned by the Research Triangle Foundation. This area comprises several thousand acres in

Durham County at its inception and now stretches over more than seven thousand acres in both Durham and Wake Counties. However, this book defines RTP as more than the footprint of the Park. It defines RTP as a set of strategies. In economic development parlance, RTP is known as a "big push," a concerted effort over years to stimulate the growth of a new industrial sector. These strategies require a range of governmental policies: the cooperation of area universities; the creation of new institutions, including nonprofits; collaborations with existing institutions; and, finally, the collaboration and ingenuity of a myriad of local governments required to provide a support structure for the technology companies located in RTP and eventually outside its borders. This book looks at RTP through the lens of a strategy both to show the scope of its ambition and to consider its successes and failures. The chapters ahead will reveal this economic strategy through the stories of those who demonstrated the vision, leadership, innovation, patience, courage, and collaboration required to implement it over many decades.

PART I

A Park Is Born

(1952–1965)

1

Brain-Drain Blues

Picture jubilant graduates in 1954 tossing mortarboards in the air with all the exuberance youth can muster. Then imagine, a few days later, a heartrending scene at Seaboard Station in Raleigh where one of those jubilant graduates turns to wave goodbye to his parents as he boards the train. Their eyes are filled with doubt and worry. They know their son *must* climb aboard—even with his new college degree, they know he can't find a fitting job in North Carolina.

A narrator's grave warning follows this emotional scene from a 1954 film produced by the North Carolina Department of Conservation and Development (today's Commerce Department): "Every year, many of our best educated young people leave, finding a place to make a living elsewhere. Of all our state's resources, these young people are most valuable, and we're still losing them by the thousands."[1] The conductor's "All aboard!" shout seems to warn of worse to come.

In the early 1950s, North Carolina's farm and industrial sectors were in steep decline. When World War II began, 40 percent of the state's population lived on the land. Only Texas had more farms, but North Carolina's were the nation's smallest at sixty-seven acres each. Government price supports had encouraged all-out farm production during the war, but after the conflict ended, subsidies dropped sharply while the cost of mechanization soared: Tractors replaced mules, herbicides ended chopping weeds by hand, and mechanical harvesters changed the rural scene even more. The mass exodus after the war left no doubt that such a large farm population could not be sustained.

Meanwhile, the mainstays of North Carolina's industrial sector—furniture, textiles, and tobacco—were going backward too; ultimately, their share of state economic output would shrink from 40 percent to 10 percent. By 1950, the state's stagnant, low-wage economy had saddled its citizens with a per capita income of $1,077, among the nation's lowest. It looked like North Carolina could not escape the nickname associated with it in the nineteenth century: the Rip Van Winkle State.

But the handwringing and dour statistics detected none of the rumblings that would transform the North Carolina economy from dirt poor to technology powerhouse in just a few decades. A Southern-born Harvard professor named V. O. Key recognized the state's capacity for change, citing its "progressive plutocracy" as a leadership asset that set the Old North State apart. Key was one of the most influential political scientists of his day. In his seminal 1949 book, *Southern Politics in State and Nation*, he dismissed the myth of the solid South, pointing to a "progressive plutocracy" that led North Carolina and differentiated it from its sister Southern states.[2] According to Key, the people of North Carolina understood the state's "lowly position.... But if there was a sentiment of inferiority, it was belligerent. And if the elegant accomplishments of others gave it an awareness of mediocrity, the mediocrity was militant."[3] In other words, North Carolina's leaders had no great legacy or historical precedents to lean on. Success would need to come from within through grit and determination. As such, North Carolina demonstrated a willingness to take risks in order to elevate the state, including founding the first public university, the first state-supported symphony orchestra, and the first public art museum and making substantial investments in its public school system.

Who were these "progressive plutocrats"? Mostly, they comprised business leaders in banking and industries such as textiles, furniture, and tobacco, centered in Charlotte, Greensboro, Winston-Salem, and Durham. According to Key, this "aristocracy... has had a tremendous stake in state policy and has not been remiss in protecting and advancing what it visualizes as its interests." As a result, state government showed "a sympathetic respect for the problems of corporate capital and of large employers."[4] The progressive plutocrats saw the state's dismal postwar economic slide as a call to action—a response to an existential threat that could not be ignored. True to form, they demanded more for the state as reflected in an ad taken by North Carolina's economic development department in the late 1940s. It read: "North Carolina wants no one to seek location within its borders expecting long hours of work at low pay. Sweatshop operators are unwelcome."[5] This sentiment had the dual benefit of protecting North Carolina businesses from outside, low-cost competition and improving the living conditions of its people.

The Mother of Invention

Given the mindset of business leaders and the context that existed in North Carolina in the 1950s, it should not be surprising that one person's vision would influence so many. The idea to build a research park to attract corporate investments to the state almost certainly originated with Romeo Holland Guest, a Greensboro businessman with a flair for promotion and a mindset of "damn the torpedoes, full speed ahead." Guest clearly was part of the progressive plutocracy. His father ran C. M. Guest & Sons (then located in South Carolina), which built manufacturing facilities, distribution centers, office buildings, and retail outlets throughout the southeastern and mid-Atlantic states.

Guest's family sent him to prep school at prestigious Phillips Exeter Academy in Exeter, New Hampshire, where he graduated in 1925. Four years later, he earned a degree in architectural engineering from Massachusetts Institute of Technology (MIT). He had barely joined the family business when the stock market crashed on October 28, 1929. In the Depression that followed, Guest helped keep the family business afloat by driving from one textile mill to the next, soliciting repair business.[6] Often, he got a foot in the door by showing photos of successful projects undertaken by the firm. That led, mostly, to small contracts to repair housing in mill employee villages. After Guest established a relationship, he had the inside track to more lucrative contracts to repair the plant itself. Guest never forgot the hard-earned lessons of face-to-face marketing in order to build trust. In 1937, he and his brother moved the firm to Greensboro, North Carolina, to be near family and larger markets.

The postwar years were lean ones. As North and South Carolina's industrial companies struggled, the need for industrial buildings and worker housing declined. That forced Guest to take a new approach. A few years before his arrival at MIT, the university established a Division of Industrial Cooperation and Research, forging ties with companies such as Eastman Kodak, DuPont, and General Electric. As a student at MIT, Guest had seen firsthand the clustering of technology-related firms on Research Row along the Charles River near Harvard and MIT. He also saw ongoing corporate research in basement labs at MIT and had been impressed by the research there for what would become the Polaroid camera.[7]

Years later, in a visit to Merck's Rahway, New Jersey, headquarters, he learned that the company would build a facility in the Shenandoah Valley and that the site's proximity to the University of Virginia had been a major factor in Merck's siting decision. Moreover, the experience in World War II, including advancements in computing, medicine, and nuclear weapons, and federal investments in places like Huntsville, Alabama, showed Guest the potential for new industries based on research and development.[8] Guest also noted the vast support for university research: "I have heard that MIT has research grants from the government through industry amounting to approximately $5 million per year and that California institutions are similarly loaded."[9] These experiences and observations sparked an idea. Instead of chasing contracts over a wider and wider geographic area, he would lay the groundwork for a new industry situated in one place. This would allow him to build labs and other research facilities for companies locating in the state.

Guest started to look at the map of North Carolina to identify the ideal location for a research park. He observed the close proximity of the state's "Big Three" universities—Duke University, North Carolina State University (a college at the time), and the University of North Carolina at Chapel Hill (UNC)—and saw how each represented the end point of a triangle. He first dubbed that area the "Golden Triangle of Research." In a journal entry on October 10, 1953, he streamlined it to "Research Triangle."[10] To leverage the output of these universities, it would be necessary to situate new industrial facilities somewhere in the middle—a logical decision but one that would have major implications for the region's development for decades to come.

One of the first officials Guest approached was regarded by many as the state's number one salesman—State Treasurer Brandon Hodges (no relation to Governor Luther H. Hodges). Elected in 1948, Hodges had made industry hunting a top priority. He helped recruit the P. Lorillard and Westinghouse plants to Greensboro and Raleigh, respectively. At his own expense, Guest traveled with Hodges in the early 1950s to recruit industry, and they frequently discussed strategy.[11] During this time, Guest pitched his concept to Hodges of a "Research Triangle" in the vicinity of the University of North Carolina, Duke University, and NC State University. Intrigued with the idea, Hodges began to open doors for Guest with industry hunters at the Department of Conservation and Development. While Hodges was reelected state treasurer in 1952, he resigned to become legal counsel to Champion Paper the next year. So impressed with Guest's concept, Hodges continued to work alongside Guest on the research park concept until his death several years later.

Although small in stature, Guest was energetic, articulate, gregarious, and something of a high-stakes gambler. On his own initiative, Guest developed a glossy print piece entitled "Conditioned for Research." He had a natural aptitude for marketing. Positioning the South for a new type of industry, the brochure emphasized the area's "refined atmosphere," scientific capabilities, "cultural living," and "acres and acres of beautiful rolling land" available for research facilities.[12] Surely, Guest's play on the words "conditioned for research" and "atmosphere" served as a subtle reminder to readers of the recent arrival of air-conditioning—an invention that would revolutionize the South and trigger a Sun Belt migration that continues to this day. C. M. Guest & Sons paid to run the brochure as an advertisement in *Fortune*, *Business Week*, *Scientific American*, and the *New York Times.*[13] Also, Guest paid Lewis Kleid Company for a list of top research directors in the United States and sent out thousands of copies of his brochure to them.[14] Guest made sure to list the point of contact for feedback as C. M. Guest & Sons.

During these early years, it appeared that Guest would face few headwinds in selling his idea. His target audience—North Carolina's political, educational, and business elite—appeared to be a blank slate he could write on. After receiving enthusiastic support within state government, Hodges began setting up meetings at the major universities. At a meeting in the fall of 1954, Guest pitched the concept to NC State College's chancellor Carey Bostian; the dean of the engineering school, Harold Lampe; the dean of the school of textiles, Malcolm Campbell; and the director of the Textile Research Center, William Newell. All four responded enthusiastically.

The meeting prompted Newell to tell Guest "there would have to be a park" to house incoming R&D facilities.[15] Newell's comment helped reshape Guest's concept from a general R&D recruitment strategy to a physical location to be situated somewhere between the area universities. A few days later, Newell sent Guest a map of the state with lines connecting the three universities and a shaded square in the middle. Newell attached a note asking, "Romeo, How's this?"[16] Such feedback only encouraged Guest to continue with his approach. There was no road map for the park concept, but leaders within government, business, and universities demonstrated a willingness to participate in the endeavor. It would take years to define their respective roles. In contrast to these constituencies, Guest had a very clear idea of his company's role as construction contractor for any business looking to locate in the park. Since Guest was volunteering his time and resources, other collaborators did not question his interests and the business aspects of the future park's development.

As Guest worked contacts in government and the area universities, he gained an important ally. In March 1954, Hodges organized a lunch to introduce Guest to Robert M. Hanes, president of Wachovia Bank in Winston-Salem and chair of the Industry Committee of the State Board of Conservation and Development. Guest used the opportunity to pitch Hanes on leading an "industrial committee" to bring life to the Research Triangle idea. Hanes deferred.[17] However, later that year, Hanes offered to introduce Guest to the state's top political leader, Governor William B. Umstead. In the end, Umstead's health prevented it.[18] In addition to these health issues, nothing in Umstead's political agenda and past actions suggested he would embrace Guest's concept. After teaching in public school and seeing combat in World War I, Umstead went to law school at Trinity College (now Duke University) and then worked as a prosecutor in Durham. He immersed himself in Democratic Party politics, rising to state chair and serving in Congress. Upon the death of Senator Josiah Bailey in 1946, Governor Robert Cherry appointed Umstead to fill the open seat. Umstead openly criticized President Truman's support for civil rights and as early as 1945 urged Truman not to run for reelection. In 1948, Umstead lost his senate seat while Truman shocked the nation with a comeback victory. Undaunted, Umstead ran for governor in 1952, calling for higher teacher pay, mandatory vehicle inspections, driver's education in high school, and a referendum to legalize liquor sales. His agenda had little connection to the industrial priorities of North Carolina's progressive plutocrats. We'll never know whether Umstead would have seen the potential benefits of a research park because he suffered a heart attack shortly after his inauguration and never fully recovered.

As Guest and other promoters of the research park waited for Umstead's health to improve, they received the sudden news on November 7, 1954, that the governor had died that morning. Now Guest would face a dramatically different landscape to pursue his vision—one that would be profoundly shaped by the person ascending to the governorship: Luther Hartwell Hodges. Hodges would provide the leadership and the commitment to collaboration often missing as Guest and others tried to get the park concept off the ground. Hodges also would bend the endeavor toward the broad interests of the state rather than the financial interests of a few.

The Right Person at the Right Time

Despite his humble beginnings, Luther Hodges embodied the ideals and mindset of the progressive plutocrats. He was born in 1898 in a four-room cabin in Cascade, Virginia—the next to youngest of nine children and one of only two to go to college. His father was a tenant farmer, but soon after Luther was born, the price of tobacco fell to five cents a pound, so his parents, James and Lovicia Hodges, moved the family to Spray, North Carolina, just across the state line and thirty-seven miles north of Greensboro. James went to work in a Spray textile mill.

Young Luther's ambition soon came to the fore. Spray had no public school, so he attended a mill school in a rundown tenement house. It had, as Luther later wrote with customary restraint, "a supervising principal who left much to be desired."[19] By sixth grade, Luther was pleading with his father to let him work in the mill, claiming he'd learn more there than in school.[20] One of his odd jobs had been peddling newspapers on passing Norfolk and Southern railway trains.

His father finally relented, and at age twelve Luther became an office boy at Fieldcrest Mills, maker of blankets, bedspreads, towels, and sheets. He got paid five cents an hour for a ten-hour day, six days a week. While there, Marshall Field & Company, a department store giant in Chicago, bought the mill.[21] Little did the ambitious lad, then in his early teens, realize that one day he would become general manager of the Marshall Field textile division.

In 1915, after two and a half years in high school, Luther left for Chapel Hill and the University of North Carolina with $62 in his pocket, saved from a summer's work at the mill. He worked his way through college in four years, waiting tables in the dining hall and earning a degree in economics. Despite the heavy demands of work and study, he got elected president of the student council and was president of his senior class. He also was a member of the Dialectic and Philanthropic Club and played on the varsity basketball team.[22] But it was campus politics that taught him the basic skills he would apply much later with great energy and confidence.

After college, he got influenza at the height of the Spanish flu pandemic. He served as an army officer and had just been shipped to an out-of-state base when he got sick. The army discharged him due to his illness. He received an offer as secretary of a Young Men's Christian Association (YMCA) but turned the job down to take a position as secretary to the general manager of the mill back home. Despite significantly less pay, the job offered other advantages. Years later, he would write, "I felt that in the long run I could do better in industry, and I also wanted to prove to certain skeptics that I could make good in my hometown."[23]

Hodges's natural leadership qualities propelled him on a rapid rise within the Marshall Field & Company textile division. Soon after Luther went to work in the mill, he was promoted to personnel manager. At about this same time, he met Martha Blakeney, a recent graduate of the Woman's College of the

University of North Carolina (UNC Greensboro today), who was teaching in a local school. They married in 1924 and would have two daughters and a son.

Meanwhile more promotions followed. At age forty, Luther lived in New York City and ran all twenty-nine Marshall Field & Company textile mills in the United States and abroad. As a big-city executive, he became active in worthy causes—the American Legion, Boy Scouts, YMCA, and many charities. He had long been active in Rotary International and ardently practiced its credo of "Service Above Self." At this time, Hodges took on several high-profile Rotary assignments—most importantly, Rotary's consultant and advisor at the founding of the United Nations in San Francisco in 1945 and at the UN Security Council in New York. In 1948, he chaired the Rotary International Convention in Rio de Janeiro. Years later, Hodges would become the president of Rotary worldwide.

On April 1, 1950, Hodges retired after thirty-two years with Marshall Field & Company, pledging in a statement to devote the rest of his life to public service. He had no particular position in mind. That same year, he joined an elite cadre of Americans called to administer the Marshall Plan to rebuild Western Europe after the ravages of World War II. The invitation came from someone he'd known and respected for many years—Robert M. Hanes, president and CEO of Wachovia Bank, the largest bank in North Carolina at the time, and a member of the Hanes textile family. Hanes was then serving as the Marshall Plan's chief of mission in Germany. He invited Hodges to become chief of the Industry Division of the Economic Cooperation Administration. Hodges accepted, moving his family to Frankfurt. His duties included oversight of funds for rebuilding industry and protecting against any buildup of German military might.[24]

After his European sojourn, Hodges returned with his family to Spray (which later merged with the nearby towns of Leaksville and Draper to become Eden) to sort out second career options. He'd barely begun when B. Everette Jordan, chair of the Democratic State Executive Committee, came calling at the suggestion of Robert Hanes. Hodges and Jordan had known each other for years through their connections in the textile industry and as avid Rotarians. Jordan urged Hodges to consider running for lieutenant governor in 1952. He received a "No, not me!" initial reaction. Jordan reminded Hodges that he had often spoken of the need for more businessmen in government. When Jordan scolded, "Practice what you preach," Hodges agreed to think the idea over.[25]

In the days, weeks, and months that followed, he made a remarkable transition from a skeptic of politics to an active aspirant: His halfhearted question "Should I give it a try?" morphed into an emphatic "I'll take the plunge!" His close friends greeted the transition with raised eyebrows and much doubt. More importantly, the state's political power brokers paid little attention to the potential candidacy of a political novice. However, Hodges's decision did not rely on such backing. If he were to run, he would run independent of any political machine. Later he would call that transition "one of the most interesting experiences of [his] whole life."[26]

His wife, Martha, was politically astute and kept his ego in check. A typical exchange occurred after a Democratic Party dinner. Hodges felt encouraged by the perfunctory encouragement of attendees. Martha advised, "I don't think most of them mean what they say."[27]

While Hodges represented a political outsider in many respects—particularly in background and temperament—he benefited from some powerful allies. Former governor and leader of the "Shelby machine," Max Gardner, appointed Hodges to the State Board of Education and the Highway Commission.[28] Hanes played a key role in Gardner's political operation after his death in 1947.[29] This enabled Hanes to activate the Shelby machine for Hodges's benefit, even if Hodges ran an independent campaign. Instead of tapping into the local Democratic Party organization, Hodges pursued a shoe-leather campaign that would take him to all one hundred of the state's counties. He crisscrossed North Carolina in a big red Buick gas-guzzler, stopping in each town at a filling station. Hodges later said he bought a dollar's worth of gas at every stop. These stops served as a mini focus group, providing insights into the local movers and shakers and their issues of concern. Also, whenever he could, he attended a meeting of the local Rotary Club. As local leaders, Rotarians offered a natural entrée and served as an indispensable arm of his campaign.

In the Democratic primary in May 1952, Hodges led a four-man field with 47 percent of the vote. His nearest competitor, state senator and establishment candidate Roy Rowe, ran sixteen points behind that. The May result shocked most political experts as well as the Raleigh press corps. At a time of the political machine, North Carolina had few precedents for such a strong showing by a newcomer with no support from the Old Boy network. Even though Rowe had the right to call a runoff, he declined. Hodges had officially arrived on the political scene.

At the time, North Carolina was a one-party state. Whoever won the Democratic primary in the spring faced little risk of defeat in the general election. Hodges campaigned lightly in the fall and crushed his Republican opponent, Warren H. Pritchett, by a vote of 783,792 to 374,530. As a practical matter, this meant that Hodges could enjoy a high degree of political independence when he was sworn into the state's second highest office.

However, his lack of political connections quickly came back to haunt him. The newly elected Durham attorney, William B. Umstead, had strong ties to the Old Boy network. After hearing during the campaign that Hodges had suggested that they work together, Umstead phoned Hodges right away and snapped, "We are *not* running together." At the time, pundits considered Roy Rowe the frontrunner for lieutenant governor, and Umstead may have felt that any tie to Hodges might hurt him with Rowe supporters.[30] Hodges's lack of relationship with Umstead would carry over into the new administration.

Umstead was a dying man when he took office. On inauguration day in January, he faced packed public events and nonstop handshaking, capped by an inaugural ball that lasted late that night. It had a brutal effect on the frail chain-smoker. As the ball ended, Umstead told Hodges his right leg was hurting. The next day, Hodges presided over his first session of the state senate. Later, he stopped by Umstead's office to offer help in getting his budget passed. It was their first policy discussion and also one of their last. That night the governor suffered a mild heart attack. Over the next twenty-two months, Umstead would spend most of his time in a hospital or in bed at the governor's mansion. He died on November 7, 1954, having delegated no responsibilities to his lieutenant governor.[31]

It is likely that one more factor caused Umstead's refusal to involve Hodges. It was no secret that Hodges's longtime friends, Robert Hanes and B. Everett Jordan, had asked him to run for lieutenant governor; in doing so, they were casting an anchor to windward. If Umstead should become incapacitated, Hodges offered a highly capable successor to take his place. Umstead must have known this. One savvy observer of the political scene would later write, "Hodges reminded him of his own mortality."[32] For all of these reasons, Hodges stepped into the role as governor with the background and network uniquely positioned to attack the brain-drain issue. Moreover, it equipped him to advance the research park concept, even if he knew little or nothing about it in November 1954.

2

Early Collaborations

Less than a month after Umstead died, Brandon Hodges and three North Carolina State (NC State) college leaders, Chancellor Carey Bostian, Dean of the School of Textiles Malcolm Campbell, and Dean of the School of Engineering Harold Lampe, briefed the new governor on the park concept. They expected him to embrace the idea and run with it. But Bostian felt that Hodges had little enthusiasm for the project. After a meeting with the governor on December 31, 1954, Guest wrote to Brandon Hodges saying the governor seemed unenthusiastic. Someone observed that as a textile man, Hodges might not understand the value of research and development.

Was this a rush to judgment or a failure to understand the way Hodges would operate? A strong case can be made for both. It should also be noted that Hodges had more pressing issues to address at this time. The day before he met with Guest, a group presented the initial response plan to the *Brown v. Board of Education* decision, an issue that could make or break any Southern governor at this time.[1]

During a long and successful business career, Hodges had learned the value of due diligence, of gathering all the relevant facts and carefully considering them before making an important decision. The suggestion that he did not understand the value of R&D seems mistaken. His worldview had been formed by many years of running manufacturing operations for Marshall Field's textile business; he had traveled the world over; and he had served under Robert Hanes as a top administrator in the Marshall Plan to rebuild Western Europe after the war. What early critics saw as indifference may well have been caution and a reluctance to commit to such a large endeavor before learning a great deal more. As a practical matter, these criticisms turned out to be quibbles because, in a very short time, Hodges became the project's most visible champion with full mastery of project details. One last point is noteworthy: Industry hunting was Hodges's passion; by all accounts, he believed it had unprecedented potential for changing the state's future. A new industry would only enhance the state's ability to recruit companies.

Soon after their December meeting, Hodges requested that Chancellor Bostian of NC State have an in-depth report prepared on the proposed park. It was written over the Christmas holiday by Newell, who produced an insightful report. Remarkably, it was the first such examination of the park since the idea's inception. Newell confirmed the opportunity had great potential and that the universities should play a major role in pursuing it. His report was essentially a call to action that led to a flurry of activity.[2]

After he got the report on January 27, 1955, Governor Hodges had lunch on three consecutive Tuesdays with Dean Campbell, Guest, and others to discuss strategies for moving forward. After the first meeting, Campbell still felt that Hodges lacked enthusiasm and did not take the effort seriously. During that session, Hodges characterized aspects of their promotional plans as "hucksterism." For a successful business executive, Luther Hodges found an approach that trumpeted the area to target companies in a pamphlet as shallow. He knew success would require a more comprehensive plan of action. By the end of the third meeting, Hodges bought into the concept. From then on, according to Campbell, "it was the Governor's Research Triangle."[3] The days of the project following an ad hoc, meandering path came to an end.

As Governor Hodges took ownership of the research park project, Guest encountered growing dissension among university leaders. On December 31, 1954, the same day Guest met with Governor Hodges for the first time, he also met with Gordon Gray, president of the University of North Carolina system. Gray told him he'd support the effort as long as it didn't interfere with the university's teaching mission. At about the same time, Guest briefed Arthur Hollis Edens, the president of Duke University, and got similar assurances. However, subordinates of both presidents expressed misgivings about the park project.

Guest's effort to position C. M. Guest & Sons as the intermediary between the universities and target companies soon boomeranged. One statement in particular in Guest's promotional literature irked some academics: "Under prescribed policies, these institutions will continue to cooperate with industrial research organizations in the prosecution of research in the public interest."[4] Who would prescribe these policies? Another offending phrase had advised prospects to call C. M. Guest & Sons to get linked to the right academic party. Such assertions soon brought the issue front and center among university leaders. All this prompted Guest to make more and more changes in his "Conditioned for Research" brochure. He must have sensed that the project might be beyond him.

That point became explicitly clear at a small meeting in Chapel Hill later in January 1955 when Governor Hodges, Brandon Hodges, Gordon Gray, Hollis Edens, and a few academics met with Guest. While Guest explained how he'd "sell" capabilities of university researchers to companies, William Carmichael, the finance officer for the University of North Carolina (UNC), broke in: "Let me see, Romeo, if I really understand what it is we are talking about here, you want the professors and all the rest of us to be the prostitutes and you're going to be the pimp."[5] That deflating barb became widely known and would have crushed a less determined man. It was clear that for the park to succeed, proponents needed a different liaison and more collaborative approach with the universities.[6]

Governor Hodges understood that. He hosted a luncheon for Gray, Edens, and others at the governor's mansion the following month. Instead of presenting the universities with a sales pitch, he asked each institution to conduct a detailed inventory of its faculty and facilities that would be of potential interest to a research-based company.[7] They all agreed.

Hodges then created an organizational structure in the form of a Research Triangle Development Council chaired by Robert Hanes, who had embraced the park idea prior to Governor Umstead's death. Minutes from the council's first formal meeting on May 27, 1955, reflect agreement on a vision statement: "Research Triangle is an effort to make use of the triangle educational institutions . . . in the development of a research center which will attract business investment, and which will give aid to North Carolina industry."[8]

The council formed a working committee, which, in turn, had two subcommittees. One focused on cataloguing the area's resources. The other, called the Program and Plans Subcommittee, would consider an organizational structure for the park. Minutes from several meetings reflect the close attention paid to the academic integrity of the universities. At its first meeting in July 1955, the minutes reflect, "The purpose of the Working committee is to develop a program which will not endanger the purposes of each institution, but which would use them as a background to develop a research area." At a meeting on September 12, 1955, the minutes state that "the principal functions of the Universities are to stimulate industrial research by the research atmosphere their very existence creates, and to supplement industrial-research talents and facilities by providing a wellspring of knowledge and talents for the stimulation and guidance of research by industrial firms."[9] These words delicately—if not clearly—delineate the line between university research and industrial research. These types of explicit statements suggest the universities needed time and reassurance to gain trust in the Research Triangle project. Expending that time would prove worth the effort.

One other major contribution of the Program and Plans Subcommittee related to organization. It recommended a full-time executive director to "provide a communication center for keeping all interested parties informed of all activities."[10] Minutes reflect Brandon Hodges stating, "The need of a high caliber man who has got to be a salesman and who can put himself on anyone's level."[11] This comment suggests the first hire should follow the mold of Romeo Guest. The council voted to appoint Hanes, Brandon Hodges, and one member from each of the universities to select a hire. Hanes agreed to raise the funds to open an office in Raleigh and pay for the executive director. He suggested to Governor Hodges that the council take the form of a nonprofit organization so that donors could receive a tax deduction to make fundraising easier.

In March 1956, William C. Friday succeeded Gordon Gray as acting president of the UNC system. Friday had served as Gray's assistant for four years before ascending to the presidency. Friday was only thirty-five years old and would serve as system president until 1986. Circumventing the selection committee, Governor Hodges asked Friday for a recommendation. That overture underscores the deference paid at the time to university sensitivities as well as the importance of this hire to the entire project. Without hesitation, Friday suggested George L. Simpson Jr., a sociology professor at UNC who earned his PhD under Howard Odom, a highly regarded sociology professor at UNC. Odom had first articulated the idea of a research center for the "study and use of Southern resources—human, natural and social."[12] Later, Friday said he suggested Simpson based on his deep understanding of the universities, his familiarity with academic management, and his ability to relate to the public.[13] Friday agreed to reach out to Simpson about the new position, which would require a one-year leave of absence from UNC. Reflecting on his decision to accept the task, Simpson said

Odom's vision had inspired him. It was clear the South required a new start—"a self-starting mechanism for industrial development." He continued: "Research was in the air. On the one hand, I thought that the Triangle idea might just barely be realistic, on the other hand, that it was essential."[14] Reflecting on this moment years later, Friday said when RTP started out:

> All the elements were there for total destruction. You couldn't put together a more violent mixture if you tried. . . . There was a very real animosity between government and industry. There was no basis to predict that industry and higher education could not only get along but work together for the benefit of both. There was no history of the three universities cooperating on the scale it would require for the Park to succeed. If you had any sense you wouldn't even have tried to make it work. And yet somehow it did. I think a vision came to them all at the same time that they were part of something unique, that could work, and everything began to fall into place.[15]

This volatile concoction required leaders who could help participants understand a higher calling. Through years of meetings and committee work, leaders within the progressive plutocracy, government, and universities saw how a research park could meet their respective needs. By working through the concerns of the disparate groups, participants began to see how the park could serve a broader public interest by advancing the state's economy.

Signifying a major step in the formation of a research park, Hanes hosted a luncheon for forty-five business leaders on September 25, 1956, at the Carolina Hotel in Raleigh. To encourage attendance, Governor Hodges sent the invitation. It would offer a chance to prime the fundraising pump for the new endeavor. At the luncheon, the governor announced the incorporation of Research Triangle Committee, Inc. Three quintessential plutocrats—Hanes, Brandon Hodges, and Governor Hodges—served as initial directors of the nonprofit corporation. The certificate of incorporation set forth the initiative's ambitious economic strategy: first, "to encourage . . . the establishment of industrial laboratories . . . primarily in, but not limited to, that geographical area or triangle formed [by the three universities]" and second, to "promote the use of the research facilities . . . through cooperation between the three institutions" to "attract the establishment of industries" and "thereby . . . increase opportunities of citizens of this State for employment and . . . increase per capita income of the citizens of the State."[16] In other words, RTP would be much more than a place: It would serve as a tool for the economic transformation of the state. The attendees understood the importance of this moment, pledging to raise over

$10,000—nearly enough to cover the annual salary of the new director. They saw the enterprise as "a good idea and good for the state."[17] Simpson would start work five days later.

It is important to note another event occurring at the same time the research park took an organizational leap forward in the fall of 1956: a statewide election. At the time, North Carolina governors could serve only one term. Since Hodges filled the unexpired term of his predecessor that began in 1952, he could run for reelection in 1956. His campaign platform focused on raising the minimum wage, serving as chief "industry hunter" for the state, and creating industrial training centers to train workers. He won in a landslide with 66 percent of the vote. The magnitude of this victory put Governor Hodges in a position to exercise significant political capital to advance his priorities.

His successes in his next term show just how much capital he enjoyed. For example, North Carolina would become the first Southern state to pass a minimum wage law. During the preceding twenty years, seven General Assemblies had failed to act on the issue.[18] Likewise, Hodges asked the legislature for $2 million to establish a number of training centers to prepare high school graduates for better paying jobs in industry and to make the state more attractive as an expansion site for out-of-state companies. By the end of the Hodges administration, enrollment in these centers passed the 20,000 mark. The Industrial Education Centers set the stage for the establishment of a statewide community college system in the 1960s. In sum, Hodges's resounding victory in 1956 gave him the mandate to champion the Research Triangle with little or no real opposition. A later chapter will address Hodges's role in industry hunting, particularly as it related to RTP.

3

Inventing a New Place for a New Worker

In a stroke of luck, the first director of the Research Triangle Committee was not only someone academics could trust, but someone who came to the job with special insights into the unique economic development challenges facing the South. George L. Simpson Jr. was an only child, born and raised in Concord, North Carolina. After getting his master's degree at the University of North Carolina at Chapel Hill (UNC), he served as a gunnery officer in the navy during World War II. He fought in both the Atlantic and Pacific theaters. He returned to UNC and obtained his PhD in 1951.

Simpson's doctorate, published as a book in 1957, looked at the role of the Coker family in the economic development of South Carolina. In 1899, James Lide Coker founded the Southern Novelty Company, later abbreviated to Sonoco. Through innovation, the family business produced a type of paper that could be used in packaging and a yarn process for textiles. The Cokers also founded a university and grew the company into a major, diversified corporation.

Simpson's study of the Cokers on "the local application of science and engineering to economic development" strongly influenced his decision to take on his new challenge, and he attacked it with great vigor.[1]

Within a few weeks of his hiring, Simpson produced a memorandum setting forth a plan for the coming year. He noted the committee's mission began with the task of attracting industrial laboratories to the area, which would stimulate economic development. To accomplish this objective, Simpson described "a straight line approach" going directly to "concerns doing industrial research."[2] He would present these companies with information on the capabilities of the universities and advantages of the area. Simpson saw this as a simpler and less expensive approach than others. Without stating it, those other approaches could include government incentives or investing in a physical place, hoping companies would come.

Simpson cited a range of factors that influenced company decisions on where to locate research laboratories. Proximity to transportation networks, home offices, or production facilities or the simple desire to reach different regions of the country all could drive their decision-making. Consequently, the pitch would prioritize companies not tied to a particular geography. Simpson emphasized that marketing efforts must recognize scientists were not impressed with "high pressure campaigns."[3] Any materials would focus on facts and take a conservative tone. He identified two collateral pieces: first, an eight-page, letter-sized document that would provide basic information on the assets of the region, and second, a larger pamphlet with more details and photos of the area. The second brochure would aim at a larger audience, including the workers interested in joining companies locating in the area.

The eight-page document emphasized the importance of the three major universities—that they in fact defined the Triangle region. He recounted the number of university researchers on staff and dollar amounts of research grants and other funding. It continues, "This concentration of research people and facilities in the Research Triangle is . . . unique in the South."[4] The document goes on to describe in detail the universities' strengths in statistics, engineering, biological sciences, nuclear research, and chemistry. Drawing on his academic studies, Simpson noted the South had made great strides in industrial development in the past quarter century, such that the region could now justify the location of "major research and industrial service activities within the region . . . comparable to those in the East, the Midwest and the Far West." He suggested North Carolina "is now ready for the second great stage in her industrial development, and to take the lead in supplying the research core for the region."[5]

Simpson's meticulous care with marketing would face setbacks. For example, the state's Department of Conservation and Development (now Commerce) produced a brochure in late 1956 that violated Simpson's conservative approach. When he saw it, Simpson was livid, writing to Brandon Hodges in protest. Hodges responded immediately, trying to mollify an outraged Simpson: "While that type of ballyhoo is abhorrent, I doubt that it will have much effect." He went on to compliment Simpson's eight-page document, which, he said, "turned out real good."[6]

Besides his sensibility for the university perspective, Simpson's greatest contribution related to his ability to see a new economic epoch and position the Research Triangle within it. As a sociologist steeped in the stages of industrial development, he foresaw a new economy based on research and development. A different type of worker would thrive in this world. Certainly, Simpson was familiar with the seminal sociological works of this period, such as *White Collar: The American Middle Class* by C. Wright Mills. It described how workers had to contend with a faceless bureaucracy, which demanded conformity to the corporate environment. In contrast, a research-based economy would depend on workers capable of inquiry, innovation, and reliance on their own capabilities with little supervision. Three years later, management guru Peter Drucker would coin the term "knowledge worker" in his work *The Landmarks of Tomorrow*. Simpson could sense what was coming and how the Research Triangle could exploit its assets to attract these new types of workers.

His insights are evident in the glossy brochure entitled "A Full Life in the Research Triangle of North Carolina." It describes "a Dream and a Dilemma . . . and a Solution." He defined the dream as a full life for the individual and family "in our work, in our cultural, social, religious, and our recreational experiences." The stresses of "modern life" in the form of long commutes, fast pace, and too little time create the dilemma. "The need exists for a middle ground where the creative man and his family may live abundantly well." He believed life in the Research Triangle could solve the tension between the dilemma and the dream by offering a place to pursue a challenging career while enjoying "life in a more leisurely fashion." The brochure cites dozens of parks, amateur and professional sports, recreational events, mid-century design, culture and arts, and "hundreds of churches of many faiths in which tolerance is the way of religious life."[7] Simpson was describing the concept of quality of life as a way to attract knowledge workers to a particular metropolitan area more than a decade before it reached the public consciousness. Within four decades, the Research Triangle would routinely top the lists of best places in the United States to live and work.

In addition to targeting a new type of worker, Simpson thought of new ways to engage his university colleagues in the park concept. He gave a speech at UNC in early 1957 several months after starting work. It allowed him to play off the insecurities felt by faculty laboring in the academic backwaters of the South. To reassure his audience, he first described the various statements issued by the working committee that delineated the line between academic and commercial research. Turning to the opportunity presented by the presence of research laboratories, Simpson stated there was a tendency for industrial research to concentrate in select metropolitan areas of the Northeast and Midwest.[8] Certainly, a concentration would eventually occur somewhere in the South. However, he bluntly advised that North Carolina had failed to put to work the uses of science, which he called "the hallmarks of Twentieth Century life." He even boldly proclaimed that the Triangle area was "a relative Sahara of scientific application to industrial development"—not because of a lack of technical expertise but because of cultural reasons.[9] Simpson suggested the area universities could play a role in changing the state's culture by creating a context where industrial research could flourish. These comments came at a time the South faced fundamental social questions about desegregation. By engaging in the state's culture, faculty could shape the outcome and elevate the status of their universities. Given his credibility at UNC, Simpson was uniquely situated to deliver this message to his peers. Also, it fit well within his discipline, examining how the South could improve itself. Like Guest, Simpson was a salesman, one who could reach audiences that had not yet embraced the industrial research concept.

Through his development of collateral and engagement of faculty, Simpson embarked on a national campaign to raise awareness of the Research Triangle. He targeted senior executives of major corporations, corporate research directors, site selection and real estate specialists, and heads of government agencies. Subject experts at Duke, NC State, and UNC provided greater detail aimed at major sectors like pharmaceuticals, chemicals, and electronics. Simpson sent materials based on these drafts to targets with a request for an in-person meeting. Professors and experts at each educational institution were recruited to make visits. That put a small army at Simpson's command. Fanning out all across the country, professors met with more than two hundred companies by the end of 1957.[10] This process further engaged the three universities in the Research Triangle project. While only a few of the recipients accepted invitations to visit North Carolina, Simpson's promotional campaign did much to elevate Research Triangle's profile nationally and within the state.

No faculty member showed more dedication to the research park concept than William F. Little, the iconic chairman of UNC's chemistry department.

Little was in the first class of Morehead Scholars at UNC and now has a building named for him on the Research Triangle Institute (RTI) campus. He rose rapidly through the professorial ranks, becoming chairman of the chemistry department at age thirty-five. Little blanketed the country in 1957, proselytizing to researchers about the attributes of North Carolina. In an oral history interview in 2007, he recalled colleagues telling him, "No one's coming here. This is all just a waste of time." Such pessimism made him bristle. Based on his tireless recruiting trips, he knew it was only a matter of time before the research concept took off. Nevertheless, these trips bore no immediate fruit. These trips shaped Little's thinking about what it would take to attract companies to the Triangle. At one point in 1957, Little wrote Simpson about a visit to Eli Lilly: "There is great value in having something concrete, something that can be mapped and walked over, to place before people. Something tangible stimulates the imagination."[11]

Conceiving a New Place

By the end of 1957, Simpson heard Little's message that he needed a physical product to sell. In response, Simpson hired a planner who would shape RTP for decades to come: Pearson Stewart. Stewart grew up in Boston and went to Amherst College. He served in the Pacific Theater during World War II and was awarded the Bronze Star for his service as an aerial photographer. Returning from the war, he was one of the first graduates of MIT's graduate program in city planning. His first job brought him to the Town of Chapel Hill as a planner. Later, Governor Hodges appointed Stewart to a study group on rehabilitation after the devastating Hurricane Hazel hammered North Carolina's coast in 1954. In hiring Stewart, Simpson charged him with producing a thoughtful design for a research park that would soon emerge somewhere near the center of the Triangle area.

Stewart's colleagues describe him as detail-oriented and reserved but someone with a big vision.[12] He avoided taking credit for his work, despite the profound impact he would have on the Triangle region's future development. His respect for the environment grounded his work and would inspire him to support land conservation long after his retirement from the Research Triangle Foundation decades later. Simpson had Stewart work with Guest on considering how a park would lay out on the largely vacant land situated at the center of the Triangle. By hiring Stewart, Simpson signaled that any research park would have a unique appeal to companies and workers alike. We will see in later chapters how Stewart conceived the park after the initial land was assembled.

4

New Institutions Define RTP

While it made sense for Simpson to deploy a simple, "straight-line" strategy by marketing directly to his target audience, the promoters of the Research Triangle had long recognized that success would require a more complex and costly approach. They pursued two such paths: the creation of an independent research institute and the establishment of a physical location for companies to locate. Both strategies would require new collaborations and require institutional structures.

At one of Guest's first meetings with leadership at Duke University, Professor Paul Gross expressed interest in an independent research institute. Gross had the clout to push for it. A renowned chemistry professor, Gross was a vice president of Duke and served as president of the American Association for the Advancement of Science and vice chair of the National Science Foundation. President Harry Truman had awarded him the Medal of Freedom. Few North Carolinians enjoyed more respect among scientists nationally.[1] It's unclear what prompted Gross to push the idea, but he did so with tenacity, ultimately making it a condition of Duke's participation in the overall project.

By the time the working committee first met in 1955, there was growing awareness that a research institute was a high priority. By January 1957, three months after Simpson came on board, Hanes appointed a Research Institute Committee chaired by Brandon Hodges. Not surprisingly, the committee's first meeting occurred in Gross's office at Duke in March.[2] Within another two months, the committee reported positively about the idea of creating an institute, having corresponded with existing research centers in Boston, Princeton, San Francisco, and Los Angeles. The institute would provide a meaningful avenue for faculty to participate in the Park through fundamental and applied research.[3] The report made clear that the universities could control the organization as directors but would bear no financial responsibility for its operations. Research contracts from government and corporations would provide its income. In sum, the institute would help solidify collaboration with the universities by providing a buffer between private research contracts for industry and pure research in a university setting. It manifested the delineation between business and academic research sought by the universities from the beginning.

Tragedy struck in late 1957. Brandon Hodges, the one person who stuck with Guest and his vision from the beginning, died. Fortunately, another progressive plutocrat would fill the void. More than any leader on the Durham side of the Triangle, George Watts Hill would make sure the research park received the attention and resources it needed to succeed. After top-secret work with the Office of Strategic Services (forerunner of the Central Intelligence Agency) in World War II, Hill returned to Durham to help manage a cluster of family businesses, including the Durham Bank and Trust Company, an insurance company, and real estate investments. In 1955, Hill ran unopposed for Durham City Council. The following year he ran for the state House of Representatives, defeating a segregationist with the help of influential Black leaders. Governor Hodges named him secretary and treasurer of the Research Triangle Committee and chairman of the Research Institute Committee after Brandon Hodges died. In these roles, Hill would profoundly shape the Park's future, especially that of the contract research entity so vital to locking in the support of academe.

Like the Park itself, Hill was something of a desert flower waiting to bloom. At age fifty-seven, he had lived most of his life in the shadow of an immensely successful father, John Sprunt Hill. As of yet, he had not found a meaningful niche in the Hill family businesses. The Park called him to a much more public life, and he willingly embraced it. He particularly excelled at "Park politics," proving himself to be a clear-eyed strategist and an adept arm-twister. His biographer, Howard Covington, wrote, "Of all the businessmen involved in the project, Hill had more resources, access, and time at his disposal than the others. His peers were tied to day-to-day corporate responsibilities, while Hill happily broke loose from the routine at the bank."[4] After Brandon Hodges's death, Simpson recruited Hill to take a leadership role in getting the research institute established. Simpson likely wanted to find a way to engage Hill more directly in the overall effort, given Hill's strong ties in Durham and its business community, as well as his university ties.

Hill's experience as a trustee of the University of North Carolina at Chapel Hill (UNC), his alma mater, told him that the academics were right about the need to maintain separation between the research park and academic research. The academic integrity of the area universities was nonnegotiable. By his own admission, Hill was "bull-headed" and often struck his peers as an "urbane know-it-all."[5] But he was never reluctant to roll up his sleeves to dive into a project, and even small details were not beneath him. He once even turned out to help volunteer firefighters battle a blaze on future Park property.

At the time Hill joined the Research Institute Committee, the committee made a decision to establish a proof of concept to show that an institute could be self-sustaining. Dean Colvard at the School of Agriculture at NC State University suggested to Simpson that he approach Professor Gertrude Cox, one of the nation's leading authorities on statistics.[6] NC State College originally sent a letter to Iowa State in 1944, asking for recommendations for a person to lead its Department of Experimental Statistics. Before sending back its recommendations, Cox's boss showed her his list, and she bluntly asked why her name wasn't on it. She did get added, but as a footnote with the comment: "Of course, if you would consider a woman for this position, I would recommend Gertrude Cox of my staff."[7] NC State had the foresight to hire Cox. She would go on to become the first female full professor at the university and the first person in the United States to lead a department of statistics. She founded the Institute of Statistics, which was widely regarded as one of the top three such research programs in the world along with Iowa State and the London School of Economics.[8] She expanded the Institute of Statistics to UNC under the Department of Mathematical Statistics and later helped establish the Department of Biostatistics, also in Chapel Hill. Statistics would become a fountainhead for commercialization in the Triangle with two of the largest local companies, SAS and Quintiles, emerging from these programs in later years.

Cox responded favorably to Simpson's offer. She had more opportunities for commercial research contracts than she could handle. She believed she could position the institute for rapid growth and indeed she did. Hill and his committee worked closely with Cox to conceive how her institute could integrate into a new, freestanding entity that would tap into the expertise of partner universities. Hill even convinced his father to contribute Wachovia Bank stock valued at $15,000 for the endeavor.[9] In essence, Cox's institute would serve as the prototype for the new research institute, showing whether it could survive on government and corporate research contracts. Cox enlisted faculty to help plan for staffing, salaries, and relationships to the universities. She devoted nearly six months to this effort; it profoundly shaped the identity and structure of the nascent institute.[10] Cox would bring the new research institute its first contract, and eighteen of its first twenty contracts were in the field of statistics. Suffice it to say that Cox played a pivotal role in convincing faculty that the new endeavor would create opportunities for consulting work and adjunct professorships that were previously unavailable—in effect, it would be a strong catalyst for the area's research ecosystem.

After proof of concept, Gross, Duke's representative, encouraged the Research Institute Committee to identify a new director for the institute. Hill took the lead. A call to Jesse Hobson, former head of the Stanford Research Institute (SRI), pointed him in the right direction: George R. Herbert.[11] Herbert had the perfect résumé for the job. He had graduated just as World War II ended from the US Naval Academy with a degree in electrical engineering and dreams of becoming an admiral. By then, defense demobilization had rendered his dream impractical. He then joined the faculty at Michigan State University as an instructor of electrical engineering. But low pay and the demands of a young family soon prompted him to look elsewhere. Herbert happened to have served in the Navy with Jesse Hobson, who, in 1946, had become executive director of the newly formed SRI in Menlo Park, California. After reconnecting with Hobson, Herbert was hired as his administrative assistant, and by 1955, Herbert had climbed the corporate ladder to the number two position at SRI. A colleague from that period praised him for having "infinite patience and great vision."[12]

Herbert knew, however, that without a PhD he'd never get the top job at SRI. So he left in 1956 to become treasurer of a New York utility holding company with the prospect of becoming CEO. He'd barely settled at his desk when he got invited to North Carolina to discuss fast-moving plans to establish the Research Triangle Institute (RTI). Hill's committee quickly realized he would be perfect for the job. Herbert's modest demeanor, quiet self-confidence, and record of managing people, programs, and money gave the committee the confidence to make an offer, despite his lack of scientific background. Herbert's main reservation in accepting centered on the scope of the institute. He understood that a successful industrial research institute needed to operate on a global level.

Otherwise, it could not compete with other emerging technology centers. Governor Hodges assuaged his concern, informing him that contract sponsorship could go far beyond the borders of North Carolina.[13] With that feedback, Herbert signed on as the first director of the new institute before it even formally existed as a corporate entity. He took up his new duties on December 1, 1958.

As the year came to a close, Herbert refined a structural model for the institute. He looked closely at other new institutes, including those in Kansas City, Birmingham, Stanford, and San Antonio. All existed as not-for-profit organizations. As such, the new institute would provide services to a clientele of government agencies and research-oriented corporations. Any surplus income from operations would go back to the organization for facilities, additional research, or public purposes. The new institution would offer scientists an alternative to research careers in an academic institution, a government laboratory, or a captive research center of private industry. Herbert was sure such an organization would appeal greatly "to the scientist who enjoyed the challenge of being an entrepreneur, of identifying a real-world need, selling the idea to a company or government agency, and leading the research to fill that need."[14] In one important respect, this new institute differed from other independent ones: It existed as part of an overall strategy to address a state's profound economic challenges in the 1950s.

In Herbert, the new institute got an urbane man of the world with a collegial approach. He was a gracious host and ardent partygiver, who invited RTI colleagues and others to his home for large and enthusiastic gatherings. His guest lists resembled a rainbow coalition or a mini–United Nations General Assembly. In time, these social occasions came to the attention of the Ku Klux Klan, which soon papered trees and utility poles in and near Herbert's yard with warnings about the evils of race mixing. Herbert shrugged off the implied threat and kept giving parties with socially and racially mixed guests.[15] He led RTI for thirty years and put a framework in place that made academics not only willing but also proud to cooperate. Among RTI's many seminal discoveries was the miracle drug Taxol®, a main treatment for early-stage and late-stage breast cancer, as well as ovarian cancer. Also importantly, RTI would anchor RTP, serving as one of the Park's few physical locations in the early years. Later chapters will reveal how RTI shaped RTP.

Acquiring the Land

As noted, by the end of 1957, leaders saw the need to have a site to show companies interested in moving there. The failure to attract businesses even for a visit made the need more urgent. Of course, from the beginning, Guest envisioned an area available for industrial research. He described such a place generally as equidistant to the three university partners and in proximity to Raleigh-Durham International Airport. While Guest sought to promote the Park by creating and mailing brochures and running ads in national media outlets, he also worked diligently on a plan to assemble thousands of acres of scrub pinelands near the center of the Triangle. A large swath of land could be assembled there in a Triassic basin, where poor drainage made farming impractical and commercial development difficult without expensive infrastructure. This area sat largely vacant due to its poor soils.

After the Chapel Hill flare-up early in 1955 when William Carmichael likened him to a pimp, Guest turned more and more to the new governor for overall leadership and focused his attention on land acquisition. Because he lacked the personal financial resources to assemble a large tract, funding would have to come from somewhere else. Promoters of the research park in government and academe did not see land acquisition as their responsibility. Funding would have to come from the private sector. In order to move forward, Governor Hodges turned to one of his oldest friends: William P. Saunders, director of the Department of Conservation Development. Saunders had been the governor's roommate at UNC and a member of the baseball team Hodges had managed. Saunders's astute management of a Pinehurst textile mill owned by a retired New Yorker, Karl Robbins, had led to windfall profits for Robbins. At Hodges's behest, Saunders invited Robbins to have breakfast at the mansion on April 12, 1955. They'd just begun their pitch for investment in the research park when Robbins interrupted: "You need not say anything more, Luther. I understand. It is a wonderful idea and a money-maker. I'll back you and will put up a million dollars for the project."[16]

Soon after that, Saunders asked Guest, who'd done construction work for Robbins, to go to New York to pin down details of the investment. When he arrived, Robbins was out, so Guest dictated a letter for Robbins's signature, authorizing Guest to sign options for up to 5,000 acres. A short time later, Robbins sent a check for $30,000. A month or so later, Guest let Robbins know he'd hired William Maughan, a Duke University forester, on the recommendation of Duke faculty, and that Maughan was securing options on heavily forested land to the south of Durham. By the end of June 1955, Maughan had signed options on 800 acres operating under cover as Evergreen Farms. Maughan made rapid headway. In September 1955, Guest incorporated a development company called Pinelands to own the property that would compose the research park. He listed himself as president and treasurer.

By the end of 1957, Guest had 3,550 acres under option or purchased at a total cost of $700,000, with $275,000 received from Robbins. The average cost per acre was $161. Guest would receive a customary commission on land sold. In conjunction with the assembling of property, Guest studied how to develop the area. As mentioned, its location in a Triassic basin presented issues. The Triassic basin sits on sedimentary rock, impeding the migration of water. To support development in the area, water would require piping from the closest municipality with capacity: in this case, the City of Durham.

Despite Guest's progress in tying up land, the research park was heading for a crisis. Some of the options began to expire by the end of 1957. Despite the efforts of Guest, Simpson, and others to entice research facilities, no companies had yet shown a willingness to acquire property in the Park. Moreover, the United States had entered a deep recession at the time. Robbins was cooling on his investment commitment. He wanted North Carolina investors to kick in too—ideally acquiring a 49 percent stake in Pinelands. He had also learned of the water issues. In the face of this brewing crisis, Secretary Saunders of the Department of Conservation and Development stepped forward. With the permission of Governor Hodges, Saunders made a personal loan of $100,000 to prevent acreage from being lost.[17]

On January 8, 1958—which would prove to be a fateful year for RTP—the governor wrote Robbins about signs that he was backing away. "I do not want to see any misunderstandings or difficulties arise," Hodges advised.[18] The immediate sticking point was Robbins's concern about the City of Durham's reluctance to supply water. In response, Simpson contacted Hill, who had just been appointed to lead the Research Institute Committee, to use his influence with Durham's mayor and city council to get the water problem solved. This issue ultimately would take years to resolve.

To keep the RTP concept alive, Guest had to find more investors for Pinelands. Robbins felt uncomfortable with too much exposure in the deal. He wanted to share the risk with others, especially given lingering questions about the Park's infrastructure needs. Hodges and Hanes recognized the urgent need to change tactics. The Park would require someone other than Guest to lead the effort to identify investors before the options expired. As in so many instances in the history of RTP, the right person would emerge in a time of need.

Archie Davis's Involvement

Logically, Hanes would serve the role of fundraiser. He had led the successful effort to solicit funds for the operations of the Research Triangle Committee and many other causes. However, other considerations would influence Hanes's thinking. There is no record of when Hanes learned of his health issues in 1958, but his health deteriorated rapidly over the course of the year. Hanes knew that someone else would need to take the reins, given the urgency and energy required to secure the Park's land before the options expired. In another fortuitous event, Hanes called on his trusted successor as CEO of Wachovia Bank: Archie K. Davis. By any measure, Davis was a progressive plutocrat and, next to Hodges, the most impactful leader in Park history. Robert Hanes, scion of one of Winston-Salem's most prominent families and longtime president of Wachovia, became Davis's mentor when he joined the bank in 1933. Davis had planned to go to graduate school at Princeton, but the scarcity of good jobs in the Great Depression led him to accept Wachovia's offer. He would remain with the bank for his entire professional career, retiring in 1974 after eighteen years as chairman of the board.

Davis had an impeccable education: He attended Woodberry Forest, a boarding school in Virginia, and earned a degree in history from the University of North Carolina where he graduated Phi Beta Kappa. Upon retirement, Davis reenrolled at the University of North Carolina and earned an MA in history, showing his passion for learning. He served as president of both the US Chamber of Commerce and the American Bankers Association, the only person to occupy both posts at the same time. He was a state senator at the time Hanes approached him to assist with the research park. He held that position in the legislature from 1958 to 1962. Bill Friday, who was friends with Davis for more than fifty years, later observed, "The important thing in his life is what an exemplary man he was. . . . I never heard him be profane or denigrate anyone or put people down." By all accounts, Davis was charming, courteous, persistent, and not to be denied.

After Hanes approached Davis with a general appeal for his help, Hanes called Davis and Governor Hodges to an urgent meeting at his beach home at Atlantic Beach in August 1958. The purpose of the meeting was to get Davis's firm commitment to raise money for Pinelands before the end of the year. Much to their surprise, Davis bluntly warned both men that the current structure of Pinelands was an albatross.

"If this [Pinelands] indeed was designed for public service," Davis told them, "it would be much easier to raise money from corporations and institutions and the like, who [are] interested in serving the State of North Carolina, by making a voluntary contribution."[19] Davis stressed three important advantages of a nonprofit approach: Donors would get a tax deduction; government could fund infrastructure costs such as roads; and perceptions of conflicts of interest and other improprieties could be put to rest. In offering the approach, Davis reminded them of what he called the Tar Heel "generosity of spirit."[20] Clearly, Davis embodied the progressive plutocrat's ethos of enlightened self-interest.

Hodges agreed on the spot, but Hanes thought the magnitude of the task could be impractical for a nonprofit. Nevertheless, they agreed to move forward with a goal of raising at least $1 million for a nonprofit that in time would replace Pinelands. They further agreed that Davis should take a leave of absence and hit the road to solicit contributions from high-net-worth individuals across the state.

Shortly after the meeting in Atlantic Beach, all of the central figures involved in the research park project gathered at the governor's mansion. Attendees included Archie Davis, William Friday, Paul Gross, Romeo Guest, George Watts Hill, William Saunders, George Simpson, and Pearson Stewart. This meeting came at a defining time for the research park and represented the culmination of years of collaboration. Discussions focused on matters of money, goals, principles, and policies that could aid Davis in his fundraising blitz. Davis wanted to make sure they were all in accord on the big-picture issues. Hill's meeting notes reflect nothing adversarial. All agreed with Friday that without the research institute, RTP was nothing. They must find a home for it. Davis agreed but saw the institute's board reporting to the foundation owning the park. Gross insisted that the universities must control RTI—that there would be "strenuous objection" if control should rest with another body, no matter how friendly. "It's not separation but cooperation," Gross held. "RTI needed the best manager possible," Gross added, "but the [real estate] Foundation will not be allowed to select him."[21] Friday confirmed that RTI would be "protected organizationally," meaning it would be under university governance. Based on this tacit agreement, Davis went forth with a charge to raise more than $1 million to close on the land, with $500,000 going to RTI for start-up costs.

Relying mainly on Hanes's contacts, Davis raised nearly $1.5 million from 850 donors in less than ninety days. More money came from Winston-Salem than anywhere else, including the Triangle.[22] Remarkably, no one turned Davis down. He'd been right: An appeal to civic pride and love of the state worked. For the first time, the park project had funding to assemble a sizable site and launch a research institute that would symbolize the university's engagement in the effort. The Davis strategy marked a defining feature of RTP.

As 1958 came to a close, RTP had passed a crucible. Its founders had risen to the challenge after years of collaboration. One of the most historic moments in the life of the state occurred on January 9, 1959, when the governor announced to a packed house of six hundred in the Virginia Dare Ballroom of Raleigh's

Sir Walter Hotel that funds had been raised to proceed with the research park. Hodges advised that the Research Triangle Committee would become the Research Triangle Foundation, vested with responsibility to acquire and sell land. Guest and Robbins agreed their financial commitments would roll over from Pinelands to the new nonprofit. Other uses of funds would include a building to house RTI. Hodges announced that the new building would be named in honor of Robert Hanes, whose photograph in the *News & Observer* the next day reflected the ravages of cancer. Hanes died a few months later.[23]

Four days after the announcement, Guest resigned as president of Pinelands. The governor later wrote him, "May I thank you for what you have done, and I again say to you as I have said to many, many other people that you are really the person who gave birth to the Research Triangle."[24] This was a prime example of Hodges's willingness to give credit to others. In his autobiography, *Businessman in the Statehouse*, he did that time and time again.

Guest would later say the project had been a success for many but a disaster for him.[25] He had coined the memorable phrase "Research Triangle," which served the effort admirably. It's unclear who added the word "Park," but it too was definitive. C. M. Guest & Sons would not benefit directly from the development of RTP. Ironically, a local firm, Nello Teer, would acquire Guest's company in 1974 but did little with it other than using its moniker. The Nello Teer Company built many of the iconic buildings that came to define the park.

As the 1950s came to a close, the RTP founders could take pride in a singular accomplishment: They had forged a level of collaboration that would endure for decades to come.

5

Bridges to Success

The establishment of the Research Triangle Institute (RTI) to engage faculty and the Research Triangle Foundation (RTF) to own and manage the development of the Park marked an important milestone for RTP. However, RTP's success would require additional ingredients: early research successes, active recruitment of companies, and adept navigation in the changing social landscape. RTI provided the early research success. Governor Hodges embarked on the largest mission in state history to recruit companies from Europe. He also would launch the industrial training centers that later became the community college system. At this time, the state also faced a seismic social and political challenge in the wake of *Brown v. Board of Education*. How North Carolina handled the dismantling of segregation would deeply affect its ability to attract the types of facilities sought by RTP. And, finally, with the initial land acquired for RTP, the RTF needed to create a plan for the Park and the surrounding area to ensure that companies and workers in RTP would thrive.

RTI Carries the Water

From the beginning, George Herbert faced considerable pressure to produce tangible results. The Park was by no means universally embraced. Critics called it a waste of money, one that would drain away leading professors from the Big Three universities. It was a given that the Park's real estate arm, the RTF, would need a minimum of one to two years to generate land sales. That meant the burden of proving the Park's viability would fall heavily on RTI. Herbert's mandate was to achieve self-sufficiency in two years, a daunting challenge to be sure. He would have to do that with an endowment of $500,000 from the $1.5 million raised late in 1958 by Wachovia's chairman, Archie Davis.

Gertrude Cox had established proof of concept for RTI during its formation. As noted in chapter 4, she helped bring numerous research contracts to RTI in its early years, securing RTI's reputation in the field of statistics. RTI's second development represented a paradigm shift—a $2.5 million grant from the Camille and Henry Dreyfus Foundation in New York that would fund a ten-year basic research program in polymer physics and chemistry. The grant would give RTI the country's first laboratory devoted to the fast-emerging field of polymer compounds such as plastics.[1] The grant specified that proceeds would, in part, be used to erect a laboratory building ($500,000) and provide equipment ($200,000).

Herbert had known from the start that he would have to build RTI from the top down. In practice, this meant hiring the best scientists he could find—even from abroad—and then leveraging their reputations to staff up new RTI laboratories and programs. He spent a year looking for a director of the new polymer lab, interviewing more than a dozen scientists in the United States and six from Europe. He settled on Dr. Anton Peterlin, a highly regarded Yugoslav theoretical physicist and mathematician, who had been a professor at the University of Ljubljana in Slovenia. It was an astute hire because Peterlin was the editor of the leading polymer journal in Germany and drew worldwide attention to RTI's Camille Dreyfus Laboratory. After Peterlin accepted Herbert's offer, he convinced several other European polymer scientists to join him at RTI.[2]

Herbert also hired Dr. Vivian Stannett, a Londoner at Syracuse University, as associate director of the polymer lab. Stannett later became Distinguished Professor of Chemical Engineering at North Carolina State University and later the dean of its graduate school. Her arrival shows how the universities benefited from talent recruited to RTI. One other hire in Herbert's top-down push bears mention: Ralph Ely Jr., an atomic scientist with deep connections to the Atomic Energy Commission (AEC). Hiring Ely was a key step in landing AEC funding for an isotopes development lab at RTI.

Joel Lawson Williams, who grew up on a tobacco farm in Duplin County that bordered the Cape Fear River, was hired at the new polymer lab in 1962 while still a chemistry student at North Carolina State University. The school would later award him its first doctorate in fiber and polymer science. At the time, the university offered the only doctoral program of its kind in the United States. Plastics were just beginning to replace glass bottles, wooden objects, and heavy metal parts, and the polymer field was about to explode in importance: Worldwide polymer consumption then was only about two billion pounds a year; today it's six hundred billion.

RTI assigned Williams badge 147; that meant he was the 147th employee hired. He got to know George Herbert and says, "He was as smooth as silk.... In the early days, the [polymer] lab was better known internationally than RTI."[3] Visitors from abroad came often, and Williams frequently picked them up at RDU airport in his well-traveled Volkswagen Beetle. He remembers well their surprise when he turned onto dirt roads as they approached RTI's 180-acre campus. "In those days," Williams recalls, "some of the roads nearby—especially NC 54—had potholes big enough to swallow a Sherman tank."[4]

Williams became a star scientist at the lab. His process for making microporous plastics was patented and assigned to RTI and later licensed to the Celanese Corporation. Because it was far more permeable to air than normal plastic was, it could be used in a wide variety of products, including baby diapers. This was the first patent that RTI owned, licensed, and earned royalties on. Williams also pioneered the development of elastic fibers that could be stretched 600 percent. In 1999, he received the International John W. Hyatt Award for outstanding contributions in the field of plastic technology.

In 1974, Williams left RTI to start and lead the Materials Research Department at Becton Dickinson (BD), a Fortune 500 medical-device company that sourced and developed biotechnology and life science technologies in RTP. One of his high-profile successes there was a radiation sterilization method for syringes and other medical products that killed bacteria on contact. It helped boost BD's annual sales from $200 million to over $8 billion. Almost overnight, BD's market share in the worldwide syringe market went from 14 percent to 35 percent.[5]

When he left RTI in 1974, Williams received a warm farewell letter from George Herbert: "During your years here, your research accomplishments have been substantial and are much appreciated by the Institute. Farewell from your friends—and I am proud to be included among them."[6] That was typical of George Herbert's generosity and approach to employee relations.

Two other early hires at RTI by George Herbert would discover one of medicine's most impactful drugs. In the early 1960s, George Herbert hired Dr. Monroe E. Wall to head RTI's Natural Products Lab. At the US Department of Agriculture (USDA), Wall studied hundreds of plants for medicinal properties with funding from the National Cancer Institute (NCI). NCI funding followed Wall to RTI where he continued his research. Wall in turn recruited star scientist Dr. Mansukh Wani to the Natural Products Lab. Together, they found properties in the Pacific yew tree that would lead to the anticancer drug Taxol®, a leading treatment for breast, lung, and ovarian cancer. The two men could not have been more different. Wall was a hulking man, who often filled rooms with bombastic declarations. Wani, in contrast, was modest and self-effacing. He was a quiet, attentive listener who never sought the limelight. Wani had grown up in India and earned BS and MA degrees from Bombay University. He had come to the United States in the late 1950s to earn a PhD at Indiana University. In the early 1960s, as a postdoctoral student at the University of Wisconsin, he learned about an opening at RTI in the Natural Products Lab.[7]

When he told colleagues that he planned to interview for the job, alarm bells went off. "Are you crazy?" someone asked. "Don't you know what's going on down there?" With racial unrest sweeping the South at the time, they gravely warned that he would be subjected to blatant discrimination. "They thought he'd stick out like a sore thumb," says Nick Oberlies, a chemist, who worked under Wani for many years at RTI and became quite close to him. "His skin color was a deep tan, but that didn't deter him at all. He told them: 'I'm going anyway; I want to check it out.' To be honest, I think he was most drawn toward the chemistry they were doing at RTI and wanted to be part of it."[8]

When Wall first moved to RTI, he brought a promising natural product lead with him known as camptothecin, which had been isolated in the bark of *Camptotheca acuminata*, a tree native to China, known there as the Happy Tree. One of Wani's great strengths was defining a crystal structure that identified the ordered arrangement of atoms, ions, and molecules. It took many years to do that, but he finally found a crystal structure. The studies leading to this discovery were set forth in 1966 in the first coauthored manuscript by Wall and Wani. Although clinical trials in the early 1970s found toxicity in camptothecin, Wall and Wani worked on many second- and third-generation analogues. In 1997 major drug companies started marketing cancer chemotherapy products based on their work. Suffice it to say, Wani thrived at the Natural Products Lab. He encountered discrimination only once, according to Oberlies: "That was at a fast food franchise with his son when a cashier ignored his order. When Wani gave him a questioning look, the cashier gave his manager a shrug and a 'What am I supposed to do?' look. 'Just take his order,' the manager blandly replied, and that was the end of it."[9]

Parallel to their work on camptothecin, Wall and Wani began testing a second compound—this one from the bark and needles of the Pacific yew tree. It was left to Wani to find the structure of the molecule, which was quite large. After two years and no progress, Wall told Wani to call it quits—that camptothecin was their best lead, so he wanted to focus only on it—but Wani's intuition told him not to stop, so he proposed continuing to work on the molecule after work and on weekends. Wall agreed, and in 1971, Wani finally solved the molecular structure issue. In a paper published soon after that, Wani and colleagues at the lab reported that a new compound, which they called Taxol®, showed promise as an anticancer drug. Wall and Wani wanted to patent the discovery. However, they could not due to restrictions on federal funding at the time. "For the next four years," Wani would say, "it was on the shelf dying a dusty death."[10] In the 1980s, research elsewhere showed that Taxol attacked cancer in an unprecedented way. Still, natural resources for producing the drug were limited. It would take material from six yew trees to treat one patient. Taxol's revival was complete when in 1992 researchers at Florida State University invented a way to mass-produce the drug. The Food and Drug Administration approved Taxol for the treatment of ovarian cancer after Bristol Myers Squibb got it through Phase III clinical trials. Oberlies estimates the market at $3 billion per year for camptothecin, Taxol, and docetaxel, another chemotherapy drug. None of this revenue goes to RTI. The passage of the Bayh-Dole Act in 1980, which lifted restrictions on licensing discoveries based on US government–sponsored research, came too late for Wall and Wani.

Oberlies, who's now a professor at the University of North Carolina at Greensboro, says, "I'd give my right arm to discover just one compound that became a drug, and Wall and Wani came up with two. I know Dr. Wall told Dr. Wani more than once to drop it, but thankfully he didn't. If you talk to an oncologist about the days before Taxol, he or she will tell you that Taxol had a profound impact on ovarian cancer and breast cancer. Bristol Myers Squibb eventually turned Taxol into a multibillion-dollar drug. It has been said that for about ten years the company made a million and a half dollars every day, including Christmas and Easter."[11]

Oberlies traveled frequently with Wani and vividly remembers people coming up to Wani in tears on planes when they learned that he discovered Taxol. "They would tell him the drug had saved a wife, mother, or a sister's life. And the next thing you know, a complete stranger was giving us a ride home from the airport. They'd tell me: 'Young man, you bring his luggage; this is a great man.' They were nearly always in tears and could not thank him enough."[12] Wani was invited to Stockholm, Sweden, by the Nobel Prize Committee, although he did not receive the prize. A building at RTI named for University of North Carolina chemist Bill Little bears a historical landmark issued by the American Chemical Society for the discoveries made there by Wall and Wani.

Along with the likes of Gertrude Cox, Anton Peterlin, Vivian Stannett, and Ralph Ely, Herbert amassed a reservoir of talent at RTI within its first few years. Those hires ensured RTI could anchor RTP during its early years when the Park had little other activity. They allowed corporate recruiters to show companies what the future of RTP would look like. Just as importantly, such talent would drive RTI's growth in the coming years, ultimately making it one of the premier research institutes in the nation.

Industry Hunting and Industrial Training Centers

Early in his administration, a newspaper cartoon depicted Hodges returning from the wilds with a musket slung over one shoulder and a big sack of game over the other—ready to fill a giant cookpot being stirred by the mistress of North Carolina. That image was well earned and carefully cultivated because Hodges employed strategies rarely, if ever, used before.

Bob Leak, who later became president of RTF, observed firsthand how Hodges's policies unfolded. After earning a degree in geology from Duke, Leak went to work in Louisiana but soon decided to return to North Carolina. In an interview at the State Personnel Office in Raleigh, he was told there were no openings for geologists, but the state was looking for industry hunters.

"What's an industry hunter?" Leak asked.

"I don't know," the personnel officer replied. "But I do know that Governor Luther Hodges is really keen on this industry hunting."[13]

Leak got hired for such a job in his mid-twenties. He was interviewed for this book in his late eighties—still in good health and living in an upscale retirement community in North Raleigh. Despite his youth, Leak had frequent access to Hodges—most often when wooing senior corporate executives from out of state. The last stop for visiting moguls was the governor's office where Hodges tried to close the deal.

"He was a great salesman," Leak says. "I was mesmerized by the effect he had. The next time I saw him, he'd always ask, 'How'd I do? . . . How'd I do?' He took good care of us: We were the only state employees who got an air-conditioned state car—a snazzy baby blue Dodge Matador. He wanted the CEOs we squired around to ride in comfort."[14]

Leak says Hodges was the first US governor to lead industry hunting missions out of state and abroad. Beginning in the fall of 1957, he took large delegations to New York, Philadelphia, and Chicago to promote North Carolina as a site for business expansion. The message was, "When you build a new plant, take a close look at North Carolina—especially our assets in people, climate, research, education, and recreation."[15]

The Department of Conservation and Development planned each weeklong mission in minute detail. Calls first went out across the state for volunteer "ambassadors" who would pay their own way. About seventy-five prominent leaders signed up for the trip to New York. They made personal calls in pairs to about 250 prospective companies. Appearances by Hodges on twelve television and radio shows generated national exposure. His appearances were booked by the Honorary Tar Heels, a loosely organized group of writers, commentators, advertising executives, photographers, and media specialists who lived in New York.

Hodges insisted that his ambassadors advocate for the state as a whole—not for their hometowns. When all was said and done, these expeditions—Hodges called them "caravans"—raised the state's visibility enormously at little or no expense. Based on the positive results, Hodges led 122 ambassadors to Philadelphia in the fall of 1958 and groups of similar size to Chicago and New York in 1960.

All this gave rise to another likely first for any state: a two-week mission to Europe with sixty-eight ambassadors in 1960. Having established RTP, Hodges had something new to sell on this mission. That delegation was split into three groups that fanned out across Western Europe, keeping up a relentless pace in Paris, Brussels, Hamburg, Zurich, and elsewhere. In all, the delegation reached 1,600 business leaders in ten cities. Specific metrics were tracked: For example, seventy-nine prospects for state ports were identified, and twelve firms wanted to visit the Research Triangle. Soon after the delegation got home, a Hamburg pump manufacturer announced plans to build a factory in Statesville with five hundred employees. Media throughout the United States covered the Tar Heels to Europe roadshow, distinguishing North Carolina from other Southern states.

Years later, Governor Jim Hunt would follow Hodges's example, leading delegations on industry hunting trips. Hunt recalled on his first recruiting trip to Europe, a German businessman approached him excitedly and exclaimed, "Governor Hodges!" This incident suggested both the rarity and impact of Hodges's visit years before. Combining the strategy of industry hunting with a new product for companies looking to expand research facilities proved providential for RTP. A number of the companies Hodges visited in 1960 ultimately came to RTP. Industry hunting remains a linchpin for RTP today.

Another priority for Hodges related to the establishment of industrial education centers. Hodges envisioned these centers as a place to train workers for jobs that do not require a four-year degree. North Carolina pioneered the concept in the United States. Such training would develop into one of the most effective recruiting tools for companies locating to the state. Hodges and his successors offered customized training to workers for new jobs created by any relocating company for free.

This offer was a difference marker for companies requiring highly technical positions specific to the technologies and applications of novel ideas to industry. Hodges housed the offices of the industrial training centers in the same building as the RTF on Edenton Street in downtown Raleigh. Governor Sanford would expand the program and rebrand it as the community college system. The offer to train workers often proved more enticing than the tax breaks offered by other states. It shows the state's understanding that talent ultimately drives the success of technology companies. By building on the legacy created by Governor Hodges, North Carolina's community colleges made the state a perennial leader in business recruitment even today. Later chapters will address the evolution of this tool and how it has impacted RTP's ability to compete for business.

Designing a New Work Environment

While promoters of the research park understood the need to have a physical location, they paid little attention to what form any development should take. Hodges once approached a prominent local developer, Willie M. York, who had developed Cameron Village in Raleigh (now the Village District), asking if he would develop RTP.[16] York had served as chairman of the Urban Land Institute and built one of the first shopping centers in the South modeled after the famous Country Club Plaza in Kansas City. However, York turned down the offer due to other commitments. By the time the founders of RTP had created the RTF, the decision was made to take a different approach. The RTF would own the initial land assembly and establish basic parameters to control future development undertaken by each individual landowner. There would be no detailed master plan. This decision would have significant implications for the future course of RTP.

Archie Davis created a separate for-profit entity called the Triangle Service Center, Inc., in June 1960. It aimed at developing a future area near RTP to accommodate shopping and leisure activities. This would keep such uses outside the confines of RTP proper while providing some conveniences and amenities for workers. Several years later, Hodges announced at an RTF board meeting the conveyance of ninety-two acres along the edge of RTP from the RTF to this entity. It eventually would host a local landmark, the Governor's Inn. The RTF's current efforts to reimagine RTP have focused on an urban hub at the Service Center property, which will be explored later. Regardless, the service center simply operated as a placeholder concept at the outset of RTP.

To create a general plan for RTP, Guest engaged a New York–based firm, Voorhees, Walker, Smith, Smith & Haines. Of course, no one had designed a research park on this scale. Certainly, corporations had begun the migration to the suburbs by this time. But what would a large land area with research labs look like? As noted in chapter 3, Simpson hired Pearson Stewart to oversee planning efforts. Stewart hired his own team, employing noted local modernist architects, Jim Webb and Bob Anderson.[17] The three of them worked with the NC Department of Transportation to create a plan for the initial 4,000-acre assemblage. In 1960, Stewart and Anderson traveled to New York to meet with the Voorhees firm. Voorhees rolled out a boilerplate plan that could be Anywhere, USA. It bore no relation to the site in North Carolina. Stewart threw the plan away and forged ahead without it.[18]

In particular, Stewart wanted a plan that respected the area's environmental features. He identified building sites and roads on the three ridges running north-south between Highway 54 and beyond Cornwallis Road. He planned for sewer and water infrastructure in the valleys. Stewart also led the charge to secure zoning from Durham County. RTP would have a zoning of research district.[19] Such zoning prohibited residential and industrial uses, which would have profound implications for the future of RTP. Stewart aimed for a bucolic setting where workers would have a sense of seclusion. Nature would surround buildings. Stewart accomplished this through strict limitations on lot coverage and large building setbacks.

Stewart also wanted to ensure RTP developed in concert with a larger region. In answering a question about the layout of RTP, Stewart said, "We made a point of looking at the whole region—Chapel Hill, Raleigh, and Durham—not just the physical boundaries of the park."[20] In 1959, the General Assembly created a Research Triangle Regional Planning Commission. Governor Hodges attended the first meeting on September 23, 1959. The commission aimed at encouraging cooperation among local jurisdictions to "achieve a soundly developed Research Triangle." Stewart served as its secretary and half-time executive director. The commission was housed alongside the offices of the RTF and the industrial training facilities on Edenton Street in Raleigh. At its second meeting, the commission raised fundamental philosophical issues that have persisted. How should urban development proceed as RTP grows? What are the implications to public finance when a major portion of the region's future commercial tax base will exist outside the taxing authority of a city? How can the region meet future demands for water, sewer, schools, highways, and utilities? The commission agreed to embark on a range of technical studies on these topics with the goal of producing general policies.

In September 1960, the commission published a guide for the Research Triangle. The guide states the expectation that RTP will attract employment to the area but also spur "future urban development."[21] The guide set forth three alternative schemes to accommodate a population three to four times the present. Scheme A contemplated compact development in the existing urban centers of Raleigh and Durham served by rail or bus transit. Scheme B described a nucleated pattern with the creation of new towns of up to 25,000 residents. This pattern relied primarily on automobiles. Scheme C directed growth into corridors following natural drainage courses. The guide advised that anticipated growth would require regional planning as well as public education about the need to plan.[22] Many of the themes described in the guide would reappear in the decades ahead: the need for regional planning, transportation options, and choices among different scenarios. Through these types of scenario planning exercises, Stewart established a framework for engaging local governments and citizens in thinking about future growth and the pressures it would bring.

Managing the Onset of Desegregation

As Governor Hodges pursued his ambitious agenda to change the economic trajectory of the state, he faced a public policy upheaval that would profoundly alter a social order that had barely changed since the Civil War. On May 7, 1954, the US Supreme Court held in *Brown v. Board of Education of Topeka* that racial segregation in public schools was unconstitutional—separate but equal would no longer stand. That historic decision would test the entire nation's commitment to integration over the next decades. However, its initial focus was on the South. The *Brown* decision served as a litmus test for whether the South had a willingness to treat all of its citizens on an equal basis. Research companies would not risk putting highly trained workers into a volatile environment of social unrest. Navigating the transition to integration posed a crucial step for RTP to succeed.

Observing the public outcry in other states to the *Brown* decision, Governor Umstead resolved to avoid damaging the state's reputation for moderation in race relations. While Umstead firmly supported segregation, he was appalled by the aggressive tone of political leaders in Virginia, South Carolina, and Georgia, some of whom even threatened school closings to avoid integration. In a typical response to the Supreme Court ruling, influential Alabama State Senator Sam Engelhardt vowed, "We are going to keep every brick in our segregation wall intact."[23]

By the 1950s, North Carolina enjoyed a positive image in public education and on race relations compared to other Southern states. As reflected in the observations of Harvard political scientist V. O. Key, North Carolina leaders worked assiduously to raise the living standards of its citizens, and leaders saw public education as the primary way to achieve that goal. Furthermore, state investments in public education extended beyond white schools. For example, North Carolina led the South in terms of the numbers of Black educators, percentage of Black students enrolled in school, average salaries for Black teachers, and accommodations for Black students.[24] These generational efforts reflected a consensus among state elected leaders that public education deserved priority and protection.

With an eye toward avoiding a calamity to the state's public school system, Umstead appointed a special advisory committee to evaluate options. He chose Thomas Pearsall, a close political ally from Rocky Mount and a former Speaker of the House, to lead it. There were nineteen committee members, mostly school superintendents and university leaders. He included three Black educators on the committee.

The Pearsall committee, as it was called, established two paramount objectives: first, preserving the public school system and, second, avoiding civil unrest. Pearsall called on the Institute of Government at the University of North Carolina to evaluate strategies to sidestep immediate desegregation without incurring federal intervention. They settled on an approach of transferring authority over pupil assignment to counties and local school boards that would follow local criteria in making pupil assignments. By decentralizing administration and decision-making, courts would have a difficult time quickly invalidating local plans unlike a unitary, statewide policy.

Umstead died just as the committee was preparing its initial report. Hodges had served just over a month when, on December 30, 1954, the committee sent him its initial report. As noted, Hodges received the report the day before Guest first met with him about the research park concept. It underscores the significant and challenging issues presented to Hodges in his first days in office. In his State of the State address the following week, Hodges read the Pearsall findings to the General Assembly. The report concluded that immediate desegregation of schools would alienate the public to such an extent that public schools could not operate in the best interest of students.

That spring, further court rulings indicated states would have ample time to comply with the *Brown* decision. Hodges reconstituted the Pearsall committee by shrinking it to eight members who each had a legislative background. He appointed no Black members, which led to criticisms by Black leaders. Hodges directed the committee to write legislation to present to legislators the following year.

In April 1956, Hodges launched his gubernatorial campaign shortly before delivery of the final "Pearsall plan." In sum, the plan centered on voluntary desegregation based on local preferences. It included a provision for parents to appeal assignments to integrated schools, offering vouchers to cover tuition and other costs at private schools. Hodges characterized these aspects of the plan as a safety valve. The plan also delegated to local authorities the option of closing a public school if tensions warranted it. The Pearsall plan took the form of eight separate bills introduced in the summer of 1956. Hodges campaigned hard for its passage, seeking support from the media and respected leaders. The plan passed overwhelmingly. Support spanned the political spectrum, including legislator and future governor Terry Sanford, as well as television commentator and future US Senator Jesse Helms. The most noteworthy critic was evangelist Billy Graham, who condemned segregation as un-Christian.

During this time, numerous pro-segregation groups sought to stir violence. The Pearsall committee's mailbox overflowed with letters decrying its willingness to allow "miscegenation." A Klan leader in Salisbury, North Carolina, warned, "If the Pearsall Plan doesn't work, the Smith and Wesson [gun] Plan will."[25]

Only one noteworthy episode of violence occurred in North Carolina. On January 18, 1958, the Knights of the Ku Klux Klan staged a rally to burn crosses in a leased field near Maxton in the south-central part of the state. Recent cross burnings in the area had convinced the Lumbee Tribe and Black locals that the Klan rally could easily get out of control. Several hundred armed Lumbee Indians confronted the Klansmen. They exchanged heated words, and shots were fired. The Klansmen fled into the woods, leaving the field littered with their fallen flags, crosses, and other paraphernalia. Fortunately, no one was seriously injured. The Lumbees and local Black citizens later celebrated what became known as the Battle of Mills Pond.[26]

Hodges navigated this period as a hard realist. Rather than imploring the white population to accept the Supreme Court ruling, he asked the Black community to remain patient. The National Association for the Advancement of Colored People (NAACP), which litigated the *Brown* case, criticized the slow pace of desegregation and threatened more lawsuits. Hodges reacted negatively. In one televised speech, he criticized the NAACP for sowing "distrust, antagonisms, resentments and confusion."[27] In his speeches to Black audiences, Hodges struck a tone of impatience as though he expected Black citizens to share his concern about inflaming segregationists who would shutter public schools to avoid integration. After enduring slavery and a century of Jim Crow, the Black community wanted action. A voluntary plan represented a bitter pill to swallow. Woefully lacking in voting power, the Black community could rely only on moral persuasion and intervention by the courts.

Although the Pearsall plan operated as a delaying tactic to integration, it avoided the backlash experienced in other Southern states. No schools shuttered. No one exercised the right to use private tuition to avoid desegregation. As school systems, including those in Craven County, Wayne County, Durham, and Chapel Hill, chose to desegregate, Hodges applauded their decisions as an example for others. This process provided time for biracial committees and Good Neighbor Councils at the local level to build support for desegregation. By the early 1960s, localities such as Raleigh, Winston-Salem, Charlotte, and Wilmington integrated all public facilities. A process that encouraged these local collaborations would pay dividends after the passage of the Civil Rights Act in 1964 when the Triangle community had to deal with federally mandated busing and other measures for integration. Later chapters will examine how these local collaborations led to a novel approach to public schools in Wake County that ensured RTP workers an attractive educational option.

The Pearsall plan charted a unique path in the South by giving local control and a safety valve as Black students were admitted into previously segregated schools. While North Carolina did not lead the South in rates of integration, the state's reputation for stable race relations remained largely intact. That reputation would prove crucial, positioning RTP for economic success in the years ahead, as will be seen.

Moderation's Rewards

The outcome of the 1960 election offers additional evidence that North Carolina's measured approach to integration had an upside. I. Beverly Lake, a former assistant attorney general who represented North Carolina before the US Supreme Court in its deliberations leading to the *Brown* decision, challenged former State Senator Terry Sanford for governor in 1960. Hodges had refused to fire Lake for inflammatory statements he made about segregation. Instead, Hodges isolated Lake, disregarding his recommendations in favor of continued segregation. Hodges did not want to give Lake a bigger platform. In the Democratic primary run-off between Lake and Sanford, desegregation took center stage. Sanford received an endorsement from Pearsall and others who supported a continuation of the state's moderate approach to integration. Lake took a hard line in favor of segregation similar to other Southern states. Sanford won decisively with 352,133 votes to Lake's 275,905.[28] The outcome of this election reverberated for decades to come. It demonstrated a reservoir of public support for the incremental advancements toward desegregation led by Hodges.

Sanford struck a nuanced shift in tone in favor of integration. His words acknowledged the frustration experienced by the Black community. At his inauguration, Sanford pointedly announced: "We are not going to forget, as we move into the challenging and demanding years ahead, that no group of our citizens can be denied the right to participate in the opportunities of first-class citizenship."[29] In an important public gesture, Sanford also enrolled his children in a desegregated Raleigh school.

Finally, Sanford took the gamble of backing John Kennedy in the 1960 presidential primary. Most Democratic leaders, including Hodges, backed Lyndon Johnson. After Sanford made the second nominating speech for Kennedy at the Democratic Convention in Los Angeles, he faced backlash back home.[30] Many voters viewed Kennedy's Catholicism and tenor on civil rights with deep suspicion. However, Sanford's endorsement proved a point he also made in his 1961 inaugural address: "I want North Carolina to move into the mainstream of America and to strive to become the leading state of the nation."[31] Kennedy's victory in North Carolina ensured his electoral victory nationally. Not only did Sanford secure political capital with the new administration, Sanford's victory in the same election furthered the state's moderate reputation on civil rights and an openness to building a new economy.

Chemstrand

By the end of Hodges's tenure as governor, RTP finally captured its first success. Chemstrand, a chemical company based in Decatur, Alabama, undertook an extensive search for a new location in 1958 that would house a facility for research scientists. At the time, competition for this type of talent was fierce, and the company no doubt saw this move as an opportunity to find a location attractive to a highly educated workforce.

Chemstrand made an initial decision to open its research facility in Princeton, New Jersey. Undaunted, William Little saw an opening during a chance meeting with Bruce Ballentine who had come to the Triangle in the spring of

1958 to recruit graduates from the University of North Carolina to work at Chemstrand. Little showed Ballentine a Park brochure and got a positive reaction. Ballentine agreed to show the brochure to the company's vice president of research in Decatur. Shortly thereafter, a faculty delegation representing all three Triangle universities visited Decatur. Chemstrand reversed course and decided to locate its new research facility at RTP.

This was a much-needed shot in the arm. Chemstrand purchased more than one hundred acres of land from RTF and began construction in early October 1959. The new Chemstrand Research Center was dedicated on February 1, 1961, with new Governor Terry Sanford and the Kennedy administration's new Commerce Secretary, Luther Hodges, in attendance. Paul Gross delivered the dedication address. Publicly, Chemstrand stated, "A principal factor in [our] decision was the stimulating research climate already established in the Triangle, with its proximity to 900 scientists at State College, Duke University, and the University of North Carolina, and to the research staff of the new Research Triangle Institute." The company also cited the area's cultural and recreational activities in its decision.

Privately, Chemstrand had other reasons. The company dispatched a team of consultants to assess the site, including a look at the state's social stability. If part of the motivation was to find a location attractive to scientists, it did not make sense to duplicate the same challenges present at Chemstrand's facility in Alabama. The consultant's report (marked confidential) showed that the company paid particular attention to the risk of school closings in response to desegregation. After consulting with the governor, businesses, and university faculty, "many of whom have a northern background," the report concluded that "the situation is sufficiently well under control and the prognosis sufficiently good as to raise no problems on these counts greater than might conceivably be faced in many northern locations. Indeed, the courage and foresightedness with which they are approaching the problem engenders a tremendous respect and presages well for the future of the state both materially and culturally."[32]

These conclusions certainly provide some support for the approach taken in North Carolina. The state's moderate stance on desegregation would serve RTP well in the years ahead.

6

IBM and Validation at Last

When the news broke in 1965 that International Business Machines (IBM) would locate a major facility in Research Triangle Park, the *Raleigh Times* informed its readers that it was equivalent to having the New York Yankees move to Raleigh.[1] That announcement was part of a shock wave that changed perceptions of RTP overnight—from a marginal success with a murky future to a comer that might morph into a world-leading tech hub. In time, its RTP site would become IBM's largest in the world.

The bombshell news of IBM, however, followed a difficult time for RTP. The Park began with a flurry of activity, including the launch of Research Triangle Institute (RTI) and the Chemstrand decision. In the years that followed, the Park attracted only a few occupants, and none of them purchased enough land to put the Research Triangle Foundation (RTF) on a sound financial footing.[2] Unlike RTI, the RTF received no public money. It depended on land sales to fund its operations, which now included several staff members.

Karl Robbins died in early 1960. The RTF could no longer delay the return of his initial investment in Pinelands, which Robbins had generously rolled into the RTF. As a result, the RTF mortgaged its real estate for $1.3 million. It used the debt to pay Robbins's estate. It also paid back the $100,000 investment from Saunders, Guest's loans, and those of three other investors. In addition, the foundation used the loan to acquire approximately 362 acres, filling in several donut holes within the assemblage. RTP now approached 5,000 acres but would require major sales to remain solvent.[3] In 1962, the RTF opened a sales office in New York City but closed it after eighteen fruitless months.[4] Years later, Elizabeth Aycock, the RTF's administrative secretary and treasurer, commented she lacked sufficient funds to purchase pencils for the office at that time.[5]

The pressure to keep RTP going fell on Hodges's successor, Governor Terry Sanford. He shared Hodges's belief that the future of North Carolina rested, in part, on the creation of a technology-based economy tied to research at the universities. Without revenue from land sales, Sanford filled the same role Archie Davis had: appealing to the civic spirit of wealthy Tar Heels to keep the Park afloat. He phoned many of them from the library at the governor's mansion with the help of Phil Carlton, a University of North Carolina law student and summer volunteer for the governor's office.

Carlton describes his role as "a flunky" and occasional driver, but he'd gotten to know Sanford well as a young Democrat in Sanford's winning 1960 campaign. With Sanford's wife, Margaret Rose, and family away at the beach, the governor offered to host young Phil at the mansion. In dialing for dollars to avoid a default on obligations of RTF, the governor and Carlton used three phones in the library. As Sanford spoke to one potential contributor, Carlton would phone another on a second line. The third line was reserved for callbacks.

This approach led to some tense moments. During one session, Sanford had just gotten on the line with a prospective donor when Charlie Cannon, the president of Cannon Mills and possibly the richest man in the state, called back. Cupping one hand over the receiver, Carlton stage-whispered to Sanford, "It's Charlie Cannon." Covering his receiver too, Sanford whispered back with a grin: "You let Charlie Cannon off the line, and you die." Carlton then told Cannon, "Sir, can you hold the line for just a moment? The governor has just stepped out of the room but won't be long."[6]

Support for the Park would come, but only after years of arduous effort, as the need for urgent calls from the governor suggest. Carlton later became a justice on the state Supreme Court. Sanford later served as president of Duke University, where he became a prodigious fundraiser. He was also elected to the US Senate. Sanford's skills as a fundraiser bridged the Park to better times.

Besides using his position as governor to cajole business leaders to keep RTP going, Sanford leveraged his close ties to President Kennedy to appoint Luther Hodges as the Commerce Secretary. That position gave Hodges a platform to promote the state on national and international levels. Even so, Sanford and Hodges struggled to convert their considerable political capital into direct economic benefits for the state.

On January 6, 1965, Sanford's last day in office, he announced that the federal government's new Environmental Health Sciences Center (later the National Institute of Environmental Health Sciences [NIEHS]) would locate a $70 million facility in RTP. It would occupy 509 acres of land where Sanford envisioned a second environmental laboratory one day. The General Assembly later appropriated $750,000 to cover the value of the land. The announcement followed three and a half years of intense effort by Park leaders and state government officials to secure the facility. Both Maryland and West Virginia competed hard for it, with the indomitable Senator Robert Byrd of West Virginia leading the charge. However, shortly before his assassination, President Kennedy chose the Triangle, mainly because of its three tier-one research universities.[7]

This new facility eventually employed roughly 1,800 federal workers, focusing on the health impacts of environmental contaminants.[8] In addition to its research role, it had an important responsibility: maintaining the national toxicology list of all carcinogens. The NIEHS also had a significant budget to fund basic research at universities, and its presence boosted such research. It brought scientific talent to the area, which in turn attracted other companies. For example, its scientific director, Martin Rodbell, received the Nobel Prize in 1994 for work he did on the components of cellular communication, including the role of G proteins. Eventually, state leaders, including EPA administrators Willis Greenstreet and William Laxton, Gov. Jim Hunt, and US Representative David Price, would secure funds to bring an EPA lab to this site in the 1990s.[9]

Another seminal event occurred in Durham in early 1965. By a razor thin vote of 7–6, the city finally agreed to allocate water and sewer to RTP. These utilities initially supported the Environmental Health Services Center. Durham's mayor, Wensell Grabarek, helped round up the votes. Not afraid of a challenge, Grabarek had fought in the Battle of the Bulge, earning a Bronze Star. He intuitively understood that RTP offered a future for Durham. Timing, however, also played a role. In early 1964, US Surgeon General Luther Terry went on television and announced that tobacco was linked to cancer deaths. At the time, seventy million Americans—42 percent of adults—smoked. The press conference proved seminal.[10] Years later, Grabarek relayed the fact that there were confidential discussions at the time with American Tobacco and Liggett & Myers. These companies informed Durham officials that the outlook for their continued operations in Durham looked dim. Plans to expand cigarette production at the Chesterfield Building were scrapped after the Surgeon General announcement.[11] This information helped swing support to provide RTP with sixteen million gallons per day (MGD), the exact amount RTP requested, and the amount of capacity Durham had available at the time. This vote finally put to rest long-simmering concerns about a source of water and sewer for the Park.[12]

The announcement about the Environmental Health Sciences Center and a decision on utilities provided a sense of relief after years of struggle. What followed in 1965 would exceed the wildest dreams of the Park's founders. In the early 1960s, a brilliant young IBM computer engineer, Frederick P. Brooks Jr., led a high-risk project to develop interoperable software that could run on hardware of varying sizes. Until then, engineers had to overhaul software programs to run on each new machine produced. It was a costly, redundant practice that IBM vowed to eliminate to enable customers to move from smaller to larger computers without the need to rewrite software.[13]

Fortune magazine called the project "IBM's $5,000,000,000 Gamble" and said the company was betting its future on the venture. At the time, rivals like Burroughs, Univac, and NCR were mounting vigorous challenges to IBM.[14] The team Brooks led developed the iconic System/360, an operating system that revolutionized computing and enabled IBM to dominate the field into the mid-1980s when new operating systems like Microsoft Windows and Apple iOS emerged.

Like the System/360, Brooks was iconic too. He had grown up in Greenville, North Carolina, and earned a degree in physics at Duke University and a PhD in applied mathematics at Harvard University. When IBM announced the System/360 on April 7, 1964, Brooks was just thirty-three. He led one of two teams working on the engineering behind the System/360, and Brooks's team would emerge from this internal competition with the preferred implementation approach.[15] He had quietly informed IBM a year earlier that he would leave after the System/360 was ready to manufacture to set up a computer science department at the University of North Carolina at Chapel Hill. But early in 1965, executives at IBM grew increasingly concerned about delays to the completion of the System/360 software necessary to deliver the machines.

At that point, Tom Watson Jr., IBM's president, invited Brooks to company headquarters in Armonk, New York, for a one-on-one lunch to ask if he would reconsider his decision to leave. When Brooks made it clear that his mind was made up, Watson asked him to stay on for a year to get the System/360 through alpha testing to confirm that everything worked properly. In return, Watson promised that IBM would hire at its expense an academic of Brooks's choosing to help set up the new department at the University of North Carolina. "And when Carolina needs a new computer, we'll help," Watson added.[16]

After careful deliberation and conversations with his wife, Nancy, Brooks accepted Watson's offer. Not long thereafter, Brooks got the System/360 through alpha testing and ready for a successful product launch of 144 new products that could send and receive data.

Brooks would have one more monumental meeting with Watson—this one on February 23, 1965, at the IBM Homestead in Poughkeepsie, New York, where senior executives from client companies stayed. Brooks would later say it was providential that the meeting was scheduled after dinner when Watson would not be pressed for time. Brooks had two closely related agenda items: first, to get IBM's help in securing a System/360 for a new Triangle Universities Computation Center (TUCC); second, to urge Watson to consider the Park as a site for a new IBM plant and lab. Brooks had encouraged the formation of TUCC because Duke University, North Carolina State University, and the University of North Carolina needed more computing power than they could afford. He also knew that Boulder, Colorado, and Manassas, Virginia, were the frontrunners for IBM's new plant and lab.[17]

"I knew IBM hadn't taken a good look here [at RTP], so I went out to the Research Triangle Park and talked to the people in charge of the Park," Brooks said in an interview just before he died.[18] "I got all the sales materials, the maps, airline schedules, and the whole works. . . . He [Watson] listened carefully for an hour and a half to the whole spiel about RTP and the new joint computing center. Then he said, 'Fred, the IBM company is not in the habit of locating laboratories for the convenience of one person.' But he then agreed to send Wis Miller, the head of the real estate division, to RTP to have a look. Miller came away from that visit impressed, and RTP got the new lab and plant. The company also rented $900,000 worth of computer time over a three-year period from when the new consortium formed by the Big Three universities."[19]

Brooks would chair the University of North Carolina department of computer science for twenty years. He became a pioneer in computer graphics and virtual reality and adapted those fields to the study of molecules in biology. He has a project management principle—Brooks's Law—named after him. It says, "Adding manpower to a late software project makes it later." This aphorism makes him an icon among software engineers to this day. Brooks won many prizes, including the National Medal of Technology and Innovation in 1985 and the Turing Award, which many consider to be the Nobel Prize of computer science, in 1999. He died on November 17, 2022, at age ninety-one.

In addition to the considerable influence of Fred Brooks, a powerful social issue of the integration of public schools had a major impact on IBM's decision to locate a large facility in RTP. With demand for the System/360 far exceeding sales projections, it was clear that new facilities would be needed, and a major reshuffling of where products got produced followed. Long before that, IBM had decided to locate new plants in the West and the South. The company chose Boulder, Colorado, in the West fairly quickly. The decision for the South finally came down to two options: Manassas, Virginia, and RTP. After assessing site characteristics—roads, airports, schools, livability, and so on—the IBM real estate division recommended Manassas. It was undeniable that the Manassas area roads and its close proximity to one of the most modern airports in the world, Dulles International, offered advantages RTP could not match. After all, the Park lacked an interstate highway and had poor roads overall. The potential IBM site within RTP also lacked a rail siding that the company needed.

However, in the end, the issue of school desegregation tilted the scales toward RTP. Unlike North Carolina, the state of Virginia had refused to accept the Supreme Court's 1954 mandate on school desegregation as the law of the land. Two years after the decision in *Brown v. Board of Education*, Virginia had embarked on a policy of "massive resistance" to the Supreme Court ruling. The term *massive resistance* had been coined by US Senator Harry F. Byrd, a former governor who exercised considerable political influence through what was known as the Byrd Machine. His influence was strongest in the rural counties of south Virginia, which had large Black populations.

In the years immediately following the high court's decision, Virginia mainly mounted legal challenges to the controversial ruling. But that changed in September 1958 when two federal judges ordered the immediate desegregation of public schools in Charlottesville, Front Royal, and Norfolk—nine schools in all. Governor Lindsey Almond promptly closed the nine schools, and thirteen thousand students were then locked out. The policy of massive resistance had suddenly morphed into one of massive displacement; the rigid wall of opposition to desegregation had been elevated.

Governor Almond soon relented on his closing policy, and seventeen Black students in Norfolk and four in Arlington entered previously all-white schools without much protest. Many more adjustments were still to be made, but the last segregated Black school in Manassas did not close until 1966.[20] As recounted earlier, consensus around the Pearsall plan had allowed North Carolina to take incremental steps toward integration without widespread disruption to schools or otherwise.

IBM CEO Tom Watson became keenly aware of this difference through a fishing buddy, Commerce Secretary Luther Hodges, who as North Carolina's governor had firsthand experience with the divisive issue. Hodges had been lobbying Watson for years to build a plant in RTP. As reflected in Chemstrand's private assessment of the school situation in North Carolina, the issue of desegregation had particular salience to companies dependent on recruiting talent. Many of these scientists and engineers grew up outside the South and needed reassurance that life there was not so different from other parts of the country. North Carolina's moderate stance on integration helped assuage those concerns. When IBM's real estate division relayed its final recommendation to put the new plant and lab in Manassas, Watson overruled them. He reportedly said, "No—we're going to Research Triangle Park instead."

Once Watson made that decision, the company implemented it with all due speed. On April 14, 1965, IBM announced that it had purchased 400 acres of land in RTP seven miles south of Durham, and that site and design studies would begin at once for a structure of 500,000 square feet. About a thousand employees—two-thirds of them local—were expected to be hired at the new facility in 1966 and 1967. That ambitious schedule called for a greatly accelerated construction schedule. Almost immediately the company began interviewing prospective employees in the basement of Hillyer Memorial Christian Church on Hillsborough Street in Raleigh; it soon announced that it would open a new employment office nearby.[21] The same announcement reported that the new IBM plant would produce data communications equipment and other units for the new System/360, including terminals and output printers.

The expedited time schedule did not come without hiccups. The manufacturing aspects of IBM's operations faced challenges. RTP's covenants and zoning did not permit manufacturing. The RTF had to revise the covenants to allow certain types of manufacturing within parts of RTP where IBM would locate. Pearson Stewart had to return to Durham to create a new zoning district called Research Applications, which allowed manufacturing when tied to a high degree of scientific input. Even with these changes to the restrictions in RTP, IBM approached local builder Willie York with an urgent request: complete a building for manufacturing on Yonkers Road in Raleigh within ninety days. York accepted the challenge.[22] The fact that IBM required an element of manufacturing would become a feature of the technological landscape in the Triangle. Later chapters will show how this aspect shaped the social and economic fabric of the Triangle region, making it distinct from other tech hubs.

IBM had five reasons for its 1965 decision to locate a large installation in RTP: First, it had an excellent workforce; second, it had great universities; third, it was a good place to live and raise a family; and, fourth, its leaders were deeply committed to collaboration. That meant those in charge of government, universities, and corporations were adept at solving problems—and nearly always were open to compromise. Of course, IBM had a fifth reason it did not want to publicize. North Carolina's ability to maintain social stability as it made a difficult transition to integration distinguished it from competitors.

Just before IBM made its final decision in 1965 to build a plant and lab in RTP, senior representatives of the company met with Governor Dan Moore, who had just been sworn in as the state's chief executive. They emphasized to Moore that a rail siding would be needed for the new plant. While most company products were shipped by truck, they needed the option to ship by rail as well.

When he heard this, Moore politely excused himself for a few minutes to make an important call. He came back shortly and told the group, "I just talked to the president of CSX, and we'll have the rail siding."[23] Was this part of a carefully staged show? The IBM representatives felt that it might have been—that the governor had been tipped off on what they wanted and had actually called the president of CSX a few days before the meeting. But that hardly mattered: The incident proved that North Carolina was a "can do" state—that public/private cooperation was a lot more than an empty phrase. At that same meeting, Governor Moore promised to build a new section of Interstate 40 through the Park to avoid traffic snarls due to inadequate roads. That roadway got built not long after IBM moved into its new RTP installation.[24]

IBM brought an important chapter for RTP to a close. It ensured the years of effort by Romeo Guest and so many others were not in vain. It told the world that any technology company looking to establish a new facility should consider North Carolina. Years later, Archie Davis reflected, "IBM was the turning point. Not only was the foundation now free of debt, but IBM's presence also validated the mission of the Park."

PART II

Big Dreams Come True

(1966–1999)

IBM's decision in 1965 marked a decisive turning point for RTP. It announced RTP as a viable location for technology companies looking to build an R&D facility in the Southeast. Part II charts RTP's rise from that event through the 1990s. During this period, RTP established itself as a global brand. Its success rested on the same factors that produced its liftoff: innovation and collaboration.

Part II begins with the continued efforts by state and local leaders during the 1970s to navigate desegregation in a way that ensured relocating tech workers had a strong public school system for their families. Success required Black and white leaders to understand the stakes involved. They had to trust in each other and make difficult decisions despite strong forces pulling them apart.

This part also addresses the willingness of state leaders to invent new institutions to forge into uncharted areas of science and technology. Such investments allowed RTP to emerge as a center for life science during a critical window for that industry. It also helped RTP gain a foothold in the dynamic and more mature information technology industry.

As research produced a number of groundbreaking discoveries, universities and academics increasingly warmed up to the idea of commercialization. During this timeframe, faculty members founded several prominent companies that became major local employers. Business leaders also became acutely aware of RTP's major weakness: infrastructure for start-ups. This period saw a wave of new tools in the form of incubators, venture capital firms, and programming all aimed at entrepreneurs seeking to bring new ideas to market. These efforts broadened the economic base of RTP and the region beyond a few large companies.

Throughout this time, RTP encouraged collaboration among local governments to provide needed amenities to workers and their families. Regional cooperation and planning efforts established a nationally recognized quality of life. By the 1990s, the combination of tech companies, scientists, and living environment established a global brand known as the Research Triangle. Economic developers routinely made a pilgrimage to RTP to study it. Countless metropolitan areas around the world sought to emulate it in the hope of achieving similar economic success. In many ways, this period represented the height of RTP's influence over the regional agenda—in terms of planning, economic development activities, public investment, and branding.

7

Creating a Viable Public School Option

As seen with the decisions to locate in RTP by Chemstrand and IBM, corporate leaders wanted certainty that workers would feel comfortable sending their children to area public schools. Images on television of defiance to desegregation and a bias against Southerners as uneducated caused fear among workers moving to RTP from the Northeast and other parts of the United States. What kind of environment would they encounter in North Carolina? Would such a move impair the educational and career opportunities for their children? Although the Triangle managed to score a couple of major successes in the 1960s, it had much more work to do on public education to build on that success and compete at the national level.

The local approach taken by the state as set forth in the Pearsall plan delayed desegregation in North Carolina. In doing so, it gave school systems a sense of control over the pace of integration. It allowed conversations among Blacks and whites through initiatives like the Good Neighbor Councils to build trust and relationships founded on a shared belief in the importance of public education.[1] Combined with the state's history of strong support for public schools, North Carolina had an advantage over other Southern states in attracting technology workers. However, white leaders could not "slow play" desegregation forever.

In 1955, the Supreme Court ruled that public school systems "must move with deliberate speed to dismantle the dual school systems and to remove the vestiges thereof."[2] Referred to as "*Brown* II," this decision required states to produce plans for desegregation or be found in noncompliance and forfeit federal educational funds. North Carolina was well positioned to respond to this mandate as one of the only states with a department of education, known as the Department of Public Instruction. The General Assembly funded this department, which oversaw curriculum for public schools. The state also funded teacher salaries, leaving school construction to localities. During his term in office, Governor Sanford raised taxes to increase teacher salaries, building on the record of previous governors to make the state a leader in public education.

The career of Dudley Flood demonstrates how North Carolina was positioned for a new economy.[3] Born in Hertford County, one of the poorest in the state, Flood attended North Carolina Central University, a historically Black college and university, graduating in 1954, the year of the *Brown* decision. Flood planned to attend law school. However, he was recruited to teach school and quickly determined his calling was education. He returned to Hertford County and "fell in love with the kids." In the late 1960s, Flood took a position as principal in the larger Pitt County. His position put him at the center of *Brown* II's directive to desegregate "with deliberate speed" and to "remove the vestiges of segregation." Flood found success in convincing white families to send their children to formerly all-Black schools. His work gained the attention of officials in Raleigh. Craig Phillips was elected state school superintendent in 1968 and served in that role for twenty years. Phillips wanted a new state framework for desegregation. He created a Desegregation Technical Assistance Team. The team offered technical assistance to schools to facilitate desegregation. Phillips plucked Flood from Pitt County to lead this team along with Gene Causby, a white educator. Their work would help North Carolina comply with federal directives while avoiding widespread violence and resistance experienced by other states throughout the country. North Carolina had 152 school systems in 1967. Each had to have a plan to show compliance to the federal Office of Civil Rights. Between 1969 and 1975, Flood and Causby visited all 152 systems. They worked closely with the schools and the communities on strategies that supported desegregation. By 1975, every school system complied with federal mandates.

While Flood developed numerous strategies to coach local districts on ways to manage desegregation, two stand out. They both center on novel approaches at collaboration. First, Flood went to trusted community institutions like churches and civic organizations to build relationships. He enlisted the leaders of these institutions to join a Principal Advisory Committee. These leaders acted as the gatekeepers of the community. They would meet in churches and pool halls and other familiar locations. Flood authorized the gatekeepers to bring concerns to the committee. If there was an immediate solution, the gatekeeper would get credit. If the solution required funds or a legal solution, the gatekeeper would communicate that back to their constituents and, if appropriate, provide mitigations in the meantime. If nothing could be done to address the concern, the gatekeepers would explain why. In this way, the community did not view the school principal as a foreign emissary within its midst. Trusted leaders actively engaged in the wrenching change experienced by families.

A second key strategy related to reframing mandated changes to create greater acceptance. This was particularly challenging in communities under a court order to desegregate. A major area of resistance related to transportation. Opponents of desegregation used the term "forced busing" to object to changes in school assignment. Flood would explain that North Carolina law required transportation if a student lived more than one mile from a school. Flood met with the KKK and other bastions of resistance. He explained that no one had to take the bus. Most of the students using buses were Black children going to majority-white schools.

Flood would help communities overcome the trap of relitigating feelings bound up in a century of Jim Crow laws. He would say, "We are not here to determine who is right. We will help you determine what is right—what will work here because every child deserves an education." He never used the word "racism," opting for "inequity," which was "not loaded." These pivots would center conversations on the best interests of the children and avoid zero-sum narratives. Parents also had concerns about the loss of school identity and the idea of racially mixed school activities. Flood would encourage schools to incorporate the colors of the school that students had left behind. He helped teachers and parents understand that incorporating more than one tradition into an activity simply broadened participation and strengthened the cohesion of the school. Cheerleading was a major issue. The tradition of Black squads was moving side to side. The tradition of white squads was jumping up and down. If the cheerleading coach acknowledged both styles, the new squad would not exclude a particular race. The same went for the playing styles of sports teams such as basketball. These issues shaped whether a community could successfully navigate the uncharted path to desegregation. Solutions to them required these types of creative collaborations.

Wake County

The communities surrounding RTP had to face these same issues. Although RTP resided in Durham County, most of the families coming to work at RTP would live in neighboring Wake County. One of the largest school systems in North Carolina, Wake County enjoyed a demographic advantage over Durham. Wake County's minority population was approximately 25 percent, while Durham's approached 40 percent. Studies show that white parents are more likely to accept minority enrollment up to 40 percent of the student population. When enrollment exceeds that demographic tipping point, white parents remove their children from the school. This phenomenon put Wake County in a better position to manage desegregation.[4]

The first test came in the 1970s. At the time, Raleigh and Wake County had separate school systems. Both had good schools. Although the overall minority population of Wake County was approximately 25 percent, most of the Black population resided in Raleigh and attended Raleigh schools. As Raleigh schools desegregated, white families began moving outside the city—a pattern of "white flight" that took hold across the United States at this time. Business leaders saw warning signs. If white families withdrew their investment in Raleigh schools in the form of time and attention, the school system would deteriorate and workers would have fewer options of where to live. Those who remained in Raleigh would experience deteriorating schools. In addition, declining population was causing the closure of schools in Raleigh while kids had to attend class in overcrowded suburban schools. Raleigh residents objected to financing more county schools while their schools declined.

To address the social and economic challenges caused by white flight, local leaders floated the idea of merging Raleigh and Wake County schools. A merger would help obviate white flight by creating one school system that managed finances and school assignments. Local officials placed a nonbinding referendum on the ballot to merge the schools in 1973. It failed by a 3–1 margin. In an act of political courage, the local legislative delegation passed a merger bill the following year. Such acts of defiance of public opinion often meet with political backlash. In this case, it did not.

One of the local legislators, Wade Smith, explains the vote: "The local delegation would hold weekly meetings with constituents. Month after month, a group of Black leaders attended these meetings—people like John Winters," who would later serve in the state Senate.[5] They forcefully and respectfully explained to the delegation that a reversion to segregated schools would hurt the community on many levels. Smith recalls such leaders relaying "how desperately important it was" and that the community "could not afford to kick this can down the road."[6] He and other local legislators listened. Reflecting the state's more moderate attitude toward race, legislative leaders listened and were moved to action through these conversations.

The state's legacy on race also motivated Black leaders to engage in such discussions with white legislators. Flood notes that Black leaders could envision a seat at the table within the power structure due to a number of role models. An educator, Howard Lee, served as mayor of Chapel Hill and later as a state senator. Henry Frye served as a justice on the North Carolina Supreme Court. Julius Chambers graduated first in his law class at the University of North Carolina and litigated many of the seminal civil rights cases in North Carolina. Ralph Campbell, one of the first children to integrate Raleigh schools, became state auditor. These and other leaders inspired the Black community to work within the system, unlike in some other Southern states that effectively blocked any such opportunities for Blacks. According to Flood, that dynamic could lead Black leaders to protect their status as a big fish in a small pond as opposed to seeking change within the system.

RTP also played an important role in the merger. Wade Smith recounts the acute awareness local leaders had about the reputation of Wake County schools to companies in RTP such as IBM. Dick Daugherty, who led operations for IBM in the 1970s and 1980s, had to explain to incoming workers they would encounter a school system much like the one they left in New York, New Jersey, or other parts of the country. At the time of the vote, Daugherty advised Smith "the Wake County School System was one of the reasons why great companies come here."[7] He reminded Smith that IBM chose North Carolina over Virginia based on "leadership in the community" and its ability to manage tough issues like desegregation.[8] The Black community and technology companies had a shared interest in seeing a strong, integrated school system in Wake County. Given RTP's relationship to the area universities and community colleges, public schools operated as a natural extension and component of the educational ecosystem.

Flood traveled to nearly every US state as a consultant. During his travels, he met Walter Marks, a school superintendent in Montclair, New Jersey. Marks developed a magnet system for the seven schools in Montclair, giving each one a unique focus to draw white students to schools with higher minority enrollment. His work there led to a position as Wake County's second postmerger superintendent, following John A. Murphy. Marks asked Flood to join him as assistant superintendent. Not wanting to leave his position with the state, Flood declined and recommended Bob Bridges. Flood had helped recruit Bridges to the central school office in Raleigh and saw him as an administrator with immense talent. Walter accepted Flood's recommendation, placing Bridges in charge of day-to-day operations of the school system while Walter engaged with the public.

Walter moved aggressively to deploy a magnet system in Wake County designed to bring racial balance to the schools. The Wake County public school system (WCPSS) set a target for Black enrollment for each school between 15 percent and 45 percent. He did this by using Title I funds to supplement programs in schools located in Central and East Raleigh. To access some of the best educational programs at these schools, families from Cary and North Raleigh and other areas voluntarily entered their children into the magnet system. Otherwise, the school system assigned suburban students to neighborhood schools. Meanwhile, Black students were bused from inner-city neighborhoods to these suburban schools to reach the enrollment goal. Before long, inner-city schools such as Hunter Elementary, Ligon Middle School, and Enloe High School gained reputations as among the best public schools in the nation. RTP workers gladly entered their children into the magnet system, helping to reduce white flight and the resegregation of the schools.

As inner-city schools improved, it became more difficult to access Title I funds. Yet Walter continued to direct funds to Raleigh schools, generating increased pushback. After five years, he stepped down as superintendent. Bridges took over—one of four Black superintendents in the state at the time. Unlike Walter, he rarely attended public events. He maintained a low profile. He worked closely with the school board and county commission, which funded the school facilities and teacher supplements. Bridges crafted solutions that these elected officials could defend to the public, particularly as tensions increased between suburban and urban areas over competition for limited funds.

While Walter helped initiate the magnet system, Bridges ensured its acceptance and longevity. Unlike Walter, Bridges grew up in North Carolina. He avoided the spotlight. Flood shared a home in the same middle-class neighborhood as Bridges—Biltmore Hills in southeast Raleigh. They visited nearly every week. Flood's statewide and national perspective and way of framing challenging issues to enlist others in collaborative solutions rubbed off on Bridges, who deployed immense skills as a listener to process feedback into acceptable solutions. Some saw Bridges as standoffish, but his professional approach gained the respect of local leaders and increased confidence in Wake County's approach.

By the late 1980s and 1990s, Wake County schools enjoyed a reputation for excellence. Instead of a detriment to corporate recruitment, the school system bolstered the area's strong reputation for education. According to Flood, "Education sold the industrial complex and the industrial complex sold education." The two generated a virtuous cycle. Local collaborations that started in the 1960s laid a foundation for the merger of the 1970s, which in turn produced a unique magnet system with racially balanced schools. Wake County served as a model for integration—a word never uttered by Bridges or others working quietly to strengthen the school system.

Harvey Schmitt, who led the Greater Raleigh Chamber of Commerce for twenty-one years beginning in 1993, reiterated this point: "Strong public schools were critical in attracting companies from the north to the south. A good public-school system meant companies did not have to factor in private-school costs in offers to move or recruit talent. In evaluating a desirable quality of life, you always include the schools, and it was often included in market rankings. For a variety of reasons (boosting underperforming schools, improving student outcomes, broadening economic opportunities), Wake County also saw a combined district as a pathway to improved business recruitment."[9] For these reasons, the business community developed organizations such as Wake Education Partnership to ensure public schools have the funding and programs they need to excel.

The success of Wake County's schools did come with a price for RTP. It created regional tensions that bubbled over by the late 1980s when the City of Durham attempted to annex RTP. In 1985, a young, dynamic Wib Gulley won election as mayor in Durham. He saw Durham struggling with the closure of cigarette factories, including American Tobacco and Liggett & Myers. At this time, Duke University had little connection to the affairs of the city. Gulley saw realtors steering families to Wake County due to the schools. The local media and others played on Durham's reputation as a high-crime area. Most of Durham's growth occurred in Durham County, which had a separate school system. As hard as Gulley tried, he struggled to leverage any local investment from RTP. In sum, Gulley, along with other young progressives and Blacks living in Durham at the time, felt "the blessings of RTP did not extend to Durham."[10]

Against this backdrop, Durham initiated efforts to annex RTP. Durham first annexed properties to the west of RTP, setting up the potential annexation of contiguous lands in RTP. The Research Triangle Foundation (RTF) and business leaders opposed the annexation. Such annexation would introduce another layer of property taxes for owners within the Park. Just as importantly, RTP had an identity free of any particular jurisdiction. It had its own planning director and charted its own course. Becoming part of the City of Durham would fundamentally alter that governance structure.

Upon learning of the annexation effort, Dick Daugherty picked up the phone and called one of the most powerful legislators in North Carolina at the time, Senator Kenneth Royall. Daugherty said, "I know this is ticklish," because Royall represented Durham. But Royall responded immediately. "I understand. I think you're absolutely right—this is for the good of the State of North Carolina." Within days, Royall introduced a bill that shut down the annexation movement. This episode revealed understandable tensions, particularly when the region's major commercial tax base—RTP—existed just beyond the reach of a struggling urban area. The end of the annexation effort showed that powerful forces would ensure that RTP would remain independent as originally conceived and serve the entire region as an economic engine. Durham would eventually experience "the blessings of RTP," as we will see in part III, through important new collaborations.

In many ways, the 1990s marked a golden age for Wake County schools. Its schools far exceeded the national average for diversity.[11] Meanwhile, the academic performance and reputation of Wake County schools improved. This gave economic developers an important talking point to sell technology companies on RTP. At the same time, this success sowed the seeds of strife. As the population of the region grew, RTP workers usually chose to live in Wake County to access its schools. Explosive population growth made pupil assignment more challenging, especially as growth centered in western Wake County. Although educational and business leaders maintained a consensus for diversity through the 1990s, disenchanted families gave rise to school-board candidates demanding a return to neighborhood schools. Those forces would gather steam in the following decade, as will be addressed in part III.

8

The Birth of Life Science

In 1880, two young American pharmaceutical salesmen formed a company in London that would revolutionize medicine in Europe by mass-producing pills that replaced potions and powders widely used at the time. The pills were branded as "tabloids" by combining the words *tablet* and *alkaloid*. To capitalize on what soon became a sterling reputation for healing and cures, the founders, Silas Burroughs and Henry Wellcome, settled on a metaphorical mark—the unicorn—and built it into one of the most successful corporate marks of the day.[1] It was a perfect fit, because in many ways Burroughs Wellcome and Co. was a one-of-a-kind company.

At a time when traveling medical quacks were common, Burroughs Wellcome became in 1895 one of the world's first companies to market serum antitoxins for inoculation against diphtheria and tetanus. Revenues from vaccinations would prove to be a major source of income for the company for a great many years.[2] These and other new products—aspirin (previously imported from

Germany), chloroform, and iodine—became indispensable on the battlefields of World War I. The company's medical safety kits became standard issue for expeditions to unknown territory. Admiral Byrd carried them on his polar expeditions and astronauts even took them on Apollo missions to the moon. After a financial downturn in the aftermath of World War II, Burroughs Wellcome roared back with blockbuster discoveries such as the first drug for leukemia, immune suppressants for organ transplants, and antivirals like AZT, the first FDA-approved drug to treat HIV.[3] Over-the-counter products like Sudafed®, Actifed®, and Neosporin® were mass-market hits.[4]

Such breakthroughs burnished the company's reputation for scientific rigor even more and led to a doubling of sales between 1964 and 1969. In the 1920s, Burroughs Wellcome had established a US administrative and research headquarters in the village of Tuckahoe, a suburb of New York City, but four decades later it had become woefully inadequate. With no room in Tuckahoe for expansion, the company began looking for a new home to meet its managerial, research, and manufacturing requirements.[5]

Several sites were considered, but RTP quickly became the first choice. Factors in the company's decision included the presence of the area universities, the National Institute of Environmental Health Science (NIEHS), and the National Center for Health Statistics.[6] An able workforce and wide selection of building sites to choose from offered advantages as well. After the company made the decision, it bought sixty-six acres in the center of the Park and held a groundbreaking on August 21, 1969, for a new administrative and research headquarters building. It also announced that all its products (of which there were more than ninety at the time) would be manufactured at a 600,000-square-foot plant staffed by six hundred employees in Greenville, North Carolina, just over an hour east of Raleigh.[7] The Greenville facility represented an important milestone. It showed that RTP could be leveraged to spur advanced manufacturing throughout the state—one of the original goals of the Park's founders.

In many ways, the company's move to North Carolina was the perfect marriage: Burroughs Wellcome got a dramatic increase in production capacity and a working environment that would help lure the knowledge workers it relied on. For North Carolina, a new flag of great consequence and potential was being planted. The Park's founding governor, Luther Hodges, told the groundbreaking audience, "Today is the first time in the history of this state when an international organization breaks ground to establish their USA headquarters [here]. . . . If we had attempted to make a selection, we could not have found a more outstanding firm than Burroughs Wellcome and company."[8]

The governor's words were far from political hot air, because the arrival of Burroughs Wellcome opened the door to what has become one of the world's great centers of excellence in life science. In the vast field of life science, biotechnology features most prominently as a toolbox to create solutions to many intractable problems in food production and in medicine and vaccines to fight life-threatening diseases. At the time, no one understood the vast potential of the biotech industry and that RTP would emerge as one of its great hubs. That would take many more steps.

At the groundbreaking, Burroughs Wellcome also introduced a stunning architectural design for its new RTP headquarters building. It evoked a spaceship floating in the void for some and an Aztec temple for others. Its S-shaped structure featured 300,000 square feet of floor space on five levels. Positioned at the highest point in the Park, it appeared to extend the hill it sat on. Its estimated cost was $10 million, and it certainly evoked the company's one-of-a-kind unicorn brand.

The architect was Paul Rudolph, a staunch adherent of Brutalism, a style of architecture that emerged after World War II in civic spaces and revitalized urban neighborhoods. Rudolph had studied at Harvard under Walter Gropius, founder of the Bauhaus School, which influenced many iconic architects like Mies van der Rohe as well as faculty at the renowned NC State College of Design. Rudolph went on to earn a master's of architecture at Yale University, and after several years in private practice, he became chairman of the School of Architecture at Yale University. His design of the Yale University Art and Architecture Building remains his most notable and controversial work.

Among his many connections to Yale University was a former classmate, Fred Coe, the new president and CEO of Burroughs Wellcome, who had pushed hard as vice president to move to RTP, despite the opposition of the company's president at the time. In his remarks at the August 21, 1969, groundbreaking, Coe told the audience Rudolph's design would achieve "an ingenious combination of striking aesthetics and functional efficiency. . . . [It] will provide a splendid climate for scientific scholarship and for the exchange of ideas among scientists and administrators."[9] Most importantly, the building made a statement about RTP. The president of Preservation North Carolina, Myrick Howard, wrote later, "The futuristic architecture conveyed such confidence that it confirmed for skeptics that RTP was really going to be a big deal. The building didn't quietly sit back in the piney woods like the other buildings in the park. It was perched on a knoll overlooking the new highway. There was a real sense that 'we have arrived.'"[10]

An independent verdict of sorts was rendered on Rudolph's design in 1981, when the film studio Metro-Goldwyn-Mayer chose the building as the setting for its science fiction film *Brainstorm*. The production featured Natalie Wood, who was twice nominated for an Academy Award. Her costars were Louise Fletcher, Christopher Walken, and Cliff Robertson, each of whom had won an Oscar. Tragically, Wood drowned in a boating accident a few weeks before on-location filming ended. Her lookalike sister served as a double for the few remaining scenes to be shot.

"It's the best job I ever had in my life!"[11] Those words come from Christy Shaffer, who joined Burroughs Wellcome in 1984 while still a postdoctoral student in pharmacology at the University of North Carolina. It's a tall statement coming from a woman with her background: In 1995, Shaffer became president and CEO of Inspire Pharmaceuticals, where she raised more than $300 million in investment funding and took the company public five years later. Her observation is further magnified by the fact that *The Scientist* magazine named Inspire the "Best Place to Work for Scientists."[12]

Shaffer was exhilarated by the ambience and vibe of Burroughs Wellcome; the animated conversations in the cafeteria, where she could sit with two winners of the Nobel Prize; the mindset of "science must always come first"; the feeling of being part of a team—a family even; and a place where scientists actually worried about head lice in the Third World. No wonder she proudly wore her lab coat with the unicorn emblem.[13]

Indeed, her new company was different. It demonstrated a willingness to pursue treatments for any orphan disease (one with a global population of a thousand or so) no matter how small the pool of patients. Scientists and others at the company felt a moral obligation to find cures. Shaffer worked on a treatment for pulmonary hypertension, the first drug approved for that condition. While the disease was extraordinarily rare, the treatment became a multi billion-dollar success when eventually brought to market by United Therapeutics.[14]

One of Shaffer's role models was Gertrude B. Elion, the daughter of immigrants, who shared the Nobel Prize in 1988 with her colleague at the company, George Hitchings. Elion's grandfather died of stomach cancer just before she entered Hunter College in New York, and her fiancé died of pneumonia just after she received her chemistry degree. These losses strongly influenced her decision to dedicate her life to medicine. It was especially hard that the antibiotic amoxicillin could have saved her fiancé's life if discovered a few years earlier. Elion once told Shaffer: "I've got to find cures, so people don't die unnecessarily."[15]

Elion's influence helped galvanize Shaffer's decision to work on pulmonary hypertension.

Elion was a Phi Beta Kappa in college and wanted to become a lab scientist. Unfortunately, she couldn't get admitted to a PhD program because of her gender. Even finding work proved difficult. To gain experience, she went to secretarial school and then took several temporary jobs. While earning her MS in chemistry at New York University (NYU), she worked part-time as a receptionist in a doctor's office. She finished her degree in 1941 after working nights and weekends in the NYU chemistry lab. Her credentials were impressive enough to Hitchings that he hired her as his assistant at Burroughs Wellcome in 1944. Elion then enrolled part-time at Brooklyn Polytechnic Institute to earn a PhD but dropped out when told she had to be a full-time student; her new job was too interesting for that. She collaborated with Hitchings for forty years and never worked anywhere else.[16]

Elion's battle with discrimination encouraged Shaffer to strive even harder. "Burroughs Wellcome found a spark in me," Shaffer now recalls, "and they allowed me to grow and never let me fall. I got great leadership training there as an international project leader. . . . You were truly valued."[17]

Few companies can boast of having one Nobel Prize winner, let alone two. Hitchings, Elion's co-recipient, earned a PhD in biochemistry at Harvard University in 1933 and spent the next nine years as a teaching fellow—first at Harvard University and later at Case Western Reserve. Because no one was interested in his field of specialization—the metabolism of nucleic acids, the building blocks of DNA—he couldn't find another job. Burroughs Wellcome hired him in 1942, and he resumed his work on nucleic acids. He rose to vice president of research in 1967 and held that job until 1975, when he became scientist emeritus.[18]

Elion and Hitchings collaborated for nearly forty years. While she began as his assistant, she soon became Hitchings's peer. Their pioneering work led early on to new drugs that could block the replication of pathogens, or cells. In the early 1950s, they discovered an important treatment for leukemia; in 1957, they found a compound to treat severe rheumatoid arthritis. They later discovered a treatment to suppress the rejection of organ transplants, as well as effective treatments for gout, malaria, and urinary tract disease.[19]

These discoveries alone did not win Hitchings and Elion the Nobel Prize. Instead, they won the award for Physiology of Medicine for their groundbreaking work on the principles of drug design. They replaced the traditional trial-and-error approach with a new method that focused on understanding the target of the drug. Elion was the fifth female Nobel Prize laureate in medicine, the ninth in science in general, and one of a handful of laureates in medicine without a doctoral degree.[20] One of her passions in retirement was urging young women to pursue careers in science.[21]

An unorthodox and complex corporate structure led to Burroughs Wellcome's demise. In 1895, Silas Burroughs died of pneumonia in the south of France. After that, Henry Wellcome had problems sorting out ownership with Burroughs's widow, Olive Chase. After Wellcome's death in 1936, a provision of his will stipulated that all assets of the foundation be transferred to a charitable trust called the Wellcome Trust. Its charge was to allocate all income to medical research and to supporting medical museums and its vast collection of medical devices and literature. As a practical matter, this proved to be an unwieldy structure. In effect, it meant that the trust in London owned sixty independent and relatively autonomous operating companies worldwide. The largest, Burroughs Wellcome and Company USA, had no say in what its trustee overlords in London did.[22]

Problems came to a head when a wave of consolidations hit the drug industry in the 1990s. These combinations aimed to reduce overhead and capitalize, where possible, on complimentary products. The shoe dropped in 1995 when early in the morning of January 23, John Robb, president and CEO of the Wellcome Trust, got an unexpected phone call from Sir Richard Sykes, his counterpart at Glaxo, the world's second largest drug company behind Merck. Sykes informed Robb that Glaxo was making an offer of $14 billion for the trust's shares in what amounted to a hostile takeover.[23]

Sykes said he believed the combined companies could be more competitive. Governments, hospitals, doctors, and others worldwide were exerting intense pressure on drug companies to keep a tighter hold on prices. Sykes stressed at the news conference: "We don't want to sit around and be carried along by consolidation. We wish to be leaders in the process."[24] It was a big bite, but Glaxo, as the world's second largest drug company, could easily absorb Wellcome, the world's twentieth. The new company was GlaxoWellcome, but the Wellcome name was dropped in 2000 when Glaxo merged with SmithKline Beecham. It later became GlaxoSmithKline.

The Wellcome name lives on because in 1955, Sir Henry Dale, one of the Trust's original trustees, and William N. Creasy, who headed its US subsidiary, decided to establish a US version of the Wellcome Trust called the Burroughs Wellcome Fund (BWF) in RTP. In 1993, the Wellcome Trust gave BWF a gift of $400 million that enabled it to become an independent foundation.[25] Today, a large unicorn stands in the BWF lobby, a reminder of the halcyon days when

Silas Burroughs and Henry Wellcome established an early adopter of technology that revolutionized the field of medicine.

More importantly to RTP, the arrival of Burroughs Wellcome in 1969 established the region as a haven for life science. It brought talent to the Triangle. Fred Hutchison, who has represented many start-ups in biotech and other industries, explains the long-term impacts to RTP from Burroughs Wellcome. He cites the sale to Glaxo in 1995 and the subsequent formation of GlaxoSmithKline in 2000 as providential. He points out:

> With each of these mergers, many talented employees in the Research Triangle lost their positions. Although this might appear to be a setback for the Triangle, these two mergers had a huge beneficial effect on the growth of the life science industry. Many displaced executives and scientists started their own life science companies, advised start-up companies, sat on their boards of directors or invested in these start-ups. The Triangle's academic talent from its research universities was now combined with the commercial talent of these displaced pharmaceutical executives and scientists. The effect on the Triangle was immense. It grew from two pharma companies in 1981 to more than 800 life science companies today.

Shaffer, who worked at both Burroughs Wellcome and Glaxo, reflects on the former's legacy in the Triangle: "Wellcome had proven that the [RTP] ecosystem was viable. It was known they could recruit top talent, which certainly helped Glaxo determine RTP was a good area for their own US headquarters. . . . The establishment of headquarters here was pivotal at a key time for our region." Their presence made RTP "a much more robust and flourishing ecosystem in the life science space." The legacy continues today and is one of the reasons the region now attracts "many great bio-manufacturing" companies, as will be seen in part III. Burroughs Wellcome showed RTP could be a major center for life science. Like IBM, it provided evidence RTP worked as an economic development strategy. These types of successes would encourage additional extraordinary measures to build RTP into a major life science sector.

9

A First Mover in Biotech

The arrival of Burroughs Wellcome in 1969 put RTP on the map as a location for life science. The presence of two Nobel Prize laureates in medicine burnished the area's reputation in the field. This success should not have been too much of a surprise as RTP's founders had originally included pharmaceuticals on the list of disciplines in which the area excelled. This sector would only grow in the years to come. However, no one could anticipate the dynamism of life science. Such dynamism gave RTP the opportunity to get on the ground floor of entirely new subdisciplines of life science, including one that would revolutionize treatment options in the decades following the 1970s known as biotech. Biotechnology, or biotech, involves the use of cellular and biomolecular processes to produce products and technologies to improve the human condition. The timing of RTP's foray into life science happened to coincide with a crucial moment when biotech first emerged as commercially viable and would help establish the region as a national hub.

A number of factors played into the events of the 1980s. However, a well-thought-out letter in 1981 from a constituent to then–state Senator Gerry Hancock of Durham, encouraging him to look into the future of biotech as a field, sparked important steps to position RTP as a first mover in this emerging sector. Instead of writing back a perfunctory reply, Hancock began reading up on the subject.[1] The timing of Hancock's literature search was crucial. Certainly, RTP had clear advantages for biotech, especially with the university strengths in chemistry, medicine, pharmaceuticals, plant science, and related fields. These disciplines had influenced the decision by Burroughs Wellcome to locate in RTP, deepening awareness of the area's strength in life science.

Also, the letter to Hancock in 1981 occurred in a particular context. It followed closely on the heels of several high-profile events for biotech, all occurring in the last quarter of 1980.[2] They included a call from Sweden on October 14 to Paul Berg at Stanford University informing him that he won the Nobel Prize for chemistry based on research into nucleic acids and for "certain aspects of recombinant DNA."[3] Frederick Sanger and Wally Gilbert shared the prize for sequencing DNA. On the same day, Genentech, a relatively new biotech company that could alter human genes through recombinant DNA techniques, went public. The success of its stock led other new biotech companies to go public in the coming months. Finally, President Jimmy Carter signed the Bayh-Dole Act into law on December 12. This bipartisan bill gave universities and nonprofits permission to own intellectual property created through federal grants. The law would be a boon to the biotech industry in the coming years.

These events and other factors resonated with Hancock. He concluded that his constituent was right about the potential for this industry in North Carolina. The year before, Governor Jim Hunt elevated the Board of Science and Technology to a cabinet-level function. A trusted advisor, Quentin Lindsey, directed the board and issued a report in 1980. The report advocated for two major efforts on the "frontiers of science that show promise of high technology and industrial application."[4] Those efforts included microelectronics and recombinant DNA. Similar to RTP's Working Committee in the 1950s, the board appointed a technical committee to review the state's assets. It recommended the formation of a state-funded nonprofit to promote the development of biotechnology. The report underscored the new organization would not compete with the universities in research but act as an intermediary to support and coordinate existing research activities.

After this initial report, Hunt pressed forward to establish the Microelectronics Center of North Carolina (MCNC), encouraged by General Electric's announcement to invest $100 million in a semiconductor research and development facility in RTP. Hunt secured $24.4 million for MCNC in 1981. The biotech initiative languished until Hancock approached Hunt to resurrect the idea. With the full support of Hunt and his senior staff, Hancock proposed to fellow legislators that a legislative study commission on biotech be formed and funded in the $150,000 range. That was enough for Hancock to engage three scientific consultants, hold hearings with expert witnesses, and make recommendations on the potential of biotechnology in the Tar Heel state.[5] The commission held a dozen or so half-day hearings in 1983 and 1984 and concluded that the potential of biotechnology in North Carolina was vast—that the state had underlying strengths in the life sciences of medicine, pharmaceuticals, animal and plant agriculture, and forestry. Expert testimony focusing on how biotechnology improved crops and other agricultural techniques helped legislators to rally around the concept and overcome doubts about human applications.

At the time, the Bay Area in California and Route 128 in Boston had indisputable leadership in life sciences, but the field was in its infancy. Many people in the know wondered where the next center of excellence might spring up. "We thought we had as good a chance as anyone to become the next [life science center]," Hancock recalls. "It was abundantly clear that economic development follows science. . . . What we needed was investment to improve our capacity—to fund something like our own Manhattan Project."[6] The study commission recommended just that: the founding of an organization to enable the state to gain a strong comparative advantage in biotech. In its final report in 1984, the commission called for investment of $50 million over ten years. Outgoing Governor Jim Hunt took a remarkably visionary approach to technological development in his 1984 state of the state address: "We saw the world changing. We knew we had to change."[7] True to form, Hunt's 1984 budget included $4.5 million for the new effort under the auspices of a North Carolina Biotechnology Center (NCBiotech).

Hancock lost his Senate seat in the 1984 election and was then asked to serve as volunteer chairman of the board of the new organization. He accepted, a board was formed, nonprofit status was secured, and the new organization opened an office in RTP and began hiring staff.[8]

In the 1980s, genetic engineering was still in its infancy. To the public, this novel technology often sounded like science fiction. But this critical foundational work would eventually lead to many new medical possibilities, including precision medicine and technologies that could "fix" genetic errors that lead to devastating diseases. These technologies made it possible to eliminate and/or replace defective DNA code or even a single gene to attack debilitating and often fatal diseases. People knew that plants and animals had been crossed for eons; but to many, improving humans through selective breeding seemed like stamping on the toes of the almighty. This made biotech's enormous potential to manipulate genes to create new tissue and new products seem risky, even sacrilegious to many. Securing a long-term funding commitment for biotech from state legislators, let alone the public at large, was a daunting challenge for NCBiotech in its early years. Yet, the center could not sustain itself without public support and continued legislative funding.

As the world's first state-sponsored biotech center, NCBiotech had no organizational template or road map to go by. Despite many obstacles, in time the biotech industry would replace tobacco, textiles, and furniture as a mainstay of the Tar Heel economy. The results of that transition were staggering: The state would gain 225,000 biotech jobs at 810 life science companies and 2,500 life science support companies. The average industrywide salary soared to a stunning $115,000—twice the state average.[9] Nearly $2.5 billion in annual state and local revenues poured into tax coffers. All of this happened in just two generations, proving that government could stimulate remarkable results and could embrace the industries of tomorrow through astute investments. In leading the way to these stellar achievements, NCBiotech earned the trust and confidence of state government leaders, university presidents and faculty, business executives, and influential media mavens.

But statistics couldn't begin to tell the full story—of the Darwinian struggle of start-up companies to survive; of lab-bench discoveries moving slowly toward commercialization; of desperate struggles to secure venture funding; of long odds against an acquisition or the holy grail of an IPO; and, always, of the prospect of miracle cures for the sick and afflicted—occurring in a vast ecosystem of teeming organisms, all striving to become something new. In 1988, NCBiotech's lengthy search for a new chief executive came to an end with the hiring of Charles E. Hamner. The choice was astute, because in his fourteen-year tenure, Hamner would achieve widespread recognition as the father of North Carolina biotechnology. In many ways, it seemed he was overqualified for the job: When hired, he served as the chief operating officer at the University of Virginia (UVA) Medical Center and had just overseen an eight-hundred-bed expansion there. He had served more than once as acting president of UVA, and his scientific credentials were impeccable. He was the world's third scientist to achieve in vitro fertilization, a controversial method at the time, which fertilized human eggs in a lab to produce a child. He also developed the drug Reglan®, which treats, among other things, nausea and vomiting caused by chemotherapy.[10]

Hamner was tall and had a receding hairline and a face that evinced affability. He spoke with the rolling drawl of southwest Virginia, where he grew up. One of his cousins, Earl Hamner, produced and wrote *The Waltons*, a popular and long-running television series in the 1970s and 1980s. After earning an undergraduate degree from Virginia Tech, Hamner spent eight years at the University of Georgia, where he earned a PhD in veterinary medicine and a PhD in biochemistry.

One gift that served Hamner especially well at NCBiotech was the ability to communicate well with just about anyone—from ordinary citizens and taxpayers, whose support was needed to sustain the effort over a long timeline; to scientists, who spoke like medical journals read; and to state legislators and senior public officials, who required bare-bones descriptions of complexities.

He had an uncanny eye for talent too: At UVA he had hired two scientists who later won the Nobel Prize, and he helped bring Nobel laureates to North Carolina as part of an effort that dramatically raised the state's research capacity. His participation on committees of the World Health Organization and the National Institutes of Health had given him the chance to rub elbows with many gifted scientists, including superstars in biotech.

Hamner said the real reason he left his secure, high-profile, high-impact job at UVA to come to North Carolina was "to build something new—a new biotech sector—from the ground up." Accomplishing that goal, Hamner told the state's leaders, would require three things: "First, you have to build widespread public support. . . . Second, you've got to have a group of topflight scientists—not just good but the best . . . and third, to grow the economy, you have to have start-ups and other young companies and large established companies to buy small ones up and take their technologies to market."[11]

Shortly after he arrived, Hamner and Steven Burke, the center's senior vice president for corporate affairs, began a series of grassroots meetings that would take them to as many as eighty of North Carolina's one hundred counties. At each, they stressed biotech's potential to provide high-paying, satisfying jobs for the sons and daughters of those in attendance. Hamner and Burke were a study in contrasts: The folksy Hamner spoke like a family friend; Burke was a stem-winder—"one of the best speakers I've ever worked with," Hamner would later say.[12]

The meetings were well attended, interest was high, and there was no shortage of spontaneity. A session at the horse pavilion in Greenville attracted an audience of two hundred or so. An elderly state senator from a nearby town chaired the event. Burke had drafted opening remarks for the senator, who read them with the solemnity of a tolling church bell: "I envision," the senator proclaimed, "a state in which our future is improved from judicious development of genetically engineered orgasms."

The audience sat stone-faced in silence, wondering if they'd heard him right—had he meant organisms instead of orgasms? Plunging forward, the senator waxed warmly about prospects for vastly improved crop yields and more delicious tomatoes. He then ended his peroration with a second showstopper: "In closing, let's think of a future in which we can all share in the benefits of genetically engineered orgasms."[13]

At that moment, Tim Valentine, a quick-witted congressman and member of the NCBiotech board, shouted from the back of the room: "More funding for biotechnology!" A crescendo of laughter then swept the room.[14]

Hamner's second requirement for building a dynamic biotech sector was to recruit the world's best scientists to come to RTP. In 1988, his first year as NCBiotech's CEO, Hamner played a pivotal role in recruiting Oliver Smithies, a British American biochemist who won the Nobel Prize in 2007 for his work on gene modifications in mice using embryonic stem cells. It had taken a comprehensive package of financial incentives to lure Smithies, his laboratory, and graduate assistants from the University of Wisconsin to the University of North Carolina School of Medicine. An NCBiotech faculty recruitment grant had played a pivotal role. Smithies was one of many academic superstars lured to the University of North Carolina, Duke University, and NC State University with the support of the NCBiotech faculty recruitment program.[15]

Hamner and Governor Jim Hunt established a strong rapport in 1993, the first year of Hunt's third term. Hunt was proud of his role nearly a decade earlier in the founding of NCBiotech. To Hunt and Hamner, biotech was like a pod filled with seeds that could stimulate rapid organic growth and further reduce the state's dependence on tobacco, furniture, and textiles. They also saw organic growth as a welcome alternative to "beggar thy neighbor" policies in which states pilfered firms from each other. Hamner was sure Hunt would support expanding NCBiotech's faculty recruitment program. At a one-on-one meeting at the governor's office in the early spring of 1993, the two explored how to expand the program. As Hamner answered his questions, Hunt diligently wrote down the answers on a yellow legal pad.

"Where will you find these eminent scientists?" Hunt had asked.

"I know a lot of them personally," Hamner replied.

"What would it cost?"

Without batting an eye, Hamner told the governor, "Seventy-five million."

"That's a lot of money," Hunt rejoined. "I'm not sure we can get it, but I'll see what I can do."

A week or so later, Hunt called Hamner to tell him he'd gotten commitments from key legislators for at least $40 million. Hamner called it "a good start," and Hunt told him to start hiring.[16]

In the late 1980s, NCBiotech embarked on an ambitious, aggressive, two-decade push to convince the corporate giants of Europe's well-established biotech sector to establish satellite operations in North Carolina. To Charles Hamner, it was a key requirement for building a robust biotech ecosystem in Research Triangle Park.

Big companies could acquire or create joint ventures with small ones; they could sponsor research worthy of commercialization at the state's three tier-one research universities; and they were on the demand side of the labor market for workers that could be trained for biotech jobs by the state's network of fifty-eight community colleges—second only to California in size with nearly a half million students.

These were persuasive reasons to locate at RTP, but two other factors proved even more decisive: First, it was clear that the Park had become a hotbed for life sciences and thus provided a practical springboard into the lucrative North American market. Second, NCBiotech recruitment efforts were led by the state's most senior leaders, whose deep commitments to a collaborative approach engendered trust and confidence.

As Hamner put it in describing Governor Hunt's appeal at several stops in Europe in 1993: "They could tell he was speaking from the heart. It was marvelous, and he did it in fifteen or twenty minutes."[17] NCBiotech's Steven Burke served as the point man for recruitment on these trips. He made dozens of presentations throughout Western Europe and in Costa Rica, Japan, Peru, Serbia, and South Africa. These trips had the cumulative impact of elevating RTP's reputation as a cluster of excellence for international life science, agriculture, and pharmaceutical companies.

In Germany, Switzerland, and Denmark alone, targets included BASF, Schering, Hoechst, Ciba-Geigy, Rhône-Poulenc, Hoffmann La Roche, Novo Nordisk, and Bayer. Ultimately, many of these firms decided to establish operations in RTP.

Successful recruiting trips to lure big companies, hiring superstar scientists, and making biotech a priority for the man on the street were all part of Hamner's peerless legacy. But nothing pleased him more than the design and construction of an iconic, $6 million headquarters building for NCBiotech that would give its fast-growing constituency a sense of place and a neutral site where thorny issues could be thrashed out.

In 1988, the year Hamner began as CEO, the legislature—on its own initiative—appropriated $1 million for a new biotech building in RTP. The center's hierarchy (Hamner, board chairman Gerry Hancock, and Steven Burke) knew that sum was far from what was needed to build a structure that would fully reflect the creativity and dynamism of the state's burgeoning biotech sector—and one that would engender a strong sense of place among visitors from home and abroad.

Finished in 1992, the building featured a footprint in the shape of a polygon rectangle with equal sides firmly anchored to a lovely, wooded hillside. Its sharp angles were softened by a rounded exterior in front. Inside, its soaring lobby featured forty-foot walls and a glass roof. The rounded element enclosed a large auditorium and a boardroom. Hamner had insisted on the round element, citing President Thomas Jefferson's premise that round structures encourage consensus and community.[18] Funding to build the iconic structure came from several sources: $2 million from the US Department of Agriculture; state appropriations; companies like Ceiba-Geigy, which provided $750,000; and the remainder in a federal appropriation secured by then-Senator Terry Sanford.[19] The finished product radiates permanence, unity, community, and a strong sense of place.

During Hamner's tenure, two overarching principles became sacrosanct. First, the center's fundamental role would be that of a catalyst, forgoing any direct role in basic research. That policy allayed initial concerns at universities that NCBiotech would compete with them for funding. Second, Hamner strongly emphasized that NCBiotech would remain steadfastly nonpartisan in all aspects of its work. He worked closely and successfully with Governor Jim Martin, a Republican, who, like Hamner, had a PhD in chemistry. Martin became a champion of funding for the center and helped raise its profile considerably during his second term from 1988 to 1992. When Hunt began his third term in 1993, he too stressed the importance of keeping NCBiotech strictly nonpartisan in all aspects.[20]

Hamner's insight and force of personality facilitated the recruitment of superstars to RTP at just the right time. Experts have studied it from every point on the compass. One study in particular demonstrates how timing played a critical role in RTP's emergence as a center for life science and how NCBiotech helped. In 1998, Lynne Zucker and Michael Darby published an analysis of the biotech sector. The study concluded that the areas that had a few superstar scientists, as measured by groundbreaking published articles during the industry's formative years, gained a dominant position.[21] Economist Enrico Moretti notes that the private sector's close proximity to ongoing academic research in nearby universities and the personal involvement in start-ups by these superstars proved crucial to a "lock-in effect" for these regions. RTP is at the top of the list, along with San Diego, Boston, and the Bay Area. This same principle applies to the auto industry in Detroit based on innovations there during the early twentieth century, the film industry in Los Angeles after several key inventions in the 1920s, and microelectronics in Palo Alto with major breakthroughs in the 1950s. Innovations that occur in a particular place at the beginning of an industry tend to bind the industry to that place. Hamner's insight and force of personality facilitated the recruitment of superstars to RTP at just the right time.

10

Case Studies of Two Superstar Scientists

Although NCBiotech's creation and strategy helped position RTP as a biotech hub during a formative period, the area's universities, businesses, and research environment also played a key role. This chapter provides case studies of two superstar scientists. Both were academics, although one arrived for a university appointment and the other for a private-sector job. Both arrived in the Triangle area around the same time in the 1970s. Both pioneered research with historic implications for biotech. Their stories show that during this period, RTP had multiple dimensions to leverage R&D for economic development. It had new institutions like NCBiotech. It also had universities that were more supportive of applied research with commercial applications as well as companies in RTP investing in the application of such research. Together, these factors secured RTP's position as a cluster for the biotech revolution.

Dr. Mary-Dell Chilton

In the late fall of 1977, after stacking the dinner dishes in the dishwasher, Dr. Mary-Dell Chilton made a discovery that would change the world. At the time, she and her husband, Scott, lived in University City, a neighborhood within walking distance of Washington University in St. Louis, where he taught chemistry, and she spent long days in the crop science lab and teaching a course in recombinant DNA technology.[1]

That night, she made a very quick supper for Scott and their sons, nine-year-old Andrew and seven-year-old Mark. After the meal, while Scott put the boys to bed, Mary-Dell got out the items she needed for advanced calculations: a programmable calculator, a computer tape, and a raft of graph paper from the lab. They made for quite a clutter on the kitchen table as she began calculating lab data gathered that day.

Her data points came from a tobacco tumor. Her team included professors and postdocs, grad students, and a technician. Years earlier, at the University of Washington in Seattle, she had studied how agrobacterium—which is often called nature's genetic engineer—caused large tumors called crown gall to grow on plant roots and trunks and then insert their genes into the host plant. When she moved to St. Louis, her mission was "to imitate what agrobacterium had done by putting genes of my choice into plant cells—and then make sure our plants carried that gene in their seeds. . . . The goal of our team was to exploit this process." Given that success, Mary-Dell and her colleagues would be the first to prove that scientists could transfer DNA from one plant kingdom to another, thus producing the first transgenic plant.

"It was a hot issue then," she recalls, "whether genes could get transferred to a higher plant. There had been claims it was possible, so I spent the first part of my career debunking them"—on the grounds that bacterial genes from agrobacterium could *not* be recombined with plant genes because there is no common heredity between the two. "I just absolutely did not believe it. It went against everything I had ever learned in school, so I set out to prove this crazy idea was wrong. And it turned out in the process of trying to prove the idea wrong, I proved it was indeed right."[2]

The data on Mary-Dell's computer tape that night had been collected from a Packard Tri-Carb—a freezer-like device that can detect small amounts of radioactivity. Inside the Tri-Carb, a line of small bottles (she called them soldiers) sat on a belt that lowered them into a dark chamber where they were subjected to flashes of light that were coded for signs of radioactivity.

When she finished her calculations that night, Mary-Dell was delighted with what she saw: After checking and rechecking her data, she exclaimed, "Oh my God, the DNA is all still there!"[3] She went to work right away on a journal article. When she finished, she sent it to *CELL*, the leading journal in the field, where she encountered the same doubts she herself had harbored for many years. *CELL*'s editor told her the results were too astonishing to be credible with the publication's readers. The editor asked her to recheck her data three times to confirm that a transgenic transfer had indeed occurred. When *CELL* published her paper late that year, it set off a storm of questions, doubt, and praise. Her discovery opened the door to genetically modified organisms (GMOs), a breakthrough that remains controversial to this day—to such an extent that the European Union still bans GMO-based foods, despite data that confirm they are just as safe as other foods.

Dr. Mary-Dell Chilton exudes warmth and a self-effacing manner. Her mop of thick curls gives way to inquisitive eyes, and a smile lights up her face. Growing up, she was a tomboy with short straight hair with bangs. Her scant interest in academic pursuits gave no hint of the world-famous scientist she would become. Her grandmother Henrietta Dell Hayes (Nannan to Mary-Dell) paid a visit when she was three and asked her to come to Southern Pines, North Carolina, where her grandfather Claude L. Hayes (Daddy Hayes) owned Hayes Book Shop and Nannan ran Mrs. Hayes's dress shop next door, which counted among its customers many well-to-do women visiting the Sand Hills in winter for golf, riding, and shopping.

She readily agreed to go—mainly to escape an older brother who delighted in terrorizing her. The visit lasted off and on for nine years; during that time, Daddy Hayes became her best friend, and she spent many hours reading Nancy Drew novels and other books in his bookstore.

The first real signs of her academic potential came after she returned to live permanently with her parents in their rented farmhouse in Tess Way, Wisconsin. Her father traveled during the week selling insurance, but she bonded deeply with her mother, who was considered by many to be quite beautiful.

When she entered high school, she was required to take a remedial class in science and later an aptitude test given to all freshmen. Afterward, her science teacher told her, "You did amazingly well. The people who administered the test are convinced that you must have cheated somehow." He went on to suggest that she consider a career in science.

After flirting with physics and astronomy, she became a chemistry major at the University of Illinois. She remained there to pursue a PhD in chemistry but chose a subject in molecular biology for her thesis. When one of her favorite professors accepted a position at the University of Washington in Seattle, he invited her to join him and become a geneticist.

She eagerly agreed to make the move. In Seattle, she soon met and married Scott Chilton, a natural products chemist, who had earned his PhD from the University of Illinois two years before Mary-Dell. She recalls, "We loved hiking, backpacking, mountain climbing, and paddling our canoe." But by age thirty-eight, it was clear that the University of Washington offered her no opportunity for a tenure-track position though Scott had one. She began exploring options and soon found that the Department of Biology of Washington University wanted to hire them both. Scott got the offer of a chemistry laboratory and an appointment as a visiting faculty member. She became an associate professor in the Department of Biology. "Scott was a prince [about giving up tenure], bless his heart," she says.

After she achieved international acclaim, Ciba-Geigy, a Swiss agro-chemical giant, came calling in 1983 with an offer to double her salary and put her in charge of its first biotech research lab in the world. Company brass saw in Mary-Dell someone who knew the science and the top people in the field, especially in the area of AgTech (agricultural technology). Corporate leadership based in Switzerland chose RTP for the new lab. According to Mary-Dell, the area universities and emerging strength in life sciences influenced their choice. This decision brought Mary-Dell to the Triangle. It was an administrative job, but she accepted it because it was an opportunity to put her technology to work in the field to develop commercial applications for field crops. She quickly proved her mettle by overseeing construction of new buildings and eventually hiring more than one hundred scientists. The early pace was so hectic she once sketched building plans for an architect on a napkin at Raleigh-Durham International Airport.

Her discoveries led to improved yields, reduced pesticide use and runoff, increased tolerance to drought and other stresses on plants, and increased profitability for farmers. After a decade, she returned to the lab bench. Ciba-Geigy went through several mergers, acquisitions, and spinoffs, becoming Syngenta in 2000.

Tragedy struck in Mary-Dell's life in 2004: Scott died at seventy-one while climbing 12,281-foot Mount Adams in Washington State, a quiescent volcano in the Cascade Range. He and his companions camped at a high elevation. The next morning they faced a sleet storm, so they delayed their departure. Scott went back to sleep and never woke up. A lifelong mountain climber, he had conquered many peaks. He spoke six languages and was a Fulbright Fellow to West Germany during the Cold War. Mary-Dell never remarried.[4]

Mary-Dell's presence in RTP helped attract numerous other AgTech scientists to RTP—perhaps her greatest impact on the area. Over the years, Mary-Dell has received many prizes and awards. In 2002, Syngenta created the Mary-Dell Chilton Center, an administrative and conference complex in RTP. It also established on its campus the Mary-Dell Chilton Hall of Fame. She received the Ben Franklin award for life sciences, and in 2013 she was named a laureate of the World Food Prize. Many of her colleagues feel it is a travesty that she has not won the Nobel Prize. In her career, she has published more than one hundred scientific papers.

When asked how comfortable she is with some of the sobriquets used to describe her—Queen of Agrobacterium, Mother of Transgenic Plants, and Midwife of the GMO Revolution—her reply was, "I am the mother of two fine sons. No accolade can exceed that."

Dr. Robert Lefkowitz

Death was knocking at the door of the inert middle-aged patient lying on the operating room table at Mass General, a Harvard teaching hospital. His vital signs were in free fall: blood pressure plummeting, kidneys shutting down, fading in and out of consciousness. The medical team surrounding the patient at what many consider America's top hospital was baffled by what to do. A newly arrived young resident named Robert Lefkowitz approached the dying man's side and took his hand as a token of consolation. Lefkowitz instantly noticed that the patient's hand was abnormally swollen.[5]

Moments later, the medical team huddled just outside the operating room to discuss the patient's dire condition. His status as a "rookie" notwithstanding, Lefkowitz spoke up boldly: "I'm 90 percent certain this patient has acromegaly. We need to get him on prednisone right away."

Acromegaly is a rare cancer of the pituitary gland that triggers large secretions of growth hormone. By pure happenstance, Lefkowitz had observed many such cases at the National Institutes of Health (NIH), where he'd recently served as a commissioned officer in the US Public Health Service.

After prednisone was administered, the patient's vital signs markedly improved. Subsequent tests confirmed that the patient did in fact have a tumor of the pituitary gland. With the tumor removed, he made a full recovery.

Barely two weeks into his residency, Lefkowitz had made quite a name for himself: He'd become a Mass General legend who'd saved a patient's life by merely holding his hand. Lefkowitz modestly dismissed his life-saving diagnosis as "dumb luck" resulting from his observance of acromegaly patients at NIH. In the career that followed, he made many breakthrough discoveries that would profoundly change the field of medicine.

Lefkowitz grew up as a child prodigy—the nerd who skipped a grade in school and aced tests routinely, including the entrance exam for the elite Bronx High School of Science. Only a few hundred applicants from the entire city of New York got accepted there; Lefkowitz not only made the cut but excelled.

Growing up in the Bronx, he worshipped his father, an accountant who frequently coached him in math. Often they raced to add long columns of figures with young Lefkowitz using a calculator, while his father tallied by hand. When his father had a heart attack at age fifty, young Lefkowitz, then twelve, set his sights on becoming a doctor. His single-minded pursuit of that dream earned him a spot in the class of 1966 at Columbia University School of Medicine. Prestigious internships and residencies followed at Mass General and NIH.

In 1973, Lefkowitz was invited to become an associate professor of medicine and assistant professor of biochemistry at Duke University. Essentially, Duke made a "name your own price" offer to lure Lefkowitz away from Mass General and Harvard. He countered with what he later described as "preposterous" conditions, including a "brash" request for tenure. At that point, he was dead set against moving south and assumed his reply would be quickly rejected. Much to his surprise, Duke accepted all of his conditions. It was an offer he considered too good to refuse, even though it'd take him to *terra incognito*. When he broke the news to his family that he'd accepted the offer, his mother-in-law sniffed, "Duke? I never heard of it. Is it new?"

His father's chronic cardiac problems strongly influenced the direction of Lefkowitz's medical career. He'd long aspired to become a clinician making daily hospital rounds to see heart patients. His residency at Mass General was designed to train him for that, but he gradually became enamored with research. He started with a few experiments in an empty Mass General lab after work. But once he found a clear focus—the study of adrenaline receptors—he began spending all his time at the lab bench.

At the time, little was known about receptors; many scientists even questioned their existence. Adrenaline, however, was a different matter. It was well known that a rush of adrenaline gets triggered by imminent danger, such as the sudden appearance of a bear just ahead on a hiking trail. This type of threat causes blood pressure to rise and the heart to beat faster as a rush of adrenaline flows to cardiac tissue. The "fight or flight" response is thus activated. But how is that adrenaline rush regulated? How do cells "talk" to each other and receive signals from the environment? Are there sensors that were attuned to the environment, receiving signals, that is, receptors? Are receptors positioned on cell walls or membranes waiting to receive those signals? Do receptors receive all types of signals about the environment, including the presence of life-sustaining nutrients such as lipids, sugars, and proteins? Can a receptor serve as an "inbox" for such messages, and how would it pass them along? Lefkowitz became captivated by questions like these and went on to make many groundbreaking discoveries.

He confirmed that each cell has tiny receptors that sense changes in its overall environment. Moreover, the receptors then react to these signals, thus accommodating needed adjustments. He found that hormones like adrenaline did send signals to receptors. In 1969, he became the first scientist to attach a radioactive isotope of iodine to adrenaline to study the hormone's functions in detail. That finding would inform much of his subsequent research.

In 1983, Brian Kobilka joined the Lefkowitz lab at Duke University as a cardiology fellow. He had just completed a residency in internal medicine at Washington University in St. Louis. At first, Lefkowitz had modest expectations for Kobilka, but it soon became clear that his young protégé could synthesize a vast amount of data in a very short time. Working mostly on his own during his second year under Lefkowitz, Kobilka learned enough about recent advances in molecular biology to add that field to the lab's competencies. At that point, Lefkowitz told his team it was ready to join the search for "the Holy Grail" of molecular biology. It would be a quest for the gene encoding beta receptors. That receptor processes the hormone adrenaline as it flows to heart and lung tissues, as well as certain muscles.

Lefkowitz had found the beta receptor—but not its encoding gene—in the late 1960s. Finding its encoding gene among billions of cells, each with its own receptor, was a herculean but essential task for understanding how adrenaline affects the overall cellular environment. Formidable competitors at other research labs were hot on the trail of this "Holy Grail"; one would come close to besting Lefkowitz and his team near the end.

But on May 1, 1986, *Nature Magazine*, one of the world's leading scientific journals, published Lefkowitz and Kobilka's principal findings that they had identified a whole family of receptors that look alike and function in the same manner—what they identified as G protein-coupled receptors. Receptors exposed to the environment outside the cell are also connected to G proteins that are closer to the inside of the cell. These G proteins are a family of proteins that act as molecular switches inside cells. Because these receptors are paired with, or coupled, to G proteins, they are called G protein-coupled receptors. The interaction between the G protein-coupled receptors and the G protein family is a fundamental part of the process of receiving signals from the environment outside a cell and passing those signals on to the interior of the cell.

Lefkowitz and his team found that these receptors govern three of the five senses—sight, taste, and smell. In time, it would be estimated that between one-third and one-half of all drugs that are sold function by binding to such receptors.

On October 10, 2012, Lefkowitz got a phone call at 5 a.m. from Stockholm with astoundingly good news: The Swedish Academy of Medicine had just named him and Kobilka, his former trainee, as co-recipients of the 2012 Nobel Prize for Chemistry. A stream of congratulatory calls followed, including one from National Public Radio. When the radio hosts had asked what he had planned to do that day, he replied, "I was going to get a haircut this morning." The hosts roared with laughter.

As Duke's first Nobel Prize laureate (Kobilka had joined the faculty at Stanford University in 1989), Lefkowitz arrived that day to an office filled with celebrants. A reception that night attracted several hundred friends and colleagues. A steady stream of praise followed for weeks after that.

Perhaps the most enjoyable moment came when Duke's legendary Coach Mike Krzyzewski—the winner of four national basketball championships at the time—honored Lefkowitz at center court during the halftime of a game. Coach K presented him with a Duke jersey bearing the number 1. As Lefkowitz walked off the court, the boisterous Duke student body chanted "He's so smart . . . he's so smart . . . he's so smart."

Chilton's and Lefkowitz's stories illustrate the depth of talent that came to the region at a crucial time for biotech. Talent arrived through the intentional efforts of a new institution, NCBiotech, created specifically to bolster RTP's position in the burgeoning biotech industry. Oliver Smithies, Jude Samulski (discussed in a later chapter), and many others reflect the success of this approach. However, talent also arrived through ad hoc university recruitment in the case of Lefkowitz and strategic business decisions of companies like Ciba-Geigy in the case of Chilton. All of these tactics can be traced back to the strategies pursued by RTP's founders in the 1950s by leveraging the cooperation of industry, academia, and government to encourage economic development within the state.

11

Big Bets on Information Technology

At first blush, the development of an information technology (IT) industry in RTP followed a pattern similar to that of life science. An industry leader—IBM in the case of IT and Burroughs Wellcome in the case of life science—located a major facility in RTP. That company brought significant talent to the region and helped attract other companies to RTP. Early successes also encouraged political leaders to search for ways to expand the industry's footprint through nonprofit research ventures. However, one major difference separates these two sectors. RTP got into life science on the ground floor. It gained a foothold during the industry's crucial formative years. In contrast, the IT industry was more mature when RTP came into existence. This distinction led state leaders to place big bets on IT. While those bets did not always pay off, RTP managed to develop a thriving IT sector by the 1990s.

The Key Innovations of IT

IT comprises the confluence of three technologies: microelectronics, computers, and telecommunications.[1] Each one would play heavily into RTP's growth. Microelectronics traces its roots to the transistor invented by Bell Laboratories in 1947. Initiated with defense spending during the war, this technology allowed machines to communicate through electric impulses. The race to make these processing devices smaller and more powerful took a leap forward in 1951 when William Shockley created the junction transistor to facilitate information processing. After several large East Coast companies rejected his vision to commercialize microelectronics, Shockley moved to Palo Alto in 1954.[2] Within a year, Shockley formed his own company and hired several engineers from Bell Laboratories. These employees soon left Shockley to form Fairchild Semiconductors. Unlike Shockley, they saw the potential of silicon-based semiconductors or chips as a material for integrating transistors. The "Fairchild Eight" later spun out their own companies, giving rise to the moniker "Silicon Valley."

World War II encouraged scientists and engineers to pursue another major breakthrough technology—this time in the form of a powerful calculator or "computer." Defense spending eventually produced the first primitive computer weighing thirty tons. It evolved quickly and entered the commercial market in 1951.

As described in part I, IBM came to dominate the mainframe computer market in 1964 with the System/360 by making advances in computing power and scalability without having to reprogram software. However, it was the creation of a microprocessor in 1971 that set the stage for a revolution in IT. By putting a computer on a chip, innovators such as Steve Wozniak and Steve Jobs, who founded Apple, could create a microcomputer, also known as a personal computer. The explosive increase in chip power allowed microcomputers to proliferate in numerous applications and excel in functionality.

The development of telecommunications and digital networking around this same time collided with microelectronics and computers to fundamentally change society. Bell Labs produced an electronic switch in 1969. By the 1970s, integrated circuit technologies paved the way for digital switching, dramatically increasing the speed, power, and efficiency of communicating on networks. Canadian-based Northern Telecom captured a large part of the US market for digital switches in the late 1970s. By the 1990s, a number of companies, including Cisco Systems (named after San Francisco), pushed forward with broadband communication using fiber optics and lasers for transmission. The newfound capacity to transmit information was staggering and increasing each year. Along with microelectronics and computers, telecommunication advances set the stage for an entirely new way of organizing and transmitting information in the form of the internet.

In sum, the key components of IT were evolving rapidly when RTP came into existence in 1959. The scientists and engineers focusing on IT tended to cluster in Boston and Northern California. In particular, Silicon Valley had a culture and financial network conducive to taking risks on new ventures. The internet, originating in part from federal spending in response to Sputnik, suited this "computer counterculture" well.[3] Its decentralized structure through the World Wide Web encouraged entrepreneurs to find new ways for computers, microelectronics, and telecommunications to meet market demands. Emerging tech hubs such as RTP would have to adapt quickly to this dynamic environment where companies could come and go in the blink of an eye.

IBM and the Rise of Computing at RTP

On June 26, 1974, a shopper visited the Marsh Supermarket in Troy, Ohio, and handed the checkout clerk a ten-pack of Wrigley's Juicy Fruit chewing gum bearing a Universal Product Code (UPC), or barcode. When sixty-seven cents rang up on the cash register, a new era of inventory tracking and management began. Its ripple effects would soon be felt worldwide.[4] The cost of checking out customers dropped dramatically, and transaction accuracy increased significantly. Checkout speed also rose 40 percent, while in-store inventory systems greatly improved the management of stock. Stores were soon able to track customer buying habits. Between 1976 and 1980, the number of grocery stores using the UPC system shot up from 104 to 2,207, and usage was spreading around the globe.[5] The IBM team that invented the UPC barcode happened to be working at the building on Yonkers Road that Raleigh developer Willie York constructed for IBM in ninety days. A plaque now marks that historic event.

IBM's success with the UPC was based on more than two decades of research and planning. A year before Marsh Supermarket sold a pack of chewing gum using UPC technology, IBM had introduced what would become an industry workhorse: the IBM 360 Supermarket System. This included a digital cash register and a scanner to read the UPC symbol. Grocery stores then began requiring suppliers to place the code on products in boxes.[6] IBM led the development of these products through its point-of-sale division based in RTP. This group even employed psychologists to help devise ways to overcome consumers' hesitancy in purchasing products with no price tag. By the end of the 1970s, IBM dominated the market in this space.[7]

UPC technology expanded into new applications. It made it possible for schools, universities, and companies in all industries to use computing power to manage their inventories. Today, in many countries, nearly every product bought in a retail store has a UPC code printed on it and gets scanned. The UPC made manual and electro-mechanical cash registers obsolete. They'd been around since the 1880s. The barcode became a $17 billion activity by the early 2000s and was being scanned billions of times each day.[8]

IBM had another overnight success: the personal computer. On August 12, 1981, it made a surprise announcement at New York's Waldorf Astoria Hotel that it would manufacture and sell a personal computer. Shipments began two months later, and $1 billion in sales revenue followed in the first year, far exceeding company projections. It had forecast that 200,000 units would be sold over the next three years, but in year two alone, customers were buying 200,000 units per month.[9]

Much of the work in developing the new PC was done in Boca Raton, Florida. But just as misguided state policy had cost Manassas the lab and plant that went to RTP, misguided policy in Florida in the form of a so-called unitary tax caused Boca Raton to lose its PC manufacturing plant to RTP. The unitary tax hit international companies like IBM especially hard by taxing a portion of total revenues—not just revenues earned in-state.

"When it [the tax] got passed in Florida, the then-chairman of IBM, John Opel, called the governor and said, 'This is the most ridiculous thing I've seen. We're moving out of Florida,'" Dick Daugherty, who was in charge of IBM/RTP at the time, recalls. "That took a few years, and in essence my last job in IBM was helping place all the people that were made available when we left Florida. That would have been in '94 or '95."[10]

A legislator in North Carolina heard about the unitary tax and offered to propose one. When Daugherty learned this, he called Senator Kenneth Royall of Durham and told him trouble was brewing. Royall nipped the proposal in the bud in two weeks. He was chairman of the Senate Appropriations Committee and one of the most powerful members of that body. Daugherty had also called on him to stop a move on the part of Durham to annex RTP. Royall typified RTP's collaborative model—an able representative of the tripartite interests of government, universities, and private corporations that stood ready to assist RTP at a moment's notice.[11]

IBM also helped encourage the area universities to embrace the IT revolution. As noted in part I, Fred Brooks joined the computer science department at the University of North Carolina at Chapel Hill (UNC) after finishing his work on the System/360 in 1964. That same year, a professor at Duke University,

Thomas Gallie, wrote the director of the Computation Center at UNC about pursuing a grant from the National Science Foundation (NSF).[12] The next year, UNC system President Bill Friday and the president of Duke, Douglas Knight, agreed to appoint a committee to investigate a joint computing center in RTP. Ultimately, the universities secured a $1.5 million grant from the NSF to support the center. Following up on his direct request to Tom Watson Jr., Fred Brooks asked IBM to provide a System/360 for the center.[13] The center was organized as a nonprofit and named the Triangle Universities Computation Center (TUCC). Brooks joined the initial board along with Gallie from Duke and David Mason, head of the statistics department at North Carolina State University. TUCC provided the universities access to state-of-the-art information processing.[14]

IBM's stellar run with the PC was short-lived. A bloated bureaucracy had formed during the many fat years when the System/360 dominated all competitors. IBM management made serious mistakes of judgment—none more costly than the strategic decision not to retain the rights to the QDOS (Quick and Dirty Operating System). IBM had hired Bill Gates and a fledgling Microsoft to develop it for IBM PCs. Instead of expanding its footprint in the operating system space, IBM handed its rights to QDOS over to Microsoft for a paltry $75,000. By the early 1990s, Microsoft's value was pegged at $27 billion—a huge number at the time but also a pittance compared to the value of Microsoft's future control over standards for operating systems. Gates said he was lucky. IBM's share of the PC market fell from 80 percent in 1982 and 1983 to 20 percent ten years later. IBM soon got out of the PC business entirely.[15]

Despite the ups and downs in its fortunes, IBM had a dominant presence in RTP. It attracted significant talent to the region and supported numerous local companies. Eventually the RTP campus had eighteen large buildings with nearly three million square feet of space and parking for 4,150 cars. By the 1980s, there would be 12,500 IBM employees working in RTP, making it the company's largest installation in the world and North Carolina's biggest private employer.

MCNC and a Foray into Microelectronics

In 1980, Governor Jim Hunt became the first governor in North Carolina to serve a second term. At the time, a deep recession gripped the nation. Hunt had largely patterned himself after Governors Hodges and Sanford, recruiting technology companies to boost employment and wages in the state. He wanted to find new ways to spur growth. Hunt turned to the Board of Science and Technology, originally created by Sanford in 1963. He elevated it to an executive-level function and installed as director his former professor and mentor, Quentin

Lindsey. Lindsey appointed two committees: one to look at how to capitalize on the emerging field of recombinant DNA and the other on microelectronics. Lindsey issued a report in 1980, recommending major capital investment "to mobilize industrial development."[16] As noted in chapter 9, the report recommended establishment of the North Carolina Biotech Center (NCBiotech). The report also recommended the creation of a Microelectronics Center of North Carolina (MCNC).

MCNC would take the form of a nonprofit organization with government funding. Echoing discussions years before in the Research Triangle Committee, the report emphasized support rather than competition with the universities. MCNC would help coordinate research activities and act as an intermediary between the universities and industry.[17] At the time, states viewed microelectronics as a growth area. Japan posed a serious economic threat to the United States through advances in technology, including microchips. In response, the federal government was funding research to improve the competitive edge of US companies.[18]

The *News & Observer* asked Assistant City Manager Ted Vaden to investigate the viability of the industry in North Carolina.[19] Vaden traveled to Silicon Valley. He reported on the traffic, housing costs and other downsides of explosive growth in California. He also met workers in the production of microchips often toiling in low-paying, tedious, and dangerous jobs. While noting the opportunity for new jobs, the series questioned whether North Carolina could attract the best jobs in the industry. That year, Hunt led a delegation to Silicon Valley and called on a number of technology companies. He felt the state could be attractive for R&D laboratories and manufacturing. He also commented on the prospect of low-wage jobs, saying "frankly, we've got some low-skilled people in this state" [and] "many of them are unemployed, others are seasonally employed. Many of them are on welfare. I think for those people, any job would be better than no job."[20]

General Electric (GE) galvanized support for creating MCNC when, in the early 1980s, it expressed interest in opening a $100 million semiconductor facility for research and development in RTP. Before making its decision on location, GE wanted to see a state commitment to semiconductor research to attract the type of talent needed for the new facility.[21]Hunt responded immediately. In July 1980, he obtained $1 million in contingency funds to start MCNC. Hunt asked George Herbert at the Research Triangle Institute (RTI) to head the new organization's board. The following month GE announced its decision to open the facility in RTP. The governor's press release said, "General Electric's decision to build here . . . puts North Carolina on the leading edge of what can be a second Industrial Revolution—the Information and Communications Revolution."[22]

Hunt received a $24 million state appropriation the following year to construct MCNC's facility in RTP to test designs and fabrication of microchips. MCNC's board installed as its president Don Bielman, a vice president at GE. Bielman was integral to GE's decision in selecting RTP for its facility. MCNC's report stated that the organization should "not conduct in-house research itself" but should support research at the universities and provide a linkage between the universities and industry.[23] Nevertheless, the board hastily made the decision to consolidate the research function, originally planned at North Carolina State University, at MCNC's RTP location.

One of the first hires at MCNC, Holt Anderson, recalls the early days: "We hired people from Bell Labs and IBM and AT&T to come to have an appointment at MCNC and an appointment at the university to do computer science, to do physics and chemistry and electrical engineering... the skills we needed to support new industry coming to North Carolina."[24] Despite the collaboration with universities, tensions arose over MCNC's structure and funding. While MCNC planned to undertake industrial research—similar to RTI—academic leaders perceived it as competing with the universities for a limited pool of research dollars from the state. Leaders within MCNC began to hear complaints from the universities, which had powerful allies in the General Assembly.[25] Herbert relayed these concerns in a letter to Governor Hunt, quoting a professor who said, "MCNC staff just took the research outputs without consulting university researchers."[26]

In response, MCNC stepped up efforts to support the universities. Fred Brooks encouraged MCNC to design a way for UNC, Duke, and NC State University to connect together and with MCNC. This suggestion led to a microwave communications system, launching the state as an early leader with the "Information Superhighway."[27] MCNC had a control room at the center of the network, which allowed students at one university to take computer science, engineering, or physics classes at another one.[28] Governor Hunt's director of science and technology, Jane Smith Patterson, helped MCNC transition from microwave communications to fiber optics by using the power of state contracting.[29] MCNC added more universities to the network, including North Carolina Agricultural and Technical State University, the University of North Carolina at Charlotte, and East Carolina University. It also included RTI. All this activity improved the state's ability to recruit talent to the universities. The enhanced connectivity also helped the universities score well for research grants by showing strong collaborations.

In addition to expanding high-speed connectivity, the universities pushed for greater processing capacity. University leaders formed a task force to consider the pursuit of a supercomputer.[30] At this time, faculty had to send data out of state for processing, which slowed research. Ultimately, TUCC took up the cause but failed in a bid to attract a supercomputer in the mid-1980s.[31] In a twist of fate, MCNC offered a home when opportunity came knocking in 1987. Always looking for a way to support his constituents, Senator Royall called MCNC's Bielman during budget deliberations at the General Assembly. Holt Anderson recalls Royall's comment: "Mr. Bielman, I really appreciate what MCNC's doing, and the fact you're connecting these universities and everything else. What else do we need to . . . keep [North Carolina] moving forward and progressing?"[32] Bielman immediately thought of a supercomputer. This brief discussion set off a mad scramble to estimate the cost for a supercomputer. Holt Anderson came up with an answer in thirty minutes—$19 million. Senator Royall put the figure in the budget, appropriating the funds in 1988 and 1989. The facility took eighteen months to construct.[33]

The North Carolina Supercomputing Center opened as a division of MCNC in 1989. From inception, the center was almost fully utilized.[34] It supported university research that required enormous computational capacity such as meteorological data, chemistry, and physics. As noted, researchers previously had to send these jobs out of state for processing. According to Dick Daugherty, IBM also took advantage of the center's supercomputing facility during the early 1990s.[35] Nevertheless, the number of researchers needing this capacity was relatively small—fewer than fifty.[36] MCNC quickly discovered that the supercomputer required significant ongoing costs. The hardware had to be replaced every two to three years, costing several million dollars. Ultimately, MCNC would need to charge users for access to the supercomputer.

By the mid-1990s, MCNC's fortunes began to change. Governor Hunt was elected to third and fourth terms beginning in 1992. But there was a limit to the political capital he would expend to continue funding MCNC. State leaders signaled an intent to transition MCNC away from government funding. Further, the production of semiconductors continued to move overseas. GE's presence did not lead to a cluster of new chip facilities in RTP. By 1995, the state ended its financial commitment to MCNC. Without this funding, MCNC had to sell most of its assets, including valuable research equipment. It had to make painful cuts in staff. By the end of the decade, MCNC could no longer sustain the supercomputer. Despite this difficult transition, one MCNC spinout had a huge payday. In 1999, MCNC transferred components used to build a new technology called microelectronic mechanical systems (MEMS) into a private company called Cronos Integrated Microsystems, Inc. MCNC also transferred valuable intellectual property in the form of patents. MEMS components are built from a combination of semiconductor and micromachining processes and high-capacity switches. Ultimately, they played a role in important applications such as automotive airbag-deployment systems, high-resolution video displays, and ink-jet printer nozzles.

In 2000, JDS Uniphase purchased Cronos in a stock deal initially valued at $750 million. MCNC had a 33 percent stake in Cronos.[37] MCNC sold much of its stock and managed to hold on to the funds despite efforts by the General Assembly to grab it. The windfall allowed MCNC to create the North Carolina Innovative Development for Economic Advancement (NC IDEA), which provides grants and programs for entrepreneurs and has become an important part of the state's start-up ecosystem. The funds also allowed MCNC to create the Rural Internet Access Authority, which operates like a utility, helping overcome the digital divide by providing internet connectivity to rural areas. It provides health care access via telemedicine. It also has enhanced the connectivity of schools in rural areas. North Carolina now ranks among the top states for digital learning.[38]

The Rise of Telecommunications

The state's leadership with the Information Superhighway and supercomputing carried over to the private sector, where the telecommunications sector took off. As noted, Bell Labs located in RTP in the 1970s. In 1980, Northern Telecom arrived in RTP fully committed to digital networks, including the hardware to support them, such as switches and routers. As noted earlier, Northern Telecom dominated the US market at this time. Then, on January 8, 1982, US District Court Judge Harold Greene approved a settlement, mandating an end of monopoly status for the Bell systems. AT&T would control long distance but otherwise, local service transferred to seven operating entities known as the Baby Bells. Deregulation of the telecommunications industry, along with the rise of computers and microelectronics, created an opening for digital networks. In particular, it allowed tech companies to tailor solutions based on a business customer's need for flexibility and speed with a local area network.

Once again, IBM played a key role in the area's growth. Development of the System/360 at IBM sites in New York required a sophisticated, front-end networking capability. Legendary employees like IBM Fellow Ed Sussenguth worked on the Systems Network Architecture (SNA) as part of the Communications Product Division in RTP. While at IBM, Sussenguth made significant advances in SNA. When deregulation occurred in the 1980s, IBM seized the opportunity. Ed Carney arrived from IBM's Burlington facility with the directive to create a modern RTP site telecommunications network, which consisted of optical fiber transport, "Token Ring" local area networks, and integrated Private Branch Exchange switches.[39] IBM's Communications Network Division in RTP boomed during this time as it went head-to-head with Northern Telecom and other new telecommunications companies.

In 1992, Cisco Systems arrived from California, constructing a series of buildings on Kit Creek Road in the newly minted Wake County section of RTP. Unlike Northern Telecom, Cisco began as an internet company using voice-over new digital networks rather than using legacy telephone switches. Cisco came to RTP, in part, to take advantage of the area's network engineering talent.[40] Ed Carney moved from IBM to Cisco in 1996 and later became the site executive at Cisco's RTP facility. At the time, Cisco's former CEO and president, John Morgridge, cited the area's "network nerds" as a reason Cisco opened its largest facility outside of Silicon Valley in RTP.[41] By the late 1990s, Cisco announced it would be doubling its workforce in RTP, which required the state to make improvements to Interstate 40 to accommodate the influx of workers coming to and from RTP.

North Carolina's investment in higher education and in the Information Superhighway also spurred the telecom industry. In particular, NC State University gained a reputation for producing among the best networking engineers in the world. Professor Mladen Vouk managed to take hard-working kids from North Carolina's small towns and instill in them a love for network architecture and an ability to foresee new technologies. Vouk did this through personal mentorship, working directly with students in the laboratory.[42] Finally, the state's leadership with the Information Superhighway attracted telecom companies. MCNC collaborated with Nortel, Cisco, and other equipment providers to connect universities to the supercomputing center. In turn, MCNC provided feedback on the equipment, which allowed the telecom companies to advertise their use by MCNC.[43] Telecom executives routinely served on MCNC's board of directors and actively participated in efforts to overcome the "digital divide" and to deploy innovative networking solutions for educational and health care challenges.[44] North Carolina's leadership on broadband connectivity showed telecom companies that state leaders cared about their industry and wanted to see it flourish.

Conclusion

IBM carved out a place for RTP in the IT industry as the company's largest facility in the world. State leaders sought to capitalize on this success with big bets on technologies like microelectronics. Those bets did not always pan out, and it's hard to measure the return on investment in facilities such as TUCC and the Supercomputing Center. Certainly, the networking of the universities and increased processing power paid lasting dividends in the form of research dollars. They have also improved the quality of life for untold North Carolinians through digital access. But it was often unforeseen events such as the breakup of the Baby Bells and a capacious appetite for digital connectivity that generated economic growth and higher wages. RTP may not have assumed the moniker of "Silicon Valley East." However, it successfully built on IBM's fortuitous decision in 1965 and established a dynamic IT sector by the end of the 1990s.

12

Avatars of University Dynamism

In the early years, RTP had little to do with the cultivation of homegrown companies. University support for RTP hinged on a clear demarcation between academic research and applied research: "The universities saw themselves as magnets to attract research companies to the area, not as participants in those companies' research efforts."[1] RTP's success would depend on the recruitment of industry similar to the state's experience with textiles and furniture in the early twentieth century.[2] The lack of entrepreneurial tradition in the South contrasted starkly from other tech centers such as Silicon Valley. There, Stanford University embraced applied research. In the 1950s, it recruited homegrown companies such as Hewlett-Packard and Varian Associates as anchors in the newly created Stanford Research Park, where these companies got direct access to talent and research in the universities. Before long, faculty and students "bounced between college classrooms and high-tech start-ups."[3] The formation of new companies came quickly there supported by an entrepreneurial culture.

Despite the structural and historical disadvantages prevalent in the South, RTP helped slowly change the mindset at the nearby universities toward commercial enterprise. In particular, with the arrival of IBM in 1965, faculty and students began to warm to the idea of entrepreneurism, seeing business formation as a way to advance technology and find fortune. This chapter recounts the story of three wildly successful tech companies created in the Triangle. All three sprang from research at area universities around the same time. Two can trace roots back to Gertrude Cox's pioneering work at North Carolina State University and the University of North Carolina at Chapel Hill (UNC) with companies that applied statistical analysis in novel ways. The other came to life at the same moment the state invested heavily in microelectronics, although its focus extended beyond semiconductors to LED lighting. Finally, all three relied on visionaries who thrived in a university setting but had a passion for solving problems best met through business.

SAS Institute

In the 1960s, the agriculture department at NC State University participated in a program funded by the University Statisticians of the Southern Experiment Stations. This organization offered an opportunity for statisticians to network and collaborate on research. At the time, the program encouraged the use of statistics to analyze different effects on crop yields such as soil, weather, and seed varieties. Tony Barr led the program at NC State with funding from the National Institutes of Health (NIH). A student from Salisbury, North Carolina, named Jim Goodnight went to work for the program in 1967. He had taken the only computer science class offered at the university and had a curiosity about programming. The IBM System/360 had just arrived, and NC State quickly established itself as a leader in generating analytical software that could be used by members of the experiment stations.[4]

As a graduate student, Goodnight worked around the clock to develop software to run on the System/360, naming it Statistical Analysis System, or SAS. By 1969, he and Barr formally announced SAS to the users of the experiment stations. The users liked what they saw, encouraging Barr and Goodnight to continue developing SAS. In 1972, the NIH cut research funding for computing facilities when it shifted its focus to medical research. Without federal funding, Barr and Goodnight began licensing the SAS software to companies and government agencies so they could continue to fund their research. Goodnight became a faculty member during this period. In the early 1970s, NC State student John Sall and Jane Helwig at the Department of Statistics joined Barr and Goodnight to work on SAS. A pivotal moment came in 1976. A group of about 350 SAS users invited the NC State team to attend a conference near Orlando, Florida. The users greeted the latest SAS innovations with enthusiasm. It was clear SAS had a burgeoning customer base. By this time, Goodnight and the others could see the market potential and diverse applications for the software system.

To meet the growing demand for its products, Goodnight and Barr, along with Helwig and Sall, decided to focus on the business full time. Officially incorporating SAS in April 1976, they moved out of Cox Hall (named for Gertrude Cox) to the north side of Hillsborough Street across from Nelson Hall. They took part of a building built by noted modernist architect Carter Williams. Goodnight has nothing but praise for the support and nurturing he received at NC State.[5] Not only did the university encourage the development of SAS over many years, but it also allowed SAS to take its coding in return for free use of it in the future. With an existing customer base and capital contributions from the four founders, SAS got underway without the need for venture capital.

The company soon outgrew its home in Raleigh. Consistent with the trends at that time, the cofounders decided to find a large site to develop a campus. Helwig, the only partner who did not live in Raleigh, spotted two and a half acres for sale in Cary near I-40. It was a bucolic setting, overlooking a pond. Goodnight saw advantages to this location: "The campus setting in Cary . . . allows us to offer a range of amenities, such as on-site childcare, a free healthcare center, and fitness facilities, contributing to a positive work-life balance for our employees. This convenience and holistic approach to the employee experience fosters a strong sense of community and collaboration, key factors in our high employee retention rates."[6]

Goodnight saw the advantage of proximity to RTP and to all three universities, helping with the recruitment of talent. Also, the company took advantage of a common loophole that allowed companies outside of RTP to obtain an RTP post office address. To the outside world, the mailing address connected the company to RTP, and the Research Triangle Foundation condoned it, believing the practice only expanded the RTP brand.[7] For Helwig, RTP also provided a convenient spot to pick up the mail to and from the SAS campus and her home in Chapel Hill. It remains a mystery whether convenience or savvy branding or a combination of both prompted the RTP address.[8] Regardless, SAS did not use the RTP address for long as it soon acquired a new one in Cary.

By the end of the 1990s, SAS grew to seven thousand employees. It expanded its offerings to serve a range of business needs, including banking, pharmaceuticals, human resource management, fraud, and risk management. By 2024, SAS employed about 12,000 in 140 countries where it has 70,000 customers. Its revenue routinely tops $3 billion. The company has no debt and has remained profitable every year since its inception.[9] Seventy percent of its revenue comes from the recurring licensing of its software, providing financial stability. It now ranks among the largest privately held software companies in the world. As impressive as all these achievements are, what also stands out is that its annual employee turnover is only 4 percent, compared to 21 percent in 2023 for the industry as a whole. The company's commitment to work-life balance has propelled SAS to the top of best workplaces lists worldwide. It has ranked No. 1 in the United States on the *Fortune* list and No. 1 on the Great Place to Work Institute's multinational list.[10]

Beyond the jobs and economic impact of SAS, the state has reaped significant benefits from a homegrown company. Goodnight and his wife, Ann, have three children and have been married for more than fifty years. Estimates of his personal wealth range from $7 billion to $17 billion. Goodnight and his cofounder, John Sall, have supported numerous causes, with education ranking at the top of the list. Goodnight generously donated to the North Carolina Museum of Art, including its renowned 165-acre park. He financed the development of the Umstead Hotel, serving as a major amenity to the region. Goodnight has also invested heavily in real estate with numerous projects including Prestonwood in Cary and Chatham Park, a massive community in nearby Chatham County. These ripple effects show that the accrued benefits of a homegrown company extend far beyond the office setting.

Quintiles and the Rise of Clinical Research Organizations

RTP is the worldwide epicenter for clinical research organizations (CROs), a highly specialized type of company that assists drug and medical device makers with clinical trials for the US Food and Drug Administration (FDA). Those trials determine when new products can be sold to the public. The US Department of Health and Human Services estimates that clinical trials account for the largest portion of overall drug development costs, accounting for 68 percent of the R&D expense. Each drug costs an average of $117 million to bring to market. CROs play a vital role in this process as a tool to improve the accuracy, efficiency, and speed of clinical trials. Today, CROs employ approximately 24,000 workers at 151 companies in the Research Triangle area. CROs comprise 37 percent of the life science industry locally.[11] A local company, Quintiles pioneered the CRO movement.

Similar to SAS, Quintiles can trace its origins to the area's deep tradition in statistics. As noted previously, Gertrude Cox helped establish a biostatistics department at UNC in the 1940s. In 1949, she encouraged a former student, Dr. Bernard Greenberg, to lead this department. It is one of five such departments in the United States.[12] Over two decades later, Greenberg recruited Dennis Barry Gillings to UNC. A Londoner by birth, Gillings earned a PhD at the University of Exeter and had studied mathematics earlier at Cambridge University. Gillings would become the father of CROs.

Gillings's concept for a new business began to gel after a 1975 phone call with an executive of the largest drugmaker at the time, German giant Hoechst (now Sanofi). Hoechst hired Gillings to investigate why fifty-six West Germans had died after taking one of its diabetes medicines. Gillings determined that patients with kidney failure were accumulating toxic levels of the drug. Using this information, the drug went to market with an advisory to give lower doses to kidney patients.[13] That experience convinced Gillings that he could provide an indispensable service to drug companies. While drugmakers are adept at developing new medicines, they are often at a loss when interpreting the large amount of data that accumulate during clinical trials. Those trials can involve thousands of patients and dozens of doctors in fifty countries or more. Managing and analyzing the data emanating from these studies is an overwhelming task.

Gillings's new firm, Quintiles, had modest beginnings: He and five colleagues analyzed data sitting around the kitchen table in his 1,100-square-foot house in Carrboro, a small town that adjoins Chapel Hill, North Carolina, to the west. One of those colleagues, Dr. Gary Koch, worked closely with Gillings for many years, but Koch never left the UNC faculty. The company uses a standardized approach to clinical trials, relying on a physician network that signs up patients for clinical trials, makes sure doctors collect needed data, and uses a data entry staff to enter data correctly. A former colleague, Paula Brown Stafford, recalls Gillings's determination to find just the right name for the new company: "It had to be distinctive—something that clearly stood out from the competition. He began to focus on the letter Q because it seemed that no one used it." Large data sets—what his firm would analyze—were typically divided into five segments, or quintiles. "It came to him in a flash," Stafford says. "It was a good name, but I did have someone ask me once if we sold bathroom tiles."[14]

By the early 1990s, roughly 25 percent of all clinical trials used CROs. Gillings first took the company public in 1994, raising $35.5 million. In 2000, he began investing cash in client products going through trials in return for royalties after the drug began to generate sales. But Quintiles's stock price nosedived because analysts were unable to value the new revenue stream. Three years later, Gillings orchestrated a leveraged buyout, and the company remained private until 2013 when it went public again. This second public offering raised $947.4 million—far more than the $789.5 million best case projected two weeks earlier.[15] That validated Gillings's strategy on investing in client products. The reaction of drug companies was enthusiastic. For example, Eli Lilly signed up its antidepressant, Cymbalta, for the royalty arrangement. Quintiles ended up investing $110 million in the drug and another $300 million in marketing it in return for 8.5 percent of the company.[16]

Stafford, who arrived shortly after Quintiles was formed, rose quickly to upper management. She was the twenty-third employee hired, and her employee insurance card was a conversation piece: UNC's most famous basketball star, Michael Jordan, wore the same number. She too would scale the heights, eventually becoming president of clinical development and overseeing fifteen thousand employees who were working on FDA clinical trials. Along the way, she served as project manager for metformin, a popular medicine for type 2 diabetes. She recalls joining Gillings at an FDA advisory committee to seek approval of metformin. "It was clear they did not want to approve metformin because they thought there were all these horrible side effects," she remembers. "They refused to allow Dennis to speak at the morning session. But after lunch, he just came in there with all his statistical prowess . . . and he won. It was history in the making."[17]

Stafford opened the Quintiles office in London in 1988 and its office in Palo Alto, California, in 1990. She says, "We had a reputation for delivering. We had a passion for what we did. . . . We were independent because we didn't depend on government grants."[18] She says the company was always proud of its ties to RTP. In the late 1990s, it secured a post office box in RTP and began using an RTP address, even though its offices were just outside the Park. She understood the RTP address was important to a new company's credibility in the market. After acquiring numerous companies, Quintiles merged with IMS Health in October 2016. The new company was called QuintilesIMS. A year later, it became IQVIA, and in 2018, Gillings left the board. The merger cost RTP its most familiar landmark when approaching the Park on I-40 from the east. The Quintiles sign was the first thing drivers saw, perched high above the tree line on top of company headquarters.

Similar to SAS, the success of Quintiles paid dividends to the region and state. In 2007, Gillings gave the UNC School of Public Health $50 million. His gift would enable the school to make targeted investments in cutting-edge public health projects. The funds also would underwrite Gillings Innovation Labs,

Gillings Experts in Residence, and Gillings Merit Scholars. Gillings's British roots and contributions to pharmaceutical development were recognized on December 28, 2019, when Queen Elizabeth II knighted Gillings.

After finishing her career at Quintiles, Stafford and her husband, Greg, invested in a historic preservation project across from the courthouse in Pittsboro, North Carolina. Called "SoCo Pittsboro," it features six thousand square feet of four seasons dining in what was once a Chevrolet car dealership. Surveying the inviting scene, Greg once observed to Paula, "This is Quintiles money"—one of the many ripple effects a big success like Quintiles can have.

Cree Research

Neal Hunter has the sturdy build of a linebacker. He exudes confidence. He and his brother, Eric, grew up in the North Carolina mountains. Both faced tragedy at an early age when their father, a physician working in Asheville for the Veterans' Administration, took his own life. Neal was five at the time and Eric was ten. Their mother, Annabel Harrill, brought the boys back home to Ashe County, where she had grown up. There, her father, Fred Neal Colvard, and her extended family helped raise the boys. Their grandfather made quite an impression. After losing nearly everything in the Great Depression, he established Colvard Farms, which later became one of the state's first Christmas tree farms. Fred Colvard exhibited an entrepreneurial spirit, inventing a new variety of red potatoes. He established a strong relationship with NC State University's extension service, helping him test new techniques such as irrigation systems. Neal and Eric would help their grandfather work the fields, which included collecting arrowheads. Although Neal and Eric may have worn hand-me-down clothes, they had family watching out for them.

At home, there was little discussion of different colleges. Neal and Eric both attended NC State University. Eric majored in materials science and Neal in mechanical engineering. Although Neal did not break any records in the realm of academics, he had a passion for business. He and Eric watched *Wall Street Week* and compared notes constantly. They began investing in stock options. Each investment reflected hours at the NC State library reviewing company details in volumes of *Value Line*. Eric constantly reminded Neal, "Look, [IBM] started from somewhere. Hewlett-Packard started from somewhere." The two brothers had the drive to build a company. They just needed the idea.

As a materials science student, Eric had the good fortune of studying under Professor Robert F. Davis. Davis joined NC State in the mid-1970s. With funding from the National Science Foundation, Army Research Office, and Office of Naval Research, Davis began studying silicon carbide, the fourth hardest substance on earth. It offered the potential to generate more power and speed than the silicon used in semiconductor chips. In addition, Davis's research showed that silicon carbide can make a blue light-emitting diode (LED) when current flows through it. Eric seized on this property while pursuing his master's in materials science. At the time, there were red and green LEDs but not blue. With blue, "You can make any color in the spectrum."[19] That property of silicon carbide created the potential to expand the use of LEDs in multiple products such as large-format signage and outdoor video screens.

Eric began working on a business plan as both he and Neal worked their day jobs after graduating from the university. By 1987, they formally launched Cree Research, Inc., named for their father, Charles Cree Hunter. They had four other founders, all "just geniuses," according to Neal—three were graduate students at NC State and one worked at the Microelectronics Center of North Carolina, which was investing heavily in semiconductor research at the time.[20] These four founders provided mostly sweat equity and had a minority interest in the company. As this team refined its value proposition, Davis "would be helping us along the way."[21] Cree's initial value derived from a license for ten patents owned by NC State. According to Neal, the negotiation with NC State was grueling. It helped that the founders of Cree were named on the patents. In return for the license, NC State received stock in Cree, and that stock paid off handsomely in time.

Unlike SAS and Quintiles, the founders of Cree needed substantial capital to test the technology and show it could work. After quitting their day jobs to pursue Cree full time, Neal took out a second mortgage on his house and Eric maxed out his credit cards. Later, a family connection helped secure a substantial investment from several McDonald's franchisees. The funds allowed the founders to refine their process with input from Davis at NC State. Cree grew silicon carbide crystals, cut and polished them, added a thin layer of metal organic chemical vapor deposition, and then annealed or etched them. By the end of the 1980s, Cree had developed and introduced the world's first blue LED for large, full-color video screens and billboards. In 1991, Cree produced the world's first silicon carbide wafer.

After a short time, Cree decided to sell the silicon carbide material in the form of crystals directly to customers. Neal recalls that was the "best decision."[22] Eric convinced the company's board to go public in 1993. He felt it was the right time. Investment bankers advised Cree to move the company to Silicon Valley to gain greater access to venture capital. Neal and Eric held firm. They would stay in North Carolina. The IPO brought in about $11 million—enough funding to enable the company to dramatically expand marketing to several new target customer groups. The company's workforce would mushroom from three hundred to six thousand by the end of the decade. Its valuation skyrocketed to $7 billion. In 1999, Cree purchased a building in RTP that had an existing clean room. The building was situated on Silicon Drive next to IBM. Neal reflects on the connection to RTP: "We identify with RTP always. Where's your company? RTP. What are the schools? NC State, Carolina, Duke. . . . And when you're talking to anyone in the world . . . they had heard of RTP."[23] With 70 percent of Cree's market overseas, the RTP brand was crucial to the company's success.

As with SAS and Quintiles, Cree's success brought local benefits. In Cree's case, NC State benefited from the post-Bayh-Dole ability to license research derived from federal funding. For example, revenues from patents that the university licensed to Cree have been invested at NC State in more innovation through a Chancellors Innovation Fund (CIF), which awards $50,000 to start-ups for early stage research. To date, sixty-three CIF awards have gone to thirty-two start-ups with fifty-nine commercialization agreements. As of 2024, licensing revenues stand at $2 million, and follow-on research funding has reached nearly $70 million. Also, the NC State patent revenue has benefited from Professor Davis's work, who pioneered research on silicon carbide and mentored Eric and Neal Hunter. Davis's role in securing the patents made him a principal investigator (PI), and the Bayh-Dole Act provides that PIs can be compensated up to 25 percent of the university's licensing revenue stream.[24] Part IV will explore Davis's continued work at NC State on silicon carbide and Cree's evolution as a company after 2000.

Conclusion

A shift occurred in the period following IBM's arrival in RTP. Instead of sticking with academia or looking for a job at an established company, faculty and students at the area universities slowly embraced an entrepreneurial spirit. They began to think in terms of building something new. Eric Hunter's assertion to his brother Neal—"IBM started somewhere"; "Hewlett-Packard started somewhere"—took root and spread. It is no surprise that North Carolina State University led this trend. As described in part I, NC State was more receptive than Duke and UNC to applied research and to blurring the line between academics and industry. The guidance and nurturing provided by Tony Barr and Bob Davis to students at NC State reflected this ethos. Bernard Greenberg played a similar role at UNC, and Greenberg came from a legacy tracing back to Gertrude Cox at NC State. Cox had jolted the Research Triangle Institute (RTI) into existence with her industrial research contracts brought to RTI from NC State. The interaction of academia and commerce eventually led to the creation of mammoth companies, and that cooperation would increase in the new century as area universities created more tools to commercialize research. Part IV will explore this phase in detail.

13

The Emergence of a Start-Up Culture

In the late 1980s, two professors at the University of North Carolina at Chapel Hill (UNC), Michael Luger and Harvey Goldstein, began studying the impact of science parks on regional economic development. Their work came at a time when science parks proliferated. Some 116 existed in the United States and many more had been started or were in the planning stages. The data showed that most parks failed to deliver significant economic benefits and diverted investment from other sources of growth such as education and training. The study became a book titled *Technology in the Garden: Research Parks and Regional Economic Development*, published in 1991.[1] The book includes case studies of RTP, Stanford Research Park, and University of Utah Research Park. It offers a useful snapshot of RTP's first thirty years.

In large part, the authors' analysis offered a sanguine assessment of RTP as "one of the most successful research parks in the world." They concluded that nearly two-thirds of the 32,000 jobs in RTP would not exist had the Park not been established.[2] Other jobs in the region situated outside RTP also would not exist. Just as importantly, they concluded that RTP enhanced the research capacity at the area universities, bringing scientists and researchers who would not otherwise reside in the area. Given the region had "little or no technology-oriented activity or tradition," RTP serves as a model to economic developers around the world.[3] By this time, RTP hosted a range of big companies. In addition to IBM and Burroughs Wellcome, large companies such as Data General, DuPont, Northrop, Glaxo, Northern Telecom, Rhône-Poulenc, and Sumitomo located R&D facilities in RTP.

In sum, RTP had achieved many of its original goals by this time. North Carolina had a viable new industry to retain its "best and brightest" students who no longer had to seek opportunity elsewhere. Also, RTP generated high-wage jobs. In fact, wages in the Triangle area had exceeded the nation as a whole—a feat in the South, which continued to lag far behind other parts of the country. The book concluded the founders of RTP succeeded, in part, due to timing. North Carolina leaders established RTP just as the South began to grow. RTP managed to capture a burgeoning industrial sector when there was limited competition in the South for technology companies. This first-mover advantage allowed RTP to increase its lead over the next three decades.[4]

The assessment of RTP in the early 1990s also acknowledged its shortcomings. RTP had "failed thus far to stimulate economic development, particularly manufacturing production facilities, in other parts of the state to the degree that development pole theory (also known as cluster development) would predict." Similarly, North Carolina lagged in start-ups compared to other parts of the country. RTP had not yet produced "new, innovative, technology-based enterprises." However, the authors surmised that could happen with time. In fact, they expected it would accelerate "through the development of networks of business and support services as well as sources of venture capital." The authors advised that RTP could help by changing priorities and providing programs for start-ups within the Park.[5]

In fact, entrepreneurial activity—much of it below the surface or in its infancy—was happening at this time. The success of RTP had awakened a belief in the transformative power of technology. Workers in RTP, university faculty members, and government leaders increasingly saw the area as a tech center. They could also see the potential for much greater economic activity as they looked to other tech centers such as Silicon Valley. Nurturing homegrown companies was an obvious gap. To close this gap, it would take a new set of tools in the form of seed capital and a range of support services for entrepreneurs.

The first conscious step in this direction began in 1982 when an executive at Corning, Bob Gress, became chair of the Raleigh Chamber of Commerce. Gress had traveled internationally. He questioned why RTP lacked a start-up ecosystem as he had seen elsewhere.[6] Through his urgings, the Raleigh Chamber started a committee to discuss the issue. The Durham Chamber had created a similar committee led by Dennis Dougherty, who worked at the Big Eight accounting firm Touche Ross (now Deloitte) and focused on advising small businesses.

The committees merged into a joint committee on start-ups. RTP had helped produce a regional environment for entrepreneurial activity. Moreover, RTP provided a neutral space for convening meetings for the joint committee, which began meeting over breakfast at the Governor's Inn off Davis Drive. After several months of meeting, the group wanted to take action. In June 1983, it organized a program on the topic: "How to Raise Venture Capital." The meeting was held at Burroughs Wellcome. Dave Rogers, a local entrepreneur who had success raising private capital, invited Bruce Anderson as guest speaker. Anderson had cofounded a private equity firm, Welsh, Carson, and Anderson (WCA), based in Boston. The firm focused investments on emerging technology and health care companies. Within a few years of its founding, WCA had gained recognition nationally in the start-up community for its success with venture capital investments.

The joint committee hoped the meeting would attract twenty-five to thirty attendees. More than one hundred showed up.[7] When Anderson asked the audience how many were working on a business plan to start a new company, three-quarters of those in the room raised their hands. It was an epiphany. Until this moment, most attendees had operated in isolation. Some worked at universities, some at bigger companies, and some out of a garage. As a group, they were not your typical joiners active in the chambers of commerce, civic groups, or private clubs. They were entrepreneurs—passionate about a particular idea or vision. For the first time, they could see that others in the area shared a similar passion to build a successful business.

The spark ignited at the meeting carried forward. Organizers saw the need for a new organization tailored for local entrepreneurs. Several months later, the joint committee incorporated a nonprofit organization in January 1983. They named it the Council for Entrepreneurial Development (CED). A plaque at the Governor's Inn in RTP would commemorate this moment. CED's membership grew quickly, as a publication that focused on RTP called the *Leader* (later to be renamed the *North Carolina Beacon*) covered its meetings and publicized its activities. Initially, meetings addressed topics of interest to members. Over time, CED created more elaborate programs, including multiweek classes on start-up financing and the basics of business formation. Just as importantly, CED provided a place for members to build relationships. They discussed service providers, how to raise money, how to formulate a business plan, and lessons learned.

The work of the joint committee and creation of CED spurred Dougherty on to further action. He saw so many of his clients struggle to raise capital. Typically, early-stage funding presented the biggest challenge for a new company. In many cases, North Carolina entrepreneurs had to leave the state to access investors. To solve this challenge, Dougherty began looking for a new way to help his small business clients raise growth capital in North Carolina. In the mid-1980s, Dougherty heard about a model for venture capital (VC) developed in the early 1970s by Kleiner Perkins in Silicon Valley.[8] Kleiner Perkins was the first VC firm to locate on Sand Hill Road, which became a cluster for such funds. Kleiner Perkins focused on top-flight entrepreneurs with bold ideas, using targeted or special use funds to commercialize advanced technology in Silicon Valley.

It occurred to Dougherty that Duke University might support a similar model to commercialize promising technologies developed in its labs. When he raised the subject with Duke, he got a surprising answer: Kleiner Perkins's cofounder, Eugene Kleiner, was coming to Durham for a meeting of advisors at Duke's Fuqua School of Business. Dougherty was asked if he'd like to meet Kleiner. They met at Duke in 1985, and Kleiner described his firm's close ties to Stanford University and the academic superstars there, who were making remarkable discoveries in the life sciences and a promising new field called biotechnology. The firm had helped a client, Genentech, raise $300 million in the world's first biotech IPO—funding the company used to take new insulin and human growth hormone products to market. With its three tier-one research universities, Kleiner thought RTP had the wherewithal to achieve similar success.

Dougherty asked for Kleiner's help in organizing a company in RTP to do that. Kleiner agreed with one stipulation: "You've got to come see me in Menlo." Dougherty readily agreed and soon established Intersouth Partners, the first VC firm in RTP. Kleiner became its special limited partner and agreed to serve as chairman of Intersouth's first advisory board.

"Kleiner and his partner, Tom Perkins, were the fathers of venture capital," Dougherty notes. "Having him involved gave us a lot of credibility. It definitely helped us recruit people like Joe Ruvane to the board." At the time, Ruvane was the president, CEO, and chairman of Glaxo, the fastest-growing major drug company in the United States. Dougherty fondly recalls that: "Those connections made it look like I knew what I was doing even if I didn't."[9]

Intersouth Partners went on to establish seven venture funds, raise $800 million in investment funds, and fund 120 ventures. Its breakthrough success was

Sphinx Pharmaceuticals, a Duke University spinout, whose 1992 IPO raised $75 million. It was the first public offering of a North Carolina biotechnology firm. Intersouth invested seed funds in Sphinx and incubated the company in its own office. Dougherty helped the founders write a business plan that translated complex science into business vernacular.

The life science sector in North Carolina got a second important infusion of investment funds and management know-how with the establishment of Pappas Capital in 1994 in Durham. Its founder, Art Pappas, brought a wealth of relationships with major drug companies to that challenge. He'd served as an executive member of the board of directors of Glaxo Holdings PLC and as Glaxo's chief executive for international operations. Before that, he'd held high-level positions at Abbott International and Merrell Dow Pharmaceuticals.

That experience augmented considerably Pappas's ability to recruit an impressive team of venture experts, to source promising early-stage technologies, and to secure attractive exits, such as IPOs and acquisitions, for its companies. Pappas's formula for finding investments did not rely solely on North Carolina–based companies. Instead, his investment strategy was deliberately broad, with approximately one-third of capital allocated to the West Coast, one-third to the Northeast, and one-third to undercapitalized markets from Florida to Quebec, including North Carolina. The benefits of this strategy were two fold: first, investing alongside more experienced VC investors on the West Coast and in the Northeast provided access to more experienced leadership and talent when evaluating opportunities; second, Pappas was able to introduce their syndicate partners in those regions to attractive opportunities identified in the undercapitalized markets. This unique strategy attracted the Duke University endowment as the first major institutional investor in the Pappas Capital funds.

Pappas would go on to develop the capacity to evaluate more than six hundred investment opportunities each year. Over the past thirty years, the firm has raised more than $800 million across its various venture funds, invested in more than 100 portfolio companies, including eight founded or cofounded by Pappas, and guided their portfolio companies to bring a remarkable twenty-six first- or best-in-class products to the market, benefiting millions of patients. These efforts are sustained by a team of experts that include PhDs, MDs, and skilled business executives. In all, Pappas has a staff of thirty-four.

The assumption that firms like Pappas and Intersouth are inveterate and tenacious competitors is mistaken. "Life science companies require a lot of capital to bring a product to market. Our environment is competitive yet very cooperative and collegial. There's plenty of work for all of us," Pappas allows. "Ideally, RTP needs two or three more VCs," says Clay Thorp of Hatteras Ventures, another

VC based in Durham. "We have a very good ecosystem now, but two or three more firms would definitely take us up a notch."

It can't be quantified, but venture capital—as bottom-line oriented as it has to be—is not all about the money. VCs create extraordinary value—in the form of profits, yes, but also in lives saved through timely and prudent investments in miracle cures for the likes of small cell lung cancer and breast cancer. Lives saved—especially the joys of extended life—cannot be quantified either.

The creation of CED and the first VC firms in the Triangle provided crucial building blocks for entrepreneurs set on bringing ideas to the market. Just as importantly, these institutions provided a place for members to build relationships. CED's first executive director, Monica Doss, recalls the early days. She occupied a tiny office down the hall from Intersouth. Daniels & Daniels, the first tech-focused law firm located in RTP, also occupied an office in the building. At the time, one entrepreneur compared CED to the bar scene from Star Wars—a place where misfits could find common company.[10] These new organizations, collaborating together, represented the beginnings of RTP's start-up culture.

Prepping High-Tech Superstars

Besides encouraging the rise of venture capital and new programs for technology entrepreneurs such as CED, RTP also prompted leaders to consider the formation of business incubators during this time. Like Bob Gress, Dennis Dougherty, and others, Governor Hunt saw the need to grow technology companies in North Carolina. Hunt had championed RTP and understood that creating more start-ups was a natural next step in the progression of the Park. In the early 1980s, Governor Hunt's Task Force on Science and Technology recommended a new state agency called the North Carolina Technology Development Authority (TDA). The TDA would offer space to "incubate" fledgling businesses and administer an Innovation Loan Program for these businesses. The legislature supported the recommendations in the form of the New Technology Jobs Act passed in 1983.[11] Ultimately, fifteen business incubators opened across the state in communities such as Brevard, Boone, Greenville, and Ahoskie. These were not exactly hotbeds of technology, but state politics ensured these public investments touched multiple constituencies.

Initially, Raleigh served as TDA's flagship headquarters. From the start, TDA faced criticism. In particular, the investment fund raised questions because it put government in the role of picking winners and losers. In essence, a state agency stood in the shoes of angel investors, who were largely absent from the start-up ecosystem during this period.[12] Like any angel investor, TDA charged a high interest rate on its loans. Its royalty agreement called for a 50 percent share of the profits over fifteen years. One entrepreneur lamented, "I won't tell you what the interest rate was, but if they charged that in private business they would be shot at sunrise."[13] Such was the rudimentary understanding of start-up financing at this time. Nevertheless, more experienced venture capitalists like Dennis Dougherty praised the agency and invested in clients of TDA.[14]

By 1991, there was a recognition by state leaders that TDA no longer should operate as a state agency. The state pushed to reconstitute TDA as a nonprofit corporation, NC Technological Development Authority, Inc. The legislature transferred property at 2 Davis Drive to TDA.[15] The building there had housed the Triangle Universities Computation Center (TUCC) along with the iconic IBM System/360 mainframe. The legislation rebranded Governor Hunt's original 1983 concept as the First Flight System and also provided an annual appropriation.[16] The Microelectronics Center of North Carolina and NCBiotech both committed funds to TDA. TDA's director, Brent Lane, led the effort to move TDA from Raleigh to an RTP location. He envisioned "an environment where small businesses are free to make mistakes and learn from them." Lane acknowledged some skepticism toward a small business incubator within RTP—home to major corporations. He wanted to build an entrepreneurial community in RTP where "peers engaged in research who share the common struggle to development of new products and ideas" can convene.[17]

Within a few years, TDA saw its first major success. As noted previously, Burroughs Wellcome (BW) and Glaxo merged in 1995. The merger resulted in the cutting of ten thousand jobs worldwide. Burroughs Wellcome was a treasure trove of biomedical research through its trust and foundation. As noted, its stunning rise in the last quarter of the nineteenth century had been spurred by finding a way to deliver medicinal potions and powders in pill form. Such groundbreaking discoveries still were ongoing a century later, when four BW scientists—John Vane, George Hitchings, James W. Black, and Gertrude Elion—all won Nobel Prizes. Vane won for discovering epoprostanol, the first approved therapy for patients with pulmonary arterial hypertension (PAH).

A number of spinouts resulted from the merger. One such project was a follow-on and improved therapy for patients with PAH for epoprostanol that restricts the flow of blood between the heart and lungs. At the time, PAH was considered an orphan disease, a fatal one affecting a patient universe in the United States of approximately 1,200 persons. But that number hugely underestimated the total because of the reluctance of physicians to diagnose diseases with no known and approved therapy. With a projected patient population so small, drug companies had little or no incentive to commercialize the follow-up therapy BW had discovered.

Epoprostanol had been developed in the United States in a BW medical section headed by James W. Crow, a PhD pharmacologist, and Walker A. Long, MD, a senior medical advisor to the section. Both believed that applications of PAH research might be much broader than estimated. After the Glaxo-BW merger, Crow was approached by Martine Rothblatt, a cofounder of Sirius Satellite Radio, whose daughter had been diagnosed with PAH. Having formed a foundation to pursue a cure, Rothblatt wanted Crowe to serve as a director. Instead, both decided to form a spinout company named United Therapeutics (UT) in 1995 and take a direct route to commercialization of BW15AU81, the follow-on patent to epoprostanol with an improved delivery and pharmacologic profile. The use patent for BW15AU81 was held by Glaxo Wellcome.

Despite Crow's wide circle of contacts within the merged Glaxo Wellcome landscape, there were formidable obstacles to out-licensing a potential treatment for patients with PAH. Like most large technology-focused companies, the newly merged entity was highly receptive to in-licensing of technology but quite averse to out-licensing. Even so, Crowe secured the use patent from Glaxo Wellcome in three months. His final hurdle was to obtain a "composition of matter" patent, which covered the exclusive synthesis of BW15AU81 for all indications. The Upjohn Company held that patent, which was secured for UT in a matter of weeks, again with Crow using his connections at the Upjohn Company. In retrospect, Crow modestly maintains that "pure luck" was a huge factor at every step in securing those patents. In one instance, a needed approval was obtained from a vice president whose sister had PAH. "I'll do anything I can to help you," he told Crow.

Soon after UT was formed, Crow moved research operations into two large rooms at First Flight's Davis Drive location. He calls going there a significant decision because it allowed him and his team to concentrate all their energies on development and not lose focus finding office space, furniture, a copier, or other equipment. First Flight provided a receptionist, access to a conference room, and internet service as part of the space costs. Flipping on the light switch was the only requirement for occupying attractive space in the heart of RTP. Looking back, Crow says, "First Flight enabled us to hit the ground running and never lose our focus on development."

Crow maintains that UT's successful pharmaceutical research and development "could not have happened anywhere other than Research Triangle Park." It began with the culture at BW where research and patient welfare were emphasized above all else. "First Flight was our springboard," Crow says. "It has had a huge impact by providing indispensable entrepreneurial services for UT and other companies." The company brought an FDA-approved therapy for PAH to market in four years—six years less than the average timeline. By 2003, its annual sales topped $50 million. They hit $300 million in 2010. Over the years, UT's focus on innovation has continued. In 2026, it announced a new drug for PAH, which could serve a billion-dollar market.[18] It now has a subsidiary that reclaims lungs that are unacceptable for transplant. Because transplants are available to so few who need them, the company currently is working on harvesting lungs from pigs to create an inexhaustible supply for humans.

Despite successes such as UT, TDA struggled during the 1990s. It could not achieve financial independence, because its existence depended on government funding. This instability led to the departure of its director in 1993 and then his return six months later.[19] Radical austerity measures followed the whims of state appropriations. In the early 2000s, TDA would lose all of its state funding. However, it emerged stronger than ever. Private sources such as programming, rent, and grants now comprise its revenue. In 2009, it rebranded to First Flight Venture Center, Inc. (FFVC), alluding to the state moniker of "first in flight." The name makes sense according to longtime board member Mary Musacchia, given FFVC's position as the state's first incubator and its encouragement of innovation and creativity.[20] More recently, it reaffirmed a commitment to start-ups focused on science and deep technology; that is, technologies requiring long R&D timeframes. Windlift and Anuma are examples of these types of companies. First Flight has now hosted over four hundred companies and helped launch thousands of jobs.

RTP's reputation as a tech center invited comparisons to Silicon Valley, which resulted in an awareness of gaps. University, government, and business leaders would collaborate as they had in the past to generate new infrastructure to fill these gaps. Events focused on venture capital and tech start-ups in the 1980s demonstrated that a number of would-be entrepreneurs lived in the area. They just needed an outlet. In the years ahead, the ecosystem to support them would grow more robust and complex, as will be discussed in parts III and IV.

14

RTP Shapes a Region

From the beginning, the architects of RTP saw it as part of a larger region. Romeo Guest wanted RTP near all three major universities to ensure that distance would not impede the interaction between research and industry. Proximity to Raleigh-Durham International Airport (RDU) provided convenient access to and from other markets. To recruit industry, George Simpson touted the cultural and recreational amenities that resided in and around the nearby metros of Durham, Raleigh, and Chapel Hill. With direction from the founders, Pearson Stewart planned RTP as a business park only. Companies would rely on legions of workers moving to surrounding communities. Therefore, RTP needed to foster a regional vision so that a myriad of businesses, local governments, and other constituents would fill in the blanks required by a new economic powerhouse. In this sense, RTP and the greater Triangle region would meld into a single identity analogous to the connection between Stanford Research Park and Silicon Valley—only RTP would subsume the region rather than vice versa.

This chapter focuses on the key ingredients to the region's growth and eventual singular identity. They include regional planning initiatives, marketing, convenings, and actions that put a regional perspective ahead of local interests. These ingredients produced spectacular results. Between the time of the IBM announcement in 1965 and the end of the twentieth century, the "Research Triangle" became a global brand synonymous with innovation, science, and quality of life. As local leaders came to embrace this identity, RTP increasingly exerted an influence on business, civic, and elected leaders to embrace a regional agenda.

Regional Planning

As described in chapter 5, one of the first actions upon the establishment of RTP was the creation of a Research Triangle Region Planning Commission. The commission, comprising mostly local elected officials, saw its mission as twofold: creating a plan to accommodate population growth that would come with the success of RTP and gaining local buy-in for the plan. In the early days, the commission identified several key challenges for an area that had a major job center situated outside any existing urban center. The commission set forth several different scenarios for how the region could adapt to this unique spatial form, leaving it to local officials to make those decisions.

By the end of the 1960s, the commission produced a *Research Triangle Region Development Guide*. The guide—note an avoidance of the term "plan"—rested on assumptions about population growth, projecting an increase from 300,000 in 1960 to 1,140,000 in 2020. Although this assumption wildly underprojected the region's growth, which would exceed 2 million by 2020, it emphasized "positive actions" rather than "revolutionary" ones.[1] It aimed at what could be achieved by private groups and public agencies. At the same time, it called on leaders to heed the urgent need to plan in a way that preserved the area's quality of life—a term now comfortably used by economic developers to extol an area to prospective companies.

The guide emphasized basic infrastructure such as water and sewer. Reflecting Pearson Stewart's imprint, it also considered the provision of open spaces. It noted a severe deficiency in housing in terms of supply and condition, particularly for low-income residents near job centers. The plan provided that, with proper investment and locations of water, sewer, and open space networks, developers could help meet the housing crisis with all types—"high rise or low rise, for rich or for poor, single family or apartment." This approach would support the region's quality of life by producing a "fusion of town and country."[2]

Though lacking teeth, the guide shaped actions of local planners for the next two decades. It helped ensure the region met the rapacious growth to come by building two massive water reservoirs—Falls Lake serving communities in Wake County, and Jordan Lake serving communities to the west. The reservoirs triggered water-supply watershed rules that limited development in large swaths of southern Durham County and northern Wake County, shaping future patterns of regional development as well as the location of open space networks and tree canopies that define the area.

It also showed the role that the Research Triangle Foundation (RTF) played at the center of these efforts. The foundation staffed the commission and cultivated a regional perspective, which produced a unique collaboration among local jurisdictions. Several years after the adoption of the guide, the Research Triangle Regional Planning Commission changed hands. In 1972, the North Carolina General Assembly established eighteen regional planning councils. The act reconstituted the commission as the planning council for "Region J," known as Triangle J Council of Governments (TJCOG). Its geographic area expanded from the three core counties of Durham, Wake, and Orange to include Chatham, Johnston, and Lee Counties. Moore County was added later. TJCOG had its own staff rather than continuing to rely on the RTF's.

The RTF closely participated in TJCOG and continued to promote a more interconnected and collaborative region, but there were bumps along the way. Chuck Flink recounts a range of attitudes in the 1980s toward RTP's connectivity to the outside world. Now a renowned greenway planner, Flink was one of Raleigh's early greenway planners when Pearson Stewart asked him to work on a greenway plan for RTP. Flink produced a wall-sized master plan showing a network of trails throughout RTP. Stewart invited Flink to present the plan to the foundation board. In his exuberance, Flink proclaimed that one day thousands of workers would be biking and walking to RTP. An imposing figure seated in front of Flink slammed his fist on the table, declaring that RTP was envisioned, planned, and constructed as an industrial park that workers would drive to. George Watts Hill reached over and put his hand on the agitated speaker's shoulder, saying, "Now, now, I think the young man makes a valid point we should consider."[3]

Flink was shaken by the encounter, but Stewart simply laughed it off and gave him words of encouragement. Flink and his firm Greenways, Inc., would design the RTP trail system in eighteen phases over a twenty-year period. The episode reflected how Stewart's low-key manner led to tangible results. It also reveals how RTP navigated a deeply ingrained suburban model as well as its relationship to the region.

In 1989, Liz Rooks succeeded Pearson Stewart as lead planner for the RTF. She had worked for the Town of Chapel Hill and for Durham, including at the time of Durham's effort to annex RTP. Rooks recounts there was a drop-off in activity in RTP around this time.[4] Nationally, the expansion of R&D facilities dwindled in the late 1980s and competition for new ones increased sharply. Also, RTP had been slow to invest in new infrastructure.[5] Under the leadership of Jim Roberson, the RTF reenergized the Park with a large expansion—approximately two thousand acres—into Wake County with the opening of Davis Drive south of Interstate 40.

Stewart had planned this area to take advantage of the natural environmental features. Cisco Systems acquired one of the first large sites adjacent to a lake. Other companies wanted a similar setting, and a land rush commenced. For a time, Rooks notes the RTF wondered if its mission of selling off all lands in RTP would be achieved. The RTF resolved to continue managing RTP and connecting the Park to surrounding communities, regardless of its ownership position.[6]

At this time, RTP received funding support from the General Assembly. While legislative leaders made sure that Durham could not annex the Park, it established a special taxing district for "Research and Science Parks." Intended to give RTP taxing authority, the new law allowed RTP to assess properties within its "district" for certain limited purposes. RTP used the funds for recreational facilities such as softball fields and walking trails, signage, landscaping, roadside maintenance, emergency preparedness, and waste collection. Although minimal, this independent taxing authority helped address a public funding gap for RTP as an island within the metropolitan region.

Creation of the RDRA

RTP's full impact on the region's identity—both to the outside world and those who lived in the area—reached a major milestone in the early 1990s. Up until this period, the Durham Chamber of Commerce and Raleigh Chamber of Commerce conducted much of the economic development work in the region. A local leader recounts that companies looking to invest in the area would fly into RDU. Tom White from the Durham Chamber of Commerce would pick up the prospect to see sites in Durham and then drive to the Governor's Inn in RTP where Ken Atkins with the Greater Raleigh Chamber of Commerce would take over for the Wake County tour.[7]

This approach did not send a message of unity to the outside world. To inspire greater collaboration, several business leaders formed the Raleigh Durham Regional Association (RDRA) in 1990. John Atkins, who led an architectural firm in Durham; Smedes York, a former Raleigh mayor and president of York Properties (and son of early RTP supporter Willie York); and Jim Roberson at RTF were galvanizing forces behind the establishment of the RDRA. According to Atkins, the RDRA had no budget. It relied on "moral suasion" to encourage the two chambers of commerce to think and act regionally.[8] The RDRA's success largely rested on the presence of RTP, which surrounding localities saw as a key to the area's success. Moreover, RTP slowly chipped away at a parochial mindset by bringing tens of thousands of new residents into the area. These new arrivals held allegiance to RTP—not a particular locality.

The lag between the local mindset and national perspective was especially evident in a watershed event in 1993 when *Fortune* named "Raleigh/Durham" as the best city in the nation for business. The following year, *Money* magazine named the region as the best place to live in the nation. Consideration of the region as a single place required no lobbying. That's how the world viewed the area. More than anything, these accolades boosted local pride and cemented the connection between RTP and the larger region.

The *Fortune* article leaned into a number of stereotypes, as demonstrated by its opening:

> Once upon a time, a lot of backyard barbecues in Raleigh/Durham's tonier suburbs involved Sansabelted tobacco and textile executives. They would stand around grumbling about business, putting down too many bourbons, and ingesting mass quantities of charred beef. My, how things have changed. These days you will more likely find a flock of microbiologists arguing about neurotransmitters as they knock back a few Evians. . . . This chunk of piney-woods real estate in central North Carolina has smartened up over the past two decades and become a genuine intellectual capital, with one of the highest per capita concentrations of Ph.D.s in the U.S.

The article cites RTP as "the heart of the area's innovative prowess" with 34,000 scientists and researchers and many "high tech" companies. The article continues: "What makes the park work so well is a unique nexus of the business community, area universities, and state and local governments. Duke, UNC, and N.C. State oversee a central research institute [RTI] within the park where scientists and technicians from the universities tackle R&D projects, often alongside colleagues from corporations. Private-sector clients benefit when their researchers gain insights from the academic world, while university scientists get a glimpse of the commercial side of things."[9]

New York, Boston, Seattle, and Austin rounded out the top five in *Fortune*'s rankings that year. *Fortune* may have wanted to create a stir by selecting a dark horse. Regardless, its choice launched a thousand national lists that would laud the Triangle in the coming decades. The outside market clearly saw Raleigh, Durham, and other localities as one region anchored by RTP.

Economic developers took another step toward regionalism when the RDRA reconstituted as the Research Triangle Regional Partnership (RTRP). By 1995, several regions received state funding to support regional economic development. Governor Hunt embraced the idea and urged the establishment of seven such partnerships across the state. To access the funds, the RDRA had to agree to add more counties to the geographic scope of the region, including Chatham, Harnett, Johnston, Franklin, Vance, Warren, Person, Granville, Lee, and Moore Counties. The new organization quickly coalesced around the moniker "Research Triangle Regional Partnership." Its first director, Charles Hayes, recalls little debate about the name.[10] The area was synonymous with RTP. Incorporating RTP into the region's brand made sense.

The RTRP hired a staff of five with the mission of marketing the region to external audiences. It did so through branding, strategic planning, and collaboration. With limited funds, the RTRP decided to hire Development Counsellors International (DCI), based in New York City. DCI worked on "earned media" rather than paying for advertising. DCI opened the door with media outlets across the nation to feature the Triangle. For example, when DCI learned that *Good Morning America* planned to broadcast a segment on North Carolina from the Linn Cove Viaduct on the Blue Ridge Parkway, they convinced producers to shift to the Old Well on UNC's campus.

In every story, Hayes and his staff hammered two points: The area is home to the nation's largest research park and three tier-one research universities. He often repeated, "The reason for the region is the Park."[11] This message struck a chord with national media fixated on competition among metro regions. Hayes says it was rare that two months passed without a visit by national or international groups studying RTP and the region and looking for ways to gain a competitive advantage.

Acting Regionally

As a new regional identity emerged, it inspired local leaders to act regionally. For example, Nobel Prize laureate George Hitchings founded the Triangle Community Foundation with a gift in 1983. The following year, a young lawyer, Hill Carrow, put in an application for Raleigh, Durham, Cary, and Chapel Hill to host the US Sports Festival. The US Olympic Committee awarded the area the event in 1987, renamed as the US Olympic Festival. The region broke an attendance record that stands to this day: 464,000. More importantly, the event required significant coordination, including seven thousand volunteers, improvements to I-40, completion of Terminal 2 at RDU, a regional bus system, and area-wide beautification. The event's success showed local leaders how regional cooperation could elevate the area's standing and bring in tourist dollars.[12]

One person, in particular, was inspired: Jim Goodmon, president of a local broadcasting company, Capitol Broadcasting. Carrow had talked Goodmon into sponsoring the festival. Although skeptical about it, Goodmon later reflected, "We really felt like a 'region.' And that sort of hit me. So I cooked up the notion of building 'Triangle Central Park' near the airport."[13] Carrow encouraged the idea. It would house a convention center and stadium facilities, positioning the Triangle for future large-scale sports events. Goodmon tried to entice the Durham Bulls to the park after a referendum to build a new stadium in Durham failed. He ended up buying the team; however, Durham found a way to build a downtown stadium, forcing Goodmon to scrap his plan for the sports park. Despite the outcome, the concept of Triangle Central Park demonstrated growing enthusiasm for regionalism. Goodmon went on to found Leadership Triangle and serve as a cheerleader for regionalism in the coming decades.

During this period, a series of major conferences engaged the public in the possibilities of regional activity. Durham's Mayor Gulley played a key role in kickstarting these conferences. Following Durham's attempted annexation of RTP, Gulley began meeting with the mayors of Raleigh, Cary, and Chapel Hill to discuss joint issues of concern. This group asked the TJCOG to convene a meeting branded as a "World Class Region Conference."[14] The organizers established a sixty-four-member steering committee and invited former Governor Jim Hunt to chair it. Held in 1988, the conference attracted several hundred civic, business, and university leaders.

The most tangible outcome of the first World Class Region Conference related to transportation. The conference had several working sessions. Gulley cochaired the Transit Committee. He purposively avoided the term *transportation* to signal an intent to produce a regional fixed guideway transit system. The working group recommended the creation of a transit authority to oversee a regional system. Few investments could bind the region more closely together than a transit system that linked surrounding urban areas to RTP. Attendees at the conference endorsed the committee's recommendations.

Gulley and others continued to advance the concept after the conference ended. Following lengthy negotiations, Wake County leaders agreed to give half of the votes on a ten-member transit board to Orange and Durham Counties, ensuring a balance of power. Now, the group needed legislation to create a governing authority that could levy taxes. Gulley and others convinced two rising stars—a future president pro tem of the Senate, Marc Basnight, and future House Speaker Dan Blue—to back the legislation. In a bit of payback for Gulley, the bill overcame Senator Kenneth Royall's motion to table the measure. Senator Basnight called the question, catching Royall off-guard, and the bill passed. Consistent with its sudden and surprising birth, the Triangle Transit Authority would take many unexpected turns in the coming decades.

The second World Class Region Conference occurred in 1992. It featured nationally syndicated columnist Neal Peirce. Peirce captured the zeitgeist of this era with his concept of the "citistate." He wrote, "Across America and across the globe, citistates are emerging as a critical focus of economic activity, of governance, of social organizations for the 1990s and the century to come." He explained this concept has reemerged due to telecommunications, the collapse of trade barriers, and migration to urban areas. These forces have pushed power to "constellations of regional economies."[15] "Only history will tell whether American citistates can overcome their disabilities" of fragmented government and achieve "a more coherent, mutually supportive social and economic order."[16]

Publisher Frank Daniels ran "the Peirce Report" on the cover of the *News & Observer*, the state's largest daily newspaper, for multiple days at the time of the conference. It encouraged the Triangle to embrace its position as a citistate. The report cited regional leadership as "the linchpin that will hold together a world class region" and the "most critical need." It proposed a group that could "promote the win-win techniques that share the benefits and burdens of developing our region and preserving our quality of life."[17] The report emphasized certain guiding principles, including the need to strike a balance between regional orientation and respecting local autonomy. In other words, a regional body would be advisory only.

Shortly thereafter, the Greater Triangle Regional Council (GTRC) was born. The RTF's Jim Roberson took a lead role along with other business, government, and university leaders. The GTRC drew a spotlight on the area's sprawling growth. In the final World Class Region Conference held in 1998, the GTRC presented a program titled "Which Tomorrow Will We Choose?" Organizers presented three scenarios for how the region could accommodate 600,000 new residents in the next twenty years. They included suburban expansion, walkable communities, and town and country. The GTRC solicited the input of participants, explaining trade-offs presented from the different growth scenarios. Organizers understood change would require education and time.

The context of the conference was clear. Its materials stated "growth brings so many good things to our region—it can also bring problems. Traffic jams. School crowding. Threatened water and air quality. Loss of open space." By implication, it suggested the region would need to back away from continued suburban expansion to maintain a high quality of life. Raleigh's mayor, Tom Fetzer, took issue, stating on a panel that officials shouldn't try "to stuff our preferences down the throats of the people."[18] Fetzer had won election in 1993 after a failed bond referendum for a downtown convention center. He enjoyed strong political support in suburban North Raleigh, which served as a bedroom community to RTP. Residents there backed his agenda of low taxes, fighting crime, and spreading amenities broadly across the city rather than in downtown. Changing this mindset would take time.

Efforts to fight sprawl represented a growing trend among planners, architects, and local leaders who increasingly questioned auto-dependent suburban sprawl. Influential groups such as the Congress for a New Urbanism, established in 1993, advocated for more walkable communities with diverse building types. This thinking ran directly counter to the model of growth typified by tech centers such as the Triangle. Writer Joel Kotkin described such places as "nerdistans," "new urban regions built on their ability to attract the rising technological elite."[19] These tech centers tended to lack social diversity. They focused on controlling the negative externalities associated with urban areas such as crime and commercial blight while excelling in "parks, schools, and amenities."[20] Fetzer's political base in North Raleigh reflected this outlook in the 1990s.

But perhaps no community in the Triangle better represented the "nerdistan" ethos than the Town of Cary. Certainly, none had a more symbiotic relationship with RTP. Just to the southeast of RTP, Cary exploded as a bedroom community shortly after IBM's announcement in 1965. Known as the "Containment Area for Relocating Yankees," Cary provided a home to engineers and scientists who valued its low crime, low taxes, and carefully landscaped roadways. As the 1990s came to a close, a volcano erupted in Cary, and it would have profound repercussions for the next phase of RTP's life. In 1999, Glen Lang was elected mayor of Cary. He ran on a strident, slow-growth message. The town's population had doubled during the preceding eight years. That same year a Wake County school bond failed in part due to constant student reassignments in Cary. In a poll, 71 percent of residents supported growth controls and said they would pay more in taxes to implement such restrictions.[21] The consensus toward growth that RTP had fostered since its inception was heading for a reset in the years ahead.

The Governor's Inn

Despite these rumblings, RTP ended the 1990s on solid footing. In many respects, RTP had entered a golden age. It profoundly shaped a region that provided the types of neighborhoods, shopping, schools, parks, and other amenities needed for the success of RTP—just as envisioned by its founders. Local economic developers liked to relay an anecdote about a visit to Japan. One excited person in the audience exclaimed, "I have heard of North Carolina; it's located in RTP!" The Triangle's brand had gone global. RTP and the region had become one and, in some respects, so had the state. Further, the communities in the area slowly overcame parochial concerns and united behind a regional mindset driven by RTP. Eventually, that mindset encouraged regional action as reflected in so many initiatives of the 1990s.

One scene best reflected the economic and cultural sway of RTP at this time. The Governor's Inn enjoyed a central location within RTP in its only commercial area located off Davis Drive, a central thoroughfare of RTP. Built in 1972 and operated by Nello Teer, the Inn hosted a who's who of the RTP business community. Ron Hunter witnessed the scene for forty-one years as maître d'. Hunter attended North Carolina Central University when he first observed the Inn under construction. He thought it surely would be a failure out in the middle of nowhere. He now says, "I spent the rest of my life trying to prove myself wrong."[22]

Despite the slow start, the Governor's Inn prospered alongside the growth of RTP in the 1970s and 1980s. Its Golden Nugget Supper Club on the third floor provided a place to unwind before North Carolina gave counties authority to sell mixed drinks. Clients—only men at the time—kept bottles of liquor in a personal locker. Servers could mix drinks for them while they ate dinner and listened to local musical talent. A larger band played on the weekends, drawing couples out to RTP to dance and enjoy a good meal. In the 1980s, the Teers brought in a dinner theater. It routinely sold out performances from Thursday through a Sunday matinee. The Teers focused on a high level of service, replicating their experiences visiting European hotels. The general manager came from Germany. Many of the servers arrived on a work visa from Europe. The setting gave local customers and visiting business executives a unique, urbane experience.

The Inn often hosted celebrities—mostly those who participated in the Duke Children's Classic, a long-running celebrity charity golf event. They included Bob Hope, Glen Campbell, Dinah Shore, Arnold Palmer, and many others. It served as a temporary home to the cast of the movie *Brainstorm* during filming at the iconic Burroughs Wellcome headquarters in late 1981. The staff grew close to the actors, who required full attention after long days of shooting. Tragically, Natalie Woods left the Inn for a quick weekend trip back home to Los Angeles. She drowned off Catalina Island that weekend. Hunter and others at the Inn felt the loss personally. Staff rarely turned over as they shared a commitment to the important role the Inn played in the region's business and cultural life.

As RTP grew, the Inn's dining room on the first floor became the gathering place for executives to make deals and see and be seen. The Inn had a captive audience, given its close proximity to all of the companies in an area otherwise devoid of dining options. Hunter would make sure the regulars, such as George Herbert from the Research Triangle Institute (RTI), George Watts Hill, Elizabeth Aycock from the RTF, Dick Daugherty at IBM, Robb Teer of Nello Teer, and John Atkins at O'Brien Atkins, were seated at the same spot. The personal familiarity made an impression on guests. By the 1990s, the Inn reportedly had the busiest lunchtime crowd of any US hotel.

Margaret Knox, founding editor of *The Leader*, covered this scene every day. *The Leader* reported the news of RTP: new companies, important business transactions, and key figures. Hunter describes Knox as a knowledgeable, dedicated reporter. She ate lunch at the Inn each day and interviewed anyone willing to talk. On occasion, Knox would mention servers in her news stories to show gratitude and foster a bond. As Knox got older, staff at the Inn would drive her to and from home and check on her in times of sickness. Years later, after she died, her sister and nephew showed up one day. They came to spread Knox's ashes in a field across from the Inn. Knox had poured her heart and soul into this place as did so many others.

The 1990s marked a golden era for RTP. IBM gave it validation in 1965. Burroughs Wellcome helped launch a new industry several years later. RTP achieved critical mass by the 1980s as the largest job center in the area and largest research park in the United States. RTP became synonymous with the identity of the region. It cast a long shadow on the area, which grew in service to the Park's needs. RTP encouraged a regional mindset, and its leaders recognized regional cooperation would help ensure the area maintained a high quality of life. As growth posed greater challenges, RTP supported new thinking around suburban development patterns. As this new thinking gathered steam and local political leaders responded to it, RTP would have to face wrenching changes in the coming decades.

PART III

Recalibration and Resurgence

(2000–2020)

RTP experienced nearly unfettered growth from the time of the IBM announcement in 1965 through the end of the 1990s. The early 2000s would present RTP with a range of new challenges that required recalibration. Part III covers the period from 2000 through the global pandemic in 2020. It addresses a range of setbacks for RTP in chapter 15. However, it also shows the continuing effort by businesses, the universities, and the state government to adapt and expand on the RTP strategy to exploit new opportunities. Initiatives focused on a new biotech sector known as AgTech, more sophisticated networks of entrepreneurs to commercialize ideas, and efforts to make the state more attractive to advanced manufacturing. This part ends with a case study on a major breakthrough in gene therapy that reflects the culmination of intense efforts by NCBiotech and universities dating back to the 1980s. Importantly, this period demonstrates that the ecosystem forged during RTP's first forty years was strong enough to carry forward through difficult times.

15

Setbacks of the Early 2000s

If the 1990s marked a high point for RTP—in terms of regional influence, global brand, expansion into its remaining areas, and overall corporate activity—the 2000s would bring a series of setbacks. Those setbacks played out over the first decade of the century and resulted from dramatic changes in the technology industry and in patterns of urban development sweeping the country. RTP endeavored to resist these changes, sticking to its original model. This chapter explains the national context in detail and how local leaders responded to it. That response would have lasting effects on the future of RTP.

Shake-Up in Technology

After weathering predictions of a catastrophic disruption to computers from the Y2K bug, the tech industry awakened three months later to a different kind of catastrophe. The 1990s had been good to tech. With low interest rates and the rapid spread of the internet, tech-heavy NASDAQ enjoyed an 800 percent climb in value between 1995 and 2000. On March 10, 2000, the index dropped precipitously. By October of that year, it had lost 78 percent of its value, wiping out all of the gains from the late 1990s. Observers likened the event to a classic bubble similar to those that afflicted railroads in the 1840s, radio in the 1920s, and transistor electronics in the 1950s.[1]

The fallout from the bursting bubble impacted RTP in a couple of ways. First, it disproportionately affected the types of tech companies clustered in the Triangle region. As relayed in chapter 11, the telecom sector had boomed in the 1990s with the passage of the Telecommunications Act in 1996, which opened up competition to meet a voracious demand for internet access.[2] Several of the major telecoms set up shop in RTP, including Northern Telecom (later Nortel) (1980), Ericsson (1990), and Cisco Systems (1994). These companies produced fiber optic cables, switching, routing, and wireless networks to meet the needs of an expanding internet. The dot.com bubble led to overcapacity in this industry by the early 2000s. Before the end of the decade, Ericsson and Nortel shuttered operations in RTP. Nortel had employed more than 8,500 workers at one time. Cisco lost nearly 80 percent of its value but held on. IBM's network hardware division, which had boomed in the 1990s, went away.[3] Meanwhile, start-ups in the Triangle area struggled to access the limited capital available during the recovery period.

The collapse of telecom exposed RTP's reliance on "hard tech." Urban theorist Joel Kotkin coined this term to distinguish types of technology. Before the bubble's burst, he argued the new information economy had "two faces, one 'hard,' built largely around quantifiable sciences and mathematics, and a second ['soft'] that focuses on the content of the messages that flow through the expanding information pipelines." Kotkin tied the two faces of technology to certain places: "These two aspects have created a split in the geography of the digital economy. The hard side, including such activities as the development and production of fiber optics and chips, remains very much concentrated in the nerdistans of the periphery. But the soft side focused primarily on such fundamentally creatively driven fields as media, fashion, advertising, and design, has taken on a decidedly more urban cast."[4] In Kotkin's typology, RTP clearly fell into the category of "hard" tech. As seen in part II, Kotkin identified these places as homogeneous and carefully planned—essentially "overgrown suburbs."[5]

Following the dot.com bubble, soft tech would rebound quicker. These types of companies focused on ways that made the users' experience on the internet more interesting and engaging. They generated content and services to meet an exploding demand now that businesses and consumers had rapid access to the internet. The so-called FAANG companies (Facebook, Amazon, Apple, Netflix, and Google) represented the new face of technology. A renewed Apple was the elder statesman of the bunch. The others came into existence in the late 1990s or the early 2000s. They towered over a landscape littered with carcasses such as WorldCom, Global Crossing, and Pets.com. The new giants consumed investment and talent in the early 2000s, further concentrating tech on the West Coast and making it more difficult for hard tech to expand.

The second major repercussion of the bursting bubble related to changing development patterns. With interest and capital gravitating to soft tech companies after the dot.com bust, economic futurists added ammunition for critics of suburban sprawl. Of course, this movement against sprawl had been mounting for years as the arguments made by urban planners began resonating with a public increasingly disenchanted with the negative externalities of suburban sprawl such as traffic and air quality. *The Rise of the Creative Class* by regional economist and planner Richard Florida became a clarion call of the post-bubble era. Published in 2002, the book captured the moment by linking the rise of soft tech to urban areas. Florida argued that regions that attracted highly educated "creatives" would flourish in the new economy. In particular, Florida identified the core of this class as engineers, scientists, designers, and those in the business of generating content.[6] According to Florida, they gravitated to places with diverse people, a vibrant street life with an arts and music scene, and ample outdoor activities.[7] These places offer urban environments comprising funky, older buildings and afford newcomers an opportunity to engage in and shape the community rather than passively observe packaged events.

By many measures, the Triangle region scored highly in Florida's "creative class" rankings. Clearly, it had a high concentration of educated workers, technology companies, and patents granted per capita. For example, Raleigh-Durham came in second on the list of "Creative Class Regions that are Innovative, High Tech Centers."[8] Nevertheless, Florida faulted the Research Triangle for lacking the "hip" urban lifestyle found in some other places. As evidence, a study in 2003 ranked the Raleigh-Durham Metropolitan Statistical Area (MSA) as the third most sprawling in the United States in large part due to the weakness of its activity centers.[9] In his book, Florida quoted a real estate developer in the Triangle area who said, "The people I am selling space to are screaming about the cultural issues."[10] This developer suggested the Research Triangle represented an outdated model where office parks are separated from residential neighborhoods and amenities.[11] A period of reckoning for RTP was coming.

Revitalized Urban Centers

While urban theorists emphasized the changing preferences of tech workers, local politics confirmed that voters supported more urban options. The 2001 election in Raleigh and Durham ushered in new leadership willing to invest in the urban core. In Raleigh, Charles Meeker prevailed in a run-off for mayor by roughly one thousand votes over a popular incumbent, Paul Coble. Like his predecessor and ally mayor, Tom Fetzer, Coble had shown little enthusiasm for public investment in downtown. While several office buildings and museums were constructed in the 1990s, downtown had few residents and little energy. The Downtown Raleigh Alliance developed a blueprint for revitalization, and Meeker championed it. The plan included ripping out a pedestrian mall and re-opening it to traffic, improving the pedestrian experience, and building a new convention center along with several public parking structures. Meeker and City Manager Russell Allen led the charge to gain approval for financing these projects. With the improvements underway, two major corporations committed to locating new offices downtown.[12] Residential projects would follow as well as bars and restaurants in renovated historic buildings. Eventually, downtown Raleigh developed a nationally recognized food scene with several James Beard Award–winning chefs. For Meeker, public interest in and support for a more exciting urban experience came through loud and clear when 45,000 people showed up to attend the re-opening of Fayetteville Street on July 29, 2006.[13]

Bill Bell followed a similar path in Durham. However, Durham had significantly bigger challenges. It faced a higher poverty rate than Raleigh's.[14] Abandoned cigarette mills littered the urban landscape. In many ways, Bell's life story reflected the sensitive relationship between Durham and RTP and the hurdles Durham would have to overcome to join in the prosperity of the Triangle region. Bell grew up in Winston-Salem before going to Howard University, where he majored in electrical engineering. After graduating from Howard, he worked on the Pershing missile at the Martin Marietta Corporation in Orlando, Florida. Having completed the US Army ROTC program in college, Bell was called up as a second lieutenant officer in the US Army Signal Corps at Ft. Monmouth, New Jersey, in the early 1960s. After his Army service, Bell continued working as a civilian engineer in the R&D Labs and also attended New York University, where he obtained an MS in electrical engineering.

IBM came calling in 1968. There were few minorities working in the tech industry, but at the time IBM made efforts to hire a diverse workforce. Bell returned to North Carolina to work in RTP, settling in Durham near the Park. In 1972, Bell ran successfully for the Durham County Board of Commissioners.

Durham County and the City of Durham are nearly coterminous, so city and county issues blend together. Bell focused on reducing poverty "neighborhood by neighborhood." Efforts centered on jobs, health care, housing, and environmental concerns.

Understated and speaking with a rapid clip, Bell explained Durham's strained relationship with RTP. Durham County lacked infrastructure for new development despite RTP's presence in Durham. He sympathized with the attempted annexation of RTP by the City of Durham in the late 1980s. Like others, Bell observed the steering of RTP workers by realtors to live in Wake County due to the knock on Durham County schools. Ninety percent of the students in Durham city schools received free or reduced lunch. The concentration of poverty in Durham made the goal of racial balance within schools difficult to achieve. Nevertheless, Bell and other community leaders pushed forward with a school merger of the then city and county schools in 1992. The backlash cost him his seat in the next election. Bell was reelected in 1996 and again in 1998. After twenty-six years of public service on the county commission, Bell chose not to run for reelection and stepped down in 2000. Later in 2001, people Bell had known over the years socially and in politics, business, and community activism encouraged him to run for mayor.

Like Meeker, Bell defeated a popular Republican incumbent in 2001—in Bell's case by fewer than five hundred votes. Durham also had a downtown plan in the works at the time Bell became mayor. As covered previously, Jim Goodmon of Capitol Broadcasting built a new stadium for the Bulls after attempting to lure them to his Triangle Central Park concept. Goodmon completed the stadium in 1995 and elevated the Durham Bulls to a Triple-A franchise in 1998, increasing attendance at games. Downtown Durham, Inc. (DDI), produced a master plan for revitalizing Durham in 1999. The plan included refurbishing the million-square-foot American Tobacco complex next to the new stadium.[15] Goodmon optioned the complex and partnered with Bell and the city and county to construct public parking decks. Within a few years, downtown Durham enjoyed new office buildings, several boutique hotels, street improvements, and the conversion of old tobacco mills into housing. The food scene and number of visitors took off.

Two key institutions connected with RTP were instrumental in Durham's renaissance: Duke University and Glaxo. For decades, Duke existed largely in isolation from the city. As the 1990s came to a close, the university concluded that the institution would benefit from a more dynamic city. To support that goal, Duke took a novel approach. Instead of purchasing buildings in downtown, it leased space, creating demand for owners to refurbish their holdings. For example, Duke leased space in American Tobacco, the West End, and Ninth

Street, eventually occupying 2.5 million square feet. When recruiting the top scientists in the world, Duke could offer faculty lab space in unique, historic buildings such as the iconic Chesterfield Building. This new approach toward mixing academics and industry reflected a sea change in attitude by Duke toward commercial activities as compared to the early days of RTP.[16]

Bell credits Duke President Nan Keohane, Executive Vice President Tallman Trask, and the late Duke Vice President John Burness during this period. He also cites Glaxo's support. Few RTP companies had collaborated with local governments in the region. Glaxo was an exception. When Joe Ruvane became president of Glaxo in 1981, he settled in Durham and, according to Bell, "adopted" the city. Upon Ruvane's retirement as CEO and chairman of the company in 1989, his successor, Bob Ingram, followed his lead. For example, Glaxo had purchased a site next to American Tobacco to build a cephalosporin packaging plant. Ruvane intended the site to benefit Durham economically. When the need for the plant evaporated, Glaxo sold the land to Durham for $1 as part of the package to keep the Bulls in Durham. A passionate baseball fan and former Little League coach, Ingram always maintained an office overlooking the Bulls' stadium. He also remained fully engaged in the civic life of the city, even keeping his collection of vintage Porsches downtown.

Initiatives following the 2001 election helped strengthen the region's competitiveness but diminished RTP's role in setting the area's agenda. The election spurred the revitalization of downtown Durham and Raleigh. This met a longtime objective of civic and business leaders who believed vibrant urban centers were critical to the recruitment of tech companies. The reemergence of night life, new restaurants, music venues, and bustling street activity helped meet a gaping hole in the region's quality of life—a hole that had grown in the 1990s with the movement against sprawl and the changing tastes of "creative" tech workers. Downtown Durham and Raleigh also became popular locations for business incubators such as American Underground and Innovate Raleigh. While these trends filled a gap for the Triangle, they left RTP isolated.[17] In fact, the mayors of Durham, Cary, Raleigh, and Chapel Hill began meeting regularly at the regional planning offices of Triangle J Council of Governments (TJCOG) in the early 2000s to discuss regional issues such as transportation projects.[18] RTP no longer led the regional conversation.

Symbolically, the Office of Management and Budget (OMB) split the Triangle's MSA in two—one for Raleigh/Cary and one for Durham/Chapel Hill—in 2003. Economic interplay between Raleigh and Durham had fallen below OMB's threshold of 25 percent, leading to the decision. When economic activity across the region picked back up and met the threshold again in 2007, there

Figure 1. Luther Hodges is sworn in as governor in North Carolina's State Capitol on November 7, 1954, following the death of Governor William B. Umstead.

Figure 2. Robert March Hanes was the president of Wachovia Bank and a founder of Research Triangle Park.

Figure 3. The founders of Research Triangle Park in 1958, from left to right, are Pearson Stewart, a Durham city councilor, George Simpson, Romeo Guest, and George Watts Hill.

Figure 4. Before Research Triangle Park was established, the land was largely made up of smaller undeveloped tracts of land and pine forests.

Figure 5. Robert Hanes and Governor Luther Hodges appear in connection with the announcement of RTP's creation in January 1959. Hanes is gaunt from his illness and died shortly thereafter.

Figure 6. George Herbert, the first president of the Research Triangle Institute (middle), and Governor Luther Hodges (right) are at the announcement of Herbert's hiring.

Figure 7. An International Business Machines (IBM) brochure depicted the IBM building on the Research Triangle Park campus.

Figure 8. Archie Davis was a chairman of Wachovia Bank, North Carolina state senator, and founder of Research Triangle Park.

Figure 9. The "First Lady of Statistics," Gertrude Cox, founded the Department of Experimental Statistics at North Carolina State University and seeded Research Triangle Institute with many of its initial research contracts.

Figure 10. The IBM System/360 is at work.

Figure 11. The Burroughs Wellcome headquarters on the Research Triangle Park campus was designed by famed modernist architect Paul Rudolph.

Figure 12. Gertrude Elion is working with Dr. George Hitchings, who won a Nobel Prize for developing a systematic method for developing pharmaceutical drugs.

Figure 13. Dr. Mary-Dell Chilton was one of the founders of modern plant biotechnology.

Figure 14. Dudley Flood (*left*) led efforts to desegregate public schools in North Carolina as a leader for twelve years within the North Carolina Department of Public Instruction.

Figure 15. Dr. Bob Bridges (*right*) served as the first African American superintendent of the Wake County public-school system following the merger of the Wake County and City of Raleigh school systems.

Figure 16. Dr. Mansukh Wani and Dr. Monroe Wall discovered the compounds camptothecin and taxol, which are used in anticancer drugs.

WORLDWIDE
WORLDWIDE

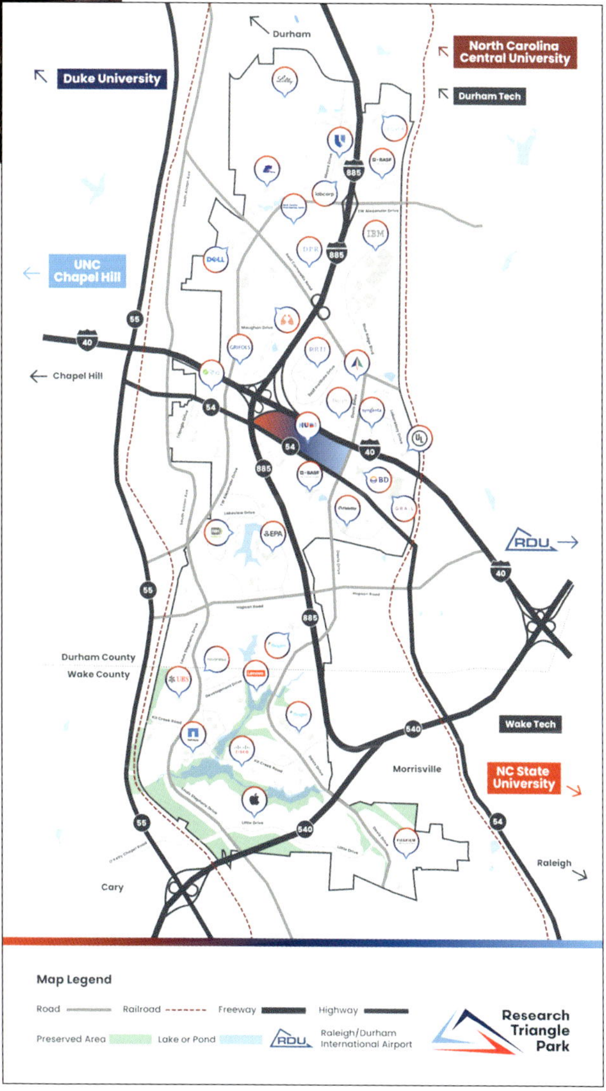

(opposite page)
Figure 17. Fayetteville Street in Raleigh opened to the public on July 29, 2006.

Figure 18. The food hall Boxyard opened at Research Triangle Park in the fall of 2021.

Figure 19. Dr. Jude Samulski, a pioneering scientist in the field of gene therapy, is seated next to Sheila Mikhail. They cofounded AskBio.

(this page)
Figure 20. Dinner is served at the Governor's Inn.

Figure 21. Durham Mayor Bill Bell came to the Triangle as an IBM engineer. He served on the Durham County Commission for twenty-six years and as Durham mayor for sixteen years.

Figure 22. A map of RTP shows the road network and locations for a number of employers

Figure 23. The Fujifilm Biotechnologies' contract development and manufacturing organization (CDMO) facility is being built in Holly Springs, North Carolina.

Figure 24. The Horseshoe, the Hub RTP's central gathering place, is under construction.

was little political energy to reunite the MSAs into one.[19] The size of MSAs help attract federal dollars, company relocations, and major league franchises, which look for a presence in the largest markets. The split dilutes the region's stature on the national stage. RTP leadership has urged unifying the MSAs.[20] However, cities in the area have been content to operate as a bigger fish in a smaller MSA.

Quest for Transit

One lifeline that could bring RTP into the conversation of urban placemaking also faced a major setback in the early 2000s. After the creation of Triangle Transit Authority (TTA) in the late 1980s, the organization settled on an ambitious plan to bring rail transit to the region. The plan had three phases: commuter rail from North Raleigh to Durham, light rail from Durham to Chapel Hill, and bus lanes and high occupancy vehicle (HOV) lanes on Interstate 40.[21] The system would provide two stops in RTP. This allowed developers and planners to map out dense, urban nodes within the Park that could serve as mixed-use centers for RTP employees. Conceivably, the rail transit system would offer new mobility options and help start filling in a regional hole, resulting from a model dating back to RTP's inception in the 1950s.

The plan took years of study and effort to arrive at a cost share of 50 percent from the Federal Transit Administration (FTA), 25 percent from the NC Department of Transportation, and 25 percent from local governments. Unlike Mecklenburg County, which passed a sales tax in 1997 to fund light rail in Charlotte, the Triangle relied on less robust local funding sources. In 2003, transit officials received news from the FTA that it approved funding for the final design of the thirty-five-mile commuter line. However, rising construction costs and anemic growth of its local funding sources caused TTA to request more funding from the FTA. Upon review, FTA officials questioned some of the key findings of TTA's travel demand models, including a projected four-hour commute from Durham to RTP. Ultimately, political leaders at the state and local level withdrew the support needed to gain approval. For the time being, regional transit was dead. RTP would have to continue its auto-dependent development pattern in the years to come.

Reality Check

As the first decade of the 2000s came to a close, the Great Financial Crisis engulfed the nation. GlaxoSmithKline announced its first major layoff—approximately ten thousand workers—in 2009. New development came to a halt. The slowdown provided a chance for area leaders to catch their breath and focus on their first regional planning initiative since the 1998 World Class Region Conference. In February 2009, 280 community leaders assembled in the Raleigh Convention Center—symbolically in a downtown rather than near RTP—to participate in the Triangle Region Reality Check planning exercise sponsored by the Urban Land Institute in partnership with Triangle Tomorrow (formerly the Greater Triangle Regional Council).[22] Participants came from fifteen counties. Facilitators organized attendees into twenty-eight groups. Each group worked around a table, placing Legos onto large maps of the region to allocate expected growth by 2030. Red Legos represented new jobs (700,000) and yellow Legos represented new residents (1.2 million). Colored yarn allowed participants to delineate open space, increased road capacity, and transit corridors. Several days after this meeting, organizers synthesized the results and presented them to an audience of five hundred.

While organizers did not reduce each table's maps to a single regional plan, Reality Check went further than the scenario planning of the 1960s and 1990s. Those exercises had simply set forth different ways the area could grow and encouraged local governments to be intentional about the coming growth. Reality Check used a software tool to generate areas of agreement and disagreement among the twenty-eight groups. The results showed strong consensus against continued suburban sprawl. Three themes emerged from the conference: encouraging vibrant urban centers, increasing transit, and maintaining green spaces. Furthermore, vibrant centers should comprise lively, mixed-use development with employment and housing.[23] At the conference, RTF President Rick Weddle explained to organizers that RTP was not changing. It would remain an office park for a variety of reasons: zoning rules, covenants, and environmental issues such as biomedical waste.[24] Since RTP's inception, the foundation had encouraged regional planning to produce a high quality of life for workers moving to the area. By 2009, such planning increasingly showed RTP as out of step with the type of development desired by area leaders and tech workers.

Not long after the Reality Check exercise, Triangle Tomorrow was folded into the Research Triangle Regional Partnership, the regional marketing group. Within a couple of years, it lost its staff, name, and independent existence.[25] Establishing a regional leadership group comprising university, civic, and business leaders had been a major goal of the World Class Region Conferences in the 1990s. Such a goal no longer resonated as a priority. The financial support for Triangle Tomorrow flowed instead to the area's Chambers of Commerce and other organizations. New initiatives focused increasingly on local matters.

An End to Consensus on Education?

As the aughts came to an end, an even more ominous event occurred. In October 2009, Wake County voters elected four new members to the Wake County School Board, producing a five-member majority that soon moved to dismantle the school system's diversity policy. The reaction was fierce. Police had to remove protesters from school board meetings. The superintendent resigned. An accrediting agency launched an investigation, and the NAACP threatened suit. The episode sent shock waves through the Triangle area, especially in the business community, which relied on Wake County schools to sell the area to tech companies.

As recounted earlier, the presence of RTP had helped lay the groundwork for Wake County's diversity policy as community leaders worked toward a program to desegregate public schools and create a high-quality system for transplants to the area. Now, the population growth generated by the Park directly undermined the approach established in the 1970s. Due in part to steering by real estate agents, much of that growth occurred on the eastern side of the Triangle. Wake County's population grew 109 percent between 1980 and 2000. Cary's population doubled in less than ten years. Four thousand new students entered the Wake County school system each year. Overall, the number of students in the Wake County system jumped from 63,816 in 1990 to 133,215 in 2007, making it one of the largest school systems in the nation.[26]

The dramatic increase in student population placed immense pressure on the Wake County system to keep up. In 1999 Wake County voters had rejected a $650 million bond. The bond had followed two others that passed in the mid-1990s. Opposition to the 1999 bond focused primarily on the increase to property taxes needed to fund the bonds. Residents enjoyed relatively low tax rates, particularly compared to those areas of the country many recent transplants had left behind. Wake County regrouped and passed smaller bonds in 2000 and 2003. While thirty-nine new schools opened between 2000 and 2006, the deficit in needed facilities increased. More and more students ended up in mobile classrooms due to overcrowding. By 2006, Wake County adopted a long-range plan that identified $5 billion in capital needs to support 94,000 new students over fifteen years.[27]

The collaboration that had produced a stable and nationally recognized school system eroded significantly during this timeframe. In 2006, the school board discussed advancing a bond package between $1.375 and $1.975 billion. In response to concerns over tax increases, the county trimmed the package to $970 million. The school board had to find ways to stretch limited dollars. This included mandatory year-round schools, which increased the capacity of each school by one-third through a tracking system. This move drew vehement opposition in certain quarters. Groups such as WakeCARES and Stop Mandatory Year-Round sprang up.[28] The school board also routinely reassigned students as new schools came online. Fast-growing western Wake County felt the brunt of the impacts of year-round schools and reassignments. As discontent over the status quo mounted, Wake County managed to pass the $970 million bond with 53 percent of the vote. The *News & Observer* reported: "With the unrelenting pressure of growth, the unpopularity of year-round school calendars and the massive reassignment of students driven by both overcrowding and diversity, permanent opposition from parents is now the norm."[29] In other words, successful passage of a large bond did nothing to solve the underlying challenges—and dissatisfaction with the status quo would grow.

For various reasons, Wake County's diversity policy became the target of public debate by 2009. Early that year the school created a new three-year student assignment plan to provide greater transparency of future changes. However, this only infuriated parents who saw their children would be ping-ponged between schools as new facilities came online. Critics started to coalesce around the idea of "neighborhood schools," where families could rely on stable assignments to a proximate school. The diversity policy stood in the way of this concept because kids who qualified for free and reduced lunch programs were bused to affluent, growing areas.[30] The incoming students reduced the number of seats available for students living nearby.

As the October 2009 school board elections approached, a battle line formed: supporters of the diversity policy on one side and neighborhood schools on the other. Wake County schools, which had largely avoided partisanship over the decades, saw local political parties gain interest in the fight. Connections among community leaders who helped find solutions to divisive issues had fragmented with the explosive growth of the area. On March 23, 2010, the new school board voted to eliminate diversity as a criterion for student assignment. The reaction to that vote gained national media attention.[31] Protests rocked the school board meetings. The years ahead would determine whether Wake County could regain its reputation for excellence and stability—qualities that eluded so many other areas of the country and had represented an advantage for the Triangle.

Conclusion

Coming on the heels of unprecedented growth and global recognition during the 1990s, the early 2000s presented new challenges for RTP. The dot.com bubble exposed a fault line in the tech industry. Places heavy on "hard tech" such as the Triangle region had to deal with massive job losses and difficulties attracting investment for new start-ups. The shape of development in the Triangle region reflected the preferences of hard tech from the carefully landscaped parkways of Cary to the abundant outdoor recreation in North Raleigh. As an office park, RTP mirrored these tastes. But the world was changing. The 2001 elections in Raleigh and Durham began to move the area toward new development patterns. Mayor Bell and Mayor Meeker would champion public investments and partnerships with the business community to revitalize the area's urban cores. Companies and tech workers increasingly sought vibrant, walkable centers. Isolated and out of steam, RTP would need to recalibrate its vision in the years ahead. In a coup de grâce, the inability of community leaders to manage explosive student growth led to chaotic results in Wake County. Frustrated parents backed candidates willing to dismantle a key feature of the school system. The ensuing reaction revealed a community divided. The challenges of the early 2000s suggested the model that fueled RTP's success was unsustainable. That model would need to change if RTP wanted to maintain a preeminent position in the tech industry.

16

Epiphany on a Plane

With a series of setbacks in the early 2000s, RTP needed to recalibrate for the years ahead. The strategies that propelled RTP as an economic engine operated as muscle memory. The building blocks created during RTP's early phase—a start-up ecosystem, university engagement in commercialization, and sophisticated talent trained in large corporations—would come together to stimulate new economic activity. This chapter details one such example—a case where university researchers pursued their entrepreneurial dreams and found the talent and local funding and mentoring to take it public. It shows how far RTP had come by this period.

Battlestar Galactica, a popular sci-fi TV series with a war of the worlds plot, first aired in 1978 and was remade in 2004; along the way, it had many spinoffs—from a Singaporean roller coaster to tabletop games, and, oddly enough, the idea for a life-saving cancer drug. In 2008, while watching a *Galactica* episode on a long plane flight, Ned Sharpless, a polymath oncologist at the University of North Carolina at Chapel Hill (UNC), was struck by the ingenious weapon the show's villains had deployed to destroy space travelers from Earth. They were using particle beams of ionizing radiation that could penetrate human bone marrow, like an x-ray, to attack the stem cells proliferating inside and, ultimately, shut down the body's repair system. It occurred to Sharpless that chemotherapy was having much the same effect on his patients.

As the show continued, he began asking himself questions like: *Could a new drug be designed to protect stem cells inside bone marrow from the ravages of chemotherapy?... Could the new drug induce a quiescent state in which red and white blood cells were put to sleep?... Could chemo treatments then continue without delays for patients to recover from its debilitating side effects? Would tumors stop growing while patients took the drug?*

In many ways, the most daunting question of all was: Could such a drug be commercialized and mass produced to treat the one million Americans taking chemo in any given year and many millions more in treatment abroad?

At the time, Sharpless was a professor at UNC's Lineberger Cancer Institute and would later become its director. In 2017, he became director of the National Cancer Institute and would serve two years later as acting commissioner of the US Food and Drug Administration (FDA). He was widely known as a visionary with an empathetic heart.

Not long after his epiphany on the plane, Sharpless and Kwok-Kin Wong, who'd been a fellow postdoc at Harvard Medical School, cofounded a company called G-Zero Therapeutics, so named for the quiescent cell state to be induced by the proposed new drug. In attempting to commercialize what amounted to little more than an idea, Sharpless and Wong faced a development cycle that could take up to fifteen years and cost tens of millions of dollars. But their bold step also set in motion a perpetual drug development cycle of seed and angel funding to validate the idea; funding rounds to bring in outside investors; extensive—and high-cost—studies to make sure the drug is safe for humans; clinical trials supervised by the FDA to obtain regulatory approval; ramp-up funding from large equity investors and/or a public share offering; mass production and marketing; and, finally, new scientific discoveries that perpetuate the cycle.

Suffice it to say that superb scientific and business expertise had to be deployed at every step through this labyrinth. Fate and sound judgment guided Sharpless in making a first hire. Right out of the gate, so to speak, he found someone who would profoundly shape the company's science going forward and add much depth to the idea that occurred to Sharpless on the plane.

As noted, in 2009 during the midst of the great financial crisis, the pharmaceutical giant GlaxoSmithKline (GSK) laid off ten thousand employees, including many scientists at its US headquarters in Research Triangle Park. Jay Strum, a biochemist who'd been with the company for fifteen years, was among those let go. At the time, he was part of a GSK international team working on a project at Harvard. A Tar Heel by birth, Strum had earned a PhD in biochemistry at Wake Forest University and did a postdoc at Duke University in molecular biology. After wrapping up his project in Boston, he returned to the Triangle and began looking for a job.

A short time later, through a friend of a friend, Strum learned that Sharpless had formed a new company that needed a biochemist. He called right away and reached Sharpless in Greensboro, where he'd taken his kids to a soccer tournament. After they established that they knew many of the same professionals, a rapport began to build. Sharpless even knew a coworker of Strum's at Harvard during his last GSK assignment.

"How come we've never met?" Sharpless asked.

Strum could hear a loud rumbling noise on the other end of the line but managed to answer, "I'm not sure . . ."

"Listen," Sharpless shouted. "My muffler is falling off. I'll call you as soon as I get home."

True to his word, Sharpless called about an hour or so later. On the way home, he'd called two professionals who both knew Strum, and both had glowing things to say about him. One even told Sharpless, "If you don't hire him, I will." A short time thereafter, Strum became G-Zero's first employee and its chief scientific officer (CSO).

Fifteen years later, Strum would say, "I've always believed fate had a hand in all that. Just think about it: A friend of a friend, who barely knew me, just happened to bump into Ned, learned that he had a job to fill, and then connected us. What if Ned's muffler had fallen off? It might have been a different story."

Strum's first task as CSO was to design a new molecule to, in effect, put cells in the bone marrow to sleep. Designing such a particle is scientific discovery verging on art. Most drugs on the market are small molecules—low-weight organic compounds designed to trigger a biological response in the human body. Antibiotics and aspirin are examples of atomic compositions that trigger a desired response. Such synthetic inventions must perform with precision and cause minimal side effects. Designing a molecule is meticulous work; often it takes years to develop and patent one. Once approved, it can be mass-produced in pill form or as a biologic that's injected. In some instances, designing and manufacturing a small molecule can cost billions of dollars.

G-Zero was incubated in Sharpless's lab at the UNC Lineberger Cancer Center, a commercialization accelerating program at UNC. Two more scientists came aboard in the early going—Patrick Roberts, a postdoc in Sharpless's lab, and John Bisi, who'd worked at GSK and had become a senior scientist.

Strum, Roberts, and Bisi all squeezed into one small room with wobbly desks at the cancer center with the dual task of finding a small molecule and securing more funding to continue their research. Soft loans from NCBiotech, totaling $500,000, provided a bridge to major and much-needed competitive grants. Between late 2009 and mid-2012, the firm won government grants worth $3.6 million. These funds enabled the team to identify and patent a candidate small molecule and also to patent a treatment for the deadliest form of lung cancer, one so aggressive that most patients die in less than a year after diagnosis. By then, the firm's funding needs had outstripped what grants could provide; venture funding was essential to continue its expansion.

Even before G-Zero was formed, Sharpless had approached Clay Thorp, an investor who'd made a lot of money by the time he was thirty. He and co-investors had spent four years in the late 1990s developing a drug discovery platform that got sold to a Swedish firm for $106.7 million in stock. Instead of relaxing on the beach, Thorp decided to pursue a recurring dream: "To start," as he puts it, "a firm that would start new companies."

Thorp gave the new enterprise a distinctive metaphorical name—Hatteras Venture Partners, so named for the Cape on the North Carolina coast facing Diamond Shoals, where countless ships have gone under. Since 1803, the Cape's famous lighthouse has guided ships through heavy storms. Instead of ships, Hatteras Venture Partners (HVP) would steer start-ups and more advanced companies through the stormy seas of the business cycle. Durham-based HVP would go on to become one of the largest venture capital firms in the Southeast. Over the years, it would invest in ninety-three medicine and life science companies. In many instances, HVP's senior management would serve as their acting CEO.

In 2009, Sharpless and Thorpe had their first discussion of G-Zero as an investment for HVP. Sharpless pitched a molecule he hoped to option from Pfizer under a material transfer agreement.

"Very impressive," Thorp allowed. "Is it your molecule?

"No," Sharpless replied. "It belongs to Pfizer."

"Well, that's not going to work for us. We're not a charity."

But Thorp's interest had been piqued enough to call a former colleague at the Pfizer Venture Fund to ask about the molecule's availability.

"You must be smoking something," he was told. "We're not going to let you option that molecule." At the time, neither Sharpless nor Thorp knew that Pfizer was on the verge of initiating clinical trials for its molecule for treatment of a hormone receptor for positive breast cancer diagnosis with potential to extend patient lives significantly. The Pfizer molecule would go on to become Ibrance®, a multibillion-dollar drug.

After his call to Pfizer, Thorp told Sharpless, "Listen, we'd love to help you, but we can't." Sharpless didn't take that as a flat turndown. It seemed that Thorp clearly understood the molecule's scientific potential—also that it addressed a big market—so he kept updating him every six months or so. Finally, in 2010, Sharpless reported that he'd hired Jay Strum, who'd been a protégé of Bob Bell, vice president of research at GSK. Bell was widely respected for his role as co-founder of Sphinx Pharmaceuticals, the first biotech firm in North Carolina to raise investment funding through an IPO.

"Jay's going to help me find a molecule with the properties I told you about," Sharpless advised.

In the all-out search for venture capital that followed, Sharpless and Strum pitched many funds but got no takers; instead, their pitch was met with glazed eyes and bored looks. While they kept updating Thorp on their efforts, his position remained the same: HVP would not invest until they owned the rights to the intellectual property for their molecule.

By 2012, G-Zero owned a library molecule (one used to study gene function) that demonstrated impressive results with animal models that indicated they could protect bone marrow from chemotherapy and radiation damage. The molecule also showed promise with small cell lung cancer, a devastating disease caused by smoking. The breakthrough impressed Thorp and others at HVP—as did G-Zero data on preclinical trials with animals.

In mid-2012 Thorp finally told Sharpless and Strum, "We'd like to invest, but we can't invest in anything with a zero in its name. That would be the same as investing in G-Loser." It was then agreed to rename the company G1 for the phase in the cycle when cell replication gets put on pause.

"Whatever you do," Thorp gibed, "don't spell it G-O-N-E or gone. That sounds about as bad as G-Zero." After that it was settled: The letter "G" followed by the numeral "1" and "Therapeutics" would be the firm's name. HVP invested $600,000 and got a 25 percent stake in the company. It was the only investor except for Sharpless's mother, who'd put in $100,000. Thorp also took a seat on the G1 board.

But Thorp planned to add something more: "You want our money," he told G1 principals, "but now I think you really need our leadership." By that he meant impressive scientific accomplishments would only take them so far. Minefields lay ahead as they prepared for and entered rigorous FDA clinical trials to make sure their proposed drug worked and was safe for humans. Even beyond that, they would have an acute need for seasoned business know-how in order to raise millions more in investment and to get the drug manufactured and sold.

Thorp knew exactly who to turn to: Christy Shaffer. Shaffer had joined HVP in 2011 as managing director of the fund's seed investment program and had had remarkable success at Inspire Pharmaceuticals, where she'd become the first full-time employee in 1995. As president and CEO, she'd grown Inspire to 250 employees and revenues of $100 million. After taking the company public in 2000, she had raised a total of $300 million, and *Scientist Magazine* had named Inspire as a "Best Place to Work."

Shaffer had a background and skill set that gave her instant credibility with GI scientists. She had a PhD in pharmacology and had held senior-level positions at Burroughs Wellcome, a firm widely admired for its groundbreaking discoveries in the life sciences. Her HVP colleagues jokingly dubbed her "the kindergarten teacher" because she excelled at helping top-flight scientists cope with arcane mysteries of the business cycle. In 2012, she became executive chair of the GI board with oversight over preparations for FDA clinical trials. The odds against success in that endeavor were long: Taking a drug to market could cost a billion dollars, and 90 percent of applicants failed.

Shaffer began meeting weekly with GI principals to assess progress toward major milestones. GI would incur significant outlays to fund studies on the effects of the proposed drug on animals and humans. One mouse study (among many) on toxicology could cost $50,000, with tests on humans much more. Consultants and/or a contract research organization (CRO) would be needed at various stages of FDA clinical trials. Shaffer had many contacts that could be leveraged throughout that process.

Along the way, she and Thorp pitched many funding sources. When one of the GI scientists questioned why so many, she replied, "You have to kiss a lot of frogs to find a prince."

Under Shaffer's leadership, GI moved forward at a pace that shaved years off the development cycle. In her first year, impressive fundraising commitments had been secured—$12 million alone in series A capital, preferred stock that institutional investors buy to implement a plan to generate long-term profitability. The series A was underwritten by HVP and MedImmune, maker of Flumist® and other products. The National Cancer Institute also provided $2.5 million in 2013, and a year later, GI moved to RTP.

In 2014, having finished what she set out to do as acting CEO, Shaffer turned the reins over to GI's first full-time CEO—Mark Velleca, who had both a medical degree and a PhD from Washington University in St. Louis. Over the next six years, he'd have a profound impact on the company, accomplishing major milestones that kept GI on its rapid growth trajectory. These included Phase I through II clinical trials resulting in FDA approval of GI's molecule and successful series B and C funding rounds with private equity and institutional investors that kept GI on track for an IPO. It sorely needed one to underwrite the high-cost testing that lay ahead. The scientific name of the product taken forward was trilaciclib, a first-in-class advanced immunotherapy. Its commercial name would be Cosela®.

GI became a public company on May 16, 2016, when Velleca rang the opening bell at the NASDAQ Stock Exchange in New York. Behind him through a wide expanse of plate glass, onlookers had a panoramic view of Times Square. Facing the luminaries of the financial press—Bloomberg, Reuters, CNBC, and others—Velleca briefly described how GI's drug, trilaciclib, would get a substantial share of the market for marrow protection in small cell lung cancer. His remarks drew enthusiastic applause from GI employees—some twenty in all. Company management had decided to take everyone to the opening, even a few who'd just been hired. Toward the rear of the arenalike enclosure, stockbrokers were already wheeling and dealing on the trading floor.

GI shares opened at $15 with the company raising a whopping $105 million, far more than the GI contingent expected. Within eighteen months of the IPO, the stock was trading at $67 per share. It was what Clay Thorp called "a home run by any measure." That night the GI entourage celebrated with high spirits in Tin Pan Alley in a private room at Oscar-winning actor Robert De Niro's Tribeca Grill. After outrageously expensive oysters, a second IPO might well have been called for.

Relationships based on resolute trust truly matter in the venture capital arena. VCs convince high-net-worth individuals and institutions to commit, say, $1 million and sign a subscription agreement. The call on that investment is at the option of the VC. The subscription agreement stipulates that the VC can take a 2 percent annual management fee. Investments then get made and if there's a payoff, the investor gets a return of invested capital, plus a pro rata share of equity profits. The VC gets 20 percent of the profits. But that may be a long time in coming, as the GI timeline illustrates: In calendar year 2024, its drug Cosela is projected to have about $70 million in sales.

The subscription document engenders trust but does not obviate personal relationships built up through periodic reports on deal status, lunch or dinner together, and even family interactions. Informal networks also can have a profound effect on interpersonal relationships. The Glaxo layoff in 2009 included many scientists in RTP. While its immediate effect was devastating for those let go and their families, an unpredicted impact was the advent of a much stronger entrepreneurial culture in RTP—what is loosely called the Glaxo effect. In essence, people like Jay Strum and John Bisi went out and started new companies. Others unaffected by the cuts—senior Glaxo executives like Fred Eshelman, who departed in 1990; Art Pappas; and Bob Bell, CEO of Sphinx Pharmaceuticals and later a mentor to Jay Strum—did the same.

It can't be quantified, but venture capital—as bottom line oriented as it has to be—is not all about the money. VCs create extraordinary value—in the form of profits, yes, but also in lives saved through timely and prudent investments in miracle cures for the likes of small cell lung cancer and breast cancer. Lives saved—especially the joys of extended life—cannot be quantified either.

Several times in interviews for this book, Jay Strum used the word "fate" as a synonym for "unexplained event"—moments like Ned Sharpless's epiphany on the plane; the "miracle" of the grandmother who got an extra five years to live; and the sheer luck of the spark Eugene Kleiner gave to the founding of RTP's first venture capital firm.

Asked if he has a spiritual side, Strum says he's been a lifelong believer. He never argues about the existence of God; instead, he points out that "there has to be a painter if there's a painting. Everything is so ordered that with a bit more gravity, the universe would implode; with a little less, it would fly apart rapidly." He then adds, "It's hard for me as a scientist to study molecule design and not see a cosmic painter's hand at work. Why else would creation exist? Why would we even be here?"

Strum is not doctrinaire about his view. He chuckles when he recalls his closest brush with fate. He joined the choir at the Methodist Church in Franklin, North Carolina, to spend more time with a girl named Susan whom he married. That, too, was an example of powerful gravitational pull.

17

AgTech Adds Depth to the Biotech Revolution

RTP's founders understood the area's strength in plant science and veterinarian science due to the presence of North Carolina State University. However, the founders had no idea how profoundly these fields would change due to the groundbreaking work of Mary-Dell Chilton and others who applied biotechnology to agricultural practices. Instead of focusing on the human genome in search of novel treatments to improve the human condition, AgTech applies such research in connection with the genetic structure of plants and animals to achieve similar results. AgTech falls within the broad term of biotech as part of the toolbox of life science. As RTP developed, NCBiotech would apply new strategies to find ways to capitalize on the area's strengths and prepare scientists for careers in life science, including AgTech. RTP would also attract global companies specializing in AgTech. One company in particular would make RTP a hub for innovation and business growth in AgTech.

NCBiotech's Focus on AgTech

From its inception, NCBiotech promoted the AgTech sector. However, NCBiotech's impact in this sector grew with the arrival of new leadership. After twenty-eight years with E. I. du Pont de Nemours, including several managing the agricultural marketing division in Geneva, Switzerland, Norris Tolson returned to his Pinetops, North Carolina, tobacco farm where he might have led the comfortable life of a country squire. Instead, he embarked on a public service career that led, ultimately, to a seven-year stint at NCBiotech that would change the trajectory of agricultural biotech, or AgTech, at RTP.[1]

Tolson had barely unpacked on returning from Geneva when neighbors began urging him to run for a House seat in the North Carolina General Assembly. After consulting local leaders, he decided to take the plunge and ended up defeating Joe Mavretic, a former Speaker of the North Carolina House.

A self-described "aggie," Tolson attended NC State University where he was elected president of the student body and won several public speaking honors. He followed Jim Hunt, who later was elected to four terms as governor, as student body president. During their undergrad days, he and Hunt cemented a lifelong friendship. Ultimately, Hunt talked Tolson into giving up his House seat and leading the Department of Commerce and later the Department of Transportation in Hunt's administration. Hunt had told Tolson: "I need a businessman." When Mike Easley became governor in 2001, he asked Tolson to serve as secretary of the Department of Revenue. These positions gave Tolson deep experience navigating complex government bureaucracies but also working in partnership with business to promote economic development in the state.

While serving as secretary of revenue, Tolson became a member of the NCBiotech board, and in 2007 he was elected president and CEO. He soon put the organization's AgTech operations on steroids by establishing a hyperactive "Ag Biotech Initiative." With many friends in high places—especially at his alma mater—Tolson assembled a star-studded leadership team that included senior executives of RTP's agribusiness giants (Bayer, BASF, Novozymes [now Novonesis], and Syngenta) and Rich Linton, the new dean of NC State's College of Agriculture and Life Sciences. Tolson had recently helped recruit Linton from Perdue; much later Linton became president of Kansas State University.

"Linton and I thought a lot alike, and we were always looking for the next curve in the road," Tolson recalls. "We focused on new science, new investment, and spinning new companies out of the labs. Obviously, the med schools at Duke and UNC were already doing that. Why not do the same at the country's third-ranked ag school? We felt State's research engines were just as strong."

Tolson and the others in the tight circle he had formed had one mantra: Monetizing science is paramount. "Unless you can monetize it," Tolson often said, "what's the point? That was what I brought to the table."

He was able to get the General Assembly to provide a modest increase in NCBiotech's budget to help with staffing and special projects that would leverage R&D and start-up activity the organization already had underway. Tolson shrewdly pushed his new initiative as a way to enhance return on investment from ongoing programs with Big Pharma and the agricultural life sciences. His small team pushed aggressively to facilitate partnerships and collaborations between the Big Three universities and the AgTech community. NCBiotech already had a strong small-loan program for start-ups, but Tolson elevated it higher under the leadership of Ken Tindall and Mary Beth Thomas. Together, they redoubled efforts to find discoveries in RTP labs that could be commercialized. A strong vetting process was backed up with coaching and counseling in planning and marketing, employee recruitment, and presentation skills.

There has always been something of a mania in RTP to catch up with giant tech commercialization programs in the Bay Area and Boston's Route 128. Tolson never succumbed to that. "Our region provided all the growth ammunition we needed—R&D people, a rich resource environment, and not the least a phenomenally strong entrepreneurial spirit," Tolson says in looking back.

Linton, who played a leading role in the AgTech Initiative, calls Tolson "a true visionary with a profound grasp of how to communicate and collaborate. He focused on building a pipeline between the universities, the Park's largest companies, and smaller firms with promising technologies. They were not well connected before the AgTech Initiative got organized. He had a strong influence on the creation of plant science and food manufacturing units at NCSU [NC State]."[2] In 2022, the state-of-the-art Plant Science Building opened on Centennial Campus at NC State. It combines the interdisciplinary study of plant science, engineering, and textiles along with resources to advance commercially focused research. The building also includes the Biomanufacturing Training and Education Center (BTEC), which serves as an important workforce training program for real-world companies. The activities housed in this building represent how far AgTech has advanced since the early 2000s.

AgTech Statistics

World population is expected to reach nine to ten billion by 2050. The World Food Organization (FAO), the lead United Nations agency for combating global hunger, estimates that it will take a 60 percent increase in output to meet that daunting level of demand. Further complicating that goal, it must be achieved while avoiding damaging environmental side effects. Dr. Chilton's pioneering discoveries and those of other scientists in and near Research Triangle Park will be in the vanguard of the planetwide battle to fend off starvation on a scale never known before.

Such innovators provide much of the impetus for what is often called RTP's AgTech sector or cluster. It has four distinct strengths: plant science (by far the largest), ag data science, food science, and animal health. Ag data science tracks and analyzes digitized AgTech data often in real time. Its analytics include predictions about yields and growing conditions, animal health, and consumer behavior.[3] As recounted in chapter 12, SAS began with statistical programs analyzing crop yields. It has continued to provide ag data analytics and recently formed a new business unit to enhance its AgTech services.

Food science, a relatively new and dynamic discipline, responds to social changes occurring in the developed world. Practitioners use chemistry, biochemistry, nutrition, microbiology, and engineering to solve real challenges like increased production of plant-based protein.[4] This is especially important in a state like North Carolina, which has more than 1,200 food manufacturers. A $30 million donation in 2024 by the Bezos Earth Fund to NC State received widespread attention. It funds research on cellular agriculture with the aim of growing meat in a laboratory. Research will entail collaborations with other universities, including Duke and North Carolina A&T, and a number of industry partners.[5]

The animal health segment of RTP's AgTech works with farmers and ranchers, government agencies, veterinarians, and other groups to make sure the health and safety of animals, humans, and the food supply are optimized. North Carolina is the number two state in pork production and number four in poultry production. RTP's AgTech cluster and all four of its segments are thriving and continue to make astounding discoveries every year.

Despite the cluster's massive size, it is still a subset of an overall life science presence at RTP that is widely viewed as a leading one in the United States. Its constituent parts include the North American headquarters of three of the world's leading science-based AgTech companies—BASF, Novonesis, and Syngenta—which help millions of farmers feed a hungry world. Other distinctive features of this presence include a world-leading concentration of plant scientists and greenhouse infrastructure; access to cutting-edge research at three tier-one universities; the dynamism of one hundred large companies interacting with a throng of start-ups vying to develop world-changing technologies; proximity to eighteen state experiment stations that can replicate temperature conditions anywhere in the world; the nation's third-ranked vet school; the phenomenon of more and more companies from the European Union and South America looking at RTP as their gateway to the United States; and a plethora of support facilitators like NCBiotech, the Research Triangle Regional Partnership, and the incubator at First Flight Venture Center.

None of the above suggests that RTP doesn't meet bumps in the road. On June 12, 2018, the German giant Bayer acquired Monsanto for $63 billion; it soon closed its RTP Crop Science headquarters and moved five hundred of its employees to Monsanto's St. Louis campus. Losing an asset of that size and importance was initially perceived as a blow to RTP's reputation. Some wondered if the bloom was coming off the rose. But a year later, BASF in RTP acquired $9 billion in Bayer assets and moved four facilities and 360 former Bayer employees to its new RTP operations.[6]

Paul Ulanch, a senior director at NCBiotech, recalls, "So they changed signs on the campus . . . and I heard from people inside that the culture of these two German companies was very similar. . . . I also heard that the merged culture in St. Louis was not a good fit. . . . We [RTP] haven't missed a beat."[7]

ARE's AgTech Infrastructure

From the street, its shimmering walls of glass suggest the presence of two or three botanical gardens; inside, its operating system runs with the precision of a Swiss watch: Robotic arms seed, fertilize, water, and rotate (for better sun exposure) 15,000 pots within an eight-hour day. Robotics may also be used to harvest the crop. The system has one other indispensable capability: Its climate controls can replicate growing conditions from almost anywhere in the world. A small firm could never afford to outlay the cost of such a system, which is why the capital-intensive nature of the farm sector favors companies at scale.

Joel Marcus, the founder of Alexandria Real Estate (ARE), saw an opening. After earning his undergraduate and law degrees from the University of California at Los Angeles, Marcus developed expertise in corporate finance and capital markets, venture capital, and mergers and acquisitions. In 1984, he became one of the principal architects of Kirin-Amgen, Inc., a trailblazing joint venture in biotech. He also served as a practicing CPA and tax manager with Arthur Young & Co., where he focused on the financing and taxation of Real Estate Investment Trusts (REITs). During this same period, he did a lot of work for REITs and for biopharmaceuticals. Marcus served on the board of directors of Intra-Cellular Therapies, a biopharmaceutical company renowned for its developments based on the Nobel Prize–winning research of Dr. Paul Greengard.

Most of this experience had practical applications in the management of a company. However, Marcus wanted to do more than manage an existing company. He had come to realize the life science field was woefully underserved, and he could help solve that problem. To buttress his planning and organization, Marcus invested $5 million of his own money and raised another $19 million to get a new enterprise underway. To distinguish the new venture, he chose the symbol of an ancient lighthouse that had stood for 1,500 years on the Mediterranean coast at Alexandria, Egypt. That city had been widely recognized for centuries as the scientific capital of the world. Marcus named the company Alexandria Real Estate (ARE). He wanted ARE to be known as the cluster capital of the life science world. Three years later, ARE management raised $216 million in an IPO on Wall Street. ARE was valued then at $4 billion.

ARE now operates life science campuses in the key hubs, including RTP, Greater Boston, New York City, the San Francisco Bay Area, San Diego, Seattle, and what is known as Maryland's "DNA Alley."[8] RTP may well have the world's largest concentration of greenhouse infrastructure. But only one—the greenhouse "LaunchLabs" of ARE in the heart of RTP—harvests crop after crop of start-ups and early stage AgTech companies. An adroit innovator, ARE is the Park's largest landowner. It bills its LaunchLabs as a premier life science start-up platform specifically designed "to accelerate the growth of transformative early-stage companies."[9]

ARE's LaunchLabs offer AgTech and life science firms in medicine the benefits that start-ups often desperately need, including move-in lab and office space, equipment sharing, a wide range of strategic and entrepreneurial support services, and access to risk capital. ARE even funds a $100,000 "pitch" competition to sharpen start-up skills in attracting many types of investment. When lab denizens need a break, they can visit the lab's fully equipped fitness center; when hungry, they can chow down at an on-site eatery; and when in need of a mental break, they can attend interesting lectures and workshops arranged by ARE.[10] The company also offers generous lease terms geared to the needs of cash-strapped early-stage firms. ARE does not require industry-standard five-year leases, which can put a firm in the position of paying for space it may never use. Instead, ARE negotiates lease renewals on an annual basis that gear space to current needs.

Providing start-ups with operational efficiencies comparable to those of corporate giants is especially important in AgTech where a handful of large firms dominate world markets for crop protection and enhancement, nutritional improvements, and other tech solutions. Fears that their technology may get replicated, or that top talent may get lured away, can make large firms slow to innovate. Smaller ones with disruptive technologies are prime candidates for acquisition by giants in need of innovative solutions.

One of ARE's tenants, Elo Life Systems, is growing bananas in a greenhouse nearly 2,500 miles north of the equator. With eight children to feed, Todd Rands and his wife could probably use a bunch of bananas every day or so. Rands earned a PhD in molecular biology from the University of Houston and went on to earn a law degree from George Mason University in northern Virginia. This unusual degree combination and success in technology commercialization qualified Rands to lead Elo Life. He likes to say the company is "reengineering the world food supply one plant at a time."

Rands says with a chuckle, "I call myself a molecular farmer." In 2021, a public company working primarily on cancer spun out high-potential food and agriculture intellectual property (IP) to Elo Life. Rands likens that IP to a Ferrari engine and says his job is to build the rest of the car. In its first two years, Elo hired thirty-five employees (eighteen of them PhDs), raised $25 million in investment capital, and began developing products for the sweetener market.

Elo is the Cherokee word for earth, and, in fact, the company has a global focus. It is applying its gene editing and molecular engineering technology to solve real-world problems in a food system Rands calls "World War II vintage."

He rues the fact that "we have obesity, heart disease and diabetes—all terrible chronic disorders—that are very much associated with the poor quality of the food in our diets. . . . As we examined this problem, we realized nature has given us interesting molecules, ingredients, flavors, spices, proteins, carbohydrates, fats, all of the things that you would ever need, but they're very hard to access. And that's what molecular farming allows us to achieve. We can go out in nature and find those really interesting, delicious, important nutritional molecules that nature's figured out through eons of evolution. We can then take those same ingredients and put them in other plants that we can grow and scale up production."

Rands cites the example of bananas, which are grown in climates where fungi, viruses, and bacteria can do great harm. These threats get in the soil, inside plant stems, and rot the fruit from inside out. They can kill trees in two to three years. Given time, Rands says, the banana will become extinct.

"Through gene editing, we can find the right genetic combination to enable the banana to grow even where that fungus is still in the soil," Rands says. "Dole Foods is on the front lines of the battle, and they've partnered with us for the last three years."

"Having a landlord like ARE that's also vested in your success, sends a strong signal that they really want this to work," says Rands. "With thirty-eight people, we need flexibility; we might have sixty or seventy in the near term—we don't know exactly what our trajectory will be. Being at ARE gives us the flexibility [to expand] as we need more greenhouse and office space."[11]

Another tenant, Mariano Alvarez, the chief scientific officer of Avalo AI, uses artificial intelligence to identify gene traits, among other unknowns, that affect drought resistance and plant tolerance to cold. For example, rising earth temperatures are pushing the Corn Belt from the upper Midwest into Canada. Thousands of gene traits come into play when the question is asked, if corn can't be grown in the Dakotas due to heat, at what latitude in Manitoba can it thrive, or even survive? Using the analytical power of AI, Avalo has developed a software package that can pinpoint where fragile plants can survive in the early spring.

Before the company was formed, Alvarez was running studies on rice because it provides more of the calories humans consume than any other commodity. Analyzing data on cold tolerance for rice, he identified eight genes that determine where rice can survive. Remarkably, three of the eight were previously undiscovered.

Shortly after that, Alvarez and Brendan Collins, Avalo's CEO, pitched Blake Stevens at ARE for funding. Stevens told them the technology was promising, that when they had more business experience, he'd consider funding them.

"At the end of the day, we were just two guys trying to figure it out," says Collins. "But actually that experience was really beneficial for us."[12] After they established the company, they were able to raise $3 million in seed funding and began hiring staff. They went back to Blake and got funded by ARE. Today, Blake is a member of the Avalo AI board. Collins calls him "one of the shrewdest investors we've ever worked with." By mid-2023, Avalo had raised $6.2 million.

Avalo has developed a core technology, according to Alvarez, "that can ingest very large and complicated data sets, interrogate them in a sophisticated way to make decisions based on the outcomes." To put the complexity of this task in perspective, there may be as many as 150,000 genes in the plant kingdom. Alvarez says, "A complicated trait [like cold tolerance] might have only five or six genes. So, many genes working together to create a trait has always been one of the more challenging parts of biology."[13] Avalo is licensing this discovery process to companies and others to augment their gene editing. Ultimately, its ambition is to own the IP surrounding the seed itself, which would have enormous value.

"I can't imagine we'll ever fully leave ARE just because the greenhouse facilities are so nice," says Collins. "It serves as a fantastic recruiting tool to be able to walk someone around the campus and say this is our home. . . . Interacting with the cadre of founders in this building is pretty powerful too—they know exactly what we're going through."

How did Avalo get its name? Alvarez's family comes from the Himalayas of India. A mythological saint there by the same name once prayed to Buddha for the wisdom to understand humanity's suffering. Buddha responded by granting the monk a thousand heads to deal with that challenge.

As the largest landowner in RTP, ARE owns forty buildings totaling four million square feet of office and lab space. Its tenant retention rate is 80 percent—about 20 percent higher than the industry average.

No one could have predicted that a force majeure in the form of COVID-19 would have such a devastating impact on conventional real estate, which saw building after building empty out. But three crucial factors enabled ARE to thrive during the pandemic's shocking economic downturn: first, the difficulty of performing lab work from home; second, a surge of demand from new and existing tenants as billions of dollars flooded into the search for vaccines; and fifteen- to twenty-year leases with industry-leading companies like Moderna, Bristol Myers Squibb, Illumina, and Takeda. These factors and ARE's ability to serve smaller upstarts provide an extra dimension to RTP that makes it more than a home for the major AgTech companies.

Conclusion

Any region of the country would covet having a biotech cluster. RTP has not just one—focused in applied research from the human genome—but two. Further, the AgTech cluster includes multiple sectors such as plant and animal science. Like its biotech cousin, AgTech took off with the arrival of superstar scientists in the field such as Mary-Dell Chilton. NC State's presence and strengths helped create an environment for companies and scientists in this field. However, institutions such as NCBiotech leveraged these assets to amplify commercialization activity. In turn, these efforts attracted major players like ARE, which provide investment and space, including sophisticated greenhouses, to AgTech start-ups. All told, RTP has leveraged the state's formidable assets in agriculture to produce a major sector in technology in that region of the United States.

18

Advanced Manufacturing Comes to the Triangle

As described in part I, the ambitions of RTP's founders extended well beyond creating a place for R&D. They included spawning new manufacturing industries in North Carolina as tobacco, furniture, and textiles faded away. An assessment of RTP in the early 1990s by economists at the University of North Carolina at Chapel Hill (UNC) noted RTP had failed to deliver on this score. That would take more time. However, success, when it did come, followed a familiar path. It began with leadership from a governor in the role of "industry hunter." Eventually, the community college system, a major university, local governments, and industry would collaborate to turbo-charge the location and growth of manufacturing companies in an ever-expanding geographic area within the state. This chapter traces the story of one of the first major manufacturing companies to take interest in North Carolina and how it helped lay the foundation for other advanced manufacturing facilities.

Emergence of a Colossus

In 1922, 510 Danes—164 of them forty-five years of age or younger—died of diabetes, the so-called sugar disease. It represented a certain death sentence at the time. Reported cases were on the rise, and in a country with just 3.2 million people, the disease posed a serious threat to public health. The only treatment was a starvation diet. Eliminating high-carbohydrate and sugary foods turned doomed patients into skeletons awaiting a painful death, often in a diabetic coma.

In the face of this grim outlook, several remarkable coincidences turned tiny Denmark into the epicenter of an all-out assault on diabetes that soon spread to the rest of Europe and beyond. In the first of these chance occurrences, an obscure Danish physiologist named August Krogh won a 1920 Nobel Prize for his groundbreaking work on how blood flows from capillaries into muscle groups during exercise and at other times. Krogh became an overnight celebrity with invitations to lecture at Harvard, Yale, the Mayo Clinic, and other prestigious US institutions. At nearly the same time, Krogh's wife, Marie, a physician, was diagnosed as diabetic. In her case, a strict diet stabilized her condition enough that she could join her husband on a lecture tour of North America.

Shortly before the Kroghs embarked on their tour, a visionary discovery occurred in Canada. In mid-1921, Dr. Frederick G. Banting and his student, Charles H. Best, of the University of Toronto began test injections of canine pancreas extracts on several humans, including themselves. (Insulin is produced in the pancreas of humans and other species.) These injections successfully lowered blood sugar, and the two doctors described the results in the *Canadian Medical Association Journal* in the spring of 1922. The *Toronto Daily Star* reported the results under a six-column headline that blared "Toronto Doctors on Track of Diabetes Cure." Despite being one of the greatest medical discoveries in history, their findings stirred little interest beyond Canada. Nevertheless, the University of Toronto managed to consummate a one-year license with Eli Lilly, which would demonstrate an ongoing focus on drugs to treat diabetes.[1]

Around the time of the Toronto news announcement, the Kroghs arrived in Boston for August's lecture tour. There, they learned of the new discovery. At Marie's behest, the couple changed their schedule to go to Toronto to learn more about the promising insulin discovery. During in-depth discussions, August engendered great trust among the Canadians—to the point that they asked themselves "who better than a Nobel laureate" to take insulin to Scandinavia? The university's Insulin Committee ended up awarding August a license for that market. It was an oral agreement because Denmark, Norway, and Sweden lacked a process for registering and patenting a drug. The parties agreed that any product sold in Scandinavia would be priced as close as possible to the cost of production. Krogh and others then formed a new company, Nordisk Insulin, to guide it through clinical trials in Denmark and to commercialize the new treatment.

On December 12, 1922, just ten days after the Kroghs returned to Denmark, experiments began on sources from which insulin could be extracted, such as fish and pork, both of which were plentiful in Denmark. Remarkably, the new company achieved production capacity within six months. At about the same time, Krogh reported that the most significant difficulties in production and standardization of manufacturing of insulin had been surmounted. Deliveries of the product began in late June 1923. These "firsts" all hinted at Denmark's soon-to-be leading role in international diabetes care.[2] And they were all made possible by Marie's insistence on learning more about the discoveries in Toronto.

Very soon after the formation of Nordisk Insulin, two employees who were also brothers—Harald and Thorvald Pedersen—left to form their own company, Novo Industri. There, they focused on new innovations for treating diabetes. In the coming years, their scientific breakthroughs would spur a bitter rivalry between the two companies, but in reality, the competition made each one stronger. By the mid-1980s, Nordisk Insulin and Novo Industri along with Eli Lilly were competing fiercely for major overseas markets for diabetes treatment in Western Europe, the United States, and Japan. Each one aimed to become the first to take a fast-acting synthetic hormone to market. Such a feat required larger and larger R&D investments. Despite the scars from their long-running conflict and competition, Novo and Nordisk began to contemplate the unthinkable: a merger. Both Novo Industri and Nordisk Insulin were 100 percent foundation owned, and their merger eventually made them the world's largest foundation.

Shortly after the merger in 1989, Mads Øvlisen became the sole president and CEO. The new company had nearly half of the world market for the treatment of diabetes.[3] A lawyer by training, Øvlisen was superbly qualified for the top job. He'd spent his junior year of high school in Cedar Rapids, Iowa, where he lived with the family of a dentist. He'd earned a law degree from the University of Copenhagen and then an MBA from Stanford University. He worked his way up the ladder at Novo Industri and became president/CEO of Novo Industri in 1981.

Arrival in North Carolina

Øvlisen's selection had significant implications for North Carolina. While at Novo Industri, Øvlisen led the effort in the 1970s to find sites in the United States for its enzyme business as well as sites to manufacture insulin and other products for humans. Although he visited many locations, the Research Triangle consistently stood out because of its three tier-one research universities and the customized training for employees offered by the state's community colleges. "Every state visited offered tax incentives," Øvlisen recalls. "But in North Carolina we encountered something quite different—what I would call knowledge incentives. They enable us to participate in top-of-the-line workforce development programs, as well as cooperate with outstanding universities on our research needs."[4]

After Novo turned its attention to North Carolina as a frontrunner for plant locations, Øvlisen met with the state's dynamic young governor, Jim Hunt, both in Copenhagen and in Raleigh. Hunt impressed Øvlisen as "a true public servant. He was very much aware of the needs of the state, but also of the potential of the state. He was very good at promoting that, and I do also remember him as a likable and charming person."[5] The company's interaction with North Carolina reflected the example set by Governor Hodges as "industry hunter" when he first helped create RTP. Like Hodges, Hunt offered an unparalleled workforce training system as the state's competitive advantage in job recruitment rather than financial incentives. This approach resonated with certain companies, including Novo. Those meetings caused Øvlisen to choose a location near RTP over one in Nebraska where enzyme source material was much more plentiful.

In 1979, Novozymes, a company managed by Novo, opened an enzyme production plant in Franklinton located about twenty-five miles north of Raleigh. The company's markets include food and beverages, animal health and nutrition, energy, fine chemicals, dietary supplements, and detergents among others. One of its by-products is biomass, which Novozymes gives away to farmers near the plant for use as fertilizer. Its products are deeply rooted in microbial science. Microbes are single-celled organisms that produce proteins, comprising the main source of enzymes. At the main Novozymes plant in Franklinton, enzyme production begins at the petri dish level and moves progressively to larger fermentation tanks, ending up in a vessel four stories tall. The company ships final products to customers in 44,000-gallon tanker trucks.

Enzyme uses are ubiquitous and found in countless items on grocery store shelves, in beer and ethanol, and in supplements for animal feed. Humans can't exist without them because they speed up metabolism or chemical reactions in the body. They produce some substances and break down others. Some enzymes are produced naturally, while others are manufactured to meet all kinds of needs. Novo Nordisk eventually spun out Novozymes (now Novonesis) as a freestanding company in 2000. However, the company continued to grow to eight hundred workers in Franklinton. Its presence there marked the beginning of a massive, advanced manufacturing movement into the greater Triangle region.

BTEC

Novo Nordisk's foray into North Carolina with advanced manufacturing would get a boost at the end of the 1990s. Cigarette manufacturers faced massive liability from the health care impacts of tobacco. To settle these lawsuits, several companies entered into a master settlement agreement negotiated by a number of state attorneys general, including North Carolina Attorney General Mike Easley. North Carolina's share was estimated at $4.6 billion. To help manage the proceeds, the state created the Golden Leaf Foundation (GLF) in 1999. It offered one of the few bright spots for communities suffering from the long decline of tobacco production. Workforce training in these areas became one of the key focus areas of GLF.

NC State University received an initial grant of $68 million from the GLF to train undergraduate and graduate students in biomanufacturing. At the time, companies lacked skilled professionals and often raided each other for talent. Over half of the NC State funds went to build and equip a new Biomanufacturing Training and Education Center (BTEC) on its Centennial Campus. The program received an enthusiastic response from industry, which prompted the General Assembly to add annual funding in the $5 million range for BTEC's operating expenses.

Gary Gilleskie became BTEC's executive director in 2017. He says the decision to locate BTEC at NC State made sense because of its large student population in biochemistry, biological sciences, and chemical engineering. BTEC typically enrolls about 450 students each year. Many of them earn a minor in biomanufacturing, in addition to their BS degree. BTEC also offers a master's degree in biomanufacturing. Nearly 100 percent of BTEC's students receive a job offer within six months. The return on state investment is extraordinary: 80–85 percent of those same grads remain in North Carolina, mainly in the greater Triangle area. In addition to its degree programs for university students, BTEC offers educational opportunities to anyone with about twenty-five courses on a range of subjects critical to biopharmaceutical manufacturing. In addition, BTEC designs and delivers customized programs for professionals from biomanufacturing companies, suppliers, regulatory agencies, and educators from other institutions.

BTEC's effectiveness caught the eye of the Danes. For over forty years, Mike Elder has worked for Novozymes, "the most famous company nobody's ever heard of," as he described it. At one point, he reported to the regional president of Novozymes North America. In that role, he became a member of the AgTech Initiative that Norris Tolson set up when he was president of NCBiotech in the early 2000s. In 2017, Elder took a delegation from NC State led by Dean Richard Linton to Denmark to meet with the executive team at Novo Nordisk. After visiting a number of universities and officials, Elder told the delegation, "There's one more place we need to go." That was the Novo Nordisk Foundation, the world's richest foundation—even larger than the one run by Bill and Melinda Gates. Its size stems from a very unusual business practice: The company returns 30 percent of its annual profits to the Novo Nordisk Foundation.

"I first thought it was a long shot, but fast forward about a year later and NCSU got a $30 million grant from our foundation in Denmark." That would open the door to even more support, because in 2019, the Danish foundation gave BTEC $27 million. A bit later, it gave the university another $17 million for carbon capture. Elder says, "Danish foundation funding has helped create a strong global relationship between NCSU and the top universities in Denmark to address important world problems." He calls this relationship the career contribution he's most proud of.

It's clear the Danes are very happy with production and research facilities in North Carolina. It's remarkable that the company did not locate at the beginning in Nebraska's corn country. Fermentation requires glucose, and glucose comes from corn or sugarcane. The company does have production in Blair, Nebraska, but it chose North Carolina, says Elder, because of the persistence of Governor Hunt and the climate for business—especially the support structure provided by organizations like NCBiotech.

With Novozymes's success in the area, Novo Nordisk launched an impressive run of manufacturing investments in Clayton, North Carolina, east of RTP starting in 1993. Investments continued in 2015, 2020, and 2024. The 2020 investment at $1.8 billion was the largest life science investment in North Carolina history. But it was dwarfed just four years later when the company announced a $4.1 billion expansion in Clayton that would create one thousand high-paying jobs. An insatiable demand for the company's traditional diabetes products, including a new prescription product for Type 2 diabetes, drove these investments. New drugs such as Ozempic® and the new weight-loss product Wegovy® have also played a role.

What started with a serendipitous trip to Toronto in 1922 has turned into a global powerhouse. Novo Nordisk has about 50 percent of the world market for 650 million diabetics. It has a workforce of sixty thousand employees and has become one of the most valuable companies in Europe. Its annual revenues exceed the gross national product of Denmark. Most importantly for North Carolina, the company's investment in Franklinton would signal the beginning of a wave of advanced manufacturing facilities, particularly concentrated in biopharma. Those investments show how RTP's strategy comprises not only the leveraging of talent in and around RTP but also the concerted effort of state leaders to recruit industry and find new ways to invest in workforce training so companies do not have to do so. Novo Nordisk saw the value proposition offered by North Carolina and it has paid huge dividends in return.

19

Gene Therapy Gains Acceptance

The AskBio Story

From the beginning, the Triangle had all the elements for a strong biotech industry. Area universities possessed programs in medicine, pharmacology, chemistry, plant science, and engineering. These assets helped the state attract Burroughs Wellcome to the area in 1969. Leaders created NCBiotech and recruited superstars at a crucial phase for the industry. In the early 2000s, the Golden Leaf Foundation invested in workforce training through the Biomanufacturing Training and Education Center (BTEC) at NC State and BioNetwork within the community college system. However, it would take decades for gene therapy to gain acceptance. It required a lengthy period of research and testing and trial and error.

In addition to the public efforts to establish a thriving biotech industry in RTP, private industry also stepped up. In the 1990s, a young lawyer named Sam Johnson saw the need for a voice on biotech policy at the state level. He had worked in the Department of Commerce under Governors Martin and

Hunt. Back in private practice, Johnson volunteered his time to build a new organization patterned on the national Biotechnology Industry Organization (BIO). By the 2000s, NCBIO came into existence. It relies largely on contributions from life science companies that see a need for advocacy. NCBIO helped establish a matching fund for start-ups that obtained federal small business grants. The organization inspired a bipartisan Life Science Caucus, which supports legislation favorable to the industry. NCBIO—now NCLifeSci—complements the work of NCBiotech and is part of an ecosystem that supports a thriving industry.

Despite all of these efforts to establish the right environment for a new industry, advances can come slowly. They require lonely work in a lab. Advances also require more than a small amount of good fortune. This chapter centers on a major milestone for RTP's biotech industry. It describes a breakthrough treatment developed by one of the most successful homegrown companies in RTP history. This story reveals the challenges facing biotech and timeframes to bring new treatments to market. It also shows how far the area has come since Gerry Hancock received a constituent's letter drawing attention to a fledgling new industry back in 1980.

The AskBio Story

The sudden death on September 17, 1999, of a Tucson teenager named Jesse Gelsinger, who was healthy enough to ride a motorcycle and had an expectant look in his eyes, quickly plunged a revolutionary new field of medicine called gene therapy into a Chernobyl-scale disaster. Young Jesse had a rare metabolic disorder that could cause a fatal buildup of ammonia in his blood. First diagnosed at two years of age, it was being managed in his adolescence with a low-protein diet and fifty pills a day.[1] When his father learned about a clinical trial at the University of Pennsylvania to test a gene therapy procedure to cure the disease in babies and eventually in others, Jesse was eagerly enrolled. Not fully grasping all the risks, his dad put him on a flight to Philadelphia alone, where Jesse would become the eighteenth person to receive the new treatment.[2] With a farewell hug, his dad told him he was a hero going off to help save the world, having no idea that the next time he'd see his son he'd be brain dead.[3]

In concept Jesse's treatment involved injection of a healthy gene into an adenovirus vector, a vehicle that delivers the good gene exactly where needed to perform the function of a bad gene. The virus vector was thought to be so benign it would cause nothing more serious than a common cold.[4] The vector cargo—ornithine transcarbanylase (OTC), a complex protein that is the building block for life itself—was to be delivered to Jesse's liver. The potential cure had been tested in clinical trials on mice and dogs.

In a twenty-year retrospective on the Gelsinger case, Meir Rinde, a freelance writer, wrote in *Distillations*, a publication of the Science History Institute, "Previous patients in the trial had experienced flu-like symptoms, but he [Jesse] had a much worse reaction. Within a day he became disoriented and showed signs of jaundice. He had an intense inflammatory response and developed a dangerous blood-clotting disorder, followed by kidney, liver, and lung failure. Four days after receiving the shot Jesse was declared brain dead and taken off life support."[5]

Jesse's death so soon after his treatment plunged the field of gene therapy into the depths of a nuclear winter. His family sued and Penn quickly settled. The university shut down its gene therapy program. The federal government halted all gene therapy clinical trials.[6] Funding from the National Institutes of Health dried up, and the term "gene therapy" became a taboo.

"Suddenly," says Sheila Mikhail, CEO and cofounder of AskBio, a leading provider of gene therapies, "our work was considered science fiction. . . . At investor conferences, people ran away from me as if I had the plague."[7] It made no difference that AskBio was developing gene therapies discovered by one of the field's leading stars, Dr. Jude Samulski, whose high forehead and circle beard give him a professorial look. He is a former president of the American Society of Gene and Cell Therapy and the first recipient of the society's Outstanding Achievement Award. In 1984, he was the first person to clone an entirely different—and much safer—vector called adeno-associated virus (AAV). The names—adenovirus (AV) and adeno-associated virus (AAV)—were too close; no one cared that the AAV package was much smaller or that it triggered a much lower immune response. Its potential to cure rare diseases—eventually genetic disorders writ large—met rejection at every turn.

Even so, Samulski's Gene Therapy Center at the University of North Carolina at Chapel Hill (UNC) would continue as a hotbed of innovation, and he'd earn many of his ninety-eight US patents there. He and his lab had been recruited from the University of Pittsburgh to the UNC School of Medicine in the mid-1990s with $500,000 from NCBiotech and $1,000,000 from the School of Medicine itself. Despite the impressive results that followed, in the aftermath of Gelsinger's death, Jude's reputation and work were ignored as fears continued to permeate the once-promising field.

All the atmospheric smoke and dust made for the worst imaginable business environment for gene therapy. And yet Samulski and Mikhail forged ahead with the founding of AskBio. A third founder joined them: Dr. Xiao Xiao, a pharmacology professor who had been a grad student and postdoc in Samulski's lab. He had led the effort to miniaturize vector payloads of a protein called dystrophin, which was delivered to muscle.[8] The cofounders were betting heavily that once the calamity faded, AAV would make the type of breakthrough that would enable the company to thrive. They knew that to continue the lab's novel research, the only revenue they might get would be contributions from parents of sick children, gifts from wealthy donors and foundations, and government awards from programs like the Small Business Innovative Research Program. They knew money problems were likely to dog them relentlessly for the foreseeable future.

Samulski and Mikhail had met not long after Gelsinger's death at a seminar at UNC, where Samulski was a pharmacology professor in the School of Medicine. Mikhail had been invited as a guest lecturer for a course for UNC doctors, "Launching the Company." In listening to her, it was clear to Samulski that she could be the perfect business partner: She had just formed a life sciences law firm that had clients like Bayer and GlaxoSmithKline, had earned a law degree with honors from Northwestern University, had an MBA in finance with honors from the University of Chicago, and had earned a BS with highest honors from the University of Illinois at Urbana-Champaign. Her steady gaze and willing smile suggest that she is anything but a hardened businesswoman. She is of Mexican American heritage and is the first in her family to attend college. In 2021, Mikhail was named Ernst and Young overall US Entrepreneur of the Year.

During the social hour that followed her talk, Samulski sought Mikhail's advice about commercializing AAV. A long conversation ensued in which the potential for collaboration became evident. Early in that encounter, Samulski had fetched Mikhail a small plate of canapés, a seemingly insignificant gesture that suggested to her he was kind and not aloof, nor did he seem overly impressed with his prodigious accomplishments. Later, Samulski probed what interest she might have in founding a company to take his AAV discoveries to market. When she agreed, he cautiously mentioned what could have been an insurmountable barrier: "I can't pay you right now. In fact, you might not get paid for quite some time. But what I can promise is that we can change the world." Mikhail was inspired by his prophecy and shrugged off the pay issue. She would say, much later, "It helped that I'm not very monetarily focused."[9]

Step by step over the next twenty years, Samulski's prediction came true: AskBio went on to become one of the most successful start-ups in terms of growth and product performance in the history of Research Triangle Park.[10] One of their first decisions was to give the company an intriguing and ambitious name: Asklepios BioPharmaceutical, Inc., or AskBio for short. Asklepios was the Greco-Roman god of medicine and the son of Apollo, god of healing, truth, and prophecy. The company's focus was first to find cures for rare monogenetic diseases, often called orphan diseases, because their tiny patient populations render commercialization of cures impractical. Given success with monogenetic disorders, AskBio would then attack diseases like heart failure with its patient population of 6.2 million. After a proven cure was developed, AskBio, a holding company, would spin off the new cure through sale or licensing to a large drug company to mass-produce AAV vectors and get them into patients. The company first targeted monogenetic diseases because they were easier to attack than multigenetic ones and had been the main focus of Samulski's research for years.[11] Because of its devastating impact, he took a special interest in Duchenne muscular dystrophy (DMD), which has an almost all-male US patient population of only 250,000. DMD causes muscle loss that robs small boys of their mobility, leaving them needing wheelchairs. Most die due to organ failure in their mid-twenties.

Among the boys in that patient population was one who had traveled the world in search of a cure. The year after the disaster at Penn, funding was running out when what Samulski calls "a guardian angel" rescued his lab. A Texas land developer had read a news story about Samulski's encouraging results with DMD. The disease already had made his son require a wheelchair and need to eat and breathe through tubes. The developer flew to Chapel Hill's small airport in his own plane and walked to Mikhail's office to meet her and Samulski. He told them he'd taken his son to India to walk on hot coals, to France to bathe in holy waters, and to Mexico to drink a magic elixir.

"So why not gene therapy?" he asked. "I don't expect any results in time for my kid . . . but I don't want any other parent to go through what I went through. I just know you can do this, I believe in the science." Before flying back to Texas, the developer wrote a $3 million check and became AskBio's first seed investor.[12]

Just as the developer's funding was running out, another guardian angel—the Muscular Dystrophy Association (MDA)—rescued the AAV program. The MDA first gave Samulski and Mikhail some important and welcome advice: form a for-profit company, which they did in 2004. The MDA explained that it was tired of making grants to academic research labs that never got potential cures into clinical trials. The MDA then awarded AskBio $1.6 million, the organization's first grant to a for-profit company.[13]

Parents of sick kids became a third group of guardian angels; they helped keep the wolf from the door by organizing bake sales, 10K races, and even concerts. Many among them were what Samulski calls "tiger moms"—mothers who refused to accept any excuse for lack of a cure. Many others who stepped forward to raise funding were parents who knew a cure wouldn't come in time to help their kids; they helped anyway, just as the Texas developer had. AskBio founded and helped fund the Columbus Children's Foundation to augment this effort.

Much of AskBio's work has been a race against time. With genetic defects claiming countless lives every day, the founders feel intense pressure to push drugs through clinical trials overseen by the US Food and Drug Administration (FDA). Getting a green light for that process is a herculean accomplishment, but it counts for little if the drug doesn't get to patients. Unless AAV vectors are made widely available, Samulski says, "It wouldn't matter if we could treat a mouse."[14] That practical reality has driven the company to expend enormous effort and resources to scale up drug production from the two liters (sixty-eight ounces) required for lab work to bioreactor output of two thousand liters.

Even so, approved gene therapy products can carry a high price tag. A treatment by Zolgensma for spinal muscular atrophy (SMA) costs more than $2 million for a single dose. But SMA is a life-shortening disease with limited treatment options. Zolgensma's treatment has extended lives and improved quality of life for children.

If Gelsinger's death in 1999 was the nadir of gene therapy, Conner Curran's inspiring battle with DMD was a storied high. On September 27, 2010, Conner and his twin brother, Kyle, were born in Ridgefield, Connecticut, to Jessica, a first-grade teacher, and Chris, who works in the buildings and grounds department of nearby Lewisboro, New York. Both boys appeared to be normal when they came home from the hospital, but soon it became evident that Conner was developing at a slower pace than Kyle. At first, his parents assumed that physical therapy would enable him to overcome that gap. But by age three they knew something was wrong, so they took Conner to a specialist, who ran tests but made no initial diagnosis. Eight more weeks of testing followed before the specialist finally concluded that Conner, then four, had DMD. During this period, Chris pressed the specialist several times about potential cures; finally, he and Jessica were told that no one had ever survived DMD and that gene therapy was too far away—that it would not help Conner.

"To us, that was a death sentence," Jessica recalls. "Basically, he told us, 'Do yourself a favor, take Conner home and just try to give him a good life, because he will succumb to this disease like everybody else.'"[15]

A second opinion at Johns Hopkins University School of Medicine confirmed that Conner would need a wheelchair at about twelve and that organ failure would claim his life at about twenty-five. Long before that, he would not have the strength to hug his mom. But Johns Hopkins did hold out one ray of hope: Gene therapy *was* progressing and soon *might* help Conner.

The bleak diagnosis filled Jessica with such despair she could barely get out of bed. But soon, after reading more about gene therapy, Chris became obsessed with what was going on in clinical trials. Eventually, he learned about studies at Bamboo Therapeutics, a unit within AskBio.

"When I learned that dogs treated by Jude [Samulski] were running and jumping, it was really exciting," says Chris. "Jude became a celebrity to us. I told Jessica that Conner was going to get Jude's drug—it's not that far away."

"Chris kept burning the midnight oil to learn all he could about clinical trials," says Jessica. He found three: two in addition to Bamboo Therapeutics—Solid Biosciences and Sarepta. They asked to have Conner included in all three, and a few weeks went by before Solid Biosciences accepted him. Jessica and Chris were elated but then got yet another keen disappointment: A child in the Solid trial had died and the FDA canceled it.

Soon thereafter, parents with a sick child, who were first in line for the Bamboo trial, got cold feet and backed out. That led to a frantic call from Bamboo to Jessica and Chris: "Can you and Conner be here tomorrow?" They agreed to go, and Conner thus became the first child to be treated for DMD. Tests carried out the next day gave him preliminary clearance to be treated, but four more months of testing followed. While they were underway, Jessica home-schooled Conner.

On the eve of Conner's infusion, Jessica and Chris got cold feet. They asked each other if they were doing the right thing. As people of faith, they prayed about that. Finally, Chris asked Jessica, "What do you think Conner would do if he could make this decision?" After taking a look at her son, Jessica answered, "Conner would want us to go for it; I know he would."

Conner's first diagnosis had taken place on April 21, 2015; his treatment finally began on March 21, 2018, when he was seven years old. By then, Samulski and Mikhail had sold Bamboo to Pfizer, because the pharma giant had the capacity to mass-produce the drug. The two-and-a-half-hour, one-time procedure to infuse the drug took place at Duke University Hospital under Samulski's watchful eye. He was especially worried about Conner's dosage: Success would depend on how much dystrophin—the key protein for maintaining muscles—was expressed in certain cell tissue. The dystrophin gene is the body's largest, but Samulski and his team had miniaturized it to fit within his carrier—the type of AAV vector he'd first cloned in 1984. Jessica and Chris waited with bated breath during the infusion. At one point Conner nonchalantly ate a pickle with the infectious smile that makes everybody want to hug him. Samulski waited anxiously throughout in a downstairs waiting room. When the infusion was over, a nurse asked if he could come up.

When he entered the room, an emotional dam burst: "We were all crying and hugging and congratulating each other," says Jessica. Dystrophin readings had gone up—and up substantially. Soon, Conner was doing things he'd never done before—among them, amazingly, running up a flight of stairs. Samulski was delighted to learn that Conner was calling the infusion his "muscle juice."

Chris is quick to point out: "Jude was the one who did this. He'd spent twenty years of his life in the lab, mouse after mouse, vector after vector, trying to figure all this out. He had something that was going to save lives and sold it to Pfizer to get it to patients."

Conner got back the gift of youth in second grade. He told his parents: "I don't watch the kids play anymore. I'm able to play." His mother calls him "a happy, well-adjusted kid with lots of friends and very well liked. He's also a good student."

One unknown weighs heavily on Jessica and Chris: When will Conner need redosing? The AAV therapeutic gets diluted as the tissue to which it was delivered turns over. Redosing is not possible now, but AskBio is working on approaches for repeat dosing.

AskBio's years of persistence and struggle were handsomely rewarded on October 26, 2020, when the company was acquired by the German pharmaceutical giant Bayer for $4 billion—$2 billion upfront and another $2 billion based on success. In its announcement Bayer stated, "To preserve its entrepreneurial culture as an essential pillar for nurturing successful innovation, AskBio will continue to operate as an independent company on an arm's length basis."[16]

The agreement's incentives are based on progress with patient redosing, further growth in manufacturing operations, advancement of current and new therapeutic programs through clinical trials, and sales-related milestones.

The transaction gave Bayer all rights to therapies in AskBio's pipeline, including Pompe disease, Huntington's disease, Parkinson's disease, and congestive heart failure, each of which was in early phases of clinical development. The transaction also conveyed AskBio's contract manufacturing at a facility it established in Spain for AAV vectors, and at TAAV Biomanufacturing Solutions for a substrate, or starter material, known as doggybone DNA (so named because of its shape).

Prior to its acquisition by Bayer, AskBio entered into two other high-value transactions. In 2014, it sold Baxter Laboratories (now Takeda) to Chatham Therapeutics for $70 million. Chatham developed and commercialized a gene therapy for hemophilia. Two years later, the company sold Bamboo Therapeutics to Pfizer for an upfront payment of $150 million and incentive payments that could reach $495 million.

Before his passing, Charles Hamner, the father of biotechnology in North Carolina, predicted that Samulski will win the Nobel Prize for Medicine. As president of the North Carolina Biotech Center, Hamner arranged the incentive package that brought Samulski's lab to the University of North Carolina. Nick Muzyczka, who was head of the Gene Therapy Lab at the University of Florida and Samulski's PhD advisor when he cloned AAV, strongly agrees with Hamner's assessment.

In the years since Conner's treatment, Samulski and the Currans have developed a special relationship. They often are invited to dinner at Samulski's home in Chapel Hill. At one point, Samulski gave Conner a book he'd put together titled "Conner's Gene Therapy Book," which his entire team had signed. A note to Conner added, "All the people who signed this book built the spaceship that you will fly for the rest of your life."

Samulski adds, "When you touch someone and you do something and it matters, then you become a part of the family. And that lasts forever."

Chris calls Samulski "a great human being. He's so humble. . . . He's been very successful financially, but I think he still drives a Prius. . . . We've formed a great relationship with Sheila too. Neither one of them seems to care much about money."

Early on, Jessica and Chris learned that Samulski is an avid gardener. One of his friends told them when he visits the garden store, he buys ugly, sickly plants that appear to be at death's door. He takes them home and gets them healthy. They said the healing gene is part of his DNA.

Chris is convinced: "He's changed the world."

That, of course, was exactly what he promised Mikhail all those years ago when they first formed AskBio in the aftermath of Jesse Gelsinger's death.

20

Big Tech and Its Progeny

As noted in chapter 15, the tech sector underwent fundamental changes in the early 2000s. Before 2000, tech companies focused on hardware and infrastructure like microchips, computers, and networks. This played well for RTP, given its focus on "hard tech" embodied by IBM and the major telecommunication companies located in RTP. The collapse of the dot.com bubble hit this sector hard. A new era in information technology emerged where investments flowed to software systems, including cloud computing and open-source. Several companies centered on the West Coast came to dominate this new era. One was an operating system (Microsoft). Another became the default search engine for the internet (Google). Amazon took over the online purchase of goods. Facebook/Meta dominated social media. And Apple produced beautiful new devices to access these products. Together, they crushed or acquired any company that dared to compete with them.

This chapter considers how these changes played out in RTP. The area experienced significant success with an innovative software operating system that competed with Microsoft. That company, in turn, led to the formation of other start-up software companies. Also, several major financial employers located operations in RTP. These companies valued the role technology played in their business and were drawn by the area's talent. Finally, the goliaths out West began making a foray to the Triangle. RTP would vie for the biggest economic development project of the century and end up landing a major new corporate hub. All the while, a cataclysmic event in the form of a global pandemic would wreak havoc on the IT sector's work environment.

Red Hat

IBM's presence in RTP would continue to have important ripple effects in the Triangle as tech transitioned to a new era. After selling the most valuable operating system in history to Microsoft in 1981, IBM would make an unlikely reappearance in this space years later. It started in the 1990s. A young Finnish student named Linus Torvalds did the unthinkable. After creating a PC operating system, he put the system's source code online for anyone to access rather than licensing it. Called Linux, the system made it possible for customers to make improvements to it, which, in turn, added value and benefited all users. The concept known as "open source" was revolutionary at the time. The internet had just begun and shaped new ways of thinking. Wikipedia would operate in a similar open-source fashion, albeit in a nonprofit form.

In 1992, IBM hired a recent college graduate, Marc Ewing, for a short-term position. Ewing arrived in Durham and quickly grew bored with his job. To stimulate his mind, Ewing began playing with Linux.[1] Ultimately, he produced more elaborate programs for certain tasks and began selling them. He named the product Red Hat after a Cornell lacrosse cap he wore in honor of his grandfather. A Canadian computer equipment salesman took notice.[2] Bob Young had struggled finding a product to sell and Linux captured his imagination. After learning of Ewing's work, Young connected with him at a tech conference in New York. Soon after, they incorporated Red Hat and set up shop in Ewing's Durham apartment.[3]

As the tech boom gained momentum in the 1990s, Red Hat began attracting attention. Microsoft's dominant Windows operating system encouraged companies to support a competitor. Intel and Netscape made investments in Red Hat. Established companies like IBM formed partnerships with Red Hat. A major breakthrough came in 1998 when *Infoworld* magazine named Linux 5.2

"Operating System of the Year" over Windows. Despite questions about its business model, Red Hat went public in 1999 shortly before the tech bubble burst. The timing was perfect. Red Hat finished the first day with a value of $3.5 billion. Within a month, Red Hat surpassed $7.2 billion, making it the most valuable public company in the Triangle. Of course, this was a time of easy money: "Two entrepreneurs would meet on an elevator going up and come down with a term sheet."[4] Venture capitalists did not require a viable business plan.[5]

After the dot.com bubble burst, Red Hat would struggle. However, Young had made an astute decision shortly before the economy tanked. He brought in Matthew Szulik, a seasoned software executive, to run the company. Szulik cut expenses and led the effort to develop a business model beyond selling code to researchers and computer programmers. Red Hat began offering enterprise customers a subscription model that included training and certifications. Companies pay a monthly fee instead of purchasing a software license. Steady revenue brought financial stability. In addition, Red Hat focused on certain sectors such as financial institutions, which tend to be on the cutting edge of technology. Customers like Fidelity and Bank of America helped establish Red Hat's credibility.[6] Success in this sector made it easier for Red Hat to move into health care, insurance, and construction.[7]

By the end of the decade, Red Hat had established a global brand. In 2010, the company outgrew its building on the Centennial Campus of North Carolina State University. The company considered a move to multiple cities, including Austin and Atlanta.[8] Ultimately, it decided on a building in downtown Raleigh—one recently vacated after a merger between Progress Energy and Duke Energy. It was a coup for Raleigh and reflected tech workers' desire for a more urban environment. With an average age of twenty-nine, these workers wanted access to restaurants and nightlife.[9] Their presence, in turn, injected new life into downtown. Red Hat even purchased the naming rights to a new downtown amphitheater. Also, the Raleigh location did not prevent Red Hat executives from mentioning their location in the RTP area, which remained an important validator to the outside world.[10]

In July 2019, the announcement came that IBM was purchasing Red Hat for $34 billion. By that time, Red Hat had more than thirteen thousand employees in forty countries. IBM had been an early investor in Red Hat. For years, IBM had a presence at Red Hat's location on Centennial Campus, showing the special relationship between the two companies.[11] Postacquisition, Red Hat has become the best-performing division of IBM, growing by double digits in seventeen of the first twenty-one quarters after IBM acquired it.[12] The contrast between Red Hat's division and IBM prompted the headline "Red Hat Saved

IBM's Bacon This Quarter."[13] Such a stellar performance helps preserve Red Hat's unique culture and fervent adherents. In a way, Red Hat helped mitigate IBM's fateful decision in 1981 to sell Bill Gates the exclusive rights to DOS. Even Microsoft has had a change of heart. In 2015, it struck a deal with Red Hat to use open-source technologies in Microsoft's cloud platform.

Beyond the wealth and attention generated by Red Hat, the company has had far-reaching impacts in the local tech community. Its lobbying efforts helped ensure a direct flight from Raleigh-Durham International Airport to Silicon Valley, fondly referred to as the "Nerd Bird." Importantly, its alumni have gone on to start other companies. Joe Colopy cofounded Bronto Software in 2002. Bronto also relies on open-source software, providing a marketing automation platform. The company expanded globally from its headquarters in the American Tobacco campus in Durham. In 2015, Oracle purchased it for $200 million. By this time, former Bronto employees had founded six more companies referred to as "Red Hat's grandchildren."[14]

Pendo in downtown Raleigh is another company tracing its roots to Red Hat. All four founders, including CEO Todd Olson, worked at Red Hat. They formed Pendo in 2013 to help product managers improve customer user experience—a challenge that's "paramount across all business," according to one of its investors.[15] Greater remote work during the pandemic only increased demand for Pendo's software. It has grown to more than 850 employees in several countries. Its valuation exceeds $1 billion, putting it squarely in unicorn territory. Like Red Hat, Pendo established its headquarters in downtown Raleigh where its workers can enjoy the benefits of an urban environment. The ripple effects of Red Hat demonstrate how deeply local ownership can benefit an area in terms of civic engagement, business formation, and continued innovation.[16]

Fintech

RTP took a big hit with the collapse of telecom in the early 2000s. Companies like Nortel and Ericsson employed thousands in the Park, and many of those jobs disappeared within a few years. Although headquartered in other places, these companies stimulated the area's economy, cultivated new skillsets, and retained college graduates in the region. Fortunately, another IT sector helped fill the void of telecom. As noted, financial service companies invest heavily in technology. They like to say, "We are a technology company doing financial services."[17] On average, 60 percent of their employees comprise tech workers. In fact, technology permeates all of the key business lines in financial services such as brokerage, charitable, asset management, and cyber security. In the fierce competition for customers, technology often provides the advantage, but it also requires major strategic investments, which can be risky.

Based in Boston, Fidelity Investments represents a pioneer in this sector. Edward Johnson II founded the company in 1946. His granddaughter, Abigail Johnson, took the reins as CEO in 2015. It remains private with employees owning 51 percent of the company. Fidelity has achieved many firsts. It provided the first toll-free number to call for a mutual fund quote and has helped democratize investing for retirement through 401(k)'s. Fidelity first established a presence outside Massachusetts in Westlake, Texas. It now has twelve such locations.

In August 2006, Fidelity announced one of its largest expansions ever. It had considered a number of states, including Texas, Kentucky, and Florida. Local television affiliates in North Carolina interrupted a heated discussion with Star Jones on *The View* with the news that Fidelity selected RTP for a facility that would employ two thousand workers. North Carolina's incentives package was the largest nonmanufacturing one up until that time. The company cited in its decision the incentives package as well as the abundant talent at area universities. However, RTP had an ace in the hole. Fidelity's Don Haile had worked at IBM in RTP prior to joining Fidelity as its CIO in Boston. IBM made the decision to outsource its health care and pension management services to Fidelity in 2002, and Haile returned to RTP to oversee the operations in October 2005. At the time, Fidelity had 450 employees working in the Triangle. In a news story, Haile talked about the company's "positive experience" in North Carolina.[18] No doubt he rooted for the outcome. Fidelity named him as site general manager.

Fidelity had planned to build a new facility in RTP. Before it settled on a location, Nortel announced its bankruptcy and intention to vacate its prominent RTP location at Davis Drive and Highway 54. Fidelity decided to take Nortel's complex of buildings. Twenty years later, Fidelity employs eight thousand workers there—nearly the same number as Nortel at its peak. Fidelity is the largest employer in RTP as of 2025. Fidelity competes for area talent against two other fintech companies: Credit Suisse (now UBS) arrived in RTP before Fidelity and employs 2,300. MetLife employs 2,600 in Cary. All of these companies work closely with the area universities and community colleges to build a pipeline of talent. They also nurture that talent. For example, Fidelity has endowed scholarships that not only fund education for deserving students but also assist with networking and mentorship with the goal of building intergenerational wealth.[19] Given the overall growth in the financial services sector and continued need for talent, RTP should remain a popular place for this industry in the years to come.

The Chase for "Big Tech"

As the Triangle economy continued to gain steam coming out of the Great Recession, it received a jolt in 2017. In September of that year, Amazon announced it would solicit proposals for a second headquarters. The prospect of landing one of the world's largest companies set off a frenzy. The new campus would cost $5 billion and house fifty thousand tech workers. More than two hundred cities entered the competition. Amazon adeptly leveraged this massive economic development project to maximize tax breaks and other incentives. Amazon's selection criteria, such as population size, educational attainment, and transportation networks, caused endless speculation about "HQ2" among economic developers and the media. Many analysts predicted Austin, Philadelphia, Denver, Washington, and New York City.[20]

Several areas in North Carolina submitted bids, including Charlotte and the Triangle. In 2018, Amazon published a list of twenty finalists. The Triangle made the cut—the only location in the state. In March of that year, Amazon officials visited the area. The visit focused on a site in RTP and one near Centennial Campus in Raleigh. That spring, an internal team at Amazon ranked potential locations as "not viable, hotly debated and top tier." A six-page internal memorandum included Raleigh in the top-tier category. A further cut put Raleigh in the top three along with Chicago and Philadelphia.

According to Brad Stone, author of *Amazon Unbound*, the company had "some heartburn" about certain legislation in North Carolina that restricted access to bathrooms by transgender individuals.[21] The law was enacted in 2016 and received substantial national attention at the time. However, it did not deter Amazon from including the Triangle among top targets. Ultimately, the company's senior leadership chose New York City and Arlington, Virginia. It dropped New York after local pushback to Amazon. Despite the outcome, the episode burnished the Triangle's reputation nationally. Many felt coming close but not winning was the best possible outcome, given the outsized impact anticipated by such a large corporate footprint.

While the Triangle did not land Amazon in 2018, speculation about Apple followed on the heels of HQ2. Apple had plans to add a campus outside of California. Apple CEO Tim Cook reportedly met with North Carolina's Governor Roy Cooper at the same time the state sweetened its incentives program to attract "transformative projects." Also, Cook had ties to the area. He attended Duke's Fuqua Business School in 1988 and worked for IBM for several years. Even then, observers noted Cook's tireless work effort—often the last to leave the campus in RTP.[22] Despite the promising signs, Apple picked Austin for the new campus. Some speculated that the transgender legislation, which was partially repealed in 2017, caused Apple to select Texas over North Carolina.[23] Tim Cook, the first openly gay Fortune 500 CEO, remained tight lipped. Now, the state had lost out on two major tech campuses in one year.

Apple continued to show interest in RTP. The state kept the company on its active target list. In late 2018, an undisclosed entity—reportedly affiliated with Apple—closed on a large site in RTP. Finally, on April 21, 2021, the Commerce Department made a major announcement: Apple planned to open an East Coast hub in RTP. It would create three thousand jobs paying an average salary of $187,000. The hub would focus on machine learning, artificial intelligence, and software engineering. It would also represent a $1 billion investment by Apple over ten years. Republican and Democratic state officials lauded the news. One compared it to IBM's decision in 1965 to locate in RTP.[24]

Since the announcement in 2021, Apple has failed to break ground in RTP. The postpandemic environment has shaken confidence in the need for real estate, especially in information technology where workers often work alone. Many of these types of companies have struggled with "return to office" policies. The specter of AI has also raised questions about the number and types of jobs needed.[25] At Apple's request, the state has extended the window for incentives through 2027. Meanwhile, Apple has added more than eight hundred jobs in the area, subleasing space in Cary.[26] Other Big Tech companies have quietly moved into the Triangle. Facebook/Meta opened an office in Durham. Google leased significant space in Durham. Since 2020, Big Tech has gained a presence, seeking access to talent gathered in and around RTP.[27]

Cree/Wolfspeed

As newer companies like Pendo race to capture greater market share, Cree's journey shows how quickly the tech landscape can change. In 2019, the company sold its lighting products division, which remains in RTP. Cree then sold its LED business in 2021. Around the same time, senior leadership at Cree made the decision to pivot from the light-emitting properties of silicon carbide to semiconductors. To reflect this new mission, they changed the company's name to Wolfspeed. As described in chapter 12, Bob Davis's pioneering research at NC State on silicon carbide had potential use for semiconductors. In contrast to first-generation semiconductors, silicon carbide has the potential for greater electrical conductivity. The scientific symbol for silicon carbide is SiC. It is a rare earth substrate formed when meteors collide with the planet.

To deploy this material as a semiconductor, Davis had to devise a chemical vapor deposition system to grow thin crystals of SiC. While working on this system, Davis made another discovery. He found a new substrate material called gallium arsenide (GaN), a by-product of aluminum processing. As an alternative substrate, GaN offered huge advantages: more electron mobility, better light absorption, less noise, less sensitivity to heat, and resistance to radiation. In sum, SiC wafers in combination with GaN substrate offer more electric power.[28] Despite these promising attributes, Cree's founders made the decision in the 1980s to focus on the light-emitting aspects of the material.

Fast forward to 2019 when Wolfspeed announced a $1 billion investment in a semiconductor manufacturing plant in Marcy, New York. New York made a grant of $500 million to incentivize the investment in Marcy. Then, in September 2022, Wolfspeed announced it would construct the world's largest SiC materials facility in Chatham County, North Carolina, vastly exceeding the production capacity of its RTP facility. The Chatham facility will create the wafers used for semiconductor chips produced in New York.

Since the 2022 announcement, Wolfspeed encountered numerous setbacks. It received a $750 million grant under the Biden administration's CHIPS Act only to find the grant held up by the Trump administration. The company raced to complete construction of the $5 billion Chatham County facility but then had to file Chapter 11 bankruptcy in 2025. New leadership reorganized the company and laid off one-third of its workforce. At the end of 2025, Wolfspeed received a $700 million tax credit and has worked to align production with market demand.[29] Its chips have a number of applications in automobiles, EV batteries, and wireless systems.

Looming over this volatility is Taiwan, which produces 60 percent of the world's chips and 90 percent of the most advanced semiconductor chips. A few tech companies such as Intel and Texas Instruments produce their own chips, but most rely on Taiwan. Biden's CHIPS Act as well as the policies of the Trump administration seek to onshore the manufacturing of semiconductors. This is not the first time US policy has encouraged domestic capacity. Like some other states in the 1980s, North Carolina dove into semiconductors with the creation of the Microelectronics Center of North Carolina and the arrival of General Electric only to find the momentum short-lived. Can Wolfspeed write a different chapter? If so, it will largely depend on Davis's work at NC State decades ago when he found novel ways to manipulate SiC and GaN into an electric powerhouse.

Conclusion

RTP's IT sector has evolved significantly since IBM's arrival. Mitch Mumma has seen these changes up close. He joined Intersouth Partners, the oldest venture capital firm in the RTP area, as its third partner in 1989. Overseeing Intersouth's tech investments, Mumma has had a hand in numerous start-ups. Many such as Accipiter did very well, finding a market where none yet existed—in that case, delivering ads on the internet.[30] Dependence on outside capital has remained a constant, with 86 percent coming from out of state. Of that, nearly 95 percent ends up in and around RTP. The frenetic activity of the dot.com era has abated. Since the late 1990s, the number of public companies has dropped 50 percent from approximately eight thousand to four thousand. Fewer public companies means fewer public offerings as a way to finance tech start-ups. Acquisitions have become more common. Often, the acquirer can be located elsewhere.

RTP is well suited for this new environment. Business executives and employees want to stay in the Triangle area. That was not always the case. During the 1980s and 1990s, Mumma found it a challenge to recruit leaders to run start-up companies. They knew their tenure was short and wanted an exit strategy. Where would they go next? "It took a while to get a critical mass [here]," says Mumma.[31] Today, executives can see a long-term career in the area. A trailing spouse can also find employment opportunities. The area's quality of life, cultivated over decades by local communities and regional leaders, makes the conversation about relocation an easy one. The pandemic and remote work have only accelerated these trends, according to Mumma.

The theme of stickiness runs throughout the story of tech in RTP. IBM may no longer have the heft it did in the 1980s, but its personal computing division remains here after Lenovo, a Chinese company, acquired it in 2005. At the time, many questioned whether the sale to Lenovo would work out.[32] However, Lenovo remains tethered to the area. It employs thousands of workers and conducts much of its R&D in RTP, its largest presence in the United States. Lenovo also has the naming rights to the stadium that hosts professional hockey and NC State Wolfpack basketball. Likewise, Red Hat remains in the area after its acquisition by IBM. Even a smaller company like Bronto still calls Durham home after Silicon Valley–based NetSuites, Inc., bought it in 2015. As the giants of technology, including Apple, Meta, and Google, filter into the RTP area, the same stickiness should apply. They are here for the talent, and the talent wants to stay. Until that changes, RTP will continue to grow.

PART IV

RTP into the Future

(2021–)

Part IV considers RTP as it faces an uncertain future. The world has changed substantially since the Park's founding in the late 1950s. The constituents necessary for its success, including the state, universities, businesses, and local governments, have had to adapt to new challenges. Competition from other regions has only increased as the technology sector has consumed an ever-larger part of the US economy. Chapter 21 examines new programs undertaken by area universities to commercialize research, breaking down barriers between once-separate disciplines. Meanwhile, the Triangle region and state are in the midst of explosive growth in biomanufacturing. While RTP spurred this growth, it has managed to expand its footprint well beyond the Park. Chapter 23 describes RTP's efforts to update its model with a major transformation to its land-use rules. RTP 3.0, as it is commonly called, will encourage the types of "innovation hubs" competitors are using to attract tech workers. Local communities also are pursuing similar changes as suburban homogeneity gives way to walkable areas with historic charm and thriving street scenes. Finally, part IV assesses RTP's track record. How has it impacted the economy? Can it be considered a success? And what are its future prospects?

21

New Leaps in University Commercialization

The stance toward commercialization has evolved significantly at the area's universities. From serious skepticism in the 1950s, to limited encouragement in the 1970s, to unbridled enthusiasm today. This chapter looks at several examples of research collaborations that are producing cutting-edge technologies and successful companies. It begins with Duke University, which has produced the most successful new technologies from the standpoint of valuation. These new technologies cover the spectrum. It then turns to North Carolina State University and the University of North Carolina at Chapel Hill (UNC), which have continued to build a joint department of biomedical engineering, showing novel ways to leverage new ideas by fermenting different academic disciplines. Besides generating new talent, these universities actively seek to find commercial applications for scientific research. Sixty-five years after RTP's creation, the area universities now represent a key component of the R&D ecosystem. However, unlike industrial research, they largely depend on federal grants. Significant cuts to these grants, beginning in 2025, could have long-term impacts on business formation in the years to come.

Duke University: An Exceptional Brood

Imagine a mother hen coaxing her chicks inside the henhouse where, once inside, she expects them to lay the golden eggs of commercialization. Her exceptional brood includes a pioneer in quantum computing and a serial entrepreneur whose metamaterials are revolutionizing satellite antenna technology. Commercial transactions must be negotiated to move each of their technologies from the so-called lab bench to the marketplace. Deals may take the form of licensing agreements; IPOs; an acquisition by a larger, more established company; and funding rounds to put drugs through the full spectrum of US Food and Drug Administration (FDA) clinical trials. At tier-one universities (where most high-impact breakthroughs are made) technology transfer offices expedite commercial transactions with staffs of highly specialized professionals—in the main, patent attorneys, financial analysts, business advisors, licensing experts, and intellectual property managers. Duke, like many large research institutions, has angel and accelerator funds to invest in early-stage companies.[1] Dollar returns from commercial success may be in the tens of millions, or even hundreds of millions—some of which the university can plow back into research with potential for commercialization.

At Duke, such commercial transactions are facilitated by the Office for Translation and Commercialization (OTC). Its mother hen is Robin Rasor, an associate vice president of Duke who entered the tech transfer field in 1991 when it was still in its infancy.[2] That was eleven years after Congress passed the Bayh-Dole Act—historic legislation that enabled universities to own, and then manage, the inventions made from federally funded research. In doing so, lawmakers set off an ongoing wave of entrepreneurship at universities that is still accelerating nearly half a century later after the passage of Bayh-Dole. Today, a professor in the physics department may well be a businessman too. The same is true of professors at the medical school, the biomedical engineering department, and other departments where leading-edge technologies are being developed. To some extent, all this goes against the grain in academe, where historically some felt commercialization could be seen as a threat to academic integrity.[3]

Before Rasor came to Duke, she managed technology licensing at the University of Michigan and before that at Ohio State University. She began her career at Batelle Columbus Labs, one of the top contract research organizations in the United States. She also served as president and chairperson of the Certified

Licensing Professionals and as president of the Association of University Technology Managers (AUTM). Her background gives her a global view of the tech transfer field, and her success at Duke, her love for her job there, empowers her to speak candidly on controversial matters: "When I started in this business, it wasn't about money," she recalls. "We were part of the university's three-legged stool: research, teaching, and benefit to society."[4]

"In recent years," Rasor observes, "many universities started deriving substantial sums from their technology transfer programs. That has led to new expectations that made some universities difficult to work with in light of their management's expectations. But we in tech transfer don't make the inventions. We just license them. People forget that unless great faculty do great research, we've got nothing to sell." When asked what expectations she has for her program, Rasor says, "Seeing companies cross the finish line—getting FDA approval of a new drug, having a successful IPO on Wall Street, or having a new company acquired by a larger, more established firm."[5]

Rasor celebrated the largest IPO in the history of Duke commercialization on October 1, 2021, when Jungsang Kim, one of the founders of IonQ, rang the opening bell at the New York Stock Exchange (NYSE). The IPO raised $636 million, by far the largest for a spinout from Duke. The transaction also vaulted Duke to the forefront of solutions to one of the great mysteries of modern physics: mastery of the qubit, a fragile, unstable unit of information that quantum computing can process at speeds and volumes that dwarf the output of bits fed into conventional computers. Bits are binary zeroes or ones. In contrast, qubits are nonbinary. They exist in a superposition of both states. Trapped ions (atomic particles that serve as qubits) are at the heart of IonQ's technology. Charged atomic particles are suspended and confined in free space using electromagnetic fields.[6]

The advent of the qubit might be compared to the invention of movable type, which made possible the publication of the Gutenberg Bible. The availability of books transformed European culture and society by making information more accessible and affordable and by encouraging literacy and learning—all of which gave rise to the Protestant Reformation. Qubits have profound transformational potential too. They can help solve large societal problems that today's conventional computers can't even address. They include greatly accelerated drug discovery; code breaking and unbreakable codes for cybersecurity; optimization of traffic flows to improve driving routes; much faster prototyping and testing in manufacturing; much more comprehensive financial modeling; identification of new materials for batteries and semiconductors; and many other uses.[7]

When Kim rang the NYSE bell in 2021, it marked a new stage in the development of quantum computing—that of hardware manufacturing and sales and new problem-solving products. Kim and a colleague, Chris Monroe, had spent more than twenty years inventing and testing a machine that was working when the NYSE bell rang in 2021. The success of their approach was driven by market acceptance, the fact that IonQ was the only quantum hardware provider with strategic partners like Amazon Web Services, Microsoft Azure, Google Cloud, and others. This was doubly important because all IonQ processing takes place in the cloud. In the month prior to its IPO, IonQ contract bookings tripled from $5 million to $15 million.[8]

Kim focused on quantum physics in his PhD program at Stanford. In 1999, at the height of the dot.com boom, Kim joined Bell Labs's Science Division. He soon moved to commercialization of leading-edge technologies, which required learning a lot about engineering. But his work on new telecom products made it clear that he was working in a mature sector where innovation would be difficult—that anything truly disruptive wouldn't go very far. By then Kim made up his mind: He'd pursue a disruptive technology. And what could be more disruptive than quantum computing? Its potential for cosmic change made it all the more attractive.[9]

Kim completed the original license to IonQ in the summer of 2016 as an all-equity deal, rather than a more "traditional license" that would have included royalties, milestone payments, and so on. Later the license was amended to add new technology for additional compensation. The OTC sold some of its shares soon after the lock-up period ended (one in which sales are prohibited in order to augment market stability) but kept a lot on Kim's advice that long-term prospects were bright.[10]

During Rasor's tenure at the OTC, seven client companies have had IPOs. Remarkably, one of them, Evolv, went public on NASDAQ at the same time IonQ went public on the NYSE. Evolv is a spinout of the Duke Center for Metamaterials led by Dr. David R. Smith, whose success with lab-to-market technologies has been prodigious. His center's technologies are currently being commercialized by seven companies. The science behind each has Duke at the forefront of a relatively new field of research on metamaterials.[11] Smith says this science has become "an engineering platform—a tool kit for manipulating sound and optical waves and making them do your bidding." Evolv has drawn off Smith's research to create a security product that detects concealed weapons, guards against unauthorized entry to closed meetings, autonomously screens participant bags, and provides crowd control. Ninety-two percent of Evolv customers renew their agreements with the company.[12]

A somewhat whimsical experiment in 2006 to demonstrate a "cloak of invisibility" brought Smith an avalanche of attention. The experiment involved the use of electromagnetic metamaterials with properties that could be adapted to make objects disappear by bending light waves around it. That inspired the teasing lead in a Scott Huler article in the May 29, 2024, issue of *Duke Magazine*—"Invisibility casts a long shadow." That line had a ring of truth about it. Smith had disavowed that any of the magical properties of Harry Potter's cloak of invisibility were at work. However, his experiment prompted a wave of curiosity over whether a person could be made to disappear. Intrigue over this question prompted a flurry of calls from reporters and landed Smith on Jay Leno, Stephen Colbert, and *The Today Show*. Smith still gets calls from reports about the cloak.[13] What largely got lost is that the experiment worked. Smith successfully split light into two waves that traveled around an object in the center and reemerged as a single wave with minimal loss due to reflections. Harry Potter would approve.

Another company originating in Smith's center, Kymeta Corporation, uses metamaterials for antennas on geostationary satellites deployed at a high altitude over the equator, which makes objects there seem motionless to the ground observer. Such deployments facilitate communication between parties that require uninterrupted connections. Kymeta says its mission is to "provide . . . intelligent, resilient communication platforms that empower critical commercial and military operations with continuous high-speed connectivity and situational awareness—anywhere, and anytime."[14]

While Kymeta has not confirmed it, some experts have speculated that a Kymeta antenna may have played a part in the April 14, 2022, sinking of the *Moskva*, the flagship of the Russian Black Sea fleet, with Ukrainian Neptune missiles. No less an authority than *RUSI Journal*, published by Royal United Services Institute, a prominent UK defense and security think tank, has suggested that a Kymeta antenna may have guided Ukraine's missiles when they struck the *Moskva*. The article ran under the headline "Uncrewed Platforms Have Been Critical to Ukraine's Success in the Black Sea." The article cites high-capacity two-way satellite communications such as Starlink and Kymeta, both of which have been observed in use.[15]

As impressive as the OTC record with IPOs is, it has facilitated many more acquisitions—a total of twenty-five—in Rasor's tenure. That metric might be compared to a small investment bank. "We make bets all the time on which technologies are going to make it," Rasor observes. "We have technologies and companies that don't make it. It may be because [they] don't make it through the regulatory process, or the market is not as large as originally predicted. In other cases, the technology doesn't scale up or work as well as we'd like." By then, the OTC may have invested what Rasor calls "a fair amount" on the technology—to get it patented, for example. "It's an economic loss for us too," Rasor adds.

She points out that very few geographic regions have three tier-one research universities in such close proximity to each other. She takes pride in the level of cooperation between the Big Three. They jointly sponsor an annual "boot camp" for start-up entrepreneurs as well as "Venture Days" where investors come to the region to hear pitches from new companies. To the question why she enjoys being at Duke, she replies, "Almost every day, somebody shows up with just a fascinating new invention. And it's true: You get to work with really creative people who are really trying to solve all sorts of problems." Early in her career she took a pay cut to go across the street (from Battelle) to Ohio State. Then with an optimistic laugh she adds, "I haven't regretted it one bit. Not one bit. It's wonderful."[16]

Lampe Joint Department at UNC and NC State

As the years passed, the Big Three became more and more adept at collaboration. In 2003, NC State and UNC established a joint department of biomedical engineering (Duke already had such a department). Although there are a handful of other joint biomedical engineering departments in the United States, the Lampe Joint Department is the only department fully joint at both the undergraduate and graduate levels with all faculty and students provided full and equal access to resources at both university campuses. It ranks third in one independent survey in number of BS degrees granted. Its full-time faculty totals fifty with an adjunct pool of one hundred scientists, engineers, and physicians.

On February 12, 2025, the joint department received a $20 million endowment from Ross W. Lampe Jr., whose family has close generational ties to NC State. His grandfather, Harold Lampe, was its dean of Engineering and part of the delegation that first briefed Governor Luther Hodges on the RTP concept in late 1954. During the telecom boom, Ross Lampe led a group at Ericsson that made many advances in cell phones. In 1994, he founded SMD Software and sold it several years later. He has maintained close ties to NC State over the years.

The Lampe Joint Endowment aims to grow the research and development pipeline for the joint department as well as to facilitate increased translation of biomedical technologies from academic research labs to the commercial marketplace. It does this by providing a variety of resources to assist faculty in entrepreneurial activities.[17] For example, it links them with savvy managers and investors who can take their discoveries to the marketplace. SonoVascular is a good example of that.

The company's technology is based on the research of Paul A. Dayton, chairman of the Lampe Joint Department of Biomedical Engineering. SonoVascular's founder and CEO is Dan Estay, who has a deep background in MedTech development and commercialization. He previously led Abbott's vascular device business in Asia for six years while he was based in Tokyo. William Starling is another cofounder and chairman of the company's board. He brings a wealth of experience as a serial entrepreneur and hands-on team member in advanced MedTech firms, having spent most of his career in Silicon Valley. SonoVascular relies on ultrasound technology to treat vascular diseases such as deep vein thrombosis and pulmonary embolisms. The Triangle has a deep history of innovation with ultrasound. Three graduate students at Duke unveiled the first commercially available 3D ultrasound in 1998.

Dayton points out that it takes ten to twenty-nine years to get a biomedical device from the lab bench to the marketplace. Getting through FDA clinical trials alone can take ten years. While early results are encouraging, Dayton sees even more promising results on the horizon. SonoVascular plans to raise another $20–25 million to get through FDA clinical trials for both clinical indications, with the first indication expected to be approved by the FDA in 2028.

Investor Bill Starling, who has homes near the UNC campus and Stanford University, applauds the encouraging culture in the Triangle: "In RTP, when a start-up becomes successful, it seems that the entire ecosystem congratulates and offers admiration for their contributions to improving lives. There's a very congenial and collaborative environment." In contrast, he has seen the money chase creep into Silicon Valley, once known for its laid-back, supportive attitude.[18] He notes that "greedy venture capitalists on Sand Hill Road will fund [copycat entrepreneurs] inspired by the success of the original start-up. Too much money chasing a cyclical phenomenon." Whether such attitudes are inevitable remains to be seen as the Triangle's innovation sector remains in its infancy.

Cuts to Research Funding

As federal research spending increased following World War II, the Triangle universities have enjoyed dramatic gains in funding. For example, Duke received $21 million in National Institutes of Health (NIH) funding in 1977. By 2022, it received $673 million, the fourth most in the nation. That same year, UNC received $588 million.[19] However, dramatic changes to the research landscape occurred in 2025. The Trump administration's Department of Government Efficiency (DOGE) implemented an across-the-board cap on administration overhead funded through federal grants. The administration also cut funding for certain types of research. For example, Duke lost two NIH grants totaling $258 million that funded HIV/AIDS vaccine development. In total, the Triangle universities lost $800 million in NIH funding in 2025. A study by the Science and Community Impacts Mapping Project anticipates a loss of $2.1 billion in 2026 funding and nine thousand jobs at Triangle universities.[20] The congressional district that is home to UNC and Duke will experience the largest cuts in federal funding nationwide.[21]

These funding cuts have an obvious impact on university research. However, they also affect the overall landscape for capital for early-stage companies. The Triangle lacks the venture capital some of its competitor regions have. Start-ups forming at universities are stretched for funds. Ben Scruggs at Hatteras Venture Partners notes the funding challenges that face "a broad platform technology that could be a riskier bet and take longer to validate."[22] Doug Edgeton, the president and CEO of NCBiotech, has seen a tenfold increase in applications for research grants it makes to universities. He fears the near-term funding crunch will impact the number of start-ups spinning out of universities in two to three years. As the activity surrounding biomanufacturing increases, the state needs to ensure that innovation continues with research and development. NCBiotech has helped bring $4 billion in venture capital to North Carolina between 2020 and 2024. It aims to bring $5 billion more before 2030.

While the area universities may have once resisted the notion of linking basic research to commercial ventures, they now embrace it. An ecosystem has built up over the decades within the universities, industry, and government to facilitate the movement of ideas to the marketplace. As uncertain and challenging the funding environment for research is, the relationship and institutional linkages remain. The universities will adapt, and the playing field will establish a new norm. The vacancy rate for life science facilities has crept up in 2025, according to Blake Stevens at Alexandria Real Estate. However, he notes other markets have a great level of oversupply and "fundamentally, innovation is accelerating [in the area]."

22

Big Pharma Embraces North Carolina

The biotech revolution exploded on the scene in the late 1970s. It showed immense promise, but the industry's ability to produce life-saving drugs and other treatments at scale would take decades. This evolution helps explain the impact of advanced manufacturing in North Carolina. It would take decades for biotech and life science companies to refine their treatments for diseases and find acceptance and a large patient base. As those treatments gained market share, companies needed to ramp up production. Eventually, these facilities would represent massive job creators in North Carolina. Importantly, these manufacturing jobs offer a career path for workers who lack a college degree. Institutions such as NCBiotech and the community college system saw the potential of expanding manufacturing jobs across North Carolina. In partnership with local governments, these institutions created training programs and infrastructure to attract biomanufacturing companies. The state now has begun to reap the benefits.

Arrival of Biogen

Biogen mirrors the story of other early biotech companies. The company was founded in 1978 in Switzerland as Biotechnology Geneva. Despite its European roots, scientists at Harvard and MIT, Walter Gilbert and Phillip Allen Sharp, respectively, pioneered its technology aimed at defeating neurological diseases. They both received Nobel Prizes—Gilbert for his groundbreaking work on DNA sequencing and Sharp for his discovery of split genes. By 1985, the company was fighting to survive. Despite raising large sums from investors, it had no products generating revenue. Raising more money was not an option. It needed a viable business plan. The company hired a proven leader, Jim Vincent, to put the company on sound footing. When Vincent took the reins, he drastically cut personnel and other costs, including projects in Biogen's developmental pipeline. He made the company's top priority a promising drug called Avonex®, which soon became a leading therapy for multiple sclerosis.[1]

Biogen had one facility spread across two buildings in a dense, urban environment at Kendall Square in Cambridge, Massachusetts. It had no backup production facilities. In 1994, Vincent began the search for a new plant to mitigate the risk of fire and other disasters as well as to build up inventories of finished and unfinished materials. He placed a company executive, Jim Mullen, in charge of finding a location. Initially, Mullen focused on New England. Meanwhile, Gary Shope, then vice president of the Research Triangle Foundation, learned of Biogen's search and decided to reach out. When Shope first knocked on Mullen's door, Shope understood that Biogen was disenchanted with doing business in the Boston area. His instincts told him that certain intangibles might favor RTP—among them the fact that Vincent had earned an engineering degree from Duke and had a son attending Duke. In addition, Vincent was a major donor to the school. Shope found an ally in Mullen. Shope and Mullen approached Vincent together and pitched RTP. After an exhausting day of site visits in North Carolina, Vincent responded, "Why wouldn't I want to be in Research Triangle Park?"[2]

The decision was made. Biogen committed to build a 110,000-foot facility in RTP. It finished the facility in 1998 at a total cost of $200 million. Given the advanced scientific processes involved in production, the facility complied with RTP's zoning limits on manufacturing uses. There, Biogen had a workforce of three hundred producing Tysabri® in addition to Avonex®. Mullen and Shope both agree that RTP's key advantage in securing the plant was its capability to train workers to Biogen specifications. Biogen would later donate a large amount of equipment to the Biomanufacturing Training and Education Center (BTEC) at its Centennial Campus at North Carolina State University to support such training.[3]

As Biogen and the biotech industry matured, the company continued to invest in RTP. Now it has a multibuilding campus in RTP creating many jobs, including a global patient services center dedicated in 2016. Its leadership continues to say that RTP's most important attribute is its history of attracting qualified employees and a diverse talent pool. Mullen and Shope believe the "secret sauce" for RTP's success has been the underpinning of industry, education, and government all working together. Biogen's foray into RTP for biomanufacturing would set the stage for a tsunami.[4]

Holly Springs

Like so many other RTP success stories, the rise of Holly Springs as a major biomanufacturing hub began as an economic development strategy prompted at the highest levels of state government. In 2003, Governor Mike Easley directed NCBiotech to produce a strategic plan for the expansion of biotech in North Carolina. With BTEC and BioWork underway, the state had the building blocks for training workers for this new industry. RTP provided a brand, but large manufacturing facilities did not belong in the Park. A key strategy sought to leverage RTP for the expansion of biotech in other parts of the state just as the founders of RTP envisioned. Biomanufacturing offered a way to accomplish this goal because it required trained workers but not necessarily the PhDs clustered in RTP.

Bill Bullock had a hand in drafting the governor's strategy. He had worked in the Department of Commerce but became the first full-time economic developer for NCBiotech in 2004, charged with executing the strategy. At the same time, leaders in Holly Springs, located in a quiet corner of Wake County, began to focus on biopharma. Jenny Mizelle served as the town's economic developer at the time. She and Bullock began discussing what it would take for Holly Springs to become a biomanufacturing hub. The town started focusing on factors to make it attractive: sufficient infrastructure, a graywater system to accommodate unique wastewater needs from biomanufacturing activities, and readily available sites. Together, the town and NCBiotech worked to position the town for incoming opportunities.

Bullock, Mizelle, and other representatives from North Carolina traveled to San Francisco in 2004 to attend the annual BIO Conference. Bullock called on an old contact at Chiron, pitching North Carolina as a site for a new facility. Mizelle made sure the list included Holly Springs, and Chiron showed interest in the town. Around this same time, Novartis acquired Chiron. Fortunately,

Novartis adopted Chiron's decision to focus on Holly Springs for its next site. In 2006, Novartis (now CSL Seqirus) announced that it would build a biomanufacturing plant in Holly Springs to produce flu vaccines to meet seasonal and possible pandemic needs. The company is on standby, even today, to provide the federal government with 150 million vaccine doses at any time they might be needed.

Irena Krstanovic now serves as Holly Springs's director of economic development. She joined that department in the early 2000s and has been its director since 2016. She brings an international perspective to the job. Born in a part of Yugoslavia that is now Serbia, she and her husband moved to the Triangle area in the late 1990s. "Our leadership—especially our mayor, Sean Mayefskie, and our town manager, Randy Harrington, as well as their predecessors, Dick Sears and Carl Dean—have had an innovative way of thinking," Krstanovic observes. "For example, we get our water from the Cape Fear River in Harnett County. Obviously, it's a finite and expensive resource. So a long time ago, our city fathers established a very robust program for graywater [derived mainly from sinks and showers, in contrast to blackwater or sewage] our biotech companies use in cooling towers. The town also invested heavily in site preparation, which meant prospects could see exactly what they'd be getting in coming here. Our philosophy is to cater to the needs of life science companies in every way we can, and that includes fast permitting. One of their mantras is 'speed to market.' We want to make that as easy for them as possible. Wake Technical Community College is also building a campus on the border of Holly Springs to create a training pipeline to funnel people hungry to get involved in this booming industry, right into their next job."[5]

"It's important to remember that all this development took place because we have a Research Triangle Park," Mayefskie added. "Without RTP, we wouldn't have access to the Biotech Center and its staff—people like Bill Bullock, who runs the center's economic and statewide development programs. What this really means is that RTP is providing many returns on all the investments that went into it. RTP is an engine of growth because it's disbursing development in the form of excellence in high-tech jobs."[6]

"Holly Springs has become a global hub for biomanufacturing," Bullock declares. "Holly Springs's economic development strategy, through Irena and her team's leadership and Jenny Mizelle before her, from the beginning embraced the importance of understanding the industry, educating their community, building necessary infrastructure, and following through on commitments. Biomanufacturing is a complex sector, so building a cluster requires an appreciation for the nuance that drives success. In my over twenty years as a life sciences economic development professional in NC, I'm often asked by communities how to attract the next big life sciences project, and I always point to Holly Springs as the model . . . one of NC's true life sciences success stories twenty-five years in the making!"

Bullock notes a major inflection point for biomanufacturing occurred in 2017.[7] "Biologics," or drugs made from living organisms, continued to emerge as a modality driving the future of pharmaceuticals, which put pressure on what was already limited availability of global production capacity. Also, the US Food and Drug Administration (FDA) started approving new classes of drugs for major markets, including new drug treatments for diabetes and obesity. The fast-growing demand for these drugs suddenly put a bullseye on places like Holly Springs—places poised to build new facilities with "speed to market." And when COVID hit, the pressure for supply only increased. Furthermore, the supply-chain problems encountered during COVID showed the importance of onshoring production capacity in the United States, the largest market for drugs. The Trump administration's focus on tariffs only adds to the reasons for constructing new facilities in the United States.[8]

A string of major economic development successes shows how Holly Springs's long-range strategy has paid off. In March 2021, Fujifilm Diosynth Biotechnologies announced that it would build a contract development and manufacturing organization (CDMO) plant in Holly Springs, replicating one Fuji constructed in Denmark. Then, three years later, Fujifilm announced an expansion, making the Holly Springs plant the world's largest CMDO. CMDOs provide a facility for multiple companies. This one affords space to manufacture complex biologic treatments for cancer, Alzheimers, and other diseases. The facility opened in 2025 at a total cost of $3.2 billion. CEO Lars Petersen says with the world's largest market for pharmaceuticals situated in the United States, drug companies prefer to "see if there's available capacity in the US before Europe." For example, Johnson & Johnson is taking at least 160,000 square feet of Fuji's new facility, where it looks to expand its US footprint.

Toshi Iida, chairman of Fujifilm Diosynth and general manager of biotechnologies and CMDOs, explains how the company got into this highly complex business: "We were founded in 1934, and our first product was to manufacture motion picture film. We were very successful doing that up until the year 2000 when film demand started to decline sharply with the advent of very high-quality digital cameras. By 2010, the global demand for photographic film fell to just 10 percent of what it had been a few years earlier."

That forced a reappraisal. "Our CEO asked what could we do to adjust to this dramatic change in our market. So then we began to focus very hard on other technologies the company had a foothold in, such as health care. In 1983, Fujifilm invented the world's first so-called computer radiography. So we began to see three pillars of health care: We already had a core strength in medical imaging and began to explore how we could duplicate that success in the areas of prevention and treatment. We soon found the opportunity to manufacture high-quality pharmaceuticals, especially biopharmaceuticals." Iida remembers vividly the indispensable reminder that Fujifilm's chairman provided at the time: "You are responsible for people's memory. So if you lose one load of film, you have lost someone's memory. Our aspirational DNA is to become a zero-defect manufacturer because we are responsible for people's memory." Iida has never forgotten those words. He calls them "words to live by" at the company's new CMDO plant in Holly Springs.[9]

In March 2021, Amgen announced that it would invest $550 million in a new plant in Holly Springs. Just three years later, the company announced that it would invest another $1 billion to expand the facility.[10] Amgen produces a range of drugs, including those that help chemotherapy and dialysis patients. Dr. Magnus Ohman joined Amgen as vice president for global development soon after the company's Holly Springs operations got underway. He brought thirty-plus years of experience at Duke and the University of North Carolina to the job along with a wealth of scientific relationships. Most recently he had served as vice chairman of medicine at Duke. He'd also been a founding member of the Duke Clinical Research Institute in the 1990s, the largest academic research organization focused on clinical research in the world. "The infrastructure in North Carolina," he added, "especially the Biotech Center is unique. When I came to North Carolina in '87, there wasn't much biotech here. So, I credit NCBiotech with making it a place Amgen wants to be a part of."[11]

Genentech is the latest Big Pharma firm to announce that it will build a plant in the Hub at Holly Springs—a $700 million, 700,000-square-foot manufacturing facility. It will employ 420 people. Genentech is considered to be a founder of the biotech industry. In welcoming the company, North Carolina Governor Josh Stein said, "These companies know that our life science workforce is ready to help them deliver their cutting-edge medicines to the world."[12] Since 2021, Big Pharma has invested $5.2 billion in new plants and brought 2,500 more employees to Holly Springs. These investments have made Holly Springs a model for how advanced manufacturing can spread across North Carolina.

Statewide Expansion

While Holly Springs offers a community model for biomanufacturing, many other communities also are finding success. Scott Hamilton, the president and CEO of the Golden Leaf Foundation (GLF), says, "Looking across North

Carolina, there has been great success in creating jobs in biotech throughout the state. When our board made its original investment in BTEC, it wanted to see benefits flow to rural counties. That has certainly happened." Hamilton cites the impact of GLF funding in fostering the growth of the Eastern Region Pharma Center at East Carolina University (ECU). The center is working with fifteen large pharmaceutical companies, who are investing $3 billion in a five-county area called the BioPharma Crescent. Community colleges in each of these eastern counties—Edgecombe, Johnston, Nash, Pitt, and Wilson—are working with the ECU center to prepare students for fulfilling, rewarding, high-paying jobs in the pharmaceutical industry. The push for new facilities never stops. Hamilton notes that the GLF invested another $25 million in 2024 for workforce development, job creation, and agribusiness growth.

Jennifer Lantz, an economic developer in Wilson, east of Wake County, has adopted the Holly Springs approach. Wilson scored a major win with Johnson & Johnson's decision to build a biomanufacturing plant in the town. Wilson Community College is building a new state-of-the-art biomanufacturing workforce training center to support Johnson & Johnson and other regional pharmaceutical companies. The prospect of a biotech corridor from RTP east to Greenville is real. This is the heart of former tobacco country. Jobs are now going to places desperate for opportunity.

NCBioImpact is a statewide workforce development network comprising a number of organizations. They include NCBiotech, the UNC system, the community college system, and the NC Life Sciences Organization. Partners take a collaborative approach to providing a pipeline of well-trained workers from community colleges and universities to biotech and biopharma companies. The network's success has long been a powerful magnet—often the main differentiator—in competitions with sister states for new facilities and investments. The community college system anchors the network with training geared to specific needs: apprentices at the entry level; process technicians, who work toward a BioWork Certificate, a required credential at many companies; and two-year degrees for more advanced work in biotechnology, biopharmaceuticals, and chemical manufacturing. Some companies provide financial support to students enrolled in these programs.

In addition to structured, off-the-shelf classes, community colleges offer customized training that meets the needs of individual companies. A program developed by Wake Tech for Eli Lilly and Company offers a good example. A company representative approached Leslie Isenhour, who runs Wake Tech's biotech programs, in the fall of 2021, well before announcing that a new Lilly plant would be located in Durham. Lilly asked if Isenhour could arrange to train quality analysts and get them up to speed quickly. It was a demanding ask because Lilly's workers would need to have expertise in using a sophisticated and expensive piece of equipment, the high-performance liquid chromatography (HPLC) system. The system allows analysts to run tests on raw materials and finished products.

The training required twenty-four hours of coursework over three eight-hour days. It was developed collaboratively by Lilly, the Wake Tech biotech department, and a network of subject-matter experts developed and operated by Wake Tech. Lilly provided the HPLC equipment and software. Wake Tech held the first class in the spring of 2022 for six students—seven months after Lilly first approached Isenhour. Additional classes ranged from three to six trainees.

"As a measure of Lilly's satisfaction," says Isenhour, "they gave us the HPLC equipment and software and specified that other companies could use it"—a magnanimous gesture in a highly competitive field. "In fact, we've already had another company use it," Isenhour notes. That, in part, prompted Wake Tech to develop a certificate for the HPLC training. The relationship with Lilly progressed to the point that Lilly made a major gift to Wake Tech. A building on its RTP campus is now called the Lilly Center for Science and Technology.

In 2024, Lilly announced it would double its investment in Concord outside of Charlotte. Ironically, the new facility is located in an old Philip Morris cigarette plant. Reflecting Lilly's ongoing competition with Novo Nordisk, the site will produce drugs to treat diabetes and obesity. Lilly announced that 60 percent of the workers are local and 70 percent come from North Carolina.[13] The plant will employ six hundred workers and wages average about $70,000, significantly higher than prevailing local wages. These announcements prompted the *Boston Globe* to take notice, acknowledging that "the picture is grim" for perennial tech powerhouse Massachusetts.[14] That state lost thirty thousand private-sector jobs between 2019 and 2024. Meanwhile, Charlotte and the Research Triangle gained about 250,000 private-sector jobs over the same period: "That's the real competition."

The recent proliferation of advanced manufacturing throughout North Carolina brings to fruition one of the dreams of RTP's founders. At the time, they understood the promise of research and development. After World War II, it seemed clear the federal government and private industry would ramp up spending on new technologies. Universities would play an important role in that new universe. No one, however, knew how those activities might translate into new industries, much less ones that did not exist at the time. Today, biomanufacturing represents nearly $90 billion in annual economic activity in North Carolina and 225,000 jobs. Importantly, those jobs provide an economic ladder for high school graduates. In 2025, the state ranked number one in the United States for biomanufacturing. Based on the momentum of investments since 2017, this sector will make a dent in the hole left by textiles, furniture, and cigarettes. The architects of RTP, especially Romeo Guest who had a dream of building new manufacturing facilities, would be pleased.

23

RTP 3.0

A popular television show, *Stranger Things*, tracks the lives of several kids growing up in the 1980s in the fictitious town of Hawkins, Indiana. The show's creators, Matt and Ross Duffer, grew up in Durham in a neighborhood off West Cornwallis Road not too far from RTP. The show's references to Durham have become a cottage industry for fans in the Triangle.[1] One reference has particular saliency. The show features Hawkins National Lab, where the government conducts secret tests to produce children with psychokinetic abilities. The lab has a dark, foreboding presence in the show just as RTP must have had for the Duffer brothers. The depiction of the lab reflects changing perceptions of research centers. Instead of providing a bright, sunny environment for workers to mine new ideas in a natural setting, these places can symbolize locations for sinister activities—isolated and claustrophobic.

As detailed in chapter 15, attitudes toward office parks shifted among tech workers in the early 2000s not too dissimilar from the sensibility expressed by the Duffer brothers. Workers began to prefer vibrant, interactive places. As vacancy rates increased in RTP during this period, leaders saw the need for a change. This chapter charts the emergence of a new framework guiding RTP's development in response to these changing tastes. It focuses on efforts by the Research Triangle Foundation (RTF) to reform its development rules to allow a wider variety of uses, including dense "innovation hubs" with the aim of maintaining RTP as a research and jobs center for the state. With more than fifty years under its belt, such a radical shift will not happen quickly. Companies located in the Park had bought into a particular physical environment, and it will take time and effort to change that. As importantly, RTP and the area have evolved certain geographic and spatial patterns based on this framework. It will take decades to see how these development changes evolve.

A New Plan

After stalling in the first decade of the 2000s, RTP faced continued headwinds with the onset of the Great Recession in 2009. The RTF depended on selling real estate to keep its operations going and sales were slow. RTP had one of the highest office vacancy rates in the Triangle region.[2] These financial issues along with ongoing critiques of the suburban model caused the RTF board to push for changes. In November 2011, Bob Geolas joined the RTF as the organization's eighth president and CEO. Geolas fills a room with energy. He speaks in grand gestures and describes himself as a "bit of a dreamer." Geolas grew up in Raleigh in a working-class family. His father repaired refrigerators, and he says the family lived hand to mouth.[3] His father got a break when Motorola hired him to sell pagers. That job allowed the family to buy a house. The power of RTP to transform the lives of people in North Carolina stayed with Geolas. He attended NC State University, worked on the Centennial Campus, and was hired away by Clemson University to run its International Center for Automotive Research.

Leading the RTF was a dream job for Geolas. He arrived with a splash, launching a bus tour of the state, seeking to reconnect the people of North Carolina with RTP. He heard the refrain repeated in different ways: "We feel like RTP is our rich cousin. We're really proud of them, but we don't hear from them anymore."[4] These meetings inspired Geolas to create "a connection point" in RTP to celebrate "the best of what we do in North Carolina around science [and] technology." That vision would underscore Geolas's five-year tenure at the RTF.

In late 2012, Geolas announced the hiring of the real estate firm Hines to develop a master plan for RTP. The plan would include three development areas within RTP, including a commuter-rail stop at the Durham end of RTP, Park

Center at Davis Drive and I-40, and an area in Wake County next to Kitts Creek Lakes. RTP's restrictive covenants and zoning would require modification. Led by Liz Rooks, the RTF spent the next two years reacquiring the properties at Park Center, such as the Governor's Inn, which was subject to a long-term land lease. Finally, in October 2015 Geolas announced plans to develop Park Center. It had taken $20 million from Durham County, $75 million from the RTF, and $10 million from the owners' and tenants' association to assemble the properties and ready Park Center for development.[5] The project would include apartments, hotels, office and retail uses, a large amphitheater, and ample public space. Geolas also saw Park Center as an opportunity to tell the story of RTP to students and other visitors. As one point of connection, he opened a former IBM building in Park Center to entrepreneurs from all walks of life called the Frontier.

With Park Center underway, Geolas announced his departure the following year. Geolas found it increasingly difficult to balance what he saw as the larger public mission of RTP with the day-to-day grind of a real estate project.[6] In 1960, Pearson Stewart established a physical template for technology companies in the form of a large, suburban office park. That template left it to companies to oversee development on property they acquired. This model did not consume the RTF's time and resources in the details of real estate development. A massive mixed-use project was entirely different. Such a project required sophisticated real estate planning, engineering, and financing. Did the RTF have the appetite and ability to execute such a venture? A new leader would have to answer this question.

Reforming the Rules

In August 2016, the RTF's board chair and former Raleigh mayor, Smedes York, announced that Scott Levitan would lead the RTF. Levitan came with substantial real estate experience in the context of higher education and research parks. He oversaw a $1.5 billion mixed-use development at Johns Hopkins University in Baltimore. Prior to that, he worked for Georgia Tech and executed Technology Square in Midtown Atlanta. Levitan has an ebullient personality but also evinces a seriousness about the task at hand. He studied architecture at Louisiana State University and then urban design at Harvard.[7] Levitan's passion for design remains, but he "fell into" a job at Harvard as director of university and commercial real estate.[8] Levitan proved adept in a role that requires navigating some of the most difficult stakeholders: higher education, government, research companies, and local communities.

After arriving in RTP, his team went to work on bringing Park Center to life. To generate activity, he brought in shipping containers to create the Boxyard, a popular outdoor dining area for RTP workers. In September 2020, the RTF broke ground on the Hub in Park Center. Levitan acknowledged that "we've bet the farm," leveraging the RTF's assets, including selling its headquarters building, with the hope that the Hub would attract users.[9] As construction progressed, the RTF signed leases and contracted with new development partners, focusing on a town square in the Hub called the Horseshoe. By 2023, hundreds of apartments with some retail amenities were underway. A hotel, lab space, and performance area will follow. The RTF team continued Geolas's concept of the Frontier, opening other former IBM buildings to multiple tenants. They now buzz with activity. Ultimately, the Hub will represent $1.5 billion in new development.[10]

With the Hub well underway, the RTF embarked on an even more ambitious task: setting up an entirely new template that allows new types of development on all seven thousand acres of RTP. Levitan calls it RTP 3.0 to distinguish it from RTP's original format (1.0) and Geolas's changes at Park Center (2.0). Similar to RTP's original model, the new framework will rely on owners to undertake the development of their property. However, the template will allow owners a much broader palette, setting up three development typologies for owners to choose from. They include an "enhanced corporate campus," which allows limited public-facing uses such as restaurants and parking decks instead of large-surface parking lots, which now comprise 20 percent of RTP's land area. The second typology, termed a "residential neighborhood development," allows residential uses and service retail such as a grocers. The final development type is a "mixed-use density node." With the help of a national planning consultant, RTF with input of the owners and tenants is producing a set of design guidelines and policies. Those guidelines could take into account development constraints such as topography and infrastructure.[11] Ultimately, an RTP Planning Board will approve development proposals. Levitan notes there will be limits to certain uses such as apartments to prevent RTP from disappearing into the densifying landscape now surrounding RTP.[12] Owners that develop property under the new regime will pay an annual assessment into the RTP Reinvestment Fund to support public purposes such as research investments, transit, and greenways.

On January 31, 2025, 96 percent of the Owners and Tenants Association voted in favor of the covenant amendments to support RTP 3.0. As with any significant shift in approach, there were questions.[13] However, the RTF team laid the groundwork for the vote with over 120 meetings and countless touchpoints with stakeholders that included owners, county officials, and chambers of commerce. Described as "a carpenter of collaboration" by community and business leaders, Levitan operates in the realm of possibility. With speculative office lagging, Levitan pivots to other uses. The pandemic wreaked havoc on society but provided an opportunity for RTP with nearly $4.5 billion in new investment, including the planned East Coast campus for Apple. While the pandemic upended downtowns everywhere, it spurred people and businesses to seek more space. RTP reaped the benefit. In particular, workers at life science companies don't have the luxury of working from home. They have to show up at a lab each day. Consequently, land values have performed well.

Levitan sees the pandemic as a short-term disruptor. The future of RTP will depend on creating more dense development. He cites as examples the "innovation hubs" such as Kendall Square in Boston and South Lake Union in Seattle. Levitan notes, "Innovation communities tend to offer more than just research and development campuses hidden behind the veil of pines, which is the model for RTP. R&D happens in multiple kinds of environments now. Some of it is more engaging, social, downtown-oriented."[14] Such areas thrive on transit-oriented development.

Levitan advocates for more regional infrastructure as traffic remains a concern to any employer in RTP. He sees bus rapid transit (BRT) as a major step in the right direction. The RTF's lead planner, Travis Crayton, is working in partnership with GoTriangle on nineteen acres at NC 54 and the NC Railroad corridor, which serves Amtrak, to create a Triangle Mobility Hub that will attract this type of urban development. The site is also close to Fidelity, the largest employer in RTP. One day this site will accommodate a dense, mixed-use center—one that relies on transit rather than automobiles. The RTF is also working closely with local governments as BRT comes to NC 54, which cuts through RTP. Crayton has a vision to make NC 54 a main street through RTP.[15] It could grow in a more urban fashion with buildings pulled up to the street rather than sitting behind large parking fields. The RTF also plans to build a ten-mile-long greenway spine that runs north to south through the Park, linking the extensive network of greenway segments within the Park and tying into the American Tobacco Trail and other regional facilities as envisioned by Pearson Stewart and planner Chuck Flink in the 1980s.

While the Triangle region now stands on its own and has multiple sites attractive to tech companies, RTP continues to drive the area's success. RTP is central to the brand of the region and North Carolina. Its vitality supports the economic health of many other constituents. According to Adrienne Cole, president and CEO of the Greater Raleigh Chamber of Commerce, RTP remains an attractive site given its global brand, location at the center of the region, and proximity to Raleigh-Durham International Airport.[16] She applauds the "expanded flexibility" of development types with RTP 3.0 "while staying true to a park anchored in research." Hub RTP now provides a place for smaller companies. Cole sees RTP 3.0 as a way to open up other areas of the Park for companies "with a fire in the belly" to innovate and grow.

Just as RTP took years to ignite, it will take years for the new development framework to show its impact. Given RTP's overall success, it is understandable that its leadership hesitated to make fundamental changes. Some say it came too late. However, no case study exists for redesigning a research park—much less the largest one in the United States. Even the Centennial Campus, the science park at NC State University, faces concerns over obsolescence, and it was designed in the 1990s. RTP's location at the center of the region, the area's growth, momentum at the Hub, and progress on transit give RTP a promising outlook for the future. Real estate development follows cycles. Projects take years to execute. It is not too hard to imagine an RTP in fifty years with vibrant innovation centers surrounded by research companies in different built environments. Of course, a canopy of green will likely remain a defining feature, greeting anyone who visits the Park.

24

"A Full Life in the Research Triangle"

As described in chapter 3, George Simpson conceived a new type of place that could appeal to tech workers by providing a challenging career without the daily grind of an urban metropolis. RTP helped achieve that goal as a bucolic work environment within easy commute of neighborhoods and abundant cultural and recreational opportunities. The diversity of offerings grew as newcomers poured into the area. As an example of the growing cultural amenities, the North Carolina Museum of Art moved in the early 1980s from the State Highway Building in downtown Raleigh to a new home designed by Edward Durrell Stone. The museum added the West Building in 2010 designed by another noted architect, Thomas Phifer. That building holds the largest Rodin collection in the southeastern United States. It is situated in the largest art park in the nation at 165 acres. In addition to the arts, the area now has the critical mass to support professional ice hockey and soccer teams to complement its long-standing strength in college sports.

The area's greenway system showcases the region's recreational amenities. It began with a design student's master's thesis that ingeniously proposed placing greenways within public easements running along the city's floodplains.[1] That student, Bill Flournoy Jr., eventually joined the planning staff in Raleigh and later became president of the Triangle Greenways Council. Known as "Mr. Green Jeans," Sig Hutchinson has championed Flournoy's vision by leading multiple open space bond campaigns that funded expansions to the greenway system. The system now stretches over 250 miles. It connects Falls Lake to the Town of Clayton along the Neuse River. It links Crabtree Creek to Umstead State Park near RDU Airport. It joins with the American Tobacco Trail, bringing joggers and bikers into the heart of Durham. It even connects to the Mountains to the Sea Trail and the East Coast Greenway. These types of amenities especially appeal to tech workers as an antidote to days and nights of strenuous mental work.

While cultural and recreational options have increased over time, growth has created significant challenges. The founders of RTP anticipated growth and encouraged local governments to prepare for it. However, few could have anticipated the pace and scale of such development. Wake County and numerous towns in the region routinely top lists of the fastest growing places in the nation. As discussed previously, the region's growth eventually compromised Simpson's vision of an idyllic workplace. The Wake County public school system became a major flashpoint. The unique, dispersed pattern of the region posed problems for a cohesive transit system that could provide commuters an alternative to cars. With few barriers to growth, the region would continue to leapfrog outward, enveloping one small town after another. This chapter considers how local leaders are navigating these challenges as they redefine "a full life in the Research Triangle" into the future.

Regional Transit Takes Another Detour

Despite the collapse of Triangle Transit's regional plan in 2006, mass transit remained a priority for the area. The region's population growth continued apace. Traffic ranked high on the list of concerns in community surveys. To pick up the pieces after 2006, the area's two transportation planning organizations and local governments appointed a Special Transit Advisory Commission (STAC) to examine the issue. This group settled on a plan similar to the one of the early 2000s, using an existing rail corridor through Raleigh, Cary, RTP, and Durham. The publicly owned NC Railroad Company controls the corridor but has a long-term lease agreement with Norfolk Southern to move freight. Funding for the proposed plan relied on federal and state funds. However, STAC recommended adoption of a half-cent local option sales tax as one other major source of funding.

The lack of robust local funding had hindered previous transit plans. Unlike Mecklenburg County, which passed a local option tax in 1998 to fund expanded buses and a light-rail system in Charlotte, the Triangle only managed to enact a rental-car tax and car registration fee. These relatively meager revenue sources did not generate sufficient local matching funds to position the Triangle in a competitive process for federal grants. This finally changed in August 2009 when the NC General Assembly passed House Bill 148, giving authority to Orange County, Durham County, and Wake County to pass a one-half cent sales tax for transit. The bill had bipartisan support with Republican Senator Richard Stevens and Democratic House member Deborah Ross leading the effort. Ross recalls last-minute negotiations when Wake County Commission Chair Joe Bryan requested a change to the bill so that Wake, Durham, and Orange Counties would not have to hold referenda on the tax simultaneously.[2] Bryan did not want pressure from the other counties to move quickly on a referendum, nor did he want a situation where Wake, the largest county, would subsidize the others. This last-minute change would have profound implications for the future of regional transit.

Bryan's concern proved prescient. Local leaders in Durham and Orange Counties moved quickly. In the wake of the Great Recession, Congress passed a stimulus package and funds flowed into the federal Capital Investment Grants program, which funds rail transit. Projects that could get through an environmental review process within twenty-four months would receive priority for funding. Durham and Orange Counties had a potential project—light rail connecting the two counties along Highway 15-501. Their transportation planning organization had studied the corridor extensively.[3] It scored well under federal criteria due to the high volume of students and patients accessing medical facilities and universities at all hours as well as the development potential along the corridor.[4] Durham led the charge to fund the project, placing a referendum on the ballot in 2011. The measure passed by a wide margin. Orange passed its referendum the following year. GoTriangle (formerly Triangle Transit) met the twenty-four-month timeframe for the environmental review with substantial assistance from the NC Department of Transportation.[5] In 2016, GoTriangle secured a full funding grant agreement with the federal government. The prospect for mass transit looked promising even though the Triangle was no longer working collaboratively on a regional plan.

Meanwhile, it was unclear when and if a less transit-friendly Wake County would proceed with its taxing authority. A spark finally occurred in June 2014, when the Urban Land Institute invited a national consultant, Jarrett Walker, to lead a day-long workshop. Walker had recently published *Human Transit: How Clearer Thinking About Public Transit Can Enrich Our Communities and Our Lives*. The workshop stimulated interest, and the fall election led to a major changeover to a pro-transit County Commission. That fall, Wake County hired Walker's firm along with Kimley-Horn, a national engineering firm with deep local roots, to assist in developing a transit plan. Wake County, Raleigh, and other local governments appointed a seventy-member advisory committee and embarked on a lengthy planning process, which included polling, surveying transit riders, soliciting public comments, and addressing more than 250 groups.[6] The final plan offered BRT in certain corridors, commuter rail to connect the region, and expanded bus service. Based on this plan, voters approved the local option tax in November 2016 by a 53–47 vote.[7]

As Wake County finally began to move ahead with a transit plan, Durham and Orange Counties encountered problems with theirs. Challenges included community concerns over station locations, which led to additional stops; major costs imposed by the NC Railroad to reduce at-grade crossings in downtown Durham; local business concerns about the loss of those crossings; and opposition by Duke University to a stop at its hospital. Ultimately, lack of support in the General Assembly proved fatal to the plan. The light-rail project depended on 20 percent funding from the state. The legislature zeroed out the funding. It was restored. Then a bill placed caps on the funding and a hard deadline to receive federal funding approval.[8] By early 2019, GoTriangle's leadership concluded the deadline could not be met and the board voted to pull the plug on the project after spending $157 million.[9] Once again, the region's transit agency failed to deliver after suffering "death by a thousand cuts."

Opinions about the outcome tend to fall into two buckets. The first relates to the national environment. Raleigh's former mayor, Mary-Ann Baldwin, has served on GoTriangle's board for eleven years. As she has stated, "There's a federal bias in favor of the Northeast," where transit systems have operated for decades. Federal criteria reward those systems by crediting existing conditions such as density along transit lines.[10] Emerging metro areas such as the Triangle do not score as well. Wib Gulley, who helped create GoTriangle in 1987 and later served as its general counsel, sees an erosion of federal funds since the system's inception, making it increasingly difficult for new transit systems to get started.[11] The second explanation focuses on the lack of regional collaboration. According to John Hodges-Copple, who served as lead planner for Triangle J Council of Governments (TJCOG), business, government, and university leaders have never coalesced around a regional transit plan.[12] That lack of consensus makes the myriad complicated barriers to implementation impossible to overcome.

There is no broad-based leadership group available to swing into action when challenges inevitably arise. Hodges-Copple notes complexity only increases "as we get bigger with more leaders to focus attention."[13]

Both of these viewpoints underscore the challenging environment facing emerging tech hubs when it comes to public transit. These areas blossomed during the auto-oriented, post–World War II era. This low-density pattern of development is not conducive to transit. The private automobile accounts for nearly 90 percent of commuting trips.[14] This helps explain why places like Austin, Nashville, San Jose, and Seattle have all faced setbacks with transit plans. However, any successful plan requires local consensus. Had the local legislation required Orange, Durham, and Wake Counties to hold their referenda together, the plan would have been different. It likely would have been regional. Now that the three counties have the local tax in place, consensus will require greater intentionality and regional collaboration rather than local action.

After thirty years of failed efforts, the region has made incremental steps on transit. In 2025, construction began on the first BRT line on New Bern Avenue in Raleigh. Durham is warming up to BRT and began studying a route from Duke University to East Durham in 2025. Similarly, Chapel Hill received a federal grant to pursue BRT north along Highway 86. In his first public comments as GoTriangle's new CEO, Brian Smith takes a measured approach. He wants to see these local BRT systems built out before looking at connectivity across the region: "I think it's important to deliver results initially."[15] The potential for a regional system got a boost when the state received a $1 billion federal grant to acquire the S Line, a rail corridor that could link Raleigh more directly to Washington, DC. The line will include commuter rail from Raleigh to Wake Forest and will intersect with the NC Railroad corridor between Raleigh and Durham, which continues to grow inter-city ridership on Amtrak.[16] Wendy Jacobs, a Durham County Commissioner who worked tirelessly on the ill-fated DOLRT, sees reason for optimism. The region's two transportation planning organizations are working closely together on a plan to integrate several transportation modes, including BRT, a Triangle bikeway, passenger rail, and a "FAST [freeway, arterial, street, and tactical] regional transit study" that links RTP, the Raleigh-Durham International Airport, and the downtowns of Durham, Raleigh, and Chapel Hill.[17]

Since RTP's inception, mobility has offered a relative advantage for the region in comparison to other metros. As traffic worsens, investors in the area anticipate a time when that's not the case.[18] When traffic becomes unbearable, it will be hard to dig out of the hole. Also, preferences of tech workers continue to evolve. Gen Z shows significantly less enthusiasm about owning an automobile than prior generations.[19] Young workers want alternatives. Experience from other cities suggests fixed guideway transit such as light rail is needed to drive the type of development that gets people out of their automobiles. Transit also eliminates the need to construct large parking structures, which are common in every new high-rise residential development in Raleigh and Durham. It will take time to see whether the pandemic has a lasting impact on federal rail funds and on commute patterns.[20] In the meantime, local leaders will stitch together a plan incrementally—one step at a time.

A New Consensus for Public Schools?

The 2009 Wake County School Board election triggered a tumultuous period. Parental frustrations with busing for diversity and school overcrowding produced a majority on the board that promised to create "neighborhood schools." Protests and controversy marked the period between 2009 and 2011 for the school system. In reaction, the board flipped in 2011 as voters elected five members who largely represented the pre-2009 status quo. However, public schools and their relationship to RTP would fundamentally change in the years ahead. In 2010, Republicans took control of the General Assembly for the first time in 112 years. The legislature's funding priorities would deemphasize the role of public schools. It would show greater support for alternatives, such as private schools, home schooling, and charter schools. This shift toward "school choice" reflects a broader national trend which has shaped the expectations for those moving to the Triangle.

Following the 2011 election, the new school board fired the superintendent previously charged with producing an assignment plan to support neighborhood schools. The board voted to reestablish the diversity policy. However, it was clear the board would tread lightly on student reassignments. Given the size of Wake County and the challenge of busing students long distances, the board can no longer rigidly adhere to the goal of limiting the number of students on free and reduced lunch to 40 percent in any given school. School board chair Chris Heagarty acknowledges the challenge: "The growth and demographic distribution in a county of more than one million limits the effectiveness of the magnet system and busing as a way to maintain diversity."[21] The board tries to avoid assigning students to schools when the student would have a bus ride of more than forty minutes. As the county segregates by wealth, it becomes more difficult to achieve economic balance in the schools. For example, western Wake County, which is culturally diverse with an influx of South Asian residents, also reflects increased affluence due to its proximity to RTP.

Through the early 2000s, education funding occupied a central place in state policy. North Carolina and Texas gained national attention for their strides in early childhood education and teacher pay.[22] A change in party control at the General Assembly in 2010 has shifted priorities on education. While overall education spending has increased some, funding per pupil and teacher pay have dropped precipitously. The state now funds a voucher program for private schools and lifted the cap on charter schools. These changes have played out in the Triangle. Wake County continues to educate the vast majority of the area's students. The fourteenth largest in the United States, Wake County's system exceeds 160,000 students in contrast to Durham County with about 32,000 and Orange County (Chapel Hill) at a little over 7,000. However, Wake County schools' explosive enrollment growth has waned. More than 25 percent of the students in Wake County are in a charter school, in a private school, or are home schooled—more than any county in the state.[23] Wake County continues to grow by about seventy-five residents per day, but public schools no longer educate as many of those incoming residents as they once did.

In this sense, the Triangle has entered a new phase. North Carolina had small, segregated school systems through the 1960s. With the arrival of IBM and RTP's liftoff, Wake County shouldered the job of educating the families of the incoming tech workers. Wake leaders navigated desegregation with the school merger and magnet system, ushering in explosive growth in enrollment and ultimately blowback to that growth. Wake continues to educate the vast majority of students in the region. Chairman Heagarty acknowledges the financial pressures felt by the school system from reduced state funding and expresses concern that residents have reached "a saturation point [over local tax increases]" to fill the gap. Nevertheless, recruiters still have a good story to tell incoming tech workers. Due to higher housing costs, which afflict nearly every part of the nation, families increasingly move to where they can find a house in their budget rather than where they can access a particular school.[24] Once there, they can opt for a magnet or neighborhood school. One of the top business recruiters for the region continues to see public schools and the offerings of a large district "as a selling point."[25] The support for K–12 education encouraged by RTP's presence has enabled the area to adapt to changing preferences and legislative priorities.

New-Era Leadership

In 2001, the same year Bill Bell and Charles Meeker changed the political landscapes in Durham and Raleigh, another local election occurred. It did not receive the same attention as those in Durham and Raleigh, but in many ways, it had equally long-lasting implications for development patterns in the region. That year, Vivian Jones won election as mayor of Wake Forest. She continued to serve as mayor through 2025. The story of Jones and Wake Forest's growth represents the future of the Triangle because it defines the region's development pattern now and in the years ahead.

Jones's life also offers an example of how RTP affected thousands of native North Carolinians.[26] Born in Randolph County west of the Triangle, Jones moved to Chapel Hill after marrying her high school sweetheart who attended the University of North Carolina at Chapel Hill (UNC). She enrolled in a secretarial course at "Women's College," now the University of North Carolina at Greensboro. After completing her coursework, Jones went to work in the Human Resources Department at Chemstrand shortly after it opened in RTP. Each day she drove down Highway 54—I-40 did not exist at the time—to Chemstrand's large building amid the vast emptiness of RTP. She recalls someone walking into her office to tell her President Kennedy had been assassinated.

She and her husband left North Carolina when he got a job at Monsanto in St. Louis. They returned to Wake Forest in 1981 so that her husband could attend the Southeastern Baptist Theological Seminary, which had acquired Wake Forest University's first campus after Reynolds Tobacco lured the university to Winston-Salem in 1956. Jones found a job in North Raleigh at Variety Wholesalers, a major homegrown company. The drive took eight minutes. It now takes twenty. According to Jones, Wake Forest residents joked at the time that they had to go to Raleigh to buy underwear.

By the end of the 1980s, her marriage ended. Jones's sister, Joyce, still living in Randolph County, decided to move to Wake Forest in 1991 where they could "share their midlife crisis" by opening a café in struggling downtown Wake Forest. They named it Jovi's Café and Catering by combining their names. The restaurant served lunch and dinner on white tablecloths: "It was not fancy but nice." After eight years, the two sisters closed the restaurant but kept the catering business going. Through the restaurant, Jones became a known entity in Wake Forest. She ran successfully for town commissioner in 1999. The next year, she closed the business for good and announced her run for mayor.

As a town commissioner attending meetings with other towns in Wake County, Jones had noticed that Wake Forest had little relevance. In particular, towns surrounding RTP, such as Morrisville, Cary, Apex, and Holly Springs, had a voice in regional decisions through groups such as the Wake Mayors Association. Wake County has twelve municipalities and Wake Forest did not engage with other towns. Jones says the town "had some dysfunction" at the time. In effect, Wake Forest was a backwater at the north end of the county. She wanted that to change through positive leadership and relationships with other localities. Jones wanted Wake Forest to have a seat at the table. She would have that opportunity after winning the election for mayor in 2001.

Jones speaks with a Southern accent and exhibits what could be described as Southern charm. However, this demeanor belies a steely toughness that enabled her to successfully pursue an agenda that helped the town prosper. One area in which Jones made her mark relates to transportation. It started over concerns when the Winn-Dixie closed in downtown. Residents in a lower-income neighborhood could walk to it. Many now had no way to get groceries without taking a taxi. Jones joined every planning initiative she could. She met David King, secretary of the NC Department of Transportation. He would go on to lead GoTriangle. He introduced her to Raleigh's transit planner, who helped create the "loop bus," providing access to Raleigh and commercial establishments along Capital Boulevard. She joined the Wake Transit Group. Eventually, Jones became a board member on GoTriangle, the regional transit-planning agency. She worked closely with the state planning the S line, which will connect Raleigh to Washington, DC, with high-speed rail. Jones has ensured it will stop at a mobility hub in downtown Wake Forest and include commuter rail between the town and downtown Raleigh.

Jones also focused on downtown revitalization. She did this through strategic property acquisition. This approach takes years. Wake Forest has worked with a number of property owners to get parcels into the hands of developers interested in bringing residential units, restaurants, and other amenities to one of the most historic towns in Wake County. The town eventually controlled the property vacated by Winn-Dixie. Now the Renaissance Center, the space holds concerts and conventions and serves as a community gathering place. The Renaissance Center helped attract an adjacent townhome development. A historic building that housed a Western Auto will be redeveloped into a food court with an attractive outdoor area along a creek. All these new developments require public investment in the form of streetscape improvements with new sidewalks and trees and burying of power lines. The town has also invested in parking to accommodate visitors.

What has happened in Wake Forest reflects the future of the Triangle. The town had a population of five thousand in 1980. By 2000 it grew to twelve thousand. Today, the town bursts with sixty thousand residents. RTP fueled growth for years as Wake Forest residents accessed the Park going west on Highway 98. Completion in 2007 of the northern outer loop, or I-540, from Capital Boulevard to RTP accelerated the town's growth. Today, new residents are not necessarily workers. Retired parents flock to Wake Forest to be near children working in the Triangle. There is no Winn-Dixie, but retail centers offer every type of retailer, including Wegman's and Target. What residents find most attractive about Wake Forest is its small-town feel. More than fifteen thousand people flock downtown for Friday Night on White (Street), held once a month during the summer. Thousands show up to listen to outdoor music on Sundays during the spring. Residents have embraced these events, which reflect a multigenerational community grounded in the past and looking to the future.

Since RTP's formation, regional leaders have engaged in scenario planning showing different ways the Triangle could grow. They have included an urban pattern with growth centered in Durham and Raleigh, a dispersed pattern, and a pattern concentrated in corridors. In significant ways, the Triangle has followed all three. Since 1960, Raleigh has grown from 94,000 residents to 500,000 in 2025. Durham's population has grown from nearly 85,000 to approximately 300,000. These two cities have captured much of the area's growth, which now exceeds two million. However, single-family neighborhoods typify much of that growth. For example, Raleigh's land area has grown by nearly five times since 1960, but its density is significantly lower than it was a century ago.[27] Downtown Raleigh contains a fraction of the city's population. At the same time, development has concentrated in certain corridors. Apartments, offices, and hotels have blossomed at Brier Creek, Midtown, Crabtree Valley, the arena area in West Raleigh, Morrisville adjacent to RTP, and Southpoint in southern Durham.

As stated previously, a composite of these patterns can be described as "nucleated." The Research Triangle Regional Planning Commission identified this typology in 1960. It is distinguishable from the small, fragmented region at RTP's outset and from a region characterized by large, suburban bedroom communities near RTP. The Research Triangle area now has multiple centers. Residents there identify with the Triangle. Many couples work jobs at different ends of the Triangle. However, residents crave a sense of place and enjoy the amenities increasingly offered by the community that makes up their daily experience. These places build on the main street that existed decades ago—places like Cary, which has a new $68 million park along Academy Street, and Apex, where Salem Street is lined with restaurants and shops. Towns like Knightdale and Holly Springs that lack a historic main street are creating a downtown area. Surrounding counties have also followed this pattern. Clayton in Johnston County has exploded with nearby advanced manufacturing facilities. There, Main Street bustles with an outdoor market, new apartments, and restaurants. Pittsboro in Chatham County and Youngsville in Franklin County have burgeoning new subdivisions and resurgent historic cores. Mayor Jones's legacy in Wake Forest shows how local leaders worked collaboratively to have a voice on regional issues but increasingly have focused on the needs of their community. Those efforts have produced a region of distinctive places.

Conclusion

Like any major center, the Triangle has experienced certain life stages. Its birth and childhood saw the creation of RTP and emergence of bedroom communities in places like Cary and North Raleigh. During its adolescence, area leaders worked to improve the area's school system and contemplate a transit system that could accommodate future population growth and connect its major centers. While that transportation system remains a work in progress, the Triangle has entered young adulthood. It now has a formative personality that will grow more pronounced with age. As the region grows outward and upward, the Triangle can anticipate a range of places competing for employers and residents based on local talent and amenities. Such competition will produce even more differentiation and choice for residents. However, issues best addressed at the regional level remain salient even if in the background. How area leaders balance local priorities and these regional challenges will define what it means to have "a full life in the Research Triangle" in the years ahead.

25

Assessing RTP's Record

Among the myriad national rankings published each year, one stood out in 2025 when Raleigh ranked among the Best Cities for College Graduates. Zumper's, an apartment-search platform, reviewed the one hundred largest cities on a number of metrics including affordability and employment. Zumper's cited Raleigh for its "blend of opportunity and Southern charm." The state officials who produced the film dramatizing the exodus of college grads from Raleigh's Seaboard Station in the 1950s (described at the beginning of chapter 1) would be astounded at the turn of events. RTP's presence not only stopped the hemorrhaging of talent: It produced a powerful magnet drawing the best and brightest to the area. Zumper's ranking, however, is only one minor anecdote among the many such marketing ploys. It does not explain how North Carolina managed such a reversal. This chapter assesses RTP from two perspectives: First, how has RTP managed to transform the area and the state? Second, can RTP be considered a success?

To answer the first question, it's instructive to look at what many consider to be the gold standards of global tech centers—Boston's 128 corridor and Silicon Valley. A quick review of these two areas only amplifies the "miracle" of RTP and why so many still make the trip to understand its ingredients. During World War II, President Roosevelt tapped the former dean of MIT's engineering department, Vannevar Bush, to run the Office of Scientific Research and Development (OSRD). OSRD coordinated scientific research for military purposes, including the Manhattan Project. Bush had witnessed the first test of the atomic bomb at Alamogordo, New Mexico, and reportedly tipped his hat to Robert Oppenheimer after the detonation. OSRD helped the United States make advances in guided missiles, radar, and penicillin to treat wounded soldiers among other breakthroughs.

Bush made his biggest contribution by transforming military spending. Instead of contracting with private companies to undertake research, he directed federal funding to universities. In doing so, he made sure MIT received many of those contracts. Funding allowed MIT to build the famous Radiation Laboratory (RadLab) among other facilities to conduct research. After the war, Bush provided a report to President Truman entitled "Science, the Endless War." In it, he advocated for continued federal funding of university basic research on a competitive basis. The report also advocated for the creation of the National Science Foundation to underwrite this research. With the Cold War well underway, such funding would continue apace in the years ahead, and MIT would continue to reap the benefits.

Bush had a student, Fred Terman, who would help lay the foundation for the nation's largest tech center. Terman grew up a "faculty rat" in Palo Alto, California, but traveled east to MIT after graduating from Stanford University, a relative backwater at the time. Bush asked Terman to join him at OSRD during the war. From his desk at OSRD, Terman wrote a Stanford colleague that the coming wave of university research presented an opportunity to "consolidate our potential strength and create a foundation for a position in the West somewhat analogous to that of Harvard to the East." After the war ended, Terman returned to Stanford and restructured its departments to produce the engineering talent needed by the burgeoning industries coalescing in Northern California. He set up the Stanford Research Park and created the Stanford Research Institute as vehicles to position the university as a preeminent research institution. As academics, Bush and Terman saw industrial research capacity as a mean to build their respective institutions—reputationally, financially, and otherwise.

Businesses clustered in Boston and Silicon Valley to feed off the research coming out of the universities—companies like Raytheon, RCA, Varian Associates,

Hewlett-Packard, Data General, and Fairchild Semiconductors. Much of their work centered on military defense. Silicon Valley and Boston's 128 Corridor became two important clusters for what President Eisenhower termed the "military-industrial complex." Billions of dollars in federal grants poured into these areas during the 1950s and 1960s. When federal spending finally slowed at the end of the Vietnam War, both Silicon Valley and Boston 128 had a critical mass of private industry, talent, inventions, and venture capital to sustain the regions in the years ahead.

As described in part I of this book, RTP followed a very different path. North Carolina played a negligible role in scientific research during World War II. Its top universities did not embrace industrial research. It was the opposite: They had deep misgivings about mixing commercial and academic research. The impetus for RTP came from a businessman—one who observed MIT's tactics up close and sensed that scientific research could lead to economic development after the war. He found a receptive audience in state government leaders anxious to bring new industries to North Carolina. Instead of a vision of institution building, their purpose centered on producing good jobs and raising the standard of living in a poor Southern state dealing with declining industries. Wisely, North Carolina leaders pursued an economic development strategy known as "the Big Push Model."[1] This approach acknowledges a need for extensive, coordinated efforts to jump-start growth in stagnant economies. To succeed, it requires engaging multiple sectors in the effort. As described in this book, strategy focused on four crucial constituents: state government, the area universities, the business community, and local government. State government embarked on a heralded workforce training system, seeded nonprofits such as NCBiotech and the Microelectronics Center of North Carolina, and ensured area universities had state-of-the-art facilities and top talent. Businesses played a pivotal role in supporting institutions such as the Research Triangle Institute and the area universities and building a start-up culture. The universities welcomed superstar researchers moving to the Triangle and ultimately embraced commercialization with evolving programs. Local governments worked hard to address growth and promote a nationally recognized quality of life for tech workers.

While the Big Push Model can achieve results, its complexity can act as a barrier, making it hard to sustain. In fact, it usually fails. Only when multiple sectors operate as an ecosystem can it move "towards a self-sustained growth path."[2] In this regard, RTP has proven crucial. The Park's scale as the largest scientific research park in the nation puts it in the public eye through rankings and other news tracking economic development. RTP's economic health serves as a gauge for the health of the region and state. As such, state government, the universities, businesses, and local government stay highly attuned to collaborations emanating from RTP. In sum, RTP operates as a constant reminder to these constituents of the founder's original goal of attracting technology companies to the area.

The state's workforce training infrastructure offers the best example of how the Big Push Model has managed to sustain itself for more than sixty years. A former system president and current Wake Tech president, Scott Ralls, captures the point: "Now, almost all states have some kind of program," but they tend to treat workforce training as a one-off incentive. "We're working with companies two or three years before they even open their facility. . . . We're selling an ecosystem that has evolved over fifty years. I think we're the best in the country, and we get visited all the time by folks who strive to get where we are."[3] Institutions like NCBiotech act as the glue for these collaborations. President and CEO Doug Edgeton regularly interfaces with universities, community colleges, and businesses, continually designing new training programs. As one recent example, he cites the NC Pharmaceutical Services Network, a collaboration between East Carolina University and Pitt Community College along with NCBiotech. It provides oral and solid-dose training on industry standard equipment. Edgeton underscores the point that collaborations beget collaborations in a virtuous cycle.

The deliberate, multidimensional approach pursued over many decades highlights the unique aspect of RTP. It helps explain why so many make the trek to the Park to learn about it. Edgeton confirms that delegations visit NCBiotech at least every quarter to see it firsthand. Certainly, there is no shortage of new initiatives and collaborations to study.

Assessing RTP's Record

While it's clear North Carolina has pursued a continuous strategy since creating RTP, what effect has it had? In particular, the Big Push Model occurred just as the South began to ride the Sun Belt wave in the 1950s. Economists can point to data showing the entire region saw an improvement in per capita income relative to the rest of the country. Much of this convergence resulted from the transition from agriculture, which was more prevalent in the South, to other economic sectors. By the 1980s, per capita income in the South approached 90 percent of the nation's.[4] However, incomes stagnated after that point. Deindustrialization and globalization hit the region hard, given its dependence on industries pursuing labor-cost savings. In sum, North Carolina would have seen improvement from its lowly status as one of the most rural states in the nation with or without RTP.

So what can be attributed to RTP? In short, a lot. The founders achieved their first goal of attracting industrial research laboratories and other facilities to the area. More than 350 companies reside in RTP with a workforce of around 65,000. A review of the Research Triangle Foundation's website in 2026 shows only two parcels for sale—a little more than fifty out of seven thousand acres. Of course, there is softness, especially with the ongoing trend of working from home. IBM announced it has moved nearly all of its employees off the four-hundred-acre campus it occupied for decades. It now leases a smaller footprint nearby. While RTP continues to evolve, companies are not leaving, and the life science clusters help ensure a demand for large facilities on large sites for the near term. Likewise, the strategy has attracted numerous companies near RTP in office parks such as Perimeter Park in Morrisville and Weston Parkway in Cary.

Data strongly suggest that RTP has had a major impact on the region's economy. According to the 2026 US Bureau of Labor Statistics, the Triangle unemployment rate is on average 0.5 percent lower than the state average (3.2 percent versus 3.7 percent). Moreover, the North Carolina unemployment rate is about 0.5 percent lower than the national rate. Note these rates have fluctuated over time. During the Great Recession, North Carolina's rate exceeded the national average due to losses in manufacturing jobs. Regardless, the Triangle has had a low rate for decades, even dropping below 2 percent during parts of the 1990s.

Similarly, per capita income of Triangle residents has far surpassed state levels and now exceeds national per capita income levels, which approached $70,000 in 2023. Three Triangle counties (Chatham, Orange, and Wake) rank among the four highest in the state, exceeding $80,000—far more than the state average of $64,000.[5] These figures are remarkable, especially considering the economic conditions in this region during the 1950s. Apart from Durham, the Triangle had little industry and lagged other urban areas of the state. In sum, the data show a powerful correlation between RTP and significant economic progress for residents in the area. Much of the state's economic dynamism and growth come from Charlotte and the Triangle with Wake County ranking the third fastest-growing county in the nation with more than seventy-five residents arriving each day. It is the most populous county in a state poised to become the seventh largest in the nation by 2030 when North Carolina surpasses Ohio.

Of course, the founders of RTP explicitly aimed to improve the overall economy of the state, believing that research laboratories in the Triangle could spur new industries. Here, the record is less compelling. North Carolina has moved up from among the lowest per capita incomes in the 1950s to a more middling ranking of thirty-fifth in the nation today. However, much of the economic growth has resulted from innovation and talent concentrated in the urban areas such as Charlotte and the Triangle region. With the recent geographic expansion of biomanufacturing and advanced manufacturing, time will tell how widespread these economic improvements are felt across the state.

WHEN THE FOUNDERS conceived RTP as a way to reverse the brain drain, they had a specific demographic in mind—a young, white, college-educated man. Today's "talent" now comprise a much larger, diverse demographic pool. And the innovation economy has garnered its fair share of critics, arguing it exacerbates economic divisions. Ironically, Richard Florida followed up *The Rise of the Creative Class* in 2017 with a more sober look at trends occurring in urban areas. He cited the Research Triangle along with other tech centers as having the highest wage inequality in the nation.[6] His analysis suggested that income inequality correlates to poverty and race as measured by the African American share of the population, especially in areas with lower rates of unionization and lower tax rates. Such inequality can be attributed to the long shadow cast by the legacy of Jim Crow on the Southern economy.

Even more troubling was a study led by Raj Chetty at Harvard and published in 2014.[7] It reviewed the administrative records of forty million Americans to measure the degree of intergenerational economic mobility. Among the top fifty metros in the nation, Charlotte ranked dead last in upward mobility. Raleigh came in third from the bottom, just above Atlanta. As factors affecting these rates, the study identified segregation, income inequality, school quality, family stability, and social capital. Not all tech centers scored poorly in mobility. For example, Salt Lake City, which has a strong tech economy, ranked number one in mobility. Again, areas such as Salt Lake City do not face the same legacy of segregation and poverty experienced in the South.

These studies underscore the point that the success of RTP has not lifted all boats, even close to home. Mayor Gulley's comment that "the blessings of RTP did not flow to Durham" could be said about a number of neighborhoods in the region. In recent years, there has been increased recognition to do more. NC Central University in Durham runs the BRITE program (Biomedical Research Institute and Technical Enterprise) to train minority students in drug discovery and translational research. NCBiotech's Edgeton notes that graduates "are highly sought after by industry." The program now includes a community engagement component that provides STEM opportunities for middle and high school students, serving more than fifteen thousand students in ninety-two counties.

As a key pathway to economic mobility, Wake Tech has taken Chetty's findings to heart. The institution looked closely at its student population of nearly sixty-five thousand and realized it did not reflect the demographics of the county. Beginning in 2020, Wake Tech instituted a number of strategies to reach potential students in low-income areas. Those efforts included engaging with organizations like the Boys and Girls Club and building a new campus in East Wake County. To reduce social isolation and improve retention, Wake Tech provides a team of advisors for students and support services such as childcare. Ultimately, Wake Tech aims to be a ladder to a four-year college or skilled trades. Wake Tech tracks its progress in terms of student population, retention, and performance in core courses such as math and English. It has made steady progress each year. These initiatives will take time. Also, research suggests that "place-based strategies" at the neighborhood level can play a critical role in mobility.[8] The legacy of intergenerational deprivation has had a lasting impact and will take multiple strategies to produce a new legacy.

Conclusion

Anyone looking for lessons from RTP must recognize its unique status among tech centers. It provides hope in that its creators formed it with the specific goal of lifting the economic fortunes of a poor state. However, the physical presence of RTP obscures the deep, interconnected, and coordinated actions of key actors over many decades. The stories of these actors reveal the true lessons of RTP. Beginning with the Progressive Plutocracy, these constituents demonstrated a willingness to collaborate out of pragmatic self-interest. Archie Davis referred to it as "a generosity of spirit." RTP's future will depend on whether this spirit continues in a larger, more diverse, fragmented region and whether complacency overtakes the militancy felt by Progressive Plutocracy.

George Simpson believed that in order to be successful, the RTP strategy had to operate as a self-generating mechanism. It could not simply rely on out-of-state companies to bring jobs to North Carolina. It needed to spawn new industries. In the fast-paced world of technology, this is an audacious goal and requires constant attention. In particular, those working within the key institutions, initiatives, and programs that collaborated to make RTP successful could benefit from periodic reminders of how RTP achieved its position. There is no end point, especially in a volatile industry driven by innovation. The journey down the "Miracle Road" continues.

And new challenges arise. The lack of affordable housing in the area has grown more acute. Traffic remains a sore spot for commuters having to navigate the region. RTI and universities have had to adapt quickly to federal cutbacks and other changes to research funding. North Carolina still ranks behind many peer states in venture capital and could use more local management talent to take fledgling start-ups to a sustainable level. State leaders created a $500 million fund called NCInnovation, but it has a directive to focus investments outside the Triangle. Understandably, policy makers believe rural areas could benefit more significantly than urban centers from such investments. However, many of the ideas poised to produce new industries throughout the state reside in the Triangle area. Advanced manufacturing that has filtered out beyond the Triangle region offers one such example. A better approach would be more thoughtful strategies to leverage the ideas emerging from RTP rather than bypassing them.

In many ways, the technology industry finds itself at a pivot point similar to that in the 1980s when visionaries saw the potential of combining personal computers and networks. AI and quantum computing will revolutionize the economy in similar ways. A visiting scholar at UNC concludes the area universities have fallen behind their peers in producing graduates with the types of skills needed to excel with artificial intelligence.[9] At the same time, IBM, Cisco, MCNC, and Duke all have initiatives underway with quantum computing. With some intentionality and leadership, the state could leverage these initiatives to establish a quantum computing test bed. Similar to MCNC's role with the information superhighway, such a network could provide access to universities and others to super-computing powers necessary to solve certain problems.[10] Even more ambitious, RTP could pursue another national lab as the Department of Energy rolls out the Genesis Mission. Likened to the Manhattan Project, the Genesis Mission seeks to integrate AI and quantum computing to revolutionize R&D in the United States. RTP's track record of collaboration and existing assets make it a promising candidate for such a lab.

How institutional leaders and new players respond to constantly evolving threats and opportunities in technology will determine whether the strategy that produced RTP remains vital. RTP's track record shows the strategy can be effective. Understanding what it takes to implement such a strategy can guide these leaders into the future and few actions would reap greater economic results than ensuring the RTP strategy remains relevant.

3D Ultrasound

DISCOVERY: Volumetrics Medical Imaging's Model 1, the first real-time volumetric ultrasound imaging system that was available commercially.

DATE: Volumetrics Medical Imaging unveiled its Model 1 on March 30, 1998, at the annual conference of the American College of Cardiology.[1]

WHO: Volumetrics Medical Imaging was founded by Olaf von Ramm, Stephen Smith, and John Oxaal. Smith and von Ramm met at Duke University while studying for their doctorates in biomedical engineering. After von Ramm published one of the earliest designs for a 2D phased array ultrasound (which would go on to be used in many commercial ultrasounds), he teamed up with Smith to develop a 3D ultrasound. As the quality of the images they were able to produce improved, they joined forces with John Oxaal, another biomedical engineer who had studied at Duke University, to form Volumetrics Medical Imaging.[2]

IMPACT: The Model 1 allowed physicians to take more detailed images of organs in an efficient, noninvasive, and timely manner. Before, 2D ultrasound technology produced one single, flat image at a time, so it could capture only a single "slice" of an organ per procedure. Physicians compensated for the limitations of this technology by taking multiple flat images (which could be a lengthy process), using expensive alternatives such as magnetic resonance imaging (MRI) or performing invasive procedures. The Model 1's 3D ultrasound technology addressed the limitations of 2D ultrasound technology by scanning organs in their entirety in an instant. Physicians were able to make more accurate decisions based on the images produced because they depicted the entire organ, not just a single "slice" of it, and represented its 3D volume.[3]

LEGACY: By 2000, Volumetrics Medical Imaging had sold almost twenty 3D scanners for use in cardiovascular and obstetric imaging. Over the years, the foundations of their technology have become widely used in medical settings in most industrialized countries across the world. Von Ramm and Smith continue to build on their research in 3D ultrasound technology to produce more effective and noninvasive methods of scanning areas of the body that are currently difficult to produce images of.[4]

Adeno-Associated Virus (AAV)

DISCOVERY: The use of AAV vectors to safely deliver corrected genes into the body. Also how to clone the adeno-associated virus was a feat never before achieved. This breakthrough set the course for gene therapy and has contributed to approved and investigational therapies for the treatment of previously untreatable diseases.

DATE: Dr. Jude Samulski first explored this challenge as a graduate student. His dissertation, published in 1982, provided a foundational approach to the now-burgeoning field of gene therapy. His vision has led to the development of advanced gene therapy and AAV technology that has helped create a future in which treating genetic disease is possible. Duchenne muscular dystrophy, hemophilia, and heart failure are among the genetic disorders that Samulski's AAV vectors have already addressed.

WHO: In 2001 Samulski cofounded AskBio with life science attorney Sheila Mikhail and Xiao Xiao, PhD, another pioneer and world-leading scientist in the field of gene therapy. Their vision led to the development of advanced gene therapy and AAV technology that has helped create a future in which treating genetic disease is possible. In 2020, they sold the company to Bayer for $4 billion. In the late 1990s, Samulski established the Gene Therapy Center at the University of North Carolina School of Medicine. He and his lab were recruited to UNC with, in part, a faculty recruitment grant from the North Carolina Biotech Center.

IMPACT: AAV technology has answered the question of how a virus can be used to safely deliver corrected genes into the body and the question of how to clone the adeno-associated virus.

LEGACY: AAV was a feat that had never been achieved. A breakthrough, it set the course for gene therapy and has contributed to approved and investigational therapies for the treatment of previously untreatable diseases.

AstroTurf

DISCOVERY: An artificial turf made of synthetic fibers that looks and feels like grass.

DATE: AstroTurf, which was called "ChemGrass" at the time, was patented and trademarked in 1965. In 1966, it was installed in the Astrodome, the world's first domed stadium, and renamed AstroTurf.

WHO: AstroTurf was created by Chemstrand, a company that specializes in the research, production, and sale of synthetic fibers and was co-owned by Monsanto (an agricultural biotechnology company) and the American Viscose Corporation (a manufacturer of synthetic fibers).

IMPACT: AstroTurf was used to replace real grass in the Astrodome, since the stadium's dome, which blocked light from the sun, made it impossible for actual grass to survive there. It quickly became a popular choice for sporting fields because it could be installed quickly and did not become soggy when it rained. The pace of sports such as baseball and field hockey increased because balls bounced higher and traveled further on AstroTurf than they did on natural grass. Ultimately, due to controversy over whether athletes were more likely to sustain injuries while playing on AstroTurf, most fields used for professional sports shifted back to natural grass. However, AstroTurf remains an incredibly popular choice for high school, college, and minor league fields because it lasts longer and costs less to maintain than natural grass.[5]

LEGACY: Today, the term *AstroTurf* is used to refer to any kind of artificial turf, and athletes across the country compete on more than eleven thousand fields made of artificial turf.[6]

Azidothymidine (AZT)

DISCOVERY: The first antiretroviral drug approved to treat HIV (human immunodeficiency virus)/AIDS (acquired immunodeficiency syndrome).

DATE: AZT was first synthesized in 1964 as a potential treatment for cancer, but it was not until March 20, 1987, that the US Food and Drug Administration approved the prescription sale of AZT as a treatment for AIDS.[7]

WHO: The research on antiviral drugs by Dr. Gertrude Elion, a biochemist at Burroughs Wellcome, provided foundational knowledge crucial to identifying AZT as an effective treatment for HIV/AIDS.

IMPACT: Before 1978, scientists felt that developing antiviral drugs, or drugs that could fight off viruses, was virtually impossible. Early antiviral drugs that were developed proved not to be very selective, making it difficult for them to target and prevent the replication of specific viruses. Additionally, these drugs were often too toxic to the host cell they were introduced to. Elion and her team changed everything when they developed acyclovir, an antiviral drug that can treat herpes viruses. Acyclovir's success proved that antiviral drugs could be selective without being too toxic. This crucial advancement in the study and treatment of viruses paved the way for the development of antiretroviral drugs such as AZT, a type of antiviral drug. Elion herself would go on to advise the team at Burroughs Wellcome that discovered AZT's efficacy in treating HIV and AIDS.[8]

LEGACY: By 1987, when the sale of AZT was approved, 32,825 cases of AIDS had been reported to the US Centers for Disease Control and Prevention, and over half of those cases had resulted in death.[9] Today, the prognosis for patients who have been diagnosed with HIV is far more positive. There are now forty-one antiretroviral drugs approved for treating HIV and AIDS. These drugs work best in combination to target the virus at different times in its life cycle. AZT is still used and is commonly included in these combinations. Today, thanks to the work of Elion, which made it possible for research into the development of antiretroviral drugs such as AZT to take place, people diagnosed with HIV are able to live long, relatively healthy lives.[10]

Fortnite

DEVELOPMENT: A free online video game and game platform that became wildly popular.

DATE: Fortnite was first released on July 25, 2017.[11] Its Battle Royale mode, which truly catapulted the game to stardom, was introduced on September 26, 2017.[12]

WHO: Fortnite is owned and operated by Epic Games, a video-game developer and publisher. The company was born as Potomac Computer Systems but was renamed Epic Games upon its move to Cary, North Carolina, in 1999, where it has been headquartered ever since.[13]

IMPACT: As of May 2024, there were 650 million registered Fortnite players.[14] Like other iconic games such as World of Warcraft and Minecraft, part of Fortnite's success lies in its ability to draw in players who aren't normally gamers.[15] The game is free to play, and it can be played on a variety of platforms, so the barrier for entry is low. Fortnite is constantly evolving and introducing new content, so players are encouraged to keep coming back for more.[16] Some of this new content is exclusive and requires in-game purchases, which provides a source of revenue for Epic Games. Fortnite often collaborates with popular media franchises and musicians to engage players even more and encourage them to spend V-Bucks, which are the game's currency.[17]

LEGACY: Fortnite has revolutionized the video-game industry. Though it was not the first video game to utilize a "battle royale" format, where players fight to be the last one standing, it massively popularized the genre. Similarly, its success in utilizing a "freemium" business model, where players can access the game for free but are encouraged to make in-game purchases, has influenced other games to adopt similar models.[18] Fortnite's influence also stretches beyond the video-game industry. Through its collaborations with various elements of pop culture, such as hosting in-game concerts and allowing players to purchase "skins" that turn their in-game personas into characters from popular franchises, it has been able to serve as a bridge between the gaming world and the mainstream.[19] Additionally, Fortnite's popularity in e-sport events and on streaming platforms (where viewers can watch gamers as they play) have helped bolster public awareness and interest in these entertainment forms.[20]

Human Transplants from Animal Parts (Xenotransplantation)

DISCOVERY: The successful transplants of genetically modified pig organs, such as hearts and kidneys, into living patients.

DATE: The first genetically modified pig heart was successfully transplanted into David Bennett, a patient with a terminal heart disease, in January 2022.[21] Another successful xenoheart transplant took place in 2023, and the first successful transplants of a xenothymokidney (a pig kidney with tissue from the pig's thymus) and a xenokidney took place on April 12, 2024, and November 25, 2024, respectively.[22]

WHO: The UHeart, UThymoKidney, and UKidney (which are the proposed trade names for the transplanted organs) were developed by Revivicor, a subsidiary of United Therapeutics, which is a biotechnology company that develops technologies to expand access to transplantable organs for patients in need.[23] United Therapeutics is headquartered in Silver Springs, Maryland, and Research Triangle Park. United Therapeutics' Regenerative Medicine Laboratory, where lungs and lung lobes are manufactured for transplant, is located in Research Triangle Park.[24]

IMPACT: As of 2024, more than 100,000 Americans were waiting for an organ transplant.[25] The demand for human organs for transplantation far exceeds the supply of them, so patients may be forced to remain on the waiting list for a lifesaving organ for years. For example, the national average wait time for a kidney transplant is five years. According to the Health Resources and Services Administration, seventeen people die each day while on the waiting list for an organ.[26] Animal organs that can be safely transplanted into humans may be able to drastically decrease the amount of time patients must wait to receive a transplant.

LEGACY: David Bennett, the first patient to receive a transplant of a pig heart, lived for two months after the transplant. The second patient to receive a heart xenotransplantation, Laurence Faucette, lived for a little over a month after the transplant. Both of these procedures were performed as experimental surgeries, as Bennett and Faucette were deemed ineligible for human heart transplants. The success of these procedures leaves United Therapeutics hopeful that they will be able to begin human clinical studies in 2025. When the company sees survival in these human studies, it plans to expand its facilities in Research Triangle Park and build two other locations near US heart and kidney transplant centers. These facilities will be able to supply about three thousand organs a year that patients will be able to live out the rest of their lives with.[27]

IBM System/360

DISCOVERY: A family of general-purpose mainframe computers unified under a single architecture.[28]

DATE: IBM introduced the System/360 on April 7, 1964.

WHO: The System/360's chief architect was the computer architect and entrepreneur Gene Amdahl. Fred Brooks, the founder of the computer science department at the University of North Carolina at Chapel Hill, was the project leader. Bob Evans, a vice president at IBM, and Erich Bloch, who later became the director of the National Science Foundation, also contributed to the development of the System/360.

IMPACT: Before the System/360 was introduced, computer software was customized to each machine, which meant that it could run only on the computer it was written for. If consumers bought a new computer, they would need new software specific to that machine as well. This made upgrading computer systems—which was often a necessity, as individual machines were generally designed to accomplish very specific types of tasks—inconvenient and expensive. The System/360 introduced a family of computers that were all compatible with the same software. Consumers could buy a small computer system and upgrade it as needed. This increased flexibility and lower barrier for access made it possible for more companies to buy a computer for the first time. Additionally, as consumers were no longer required to purchase specific machines for specific tasks, the distinction between scientific and commercial computers faded away.[29] On April 14, 1965, a little over a year after the System/360 was introduced, IBM announced that it would be building a manufacturing plant in Research Triangle Park to build parts for System/360 computers.[30]

LEGACY: The System/360 revolutionized how industry and consumers alike thought about designing, building, and using computer systems. It separated software from hardware and introduced the idea of computers as platforms. This platform business model remains popular among technology companies across a variety of industries today. It also sparked the creation of new markets as companies began creating equipment that was compatible with System/360 computers. On a more abstract level, the introduction of the System/360 marked a turning point in the study of computers by shifting the focus beyond the automation of tasks and toward managing more complicated processes through computer systems.[31]

LED Lighting

DISCOVERY: The first commercially available silicon carbide (SiC) blue light-emitting diode (LED).

DATE: Cree introduced the first commercially available SiC blue LED in 1989.

WHO: Cree, now known as Wolfspeed, was an LED lighting manufacturing company that spun out from research on SiC at North Carolina State University. Five of the company's founders—Calvin Carter, Thomas Coleman, John Edmond, Eric Hunter, and John Palmour—earned degrees from NC State from the Department of Materials Science and Engineering.[32] A sixth founder, Neal Hunter, earned a master's of mechanical engineering at NC State at the same time. Cree officially rebranded as Wolfspeed and pivoted toward a focus on its semiconductor technology rather than on LED lighting.

IMPACT: LED lighting has become wildly popular because LED light bulbs last longer and consume less power than other lighting technologies.[33] Before Cree commercialized the blue LED, LEDs were only available in red and green, which limited their potential for use. Making blue LEDs available was crucial because red, green, and blue LEDs can be combined to create any other color of light, including white.[34]

LEGACY: The commercialization of blue LEDs completed the LED color spectrum, allowing manufacturers to create full-color electronic displays. The screens of our televisions, computers, and phones rely on LEDs to create vibrant and colorful displays. Additionally, white LED light, which can only be created using blue LEDs, emits more light than traditional light bulbs can while also using less energy. It has great potential as an alternative light source that can help reduce the amount of electrical energy consumed.[35]

Plant-to-Plant Gene Transfer

DISCOVERY: How to genetically engineer plants by transferring desired genes from one plant kingdom to another.

DATE: 1983.[36]

WHO: Dr. Mary-Dell Chilton and a team of researchers from the University of Washington at St. Louis.

IMPACT: After leading the team of researchers that produced the first transgenic plant in 1983, Chilton moved to North Carolina and became the founding director and vice president of Ciba-Geigy's first biotechnology research lab, located in Research Triangle Park. Under her leadership, Ciba-Geigy, now known as Syngenta, became a global leader in the field of agricultural biotechnology and even became the first company to commercialize a biotechnology trait in corn. Chilton's foundational research allows scientists at Syngenta and across the world to develop crops that produce larger yields and are more resistant to disease, insects, and disadvantageous environmental conditions.[37] She was awarded the World Food Prize in 2013.[38]

LEGACY: Chilton's research ignited an enduring movement for ongoing development of genetically modified organisms (GMOs). Many fellow scientists believe she should have won the Nobel Prize and would have if not for obdurate European opposition to GMOs.

PyroMan

DEVELOPMENT: PyroMan, a life-sized mannequin scientists use to test the efficacy of thermal protective clothing worn by military members, first responders, and industrial workers.[39]

DATE: PyroMan has been used to evaluate the performance of fire- and heat-resistant suits since 1993.[40]

WHO: PyroMan was developed by researchers at the Textile Protection and Comfort Center, which is a part of North Carolina State University's Wilson College of Textiles.[41]

IMPACT: Flames burn at an average of 1,100 degrees Fahrenheit, so it is crucial for firefighters, members of the military, and industrial workers to have access to the most effective personal protective equipment.[42] Studying PyroMan in his fire-test chamber provides scientists with a repeatable and safe way to evaluate the performance of thermal protection gear, as well as how the body reacts to flames and intense heat. Researchers can analyze data recorded by sensors on PyroMan's body to predict whether someone wearing thermally protective clothing would experience tissue-burn injury, where that injury might take place, and how severe that injury might be.[43]

LEGACY: Research on PyroMan has inspired the creation of additional tools such as PyroHands and PyroHead that allow scientists to study the capabilities of thermal protection garments on specific parts of the body.[44] In 2021, researchers began to develop an updated version called Dynamic PyroMan that is able to move. Dynamic PyroMan addresses a major shortcoming of the original PyroMan by more accurately modeling how firefighters behave while in extreme conditions.[45] Dynamic PyroMan will help researchers better understand how thermal protection garments react in more realistic scenarios. Next, researchers anticipate developing a female version of PyroMan.[46]

Taxol® (Generic Name Paclitaxel)

DISCOVERY: A chemotherapy drug made from a compound derived from the bark of the Pacific yew tree (*Taxus brevifolia*).

DATE: Scientists at the Research Triangle Institute identified, isolated, and named the compound from the bark of the Pacific yew tree that would become Taxol® in 1967. They published their findings on the structure of the compound in 1971. A little over twenty years later, in 1992, Taxol® was first approved by the Food and Drug Administration (FDA) for use in cancer treatment.[47]

WHO: Paclitaxel was discovered by Dr. Monroe Wall and Dr. Mansukh Wani, chemists who worked at the Natural Products Laboratory at the Research Triangle Institute.[48]

IMPACT: Taxol® has been used to treat over one million patients.[49] It is approved by the FDA for use in treating ovarian cancer, breast cancer, non–small cell lung cancer, and Kaposi's sarcoma.[50] It is also used off-label to treat cervical, endometrial, gastroesophageal, prostate, head, and neck cancers, along with leukemia, lymphoma, and sarcoma.[51] In response to the drug's efficacy in treating cancer, the World Health Organization recognized it as a medicine crucial to supporting basic health care systems by including it in its Model List of Essential Medicines.[52]

LEGACY: According to the National Cancer Institute, Taxol® remains one of the best cancer treatments based on plants available. Continuing research aims to improve and expand its use in cancer treatment, as well as to better understand how it works so even better drugs can be developed. Researchers are exploring its effect on different types of cancers and how it can be used alongside other cancer drugs in combination therapy.[53] Future challenges may relate to the expensive and unsustainable nature of Taxol®'s production and remaining questions about how tumor cells develop resistance to it.[54]

Universal Product Code

DEVELOPMENT: The Universal Product Code (UPC), a scannable barcode that helps identify a product.

DATE: On April 1, 1973, a symbol selection committee organized by grocery industry leaders in search of a scannable code to be used during the inventory and purchase of items, voted in favor of the UPC. On June 26, 1974, the UPC was swiped for the first time at a Marsh's Supermarket in Ohio.[55]

WHO: George Laurer, an electrical engineer at IBM's Research Triangle Park location, led the team that developed the UPC.[56]

IMPACT: Though many—including manufacturers, who would need to spend substantial amounts of money printing barcodes on their products; labor unions, who feared machines would replace human cashiers; and shoppers, who were uncertain how accurate scanners would be—had their reservations about the usage of barcodes on products, over time, it became clear that it had a variety of benefits. Checkout lines moved 40 percent faster because cashiers no longer had to key in each item. Retailers were able to keep track of their stores' inventory, and they could analyze consumers' purchase history to anticipate demand for products. These combined factors helped to increase profit. The usage of barcodes was so successful in the grocery industry that it later spread to other industries such as factories and libraries.

LEGACY: The UPC provided manufacturers, retailers, and consumers with the ability to track and quantify product-related data. By making it possible to identify material objects digitally, it served as a precursor to modern commerce, where so many products are represented digitally. Additionally, the success of barcodes ushered in the development of strategies and technologies, such as predictive maintenance, advanced analytics, and machine learning.[57]

NOTES

INTRODUCTION

1. Enrico Moretti, *The New Geography of Jobs* (Houghton Mifflin Harcourt, 2013).

CHAPTER 1: BRAIN-DRAIN BLUES

1. John Wilson, "North Carolina's Research Triangle Park: An Investment in the Future," posted April 24, 2010, Vimeo video, https://vimeo.com/11199745.

2. V. O. Key, *Southern Politics in State and Nation* (Alfred A. Knopf, 1949), 205.

3. Key, *Southern Politics in State and Nation*, 207.

4. Key, *Southern Politics in State and Nation*, 211.

5. Mac McCorkle, "History and the 'New Economy' Narrative: The Case of Research Triangle Park and North Carolina's Economic Development," *Journal of the Historical Society* 12, no. 4 (2012): 496.

6. Transcript of oral history of Romeo Guest and William Saunders, January 27, 1980, RL.00486, Romeo Guest Papers, 1925–1987 and undated, David M. Rubenstein Rare Book and Manuscript Library, Durham, North Carolina.

7. Transcript, Romeo Guest Papers.

8. Alex Sayf Cummings, *Brain Magnet: Research Triangle Park and the Idea of the Idea Economy* (Columbia University Press, 2020), 26.

9. Romeo Guest to Senator Arthur Kirkman, January 6, 1956, in Romeo Guest Papers, box 10, Correspondence 1955; "Proposed Statement of Principles for the Research Institute of the Research Triangle," April 23, 1957, in RCP, box 11, Governor Hodges's Archival Papers, 1955–57.

10. Charles W. Wessner, ed., "Best Practices in State and Regional Innovation Initiatives: Competing in the 21st Century," National Institutes of Health, 2013.

11. Albert N. Link, *A Generosity of Spirit: The Early History of the Research Triangle Park* (Research Triangle Foundation of North Carolina, 1995), 13.

12. Romeo Guest, "Conditioned for Research," 1954, RL.00486, Romeo Guest Papers, 1925–1987 and undated, David M. Rubenstein Rare Book and Manuscript Library, Durham, North Carolina.

13. Transcript, Romeo Guest Papers.

14. Morgan P. Abbott, "North Carolina's Research Triangle Park: A Success Story of Private Industry Fostering Public Investment to Create a Homegrown Commercial Park," *Campbell Law Review* 40, no. 2 (2018): 575, https://scholarship.law.campbell.edu/clr/vol40/iss2/6/.

15. Link, *A Generosity of Spirit*, 18.

16. Link, *A Generosity of Spirit*, 18.

17. Link, *A Generosity of Spirit*, 17.

18. Link, *A Generosity of Spirit*, 17.

19. Luther Hodges, *Businessman in the Statehouse: Six Years as Governor of North Carolina* (University of North Carolina Press, 1962), 6.

20. Hodges, *Businessman in the Statehouse*, 6.

21. Hodges, *Businessman in the Statehouse*, 6.

22. Hodges, *Businessman in the Statehouse*, 6–7.

23. Hodges, *Businessman in the Statehouse*, 7.

24. Hodges, *Businessman in the Statehouse*, 9–10.

25. Hodges, *Businessman in the Statehouse*, 10.

26. Hodges, *Businessman in the Statehouse*, 12.

27. Hodges, *Businessman in the Statehouse*, 11.

28. Rob Christensen, *The Paradox of Tar Heel Politics* (University of North Carolina Press, 2010), 157.

29. Christensen, *The Paradox of Tar Heel Politics*, 114.

30. Hodges, *Businessman in the Statehouse*, 18.

31. Hodges, *Businessman in the Statehouse*, 19.

32. Christensen, *The Paradox of Tar Heel Politics*, 158, quoted in Karl Campbell, "From Resurgence to Realignment: The Shelby Dynasty, Luther Hodges, and the Election of 1952," Historical Political Campaigns in North Carolina Conference paper, Chapel Hill, September 14–15, 2012, https://dcr.lib.unc.edu/indexablecontent/14f01559-2b4e-4a4f-a886-da95643bb567.

CHAPTER 2: EARLY COLLABORATIONS

1. Arthur Larentz Carlson, "With All Deliberate Speed: The Pearsall Plan and School Desegregation in North Carolina, 1954–1966," *ScholarShip* (2011): 37, https://thescholarship.ecu.edu/items/144ee73a-b44a-48ca-b5ac-8092bf05648c.

2. Link, *A Generosity of Spirit*, 19.

3. Link, *A Generosity of Spirit*, 20.

4. Transcript, Romeo Guest Papers.

5. Link, *A Generosity of Spirit*, 29.

6. Guest wrote Governor Hodges on January 30, 1955, and asked him to take a leadership role with the park. Link, *A Generosity of Spirit*, 26.

7. Link, *A Generosity of Spirit*, 26.

8. Link, *A Generosity of Spirit*, 27.

9. Link, *A Generosity of Spirit*, 29.

10. Link, *A Generosity of Spirit*, 29.
11. Link, *A Generosity of Spirit*, 30.
12. Link, *A Generosity of Spirit*, 32.
13. Link, *A Generosity of Spirit*, 31.
14. Link, *A Generosity of Spirit*, 32.
15. Charles X. Larrabee, *Many Missions: Research Triangle Institute's First 31 Years, 1959–1990* (Research Triangle Institute, 1991), 57.
16. Link, *A Generosity of Spirit*, 34.
17. Link, *A Generosity of Spirit*, 35.
18. Hodges, *Businessman in the Statehouse*, 161.

CHAPTER 3: INVENTING A NEW PLACE FOR A NEW WORKER

1. Link, *A Generosity of Spirit*, 33.
2. George L. Simpson Jr., "Memorandum on the Research Triangle," November 14, 1956, 05081, series 2.1.1., box 17, folder 193, Research Triangle Foundation Records, 1955–1999, Wilson Special Collections Library, University of North Carolina at Chapel Hill.
3. Simpson, "Memorandum on the Research Triangle."
4. Link, *A Generosity of Spirit*, 101.
5. Link, *A Generosity of Spirit*, 106.
6. Brandon Hodges to George Simpson, December 14, 1956, 05081, box 1, series 1.1., folder 4, Research Triangle Foundation Records, 1955–1999, Wilson Special Collections Library, University of North Carolina at Chapel Hill.
7. Governor's Research Triangle Committee (NC), "A Full Life in the Research Triangle of North Carolina," in *The Research Triangle of North Carolina*, ed. George Simpson Jr. (Research Triangle Committee, 1958), 8.
8. George L. Simpson Jr., "The Research Triangle of North Carolina," February 5, 1957, Romeo Guest Papers, 1925–1987 and undated, David M. Rubenstein Rare Book and Manuscript Library, Durham, North Carolina.
9. Link, *A Generosity of Spirit*, 49.
10. Link, *A Generosity of Spirit*, 42–43.
11. William Little to George L. Simpson Jr., February 20, 1957, box 11, Romeo Guest Papers, 1925–1987 and undated, David M. Rubenstein Rare Book and Manuscript Library, Durham, North Carolina.
12. Liz Rooks, interview by Mack Paul, April 1, 2024.

CHAPTER 4: NEW INSTITUTIONS DEFINE RTP

1. Link, *A Generosity of Spirit*, 122.
2. Link, *A Generosity of Spirit*, 45.
3. Larrabee, *Many Missions*, 5.
4. Howard E. Covington Jr., *Favored by Fortune: George W. Watts and the Hills of Durham* (University of North Carolina Press, 2011), 270.
5. Covington, *Favored by Fortune*.

6. Link, *A Generosity of Spirit*, 46.

7. Austin Dunlow, "Gertrude Mary Cox: Statistical Genius, Groundbreaker and NC State History-Maker," *Technician*, March 24, 2021, https://www.technicianonline.com/arts_culture/gertrude-mary-cox-statistical-genius-groundbreaker-and-nc-state-history-maker/article_ac28b416-8d09-11eb-b76c-4f7fa58e93c4.html.

8. Larrabee, *Many Missions*, 2.

9. Larrabee, *Many Missions*, 5.

10. Larrabee, *Many Missions*, 6.

11. Larrabee, *Many Missions*, 26.

12. Lawson Williams, interview by Allen Paul, October 24, 2022.

13. Larrabee, *Many Missions*, 27.

14. Larrabee, *Many Missions*, 33.

15. Casey and Gordon Herbert (sons of George Herbert), interview by Allen Paul, May 14, 2022.

16. Link, *A Generosity of Spirit*, 52.

17. Transcript, Romeo Guest Papers.

18. Link, *A Generosity of Spirit*, 63.

19. Link, *A Generosity of Spirit*, 68.

20. Link, *A Generosity of Spirit*, 70.

21. Larrabee, *Many Missions*, 70.

22. Link, *A Generosity of Spirit*, 73.

23. Link, *A Generosity of Spirit*, 73.

24. Luther Hodges to Romeo Guest, November 17, 1959, RL.00486, Romeo Guest Papers.

25. Romeo Guest to Thomas Evans, July 22, 1977, RL.00486, Romeo Guest Papers.

CHAPTER 5: BRIDGES TO SUCCESS

1. Joel Lawson Williams (RTI inventor), interview by Allen Paul, October 24, 2022.

2. Williams, interview by A. Paul, October 24, 2022.

3. Williams, interview by A. Paul, October 24, 2022.

4. Williams, interview by A. Paul, October 24, 2022.

5. Williams, interview by A. Paul, October 24, 2022.

6. Williams, interview by A. Paul, October 24, 2022.

7. Nicholas Oberlies (research chemist), interview by Allen Paul, October 28, 2022.

8. Oberlies, interview by A. Paul, October 28, 2022.

9. Oberlies, interview by A. Paul, October 28, 2022.

10. Oberlies, interview by A. Paul, October 28, 2022.

11. Oberlies, interview by A. Paul, October 28, 2022.

12. Oberlies, interview by A. Paul, October 28, 2022.

13. Bob Leak, interview by Allen Paul, May 17, 2021.

14. Leak, interview by A. Paul, May 17, 2021.

15. Leak, interview by A. Paul, May 17, 2021.

16. Linda Harris Edmisten, *J. W. Willie York: His First Seventy-Five Years in Raleigh, An Historical Biography* (1987), 111.

17. Sabine Vollmer, "Planner Devoted Career to RTP" (Raleigh) *News & Observer*, April 8, 2007.

18. Vollmer, "Planner Devoted Career to RTP."

19. Joe Duke, "Research Zone Planned," *Durham Sun* (NC), August 3, 1958.

20. Vollmer, "Planner Devoted Career to RTP."

21. Research Triangle Regional Planning Commission, *Guides for the Research Triangle of North Carolina* (Research Triangle Regional Planning Commission, 1960), 5.

22. Research Triangle Regional Planning Commission, *Guides for the Research Triangle of North Carolina*, 14–16.

23. Carlson, "With All Deliberate Speed," 39.

24. Carlson, "With All Deliberate Speed," 87.

25. Carlson, "With All Deliberate Speed," 75.

26. Carlson, "With All Deliberate Speed," 75.

27. Carlson, "With All Deliberate Speed," 64.

28. Carlson, "With All Deliberate Speed," 78.

29. John Drescher, "Terry Sanford, North Carolina's Governor, Broke Ranks with Segregationists in 1961," *Washington Post*, January 1, 2021, https://www.washingtonpost.com/history/2021/01/01/terry-sanford-north-carolina-race-segregation/.

30. Howard E. Covington and Marion A. Ellis, *Terry Sanford: Politics, Progress, and Outrageous Ambitions* (Duke University Press, 1999), 241.

31. Covington and Ellis, *Terry Sanford*, 239; Sanford's inaugural address, January 5, 1961.

32. "Special Report: Selection of a Site for Chemstrand Research" by David Chaney, 05081, series 2.1.1., box 8, folder 91, Research Triangle Foundation Records, 1955–1999, Wilson Special Collections Library, University of North Carolina at Chapel Hill.

CHAPTER 6: IBM AND VALIDATION AT LAST

1. *The Raleigh Times* was an afternoon paper that ceased publication in 1989. See the IBM publication named *Partners in Progress*, August 1988, 05081, subseries 2.16, box 53, folder 807, Research Triangle Foundation Records, 1955–1999, Wilson Special Collections Library, University of North Carolina at Chapel Hill.

2. Wilson, "North Carolina's Research Triangle Park."

3. Larrabee, *Many Missions*, 73.

4. Wilson, "North Carolina's Research Triangle Park."

5. Wilson, "North Carolina's Research Triangle Park."

6. Phil Carlton, interview by Allen Paul, March 8, 2022.

7. Covington, *Favored by Fortune*, 239.

8. John Schelp (former director of community engagement at the NIEHS), interview by Mack Paul, October 2025.

9. Rep. David Price, interview by Mack Paul, May 9, 2026.

10. Sonya Anderson, "When the U.S. Surgeon General Shocked Americans by Announcing That Smoking Kills," *Smithsonian Magazine*, January 11, 2025.

11. John Schelp, interview by Mack Paul, October 23, 2025.

12. Nick Tennyson, email to Mack Paul, April 2, 2025.

13. Steve Lohr, "Frederick P. Brooks, Jr., Computer Innovator, Dies at 91," *New York Times*, November 23, 2022, https://www.nytimes.com/2022/11/23/technology/frederick-p-brooks-jr-dead.html.

14. Lohr, "Frederick P. Brooks, Jr."

15. James W. Cortada, *IBM: The Rise and Fall and Reinvention of a Global Icon* (MIT Press, 2019), 210–23.

16. Fred Brooks, "Big Lunch with the Big Boss," unpublished paper, May 6, 2019, provided to Allen Paul shortly before Brooks's death in 2022.

17. Fred Brooks, "Introducing Tom Watson to the Research Triangle Park," unpublished paper, July 22, 2013, provided to Allen Paul shortly before Brooks's death in 2022.

18. Frederick Brooks, interview by Allen Paul, 2022.

19. Brooks, "Introducing Tom Watson to the Research Triangle Park."

20. James Hershman, "Massive Resistance," *Encyclopedia Virginia*, December 7, 2020, https://encyclopediavirginia.org/entries/massive-resistance/.

21. "RTP Celebrates 20 Great Years of People, Products and Progress," *Siteline* 1, no. 1 (April 1985): 4.

22. Smedes York, interview by Mack Paul, August 5, 2024.

23. Smedes York, *What We Remember: Personal Recollections of Raleigh in the Mid-Twentieth Century* (Gatekeeper Press, 2021).

24. York, *What We Remember*.

CHAPTER 7: CREATING A VIABLE PUBLIC SCHOOL OPTION

1. Governor Terry Sanford created the Good Neighbor Councils in 1963 as a way to encourage diverse hiring practices and help ensure young people received better job training. Sanford appointed David S. Coltrane, commissioner of Agriculture, as chair and executive director of the Good Neighbor Councils.

2. *Broad v. Board of Education of Topeka*, 349 US 294 (1955), known as *Brown* II.

3. This chapter includes quotations from interviews with Dudley Flood conducted on August 23, 2024, and August 29, 2024, by Mack Paul.

4. Todd Silberman, "Wake County Schools: A Question of Balance," in *Divided We Fail: Coming Together Through Public School Choice* (Century Foundation, 2002).

5. York, *What We Remember*, 460.

6. York, *What We Remember*, 462.

7. York, *What We Remember*, 462.

8. York, *What We Remember*, 462.

9. Harvey Schmitt, interview by Mack Paul, December 16, 2024.

10. Wib Gulley, interview by Mack Paul, September 3, 2024.

11. Silberman, "Wake County Schools."

CHAPTER 8: THE BIRTH OF LIFE SCIENCE

1. Julia Robinson, "Hidden in the Shadow of Henry Wellcome: Silas Mainville Burroughs," *Pharmaceutical Journal*, March 16, 2016, https://pharmaceutical-journal.com/article/news/hidden-in-the-shadow-of-henry-wellcome-silas-mainville-burroughs.

2. "History of Wellcome," https://wellcome.org/about-us/history-wellcome.

3. E. M. Tansey, "Medicines and Men: Burroughs, Wellcome & Co, and the British Drug Industry Before the Second World War," *Journal of the Royal Society of Medicine* 95, no. 8 (2002), https://www.ncbi.nlm.nih.gov/pmc/articles/PMC1279970/.

4. Gabe Cipau (retired B. W. & Co. board member), interview by Allen Paul, September 11, 2023.

5. Cipau, interview by A. Paul; "History of Wellcome."

6. John Wilson, Documentary film on RTP, UNC-TV, https://dcr.lib.unc.edu/record/b6af301b-9feb-4e99-9a66-3b87566db25c/?browse_type=list-display.

7. Typescript of Burroughs Wellcome press release, August 21, 1969, 05081, series 3.3, box 140, folder 2449, Research Triangle Foundation Records, 1955–1999, Wilson Special Collections Library, University of North Carolina at Chapel Hill.

8. Typescript of Burroughs Wellcome press release.

9. Typescript of Burroughs Wellcome press release.

10. Richard Stradling, "RTP Landmark Could Soon Meet the Wrecking Ball," (Raleigh)*News & Observer*, September 18, 2020.

11. Christy Shaffer, interview by Allen Paul, July 6, 2023.

12. "Christy Shaffer, PhD," Hatteras Venture Partners, https://dev.hatterasvp.com/people/christy-shaffer-phd/.

13. Shaffer, interview by A. Paul.

14. Shaffer, interview by A. Paul.

15. Shaffer, interview by A. Paul.

16. "George H. Hitchings Biography (1905–1998)," *FAQs.org*, http://www.faqs.org/health/bios/74/George-H-Hitchings.html.

17. "George H. Hitchings Biography."

18. "George Herbert Hitchings," *Encyclopedia Britannica*, https://www.britannica.com/biography/George-Herbert-Hitchings.

19. "George Herbert Hitchings."

20. Kristine Larsen, "Gertrude Elion," *Jewish Women's Archive*, February 27, 2009, https://jwa.org/encyclopedia/article/elion-gertrude-belle.

21. Larsen, "Gertrude Elion."

22. David Ravenscraft and William Long, "Paths to Creating Value in Pharmaceutical Mergers," in *Mergers and Productivity*, ed. Steven Kaplan (University of Chicago Press, 2000), 311, https://www.nber.org/system/files/chapters/c8653/c8653.pdf.

23. Richard W. Stevenson, "Glaxo Offers $14 Billion for Wellcome," *New York Times*, January 24, 1995.

24. Stevenson, "Glaxo Offers $14 Billion."

25. "History," Burroughs Wellcome Fund, accessed March 5, 2025, https://www.bwfund.org/about/history/.

CHAPTER 9: A FIRST MOVER IN BIOTECH

1. Gerry Hancock, interview by Allen Paul, February 3, 2022.

2. Henry Greely, "The Two Months That Shaped the Future of Biotech," *STAT*, October 17, 2020, https://www.statnews.com/2020/10/17/two-months-in-1980-shaped-the-future-of-biotech/.

3. Maryann P. Feldman and Nichola Lowe, "Restructuring for Resiliance," *Innovations Tecnology Governance Globalization* 6, no. 1 (2011): 129–46.

4. Feldman and Lowe, "Restructuring for Resilience."

5. Hancock, interview by A. Paul.

6. Hancock, interview by A. Paul.

7. Hancock, interview by A. Paul.

8. Hancock, interview by A. Paul.

9. Doug Edgeton, "NCBiotech: Looking Back on 40 Years of Growing NC Life Sciences," North Carolina Biotechnology Center, February 22, 2024, https://www.ncbiotech.org/news/ncbiotech-looking-back-40-years-growing-nc-life-sciences.

10. Charles Hamner, interview by Allen Paul, December 2, 2021.

11. Hamner, interview by A. Paul.

12. Hamner, interview by A. Paul.

13. Steven Burke, interview by Allen Paul, January 12, 2022.

14. Burke, interview by A. Paul.

15. Hamner, interview by A. Paul.

16. Hamner, interview by A. Paul; Jim Hunt, interview by Allen Paul, April 27, 2022.

17. Hamner, interview by A. Paul.

18. Burke, interview by A. Paul.

19. Burke, interview by A. Paul.

20. Hamner, interview by A. Paul.

21. Lynne G. Zucker, Michael R. Darby, and Marilynn B. Brewer, "Intellectual Capital and the Birth of U.S. Biotechnology Enterprises," National Bureau of Economic Resaerch, Working Paper no. 4653, February 1994, https://doi.org/10.3386/w4653.

CHAPTER 10: CASE STUDIES OF TWO SUPERSTAR SCIENTISTS

1. This chapter segment is based on two author interviews with Dr. Mary-Dell Chilton on July 20 and July 27, 2023.

2. Joel Richardson, "Mary-Dell Chilton: The Queen of Agrobacterium," *Thrive*, Spring 2016, https://thrive.g-sdev.com/community/mary-dell-chilton.html.

3. Richardson, "Mary-Dell Chilton."

4. Mary-Dell Chilton, "My Secret Life," *Annual Review of Plant Biology* 69 (2018): 1–20, https://doi.org/10.1146/annurev-arplant-032717-090606.

5. Robert Lefkowitz, interview by Allen Paul, May 29, 2024.

CHAPTER 11: BIG BETS ON INFORMATION TECHNOLOGY

1. Manuel Castells, *The Rise of the Network Society* (Wiley-Blackwell, 1996), 39. *The Rise of the Network Society* recounts the evolution of information technology and the birth of the IT industry in the 1970s.

2. Castell, *The Rise of the Network Society*, 62.

3. Castell, *The Rise of the Network Society*, 46–51. The shock of Sputnik's launch in 1957 led the Department of Defense to charge the Advanced Research Projects Agency with

a number of initiatives, including the design of a self-contained communications system immune to nuclear attack. In response, engineers conceived a system that functioned independently of a control center. Messages found their destination along routes in a network. The first computer network went online in 1969. Before long, scientists, academics, and others had access to the network and improved its functionality. By the 1990s, commercial pressures and the proliferation of private networks led to an end of government sponsorship of the internet. Once privatized, the internet proliferated and improved rapidly with the launching of the World Wide Web.

4. "UPC: The Transformation of Retail," IBM at 100, IBM, https://web.archive.org/web/20221207211542/https://www.ibm.com/ibm/history/ibm100/us/en/icons/uPC/transform/.

5. "UPC: The Transformation of Retail."

6. "UPC: The Transformation of Retail."

7. Dennis Kekas (former director for IBM's Point of Sale Division), interview by Mack Paul, 2025.

8. "UPC: The Transformation of Retail."

9. James W. Cortada, "How the IBM PC Won, then Lost, the Personal Computer Market," *IEEE Spectrum*, July 21, 2021, https://spectrum.ieee.org/how-the-ibm-pc-won-then-lost-the-personal-computer-market.

10. Dick Daugherty, interview by Allen Paul, May 22, 2022. Daugherty was general manager of IBM/RTP from 1973 to 1988 and vice president from 1988 to 1994.

11. Daugherty, interview by A. Paul.

12. Will Sexton, "DUCC, TUCC and the Origins of Digital Computing in North Carolina," *Bitstreams: The Digital Collections Blog*, Duke University Libraries, April 3, 2020, https://blogs.library.duke.edu/bitstreams/2020/04/03/ducc-tucc-and-the-origins-of-digital-computing-in-north-carolina/.

13. Brooks, interview by A. Paul.

14. Triangle Universities Computation Center (TUCC) Records, 1965–73, Wilson Special Collections Library, University of North Carolina at Chapel Hill.

15. Daugherty, interview by A. Paul; Cortada, "How the IBM PC Won."

16. Maryann P. Feldman and Nichola J. Lowe, "Restructuring for Resilience," *Innovations: Technology, Governance, Globalization* 6, no. 1 (2011): 129–46.

17. Feldman and Lowe, "Restructuring for Resilience," 132.

18. Around this same time, the federal government made a major investment to enhance US competition in microchips through the Defense Advanced Research Projects Agency. Known as SEMATECH (Semiconductor Manufacturing Technology), the initiative represented a consortium of chipmakers, universities, research institutes, and government. It located in Austin, Texas, in 1988.

19. Ted Vaden, "Electronics Industry Brings Boom and Problems," (Raleigh) *News & Observer*, December 28, 1980.

20. Ted Vaden, "N.C. Uses Hard Sell on Electronics Firms," (Raleigh) *News & Observer*, December 31, 1980.

21. Feldman and Lowe, "Restructuring for Resilience," 133.

22. Feldman and Lowe, "Restructuring for Resilience," 133.

23. Feldman and Lowe, "Restructuring for Resilience," 136.

24. Holt Anderson, interview by Mack Paul, September 11, 2024.

25. Anderson, interview by M. Paul.

26. Feldman and Lowe, "Restructuring for Resilience," 137.

27. Governor Hunt would use this term in the 1990s as a way to describe increased connectivity in the state. It started with the universities but would continue with personal computers and internet access. As more and more institutions and individuals became connected, the goal shifted to ending the "digital divide" for rural areas.

28. Anderson, interview by M. Paul.

29. Anderson, interview by M. Paul.

30. Albert Link, *From Seed to Harvest: The Growth of the Research Triangle Park* (University of North Carolina Press, 2002), 96.

31. TUCC Records, Duke University Archives, David M. Rubenstein Rare Book and Manuscript Library, Duke University, Durham, NC. In September 1990, TUCC's board made the decision to disband the organization. MCNC had supplanted TUCC from the standpoint of possessing a supercomputer and providing network connectivity with the universities.

32. TUCC Records, Duke University Archives.

33. TUCC Records, Duke University Archives. It should be noted that as MCNC took on an increasing role in connecting the universities to computing power, the need for TUCC decreased. TUCC had pursued a supercomputer in the mid-1980s and failed to secure it. TUCC shuttered its doors in 1990.

34. Anderson, interview by M. Paul. MCNC chose to install a Cray 2 supercomputer. At the time, this model was a state-of-the-art supercomputer. There was some understandable pushback over not selecting an IBM model, given the company's large presence in North Carolina.

35. Link, *From Seed to Harvest*, 97.

36. Mark Johnson, interview by Mack Paul, February 2025.

37. Lee Weisbecker, "JDS Stock Sale Has MCNC Flush," *Triangle Business Journal*, August 28, 2002, https://www.bizjournals.com/triangle/stories/2000/08/28/story1.html.

38. Jean Davis (former director of MCNC), interview by Mack Paul, February 13, 2025.

39. Ed Carney, interview by Mack Paul, March 31, 2025.

40. Kekas, interview by M. Paul.

41. Carney, interview by M. Paul. Ed Carney cites a comment made by John Morgridge, former president and CEO of Cisco, in the local media. Morgridge acknowledged a desire to attract "network nerds" as a reason to come to RTP.

42. Carney, interview by M. Paul.

43. Johnson, interview by M. Paul.

44. Executives such as Tom Rabon, formerly of Lucent Technologies; Ed Carney of IBM and Cisco; and many others have served on MCNC's board.

CHAPTER 12: AVATARS OF UNIVERSITY DYNAMISM

1. Link, *A Generosity of Spirit*, 29.

2. Note George Simpson's research work on the Coker family's impact in South Carolina as a unique example of industrial development in the South.

3. Margaret O'Mara, *The Code: Silicon Valley and the Remaking of America* (Penguin, 2020), 32. Chapter 2, entitled "Golden State," describes the interplay between university research and industrial development. In particular, the relationship between Fred Terman, Stanford's dean of the School of Engineering, actively promoted this approach as distinct from the more conservative approach at MIT and Harvard.

4. Peter High, "An Interview with the Godfather of Data Analytics," *Forbes*, May 12, 2014, https://www.forbes.com/sites/peterhigh/2014/05/12/an-interview-with-the-godfather-of-data-analytics-sass-jim-goodnight/.

5. Jim Goodnight, interview by Mack Paul, April 9, 2025.

6. Goodnight, interview by M. Paul.

7. Email from Liz Rooks to Mack Paul, September 7, 2025.

8. Email from John Sall on September 16, 2025.

9. Andy Hayler, "SAS—Who Dares Wins in Database Analytics," *Bloor*, March 11, 2024, https://bloorresearch.com/2024/03/sas-who-dares-wins-in-database-analytics/.

10. "SAS," *Great Place to Work*, https://www.greatplacetowork.com/worlds-best-profile/sas, accessed November 6, 2025.

11. "Booming Triangle Sector Has Nearly 24,500 workers, Up 4 Percent Year-over-Year—List Insights," Research Triangle Regional Partnership, February 19, 2020, https://researchtriangle.org/news/booming-triangle-sector-has-nearly-24500-workers-up-4-percent-year-over-year-list-insights/.

12. Greenberg later became the first dean of the School of Public Health at UNC.

13. Matthew Herper, "Money, Math and Medicine," *Forbes*, November 3, 2010, https://www.forbes.com/forbes/2010/1122/private-companies-10-quintiles-dennis-gillings-money-medicine.html.

14. Paula Brown Stafford, interview by Allen Paul and Mack Paul, December 7, 2023.

15. Peter Mansell, "Quintiles Raises US$947.4 Million in Second IPO," *PharmaTimes*, May 14, 2013, https://pharmatimes.com/news/quintiles_raises_us947-4_million_in_second_ipo_1005013/.

16. Herper, "Money, Math and Medicine."

17. Stafford, interview by A. Paul and M. Paul.

18. Stafford, interview by A. Paul and M. Paul.

19. Neal Hunter, interview by Allen Paul and Mack Paul, June 8, 2024.

20. The founders who were students at NC State included John Edmond, John Palmer, and Calvin Carter. Tom Coleman worked at MCNC.

21. Hunter, interview by A. Paul and M. Paul.

22. Hunter, interview by A. Paul and M. Paul.

23. Hunter, interview by A. Paul and M. Paul.

24. Davis, interview by A. Paul.

CHAPTER 13: THE EMERGENCE OF A START-UP CULTURE

1. Michael Luger and Harvey Goldstein, *Technology in the Garden: Research Parks and Regional Economic Development* (University of North Carolina Press, 1991).

2. Luger and Goldstein, *Technology in the Garden*, 97.

3. Luger and Goldstein, *Technology in the Garden*, 76.

4. Luger and Goldstein, *Technology in the Garden*, 98.

5. Luger and Goldstein, *Technology in the Garden*, 99.

6. Fred Hutchison, interview by Mack Paul, December 2024.

7. Hutchison, interview by M. Paul.

8. Dennis Dougherty, interview by Allen Paul, 2024.

9. Dougherty, interview by A. Paul.

10. Monica Doss, interview by Mack Paul, August 19, 2025.

11. The New Technology Jobs Act, House Bill 1122, created the North Carolina Technology Development Authority as a state agency. It had a twelve-member board. The governor appointed eight members and the General Assembly appointed four. Its mandate was to "stimulate the development of existing new small businesses."

12. Mary Musacchia, interview by Mack Paul, January 7, 2025.

13. John Manuel, "Peak Interest," *Business North Carolina*, July 1990.

14. Manuel, "Peak Interest."

15. Senate Bill 919 was introduced by Senator Bob Martin of Pitt County. It made the transfer of assets effective on September 1, 1991.

16. Margaret Knox, "Science and Technology Research Center to Fold," *North Carolina Beacon*, May 30, 1991.

17. John Pickering, "First Flight Takes Wing with First Tenants," *North Carolina Beacon*, October 17, 1991.

18. Zac Ezzone, "RTP Biotech Sees Promise with New Drug," *Triangle Business Journal*, March 13–19, 2026.

19. Margaret Knox, "Brent Lane Returns to RTP as Head of First Flight, Inc.," *North Carolina Beacon*, August 26, 1993.

20. Mary Musacchia interview by Mack Paul, March 16, 2026.

CHAPTER 14: RTP SHAPES A REGION

1. Research Triangle Regional Planning Commission, *Research Triangle Region Development Guide* (1969), 2, https://digital.ncdcr.gov/Documents/Detail/research-triangle-region-development-guide-with-special-emphasis-being-given-to-plans-for-water-and-sewer-facilities-to-the-provision-of-open-spaces-both-public-and-private-. . . /3690669?item=5232313.

2. Research Triangle Regional Planning Commission, *Research Triangle Region Development Guide*, 2.

3. Chuck Flink, interview by Mack Paul, July 8, 2024.

4. Liz Rooks, interview by Mack Paul, March 20, 2024.

5. Luger and Goldstein, *Technology in the Garden*, 78.

6. Rooks, interview by M. Paul.

7. John Atkins, interview by Mack Paul, November 12, 2024.

8. Atkins, interview by M. Paul.

9. *Fortune* article by Kenneth Labich, November 15, 1993.

10. Charles Hayes, interview by Mack Paul, November 18, 2024.

11. Hayes, interview by M. Paul.

12. Hill Carrow, interview by Mack Paul, November 28, 2024.

13. York, *What We Remember*.

14. Wib Gulley, interview by Mack Paul, September 3, 2024.

15. Neal R. Peirce, Curtis W. Johnson, and John Stuart Hall, *Citistates: How Urban America Can Prosper in a Competitive World* (Seven Locks Press, 1994), 2.

16. Peirce et al., *Citistates*, 37.

17. Neal Peirce, "The Peirce Report," (series), (Raleigh) *News & Observer*, 1993.

18. *Durham Herald*, April 25, 1998.

19. Joel Kotkin, *The New Geography: How the Digital Revolution Is Reshaping the American Landscape* (Random House, 2000), 40.

20. Kotkin, *The New Geography*, 41.

21. Stuart Leavenworth, "Caryites Want to Apply Brakes to Growth," (Raleigh) *News & Observer*, September 2000.

22. Ron Hunter, interview by Mack Paul, December 4, 2024.

CHAPTER 15: SETBACKS OF THE EARLY 2000S

1. Jim Edwards, "One of the Kings of the '90s Dot-Com Bubble Now Faces 20 Years in Prison," *Business Insider*, December 6, 2016.

2. Robert E. Litan, "The Telecommunications Crash: What to Do Now?," Brookings Institution, December 1, 2002.

3. Ed Carney, interview by Mack Paul, March 31, 2025.

4. Kotkin, *The New Geography*, 16.

5. Kotkin, *The New Geography*, 29.

6. Kotkin, *The New Geography*, 8.

7. Richard Florida, *The Rise of the Creative Class and How It's Transforming Work, Leisure Community and Everyday Life* (Basic Books, 2002), 232.

8. Florida, *The Rise of the Creative Class*, 244.

9. Reid Ewing, Rolf Pendall, and Don Chen, *Measuring Sprawl and Its Impact* (Smart Growth America, 2002).

10. Ewing et al., *Measuring Sprawl and Its Impact*, 284.

11. Ewing et al., *Measuring Sprawl and Its Impact*.

12. Charles Meeker, interview by Mack Paul, December 13, 2024.

13. Meeker, interview by M. Paul.

14. Bill Bell, interview by Mack Paul, October 8, 2024.

15. William Rohe, *The Research Triangle: From Tobacco Road to Global Prominence*, (University of Pennsylvania Press, 2011), covers Durham's renaissance on pages 190–200.

16. "Duke's Role in Durham Development: A Chat with Scott Selig," *Building Bull City*, June 11, 2018, https://www.buildingbullcity.com/2018/06/dukes-role-in-durham-development-chat.html.

17. Meeker, interview by M. Paul, relaying the monthly meetings among the mayors in the early 1990s. There were no more World Class Region Conferences sponsored by TJCOG and RTP. Policy action had shifted to the cities.

18. Meeker, interview by M. Paul.

19. Blake Corbitt, Jonathan Liu, Marc Losito, and Andrew McGannon, "The Triangle's MSAs and Economic Development," North Carolina Economic Development Association, April 2021, https://www.nceda.org/wp-content/uploads/2021/12/804-NCSU-Client-Report.pdf.

20. Corbitt et al., "The Triangle's MSAs." RTF President Scott Levitan is quoted as saying, "On paper, we don't compete well. We look like two separate markets, which isn't the case. . . . [I]t takes a lot of work to get past the MSA divide."

21. Rohe's *The Research Triangle* provides a comprehensive overview of the transit plan on pages 208–18.

22. Rohe's *The Research Triangle* describes the Reality Check exercise on pages 229–33.

23. Results Report: Reality Check North Carolina Triangle Region, 1, https://townofchapelhill.org/agendas/2010/02/22/5b/5b-2-reality_check_report-reality_check.pdf.

24. TJCOG prepared materials for Reality Check participants to prepare for the exercise. They encouraged bold thinking and did not place constraints on where development occurred, including in RTP. The RTF made no formal written statement about its restrictions—only through conversations with organizers.

25. Email from Pam Wall (former executive director of Triangle Tomorrow) to Mack Paul, May 21, 2025.

26. These figures are cited in Toby Parcel and Andrew Taylor, *The End of Consensus: Diversity, Neighborhoods, and the Politics of Public School Assignments* (University of North Carolina Press, 2015), 23.

27. "Keung Hui, "Money from Bonds Will Go to Work Soon," (Raleigh) *News & Observer*, November 8, 2006.

28. Toby L. Parcel and Andrew J. Taylor, *The End of Consensus: Diversity, Neighborhoods, and the Politics of School Assignments* (University of North Carolina Press, 2015).

29. Kinea White Epps, "Wake Schools Fight Goes Year-Round," (Raleigh) *News & Observer*, July 31, 2007.

30. In January 2000, Wake County shifted its diversity policy from race to income based on the percentage of students on free and reduced lunch. This shift was approved in response to federal court cases prohibited race-based student assignments.

31. Stephanie McCrummen, "Republican School Board in N.C. Backed by Tea Party Abolishes Integration Policy," *Washington Post*, January 12, 2011; Associated Press, "US Schools Chief Criticizes NC Board over Busing," January 14, 2011.

CHAPTER 17: AGTECH ADDS DEPTH TO THE BIOTECH REVOLUTION

1. This chapter segment is based on author interviews with Norris Tolson on June 21 and July 19, 2023.

2. Richard Linton (Agtech), interview by Allen Paul, June 21, 2023.

3. "Ag Data Science," Research Triangle AgTech Cluster, https://researchtriangleagtechcluster.org/ag-data-science/, last accessed February 25, 2026.

4. "What Is Food Science?," McGill University, archived September 27, 2011, at the Wayback Machine, https://web.archive.org/web/20111228142810/https://www.mcgill.ca/foodscience/what-food-science.

5. Adam Wagner, "Bezos Fund Gives NC State $30 Million to Develop Sustainable Protein, Fight Climate Change," (Raleigh) *News & Observer*, July 24, 2025.

6. "Bayer Crop Science Makes Official Moving Jobs from RTP but BASF Deal Has Lessened Impact," *WRAL-TV Techwire*, July 18, 2019.

7. Paul Ulanch (Agtech), interview by Allen Paul, October 19, 2023.

8. "About Alexandria," Alexandria Real Estate, https://www.are.com/about.html, last accessed February 25, 2026.

9. "Purpose-Built to Accelerate Innovation & Growth: Everything You Need to Thrive," Alexandria LaunchLabs, https://www.alexandrialaunchlabs.com/, last accessed February 25, 2026.

10. "Why LaunchLabs," Alexandria LaunchLabs, https://www.alexandrialaunchlabs.com/why-launchlabs/, last accessed February 25, 2026.

11. Todd Rands (Agtech), interview by Allen Paul, October 19, 2023.

12. Brendan Collins (Agtech), interview by Allen Paul, October 17, 2023.

13. Mariano Alvarez (Agtech), interview by Allen Paul, October 17, 2023.

CHAPTER 18: ADVANCED MANUFACTURING COMES TO THE TRIANGLE

1. Kurt Jacobsen, *Novo Nordisk* (Gad Publishers, 1970), 24.

2. Jacobsen, *Novo Nordisk*, 35.

3. Mads Øvlisen, interview by Allen Paul, January 3, 2024.

4. Øvlisen, interview by A. Paul.

5. Øvlisen, interview by A. Paul.

CHAPTER 19: GENE THERAPY GAINS ACCEPTANCE

1. Meir Rinde, "The Death of Jesse Gelsinger, Twenty Years Later," *Distillations Magazine*, June 4, 2019, https://www.sciencehistory.org/stories/magazine/the-death-of-jesse-gelsinger-20-years-later/. For the monthly cost of pills, see Paul Gelsinger, "Jesse's Intent," *Guinea Pig Zero*, https://www.guineapigzero.com/jesses-intent.html, last accessed February 25, 2026.

2. Rinde, "The Death of Jesse Gelsinger."

3. "Pfizer & Gene Therapy: Breakthroughs that Change Patients' Lives," flyer issued by Pfizer Rare Disease.

4. Gelsinger, "Jesse's Intent."

5. Rinde, "The Death of Jesse Gelsinger."

6. Subsequent to Jesse's death, an FDA investigation found that researchers had broken several rules of conduct, mainly in the informed-consent process. The FDA fined the Penn Institute for Gene Therapy $500,000. The Gelsinger family sued, and the university quickly settled for an undisclosed sum but declined to take responsibility for Jesse's death. In January 2000 the FDA suspended human research at the Penn institute, and the university eventually shut the program down.

7. Sheila Mikhail, interview by Allen Paul, March 28, 2022. AskBio has commercialized several gene therapy cures.

8. Marc Derewicz, "From the Ashes, a Cure," *Carolina Alumni Review*, University of North Carolina at Chapel Hill, January 21, 2022, https://alumni.unc.edu/news/from-the-ashes-a-cure/.

9. Derewicz, "From the Ashes, a Cure"; Mikhail, interview by A. Paul.

10. Sperry Krueger (from the Intelligence Unit at NCBiotech), email to Allen Paul, August 16, 2022.

11. Krueger, email to Allen Paul; Mikhail, interview by A. Paul.

12. Mikhail, interview by A. Paul; Derewicz, "From the Ashes, a Cure."

13. Derewicz, "From the Ashes, a Cure"; Mikhail, interview by A. Paul.

14. Mikhail, interview by A. Paul; Derewicz, "From the Ashes, a Cure."

15. Jessica and Chris Curran, interview by Allen Paul, March 5, 2022.

16. "Bayer Acquires Asklepios BioPharmaceutical to Broaden Innovation Base in Cell and Gene Therapy," Bayer Global, October 26, 2020, https://www.bayer.com/media/en-us/bayer-acquires-asklepios-biopharmaceutical-to-broaden-innovation-base-in-cell-and-gene-therapy/.

CHAPTER 20: BIG TECH AND ITS PROGENY

1. Brian Gordon, "How a Little Triangle Startup Took on Microsoft . . . and Won," (Raleigh) *News & Observer*, April 30, 2023. This was the first of a four-part series authored by Gordon on the history of Red Hat through its acquisition by IBM.

2. Gordon, "How a Little Triangle Startup."

3. Gordon, "How a Little Triangle Startup."

4. Fred Hutchison, interview by Allen Paul and Mack Paul, November 19, 2025.

5. Hutchison, interview by A. Paul and M. Paul.

6. Tom Rabon, interview by Mack Paul, November 20, 2025.

7. Rabon, interview by M. Paul.

8. Brian Gordon, "After Flirting with NC Exit, Red Hat Enters the Raleigh Skyline," (Raleigh) *News & Observer*, April 29, 2023.

9. Gordon, "After Flirting with NC Exit."

10. Rabon, interview by M. Paul.

11. Rabon, interview by M. Paul.

12. Brian Gordon, "Raleigh's Red Hat Has Delivered in Five Years Under IBM," (Raleigh) *News & Observer*, November 8, 2024.

13. Ron Miller and Alex Wilhelm, "Red Hat Saved IBM's Bacon This Quarter," *TechCrunch*, July 21, 2023.

14. Miller and Wilhelm, "Red Hat Saved IBM's Bacon."

15. Mike MacMillan, "Big Money for NC Tech Stars Comes from Out of State," *Business NC*, January 4, 2019.

16. Rabon, interview by M. Paul.

17. On background, interview by Mack Paul, March 15, 2026.

18. "Fidelity Picks RTP for 2000 Jobs," *Triangle Business Journal*, December 28, 2007.

19. "Fidelity Pledges $25 Million to Support Minority Students," ABC11, January 17, 2023.

20. Zachary Eanes, "Raleigh Was a Top Three Finalist for Amazon HQ, Says New Book," (Raleigh) *News & Observer*, May 14, 2021.

21. Brad Stone, *Amazon Unbound: Jeff Bezos and the Invention of a Global Empire* (Simon and Schuster, 2021).

22. Kekas, interview by Mack Paul, 2025.

23. "After Apple's Decision the Big Question for North Carolina: 'Why Can't We Land the Big One'," *WRAL Techwire*, December 14, 2018.

24. Dan Barkin, "Comparing Apple's Impact to IBM's RTP Launch in the Mid-1960s," *Business NC*, May 3, 2021.

25. Josh Lawson, interview by Mack Paul, 2025.

26. Lauren Ohnesorge, "Apple Still Quietly Grows in NC Despite Hiccups," *Triangle Business Journal*, December 5–11, 2025.

27. Lawson, interview by M. Paul.

28. Papers of Brian Eller, assistant vice chancellor of the Office of Technology Licensing at NC State.

29. Brian Gordon, "Wolfspeed Post-Bankruptcy Gets $700 Million Through CHIPS Act for Chatham Facility," (Raleigh) *News & Observer*, December 4, 2025.

30. Mitch Mumma, interview by Mack Paul, December 1, 2025.

31. Mumma, interview by M. Paul.

32. Tim Bajarin, "The 20th Anniversary of Lenovo-IBM Deal That Reshaped the PC Industry," *Forbes*, May 6, 2025.

CHAPTER 21: NEW LEAPS IN UNIVERSITY COMMERCIALIZATION

1. Robin Rasor, interview by Allen Paul, March 6, 2024.

2. Rasor, interview by A. Paul.

3. Rasor, interview by A. Paul.

4. Rasor, interview by A. Paul.

5. Rasor, interview by A. Paul.

6. Jungsang Kim, interview by Allen Paul, December 6, 2024.

7. Kim, interview by A. Paul.

8. Kim, interview by A. Paul.

9. Kim, interview by A. Paul.

10. Kim, interview by A. Paul.

11. David Smith, interview by Allen Paul, March 31, 2025.

12. "Advanced Security Detection Technology for a Safer World," Evolv, https://evolv.com/, last accessed February 26, 2026.

13. Scott Huler, "Weird Science," *Duke Magazine*, May 29, 2024, https://dukemag.duke.edu/stories/weird-science.

14. H. I. Sutton, "Uncrewed Platforms Have Been Critical to Ukraine's Success in the Black Sea," *RUSI Journal*, August 20, 2024, https://www.rusi.org/explore-our-research/publications/commentary/uncrewed-platforms-have-been-critical-ukraines-success-black-sea.

15. Sutton, "Uncrewed Platforms."

16. Sutton, "Uncrewed Platforms"; Rasor, interview by A. Paul.

17. Lisa Coston Hill, "Transformational Investment in Biomedical Engineering Deepens Lampe Family Legacy," *Giving News*, North Carolina State University, February 12, 2025, https://news.giving.ncsu.edu/2025/02/transformational-investment-in-biomedical-engineering-deepens-lampe-family-legacy/.

18. Annalee Saxenian, *Regional Advantage: Culture and Competition in Silicon Valley and Route 128* (Harvard University Press, 1994).

19. Brian Gordon, "Funding Cut, Research Ended, Jobs Lost: How Trump 2.0 Has Altered NC's Research Triangle," (Raleigh) *News & Observer*, July 17, 2025.

20. Laura Leslie, "Triangle at the Epicenter of Proposed Cuts to Federal Funding for National Research," WRAL, August 22, 2025.

21. Leslie, "Triangle at the Epicenter."

22. Zac Ezzone, "What's Next for Life Sciences," *Triangle Business Journal*, November 26, 2025.

CHAPTER 22: BIG PHARMA EMBRACES NORTH CAROLINA

1. Gary Shope, interview by Allen Paul, August 15, 2024.

2. Jim Mullen, interview by Allen Paul, September 12, 2024.

3. Shope, interview by A. Paul.

4. Mullen, interview by A. Paul.

5. Irena Krstanovic, interview by Allen Paul, March 11, 2025.

6. Mayefskie quote provided by Irena Krstanovic, March 3, 2025.

7. Bill Bullock, interview by Mack Paul, October 7, 2025.

8. Bullock, interview by M. Paul.

9. Toshi Iida, interview by Allen Paul, December 3, 2024.

10. Robert A. Bradway, chairman and CEO of Amgen, company announcement, 2024.

11. Magnus Ohman, interview by Allen Paul, December 13, 2024.

12. Keaton Eberly and Maggie Newland, "U.S. Biotech Company to Bring 400 Jobs for New Plant in Wake County," CBS 17, May 12, 2025.

13. Miles Ruder, "Ribbon Cutting at New Eli Lilly Facility," WCCB Charlotte, June 15, 2024.

14. "'The Bigger Picture Is Grim': Yes, Mass. Snagged Hasbro but Can It Compete with North Carolina?," *Boston Globe*, October 6, 2025, https://www.bostonglobe.com/2025/10/06/opinion/hasbro-business-climate-competitiveness/.

CHAPTER 23: RTP 3.0

1. Brook Caine and Chyna Blackmon, "A List of Durham References and Hidden Clues in 'Stranger Things' Seasons 1–5," (Raleigh) *News & Observer*, December 1, 2025.

2. David Bracken, "RTP Begins Updating Its Master Plan," (Raleigh) *News & Observer*, September 4, 2010.

3. Bob Geolas, interview by Allen Paul, May 27, 2021.

4. Geolas, interview by A. Paul.

5. Editorial Board, "A Bold Plan Renews RTP," (Raleigh) *News & Observer*, October 2, 2015.

6. Geolas, interview by A. Paul.

7. "2025 Space Awards: Pillar Award Winner Scott Levitan," *Triangle Business Journal*, February 14, 2025; Laura Ohnesorge, "Space Award," *Triangle Business Journal*, February 13, 2024.

8. Ohnesorge, "2025 Space Award."

9. Zachery Eanes, "An Insider's Look at RTP's Biggest Projects and What Apple's Arrival Means for the Future," (Raleigh) *News & Observer*, June 3, 2021.

10. Ben Bokun, "RTP's New Downtown Takes Form with $1.5 Billion Project," CBS 17, April 5, 2023.

11. Scott Levitan, interview by Mack Paul, April 17, 2025.

12. Levitan, interview by M. Paul.

13. RTP companies expressed concerns about RTP 3.0 on background to the authors. Those concerns related to the lack of a master plan to control future development and inadequate infrastructure to accommodate increased density. However, these owners supported the efforts of the RTF and did not want to oppose those efforts publicly.

14. Ohnesorge, "2025 Space Award."

15. Travis Crayton, interview by Mack Paul, February 12, 2025.

16. Adrienne Cole, interview by Mack Paul, June 12, 2025.

CHAPTER 24: "A FULL LIFE IN THE RESEARCH TRIANGLE"

1. Scott Huler, "Raleigh's Amazing Greenway," *Walter Magazine*.

2. US Representative Deborah Ross, interview by Mack Paul, June 3, 2025.

3. Jeff Mann (former CEO of GoTriangle), interview by Mack Paul, June 4, 2025.

4. Mann, interview by M. Paul.

5. Ross, interview by M. Paul.

6. Wake Transit Plan timeline published by RaleighForward, https://gotriangle.org/waketransit.

7. Paul Specht, "Wake County Voters Approve Tax Hike for Transit," (Raleigh) *News & Observer*, November 9, 2016.

8. Mann, interview by M. Paul.

9. Mann, interview by M. Paul.

10. Mary-Ann Baldwin, interview by Mack Paul, May 17, 2025.

11. Wib Gulley, interview by Mack Paul, September 3, 2024.

12. John Hodges-Copple, interview by Mack Paul, February 6, 2025.

13. Hodges-Copple, interview by M. Paul.

14. Kinder Institute for Urban Research, "The Urban Sun Belt: An Overview," June 2020.

15. Zachery Eanes, "GoTriangle's CEO: BRT Could Play a Key Role in the Triangle's Future," *Axios*, June 16, 2025.

16. Sig Hutchinson (former chair of the Wake County Commission and member of GoTriangle), interview by Mack Paul, May 20, 2025.

17. Wendy Jacobs, interview by Mack Paul, November 24, 2025.

18. Eric Mulata (Dalian Development based in Washington, DC), interview by Mack Paul, November 2025.

19. Francis Rozange, "Decoding Generational Shifts in Vehicle Ownership: From Possession to Experience," *Automotive Market Research*, February 27, 2025.

20. Mann, interview by M. Paul, June 4, 2025; Will Allen (who served on the GoTriangle board and resigned in 2024 after the board voted to forgo commuter rail), interview by Mack Paul, August 8, 2025.

21. Chris Heagarty (chair of Wake County Public Schools), interview by Mack Paul, May 15, 2025.

22. J. B. Buxton (former deputy superintendent of the NC Department of Public Instruction), interview by Mack Paul, June 5, 2025.

23. David Bass, NC Private, "Home and Charter School Enrollment Continue Upward Trend," *Carolina Journal*, June 6, 2024.

24. Becky Harper, Compass Realty, interview by Mack Paul on June 11, 2025.

25. Cole, interview by M. Paul.

26. Vivian Jones, interview by Mack Paul, May 23, 2025.

27. City of Raleigh 2030 Comprehensive Plan, Framework, chapter 2, https://user-2081353526cld.bz/2030Comprehensiveplanupdate.

CHAPTER 25: ASSESSING RTP'S RECORD

1. Moretti, *The New Geography of Jobs*, 197–203.

2. Ojugbele Bakre, "Big Push Economic Development Theory for Sustainable Growth in No Poverty," Encyclopedia of the UN Sustainable Development Goals (2021).

3. Scott Ralls, president of Wake Tech Community College, interview by Allen Paul and Mack Paul, November 6, 2023.

4. David Carlton and Peter Coclanis, "Southern Economic Commentary in Historical Perspective," in *A Way Forward: Building a Globally Competitive South* (UNC Global Research Institute, 2011).

5. The figures come from the Federal Reserve Bank of St. Louis, which maintains comprehensive economic data on all states.

6. Richard Florida, *The New Urban Crisis: How Our Cities Are Increasing Inequality, Deepening Segregation, and Failing the Middle Class and What We Can do About It* (Basic Books, 2017), 85.

7. Raj Chetty, Nathaniel Hendren, Patrick Kline, and Emmanuel Saez, "Where Is the Land of Opportunity? The Geography of Intergenerational Mobility in the United States," *Quarterly Journal of Economics* 129, no. 4 (2014): 1553–1623.

8. Raj Chetty, Nathaniel Hendren, John Friedman, Maggie Jones, and Sonya Port, "The Opportunity Atlas: Mapping the Childhood Roots of Social Mobility," Working Paper no. 25147, National Bureau of Economic Research, October 2018.

9. Randy Avent, "Artificial Intelligence at UNC," *Visiting Scholar*, July 3, 2025.

10. Phil Emer (senior director for innovation at MCNC), interview by Mack Paul, December 9, 2025.

1. Volumetrics Medical Imaging, "Volumetrics Medical Imaging Inc. Unveils First Commercial Real-Time Volumetric Ultrasound System," *Newswise*, March 30, 1998, https://www.newswise.com/articles/volumetrics-medical-imaging-inc-unveils-first-commercial-real-time-volumetric-ultrasound-system.

2. Duke University Pratt School of Engineering, "The Pioneers of 3D Ultrasound," Innovation Development Institute, April 1, 2019, https://www.inknowvation.com/sbir/story/pioneers-3d-ultrasound.

3. Volumetrics Medical Imaging, "Volumetrics Medical Imaging."

4. Duke University Pratt School of Engineering, "The Pioneers of 3D Ultrasound."

5. Jennifer Weeks, "Turf Wars," Science History Institute Museum and Library, October 3, 2015, https://www.sciencehistory.org/stories/magazine/turf-wars/.

6. Weeks, "Turf Wars."

7. Celia Hooper, "The FDA Granted Final Approval for Sales of AIDS Drug AZT," United Press International, March 20, 1987, https://www.upi.com/Archives/1987/03/20/The-FDA-granted-final-approval-for-sale-of-AIDS-drug-AZT/8964543214800/.

8. Catharina Goedeck, "Gertrude B. Elion and the 'Antiviral Odyssey,'" ChemistryViews, last modified February 21, 2024, https://www.chemistryviews.org/gertrude-b-elion-and-the-antiviral-odyssey/.

9. Hooper, "The FDA Granted Final Approval."

10. Alice Park, "The Story Behind the First AIDS Drug," *Time*, March 19, 2017, https://time.com/4705809/first-aids-drug-azt/.

11. Lucas Stolze, "How Old Is Fortnite? A Timeline of Its Evolution," *ExitLag*, October 17, 2024, https://www.exitlag.com/blog/how-old-is-fortnite/.

12. Fortnite Team, "Announcing Fortnite Battle Royale," Epic Games, September 12, 2017, https://www.fortnite.com/news/announcing-fortnite-battle-royale.

13. "The Evolution of Epic Games," Vox Media, accessed March 9, 2025, https://apps.voxmedia.com/at/polygon-a-history-of-epic-games/.

14. Josh Howarth, "Fortnite User and Growth Stats 2024," *Exploding Topics*, March 5, 2025, https://explodingtopics.com/blog/fortnite-stats.

15. Hayley Tsukayama, "Everything You Need to Know About Fortnite and Why It's So Popular," *Washington Post*, April 3, 2018.

16. Zack Arnold, "Fortnite: The Cultural Phenomenon That Changed Gaming Forever," *Medium*, February 21, 2024, https://zacarnold.medium.com/fortnite-the-cultural-phenomenon-that-changed-gaming-forever-77be7433487d.

17. Akhilesh Ganti, "How Does Fortnite Make Money?," *Investopedia*, September 10, 2020, https://www.investopedia.com/tech/how-does-fortnite-make-money/.

18. "How Has Fortnite Impacted the Gaming and Media World?," *DigitalCommerce360*, March 22, 2023, https://www.digitalcommerce360.com/2023/03/22/sponsored-content-how-has-fortnite-impacted-the-gaming-and-media-world/.

19. Samantha, "Fortnite's Evolution: From Early Days to Esports," *Z League*, January 2, 2025, https://www.zleague.gg/theportal/fortnite-evolution-esports/.

20. Anjali Bhati, "Fortnite and Its Impact on Gaming Culture," *Driffle*, October 1, 2024, https://driffle.com/blog/fortnite-impact-on-gaming-culture-a-detailed-analysis/.

21. Deborah Kotz, "University of Maryland School of Medicine Faculty Scientists and Clinicians Perform Historic First Successful Transplant of Porcine Heart into Adult Human with End-Stage Heart Disease," University of Maryland School of Medicine, January 10, 2022, https://www.medschool.umaryland.edu/news/2022/university-of-maryland-school-of-medicine-faculty-scientists-and-clinicians-perform-historic-first-successful-transplant-of-porcine-heart-into-adult-human-with-end-stage-heart-disease.html.

22. "United Therapeutics Announces World's First Successful Xenothymokidney Transplant," United Therapeutics, accessed January 9, 2025, https://ir.unither.com/press-releases/2024/04-24-2024-140050479; "United Therapeutics Announces Successful World's First UKidney Transplant," United Therapeutics, accessed January 9, 2025, https://ir.unither.com/press-releases/2024/12-17-2024-120130031.

23. "United Therapeutics Announces Successful World's First UKidney Transplant."

24. "United Therapeutics Corporation History," United Therapeutics, accessed January 9, 2025, https://www.unither.com/about-us/history.

25. "Organ Donation Statistics," Health Resources and Services Administration, accessed January 9, 2025, https://www.organdonor.gov/learn/organ-donation-statistics.

26. "Organ Donation Statistics."

27. Tad Dickens, "Southwest Virginia Scientists Are Gene-Editing Pigs for Human Transplants," *Cardinal News*, December 19, 2023, https://cardinalnews.org/2023/12/19/southwest-virginia-scientists-are-gene-editing-pigs-for-human-transplants/.

28. "IBM System/360," Computer History Museum, accessed December 12, 2024, https://www.computerhistory.org/revolution/mainframe-computers/7/161.

29. "The IBM System/360," IBM, accessed December 12, 2024, https://www.ibm.com/history/system-360.

30. Research Triangle Foundation, "IBM Celebrates 50 Years in the RTP," interview by Fran O'Sullivan, Research Triangle Park, 2015, https://www.rtp.org/2016/02/ibm-celebrates-50-years-in-rtp/.

31. "The IBM System/360."

32. Engineering Communications, "Growing at Wolfspeed," College of Engineering News, North Carolina State University, January 19, 2024, https://engr.ncsu.edu/news/2024/01/19/growing-at-wolfspeed/.

33. Tom Harris, Chris Pollette, and Wesley Fenlon, "How Light Emitting Diodes (LEDs) Work," *HowStuffWorks*, accessed January 9, 2025, https://electronics.howstuffworks.com/led.htm#pt4.

34. Lidiya Kukova, "Q&A: What Makes Blue LED Light So Special?," Yale Scientific, January 18, 2015, https://www.yalescientific.org/2015/01/qa-what-makes-blue-led-light-so-special.

35. Kukova, "Q&A."

36. Steve Hendershot, "Pioneer in Her Field: Mary-Dell Chilton Receives U of I Alumni Association Achievement Award," University of Illinois Urbana-Champaign, last modified July 1, 2016, https://las.illinois.edu/news/2016-07-01/pioneer-her-field.

37. Syngenta, "Mary-Dell Chilton, Distinguished Science Fellow: Innovator in Modern Plant Biotechnology," accessed May 14, 2024, https://www.syngenta-us.com/biotechnology/mary-dell-chilton.

38. "Mary Dell Chilton One of Two UI Alums Named Winner of World Food Prize," University of Illinois Urbana-Champaign, July 1, 2013, https://chemistry.illinois.edu/news/2013-07-01t153846/mary-dell-chilton-one-two-ui-alums-named-winner-world-food-prize.

39. "Pyroman™," Wilson College of Textiles, North Carolina State University, accessed March 16, 2025, https://textiles.ncsu.edu/tpacc/heat-and-flame-protection/pyroman/.

40. Sean Cudahy, "TPACC Researchers Unveil 'Game-Changing' Technology to Test Firefighter Thermal Wear," Wilson College News, North Carolina State University, March 18, 2024, https://textiles.ncsu.edu/news/2024/03/tpacc-researchers-unveil-game-changing-technology-to-test-firefighter-thermal-wear/.

41. Sylvia Adcock, "Burning Man," *NC State Magazine*, North Carolina State University, October 28, 2024, https://magazine.ncsu.edu/2024/burning-man/.

42. Cudahy, "TPACC Researchers."

43. "Heat and Flame Protection," Wilson College of Textiles, North Carolina State University, accessed March 16, 2024, https://textiles.ncsu.edu/tpacc/heat-and-flame-protection/.

44. "Heat and Flame Protection."

45. Cudahy, "TPACC Researchers."

46. Adcock, "Burning Man."

47. Beth Weaver, "How Taxol/Paclitaxel Kills Cancer Cells," *Molecular Biology of the Cell* 25, no. 18 (2014): 2677–81, https://pmc.ncbi.nlm.nih.gov/articles/PMC4161504/#B54.

48. "Discovery of Camptothecin and Taxol," American Chemical Society, accessed February 17, 2025, https://www.acs.org/education/whatischemistry/landmarks/camptothecintaxol.html.

49. Julia Gallego-Jara et al., "A Compressive Review About Taxol: History and Future Challenges," *Molecules* 25, no. 24 (2020): 5986, https://pmc.ncbi.nlm.nih.gov/articles/PMC7767101/#.

50. Ayoola Awosika, Maela Farrar, and Tibb Jacobs, "Paclitaxel," StatPearls, accessed February 17, 2025, https://www.ncbi.nlm.nih.gov/books/NBK536917/.

51. Weaver, "How Taxol/Paclitaxel Kills Cancer Cells."

52. "A Story of Discovery: Natural Compound Helps Treat Breast and Ovarian Cancers," National Cancer Institute, accessed February 17, 2025, https://www.cancer.gov/research/progress/discovery/taxol.

53. "A Story of Discovery."

54. Gallego-Jara et al., "A Compressive Review."

55. "The UPC," IBM, accessed December 29, 2024, https://www.ibm.com/history/upc.

56. "George Laurer," IBM, accessed December 29, 2024, https://www.ibm.com/history/george-laurer.

57. "The UPC."

INDEX

3D ultrasound, 203, 239–40

AAV (adeno-associated virus), 178–84, 240–41
adeno-associated virus (AAV), 178–84, 240–41
adenovirus (AV), 177–78
agricultural technology (AgTech), 92–93, 139, 160–68, 174
AgTech Initiative, 161–62, 174
Alexandria Real Estate (ARE), 164–68, 204; LaunchLabs, 165
Amazon, 190, 200
Amdahl, Gene, 245. *See also* IBM System/360
American Tobacco Campus, 145–46, 188. *See also* downtown revitalization
American Tobacco Company, 57–58, 71
American Tobacco Trail, 218, 211. *See also under* regional amenities
Amgen (Kirin-Amgen), 164, 210
Anderson, Bruce, 120
Anderson, Holt, 103–4. *See also* Microelectronics Center of North Carolina (MCNC)
Apple, 190–91, 193, 218
ARE (Alexandria Real Estate), 164–68, 204; LaunchLabs, 165
AskBio, 178–84, 240–41
AstroTurf, 241. *See also* Chemstrand
Atkins, John, 130–31, 137
Atkins, Ken, 130. *See also* Chamber of Commerce
AV (adenovirus), 177–78
Avalo AI, 167–68
Aycock, Elizabeth, 56, 137. *See also* Research Triangle Foundation (RTF)
Azidothymidine (AZT), 74, 241–24. *See also* Burroughs Wellcome & Company (BW)
AZT (Azidothymidine), 74, 241–42. *See also* Burroughs Wellcome & Company (BW)

Baldwin, Mary-Ann, 223. *See also* regional transit
Bamboo Therapeutics, 182–83. *See also* AskBio
Barr, Tony, 109–10, 116. *See also* SAS Institute
BASF, 86, 161, 163–64
Basnight, Marc, 134. *See also* regional transit
Battlestar Galactica, 152–53
Bayer, 161, 164, 179, 183, 240
Bayh-Dole Act of 1980, 44, 81, 116, 198
Bell, Bill, 144–46, 151, 226. *See also* downtown revitalization
Bell, Bob, 156, 159. *See also* Sphinx Pharmaceuticals
Bell Laboratories, 200, 98, 103–5; Baby Bells, 105, 107
Bielman, Don, 103–4. *See also* Microelectronics Center of North Carolina (MCNC)
Big Push Model, 5, 233–34
Biogen, 206–7
biomanufacturing: Holly Springs hub, 207–8, 210; industry growth, 195, 204, 207, 212–13, 236; workforce development programs, 162, 173, 176, 205–7, 211
Bisi, John, 154–55, 159. *See also* G1 Therapeutics (G-Zero Therapeutics)

Black, James W., 124. *See also* Burroughs Wellcome & Company (BW); Nobel Prize: winners
Blue, Dan, 134. *See also* regional transit
Board of Science and Technology, 81, 101–2
Bostian, Carey, 13, 19–20
Boxyard, 217. *See also* Hub RTP; Research Triangle Foundation (RTF): Park Center
brain drain, 9, 18, 119, 188, 231, 236
Brainstorm, 76, 136–37. *See also* Burroughs Wellcome & Company (BW)
Bridges, Bob, 70–71. *See also* desegregation in public education
Bronto, 188, 193
Brooks, Frederick P., Jr., 58–60, 100–101, 103, 245. *See also* IBM (International Business Machines Corporation); IBM System/360
Bryan, Joe, 222. *See also* regional transit
Bullock, Bill, 207–9. *See also* biomanufacturing: Holly Springs hub; Holly Springs
Burke, Steven, 84, 86. *See also* North Carolina Biotechnology Center (NCBiotech)
Burroughs, Silas, 73, 78–79. *See also* Burroughs Wellcome & Company (BW)
Burroughs Wellcome & Company (BW), 73–80, 124–25, 241–42
Bush, Vannevar, 232
BW (Burroughs Wellcome & Company), 73–80, 124–25, 241–42

Camille Dreyfus Laboratory, 41; Anton Peterlin, 41, 45. *See also* Research Triangle Institute (RTI)
Campbell, Malcolm, 13, 19–20
camptothecin, 43–44. *See also* Taxol (Paclitaxel); Wall, Monroe E.; Wani, Mansukh
Cannon, Charlie, 56
Carlton, Phil, 56
Carmichael, William, 21, 35
Carney, Ed, 105–6
Carrow, Hill, 132–33
Carter, Calvin, 246. *See also* Cree (Wolfspeed)
Cary, NC, 135, 151, 229–30; businesses in, 110–11, 189, 191, 235, 243
Causby, Gene, 66. *See also* desegregation in public education
Chamber of Commerce: Durham, 120, 130; joint committee on start-ups, 120–21; Raleigh, 119–20, 130
Chatham County, 3, 111, 129, 132, 192, 229, 235
Chatham Therapeutics, 183. *See also* AskBio
Chemstrand, 53–55, 65, 241
Chetty, Raj, 236
Chilton, Mary Dell, 90–93, 96, 160, 163, 168, 246–47. *See also* agricultural technology (AgTech); Syngenta (Ciba-Geigy)
Ciba-Geigy (Syngenta), 86, 92, 96, 246–47
Cisco, 98, 106, 130, 142, 238
Clayton, NC, 174, 221, 229
clinical research organizations (CROs), 111–12
Coble, Paul, 144. *See also* downtown revitalization
Coe, Fred, 75. *See also* Burroughs Wellcome & Company (BW)
Cole, Adrienne, 218–19
Coleman, Thomas, 246. *See also* Cree (Wolfspeed)
Collins, Brendan, 167. *See also* Avalo AI
Colopy, Joe, 188. *See also* Bronto
Commerce Department (Department of Conservation and Development), 9, 12, 27, 35–36, 46, 161, 176–77, 191
Cook, Tim, 190–91. *See also* Apple
Cooper, Roy, 190
Cox, Gertrude, 32–33, 41, 45, 109–10, 112, 116–17
Cree (Wolfspeed), 114–16, 191–92, 245–46
Cronos Integrated Microsystems, 104–5. *See also* Microelectronics Center of North Carolina (MCNC)
CROs (clinical research organizations), 111–12
Crow, James W., 125–26. *See also* United Therapeutics (UT)
CSL Seqirus (Novartis), 207–8
Curran, Chris, 181–84. *See also* AskBio
Curran, Conner, 181–84. *See also* AskBio
Curran, Jessica, 181–84. *See also* AskBio
Curran, Kyle, 181. *See also* AskBio

Daugherty, Dick, 69, 72, 100, 104, 137. *See also* IBM (International Business Machines Corporation)
Davis, Archie K.: background, 36–37; fund-raising efforts, 38, 41, 56; on "generosity

of spirit," 37, 237; on IBM (International Business Machines Corporation), 62; on importance of a non-profit structure, 37–38; Triangle Service Center, Inc., 47–48
Davis, Robert F., 114–16, 191–92. *See also* Cree (Wolfspeed)
Dayton, Paul A., 203. *See also* university commercialization programs
Department of Conservation and Development (Commerce Department), 9, 12, 27, 35–36, 46, 161, 176–77, 191
desegregation in public education: *Brown v. Board of Education*, 3, 19, 49, 52, 60, 66; "*Brown* II," 66–68; impact on companies relocating to Research Triangle Park, 54, 60–61, 65, 69, 226; Pearsall Committee, 50–51; Pearsall Plan, 51–52, 60, 65; response of Southern states, 49–50, 60; Wake County, 68–72, 226
Doss, Monica, 123. *See also* start-ups
Dougherty, Dennis, 120–24. *See also* Intersouth Partners
downtown revitalization, 144–46, 151, 187, 228
Drucker, Peter: *The Landmarks of Tomorrow*, 27. *See also* "knowledge worker"
Duffer brothers, 214–15. See also *Stranger Things*
Duke University, Durham, 71, 145; regional transit, 223; Hospital, 182; Research Triangle, 12, 35, 54; Research Triangle Institute (RTI), 30–31; role in Park formation, 21, 30-31; staff, 56, 85, 94–95, 146; students, 14, 58; Triangle Universities Computation Center (TUCC), 59, 100–101; university commercialization, 121–22, 146, 197–202; venture capital, 122
Durham, NC: attempted annexation of RTP, 71–72, 100, 130, 133, 145; decline, 71–72; Durham Bulls, 133, 145–46; regional tensions, 71–72, 144–45, 236; water supply from, 36, 57–58; zoning, 48, 61
dystrophin, 179, 182. *See also* AskBio

Easley, Mike, 161, 173, 207
economic growth, 27, 119, 130, 132, 188
economic mobility, 236–37
Edens, Arthur Hollis, 20–21
Edgeton, Doug, 204, 234, 236. *See also* North Carolina Biotechnology Center (NCBiotech)
Edmond, John, 246. *See also* Cree (Wolfspeed)
Elder, Mike, 173–74. *See also* Novozymes (Novonesis)
elections: 1940s, 12, 14; 1950s, 12, 14, 17, 24; 1960s, 52–53, 66; 1980s, 71, 82, 101; 1990s, 135, 104, 145; 2000s, 144–46, 151, 225–28, 149–50; 2010s, 225
Eli Lilly and Company, 29, 112, 170–71, 211–12
Elion, Gertrude B., 76–78, 124, 242. *See also* Burroughs Wellcome & Company (BW); Hitchings, George
Elo Life Systems, 166–67
Ely, Ralph, Jr., 41, 45. *See also* Research Triangle Institute (RTI)
Environmental Health Sciences Center. *See* National Institute of Environmental Health Sciences (NIEHS)
enzyme production, 171–73. *See also* Novozymes (Novonesis)
Epic Games, 243. *See also* Fortnite
epoprostanol, 124–25. *See also* United Therapeutics (UT)
Ericsson, 142, 188, 202
Eshelman, Fred, 159. *See also* Glaxo
Estay, Dan, 203. *See also* SonoVascular
Evolv, 200–201
Ewing, Marc, 186. *See also* Red Hat

FAANG companies (Facebook, Amazon, Apple, Netflix, and Google), 143
Facebook (Meta), 191, 193
federal cutbacks, 197–98, 203–4, 233, 237
Fetzer, Tom, 135, 144
Fidelity Investments, 187, 189, 218
fintech, 188–89. *See also* Fidelity Investments
First Flight Venture Center (FFVC). *See* Hunt, James: North Carolina Technology Development Authority (TDA); North Carolina Technology Development Authority (TDA); start-ups: North Carolina Technology Development Authority (TDA)
Flink, Chuck, 129, 218. *See also* regional amenities

Flood, Dudley, 66–71. *See also* desegregation in public education
Florida, Richard, 143, 236
Flournoy, Bill, Jr., 221. *See also* regional amenities
Fortnite, 242–43. *See also* Epic Games
Franklinton, 172–73, 175. *See also* Novozymes (Novonesis)
Friday, William C., 22–23, 37–38, 101
Fujifilm Diosynth Biotechnologies, 209–10. *See also* biomanufacturing: Holly Springs hub; Holly Springs

G1Therapeutics (G-Zero Therapeutics), 153–59
GE (General Electric), 11, 102–4, 192
Gelsinger, Jesse, 177–79, 181, 184. *See also* gene therapy
Genentech, 81, 121, 210
General Electric (GE), 11, 102–4, 192
gene therapy, 176–84
genetically modified organism (GMO), 91, 93
Geolas, Bob, 215–17. *See also* Hub RTP; Research Triangle Foundation (RTF)
Gilbert, Walter, 81, 206. *See also* Nobel Prize
Gillings, Dennis Barry, 112–14. *See also* Quintiles (IQVIA)
Glaxo: BW15AU81 patent, 125; layoffs, 147, 153, 158–59; mergers, 78–79, 124–25; relocation to RTP, 79, 119; support of Durham, 145–46
GLF (Golden Leaf Foundation), 173, 176, 210–11. *See also* workforce development
GMO (genetically modified organism), 91, 93
Golden Leaf Foundation (GLF), 173, 176, 210–11. *See also* workforce development
Goldstein, Harvey, 118–19. *See also* Luger, Michael; research parks: *Technology in the Garden: Research Parks and Regional Economic Development*
Goodmon, Jim, 133, 145–46. *See also* downtown revitalization
Goodnight, Jim, 109–11. *See also* SAS Institute
Google, 191, 193, 199
Governor's Inn, 48, 120, 130, 136–37, 216
Grabarek, Wensell, 57–58. *See also* Durham, NC
Gray, Gordon, 20–22
Greater Triangle Regional Council (GTRC), 134
Greenberg, Bernard, 112, 116. *See also* Gillings, Dennis Barry
Gress, Bob, 119–20, 123. *See also* Chamber of Commerce
Gross, Paul, 30–31, 33, 38, 54
GTRC (Greater Triangle Regional Council), 134
Guest, Romeo: C. M. Guest & Sons, 11, 13, 21, 39; early life, 11–12; formulating Research Triangle Park idea, 11–12, 127, 213, 233; gaining support, 12–14, 19–22, 28, 30, 35, 50; legacy, 39, 62; Pinelands, 35–36, 39, 56; Research Triangle Foundation (RTF), 38–39
Gulley, Wib, 71, 133–34, 223, 236
G-Zero Therapeutics (G Therapeutics), 153–59

Haile, Don, 189. *See also* Fidelity Investments
Hamilton, Scott, 210–11. *See also* Golden Leaf Foundation (GLF)
Hamner, Charles E., 83–88, 183–84. *See also* North Carolina Biotechnology Center (NCBiotech)
Hancock, Gerry, 81–82, 86, 177. *See also* North Carolina Biotechnology Center (NCBiotech)
Hanes, Robert M.: formation of Research Triangle Park, 14, 21–23, 31, 36–39; Luther Hodges, 16–18, 20
Hatteras Venture Partners, 122–23, 155–58, 204. *See also* venture capital
Hayes, Charles, 132. *See also* Raleigh Durham Regional Association (RDRA)
Heagarty, Chris, 225–26. *See also* Wake County public school system
Helwig, Jane, 109–10. *See also* SAS Institute
Herbert, George, 33–34, 41–43, 45, 102–3, 137. *See also* Research Triangle Institute (RTI)
Hill, George Watts, 31–33, 37, 129, 137
Hitchings, George, 76–78, 124, 132. *See also* Burroughs Wellcome & Company (BW); Elion, Gertrude
Hobson, Jesse, 33. *See also* Herbert, George
Hodges, Brandon: death, 31–32; George Simpson, 23–23, 27; Research Institute Committee, 31; Research Triangle Council, 23; Romeo Guest, 12–14, 19, 21, 31
Hodges, Luther Hartwell: business career, 15–16, 20; Chemstrand, 53; desegregation, 49–53; development of industry, 20, 24, 40, 45–47, 101, 172; early life, 14–15; elections,

16–18, 24, 42–43; formation of Research Triangle Park, 14, 19–23, 34–39, 50, 53, 56–57; impact on other governors, 101, 172; later political career, 54, 57, 61; Marshall Plan, 16, 20; public speaking, 1, 38–39, 74; Rotary International, 16–17; Triangle Service Center, Inc., 47–48
Hodges, Martha Blakeney, 15–17. *See also* Hodges, Luther Hartwell
Hodges-Copple, John, 223–24. *See also* regional planning
Hoechst (Sanofi-Aventis), 86, 112
Holly Springs, 207–11, 227, 229. *See also* biomanufacturing
Hub RTP, 48, 217, 219. *See also* Boxyard; Research Triangle Foundation (RTF)
Hunt, James: industry hunting, 46, 86; Microelectronics Center of North Carolina (MCNC), 81–82, 101–4; NCBIO, 176–77; Norris Tolson, 161; North Carolina Biotechnology Center (NCBiotech), 81–82, 85, 87, 102; North Carolina Technology Development Authority (TDA), 123–24, 164; Novo Nordisk, 172; Novozymes (Novonesis), 174; Raleigh Durham Regional Association (RDRA), 132; World Class Region Conference, 133
Hunter, Eric, 114–16, 246. *See also* Cree (Wolfspeed)
Hunter, Neal, 114–16, 246. *See also* Cree (Wolfspeed)
Hunter, Ron, 136. *See also* Governor's Inn
Hutchinson, Sig, 221. *See also* regional amenities
Hutchison, Fred, 79. *See also* Glaxo

IBM (International Business Machines Corporation): downsizing, 235; information technology, 105–7, 142, 185, 193; Lenovo, 193; personal computer, 100–101, 193; quantum computing, 238; Red Hat, 186–88, 193; relocation decision, 59–63, 65, 69, 191; relocation to Research Triangle Park, 55, 59, 61–62, 119, 128, 245; Systems Network Architecture (SNA), 105–6; unitary tax, 100; Universal Product Code (UPC), 99–100, 248–49; zoning for manufacturing, 61
IBM System/360, 244–45; development, 58–59, 100, 105, 109; industry dominance, 98, 101; manufacturing, 60–61; Statistical Analysis Software (SAS), 109; Triangle Universities Computation Center (TUCC), 101, 125. *See also* IBM (International Business Machines Corporation)
industry: decline of traditional sectors, 9–10, 169, 213; hunting, 12, 20, 24, 45–47, 169, 172, 175; Industrial Education Centers, 24, 47
Information Superhighway, 103, 105–6, 238. *See also* Microelectronics Center of North Carolina (MCNC)
Ingram, Bob, 146. *See also* downtown revitalization; Durham: Durham Bulls
"innovation hubs," 195, 215, 218
International Business Machines Corporation (IBM): downsizing, 235; information technology, 105–7, 142, 185, 193; Lenovo, 193; personal computer, 100–101, 193; quantum computing, 238; Red Hat, 186–88, 193; relocation decision, 59–63, 65, 69, 191; relocation to Research Triangle Park, 55, 59, 61–62, 119, 128, 245; Systems Network Architecture (SNA), 105–6; unitary tax, 100; Universal Product Code (UPC), 99–100, 248–49; zoning for manufacturing, 61
Intersouth Partners, 121–23, 193. *See also* Dougherty, Dennis
IonQ, 199–200
IQVIA (Quintiles), 32, 111–16
Isenhour, Leslie, 211–12. *See also* workforce development

Jacobs, Wendy, 224. *See also* regional transit
Johnson, Abigail, 189. *See also* Fidelity Investments
Johnson, Edward II, 189. *See also* Fidelity Investments
Johnson, Sam, 176–77
Johnson & Johnson, 209, 211. *See also* Wilson, NC
Jones, Vivian, 227–29. *See also* Wake Forest
Jordan, B. Everette, 16, 18. *See also* Hodges, Luther Hartwell

Key, V. O.: on public education, 50; progressive plutocracy, 10–11, 14, 23, 31, 37–38, 237
Kim, Jungsang, 199–200. *See also* IonQ
King, David, 228

Kirin-Amgen (Amgen), 164, 210
Kleiner, Eugene, 121, 159
Kleiner Perkins, 121. *See also* Kleiner, Eugene
"knowledge worker," 27, 74
Knox, Margaret, 137. *See also Leader (North Carolina Beacon)*
Koch, Gary, 112. *See also* Quintiles (IQVIA)
Kotkin, Joel: "hard tech," 142–43, 150–51, 185; "nerdistan," 135, 142; "soft tech," 142–43
Krogh, August, 170–71. *See also* Novo Nordisk
Krogh, Marie, 170–71. *See also* Novo Nordisk
Krstanovic, Irena, 208. *See also* biomanufacturing: Holly Springs hub; Holly Springs
Ku Klux Klan (KKK), 34, 51, 67
Kymeta, 201

Lake, I. Beverly, 52–53. *See also* desegregation in public education; Sanford, Terry
Lampe, Harold, 13, 19, 202
Lampe, Ross W., Jr., 202. *See also* Lampe Joint Department of Biomedical Engineering
Lampe Joint Department of Biomedical Engineering, 202–3
Lane, Brent, 124. *See also* North Carolina Technology Development Authority (TDA)
Lang, Glen, 135. *See also* Cary, NC
Lantz, Jennifer, 211. *See also* Wilson, NC
Laurer, George, 249. *See also* IBM
Leader (North Carolina Beacon), 120, 137
Leak, Bob, 45–46. *See also* industry
LED (light-emitting diode) lighting, 109, 115, 191, 245–46. *See also* Cree (Wolfspeed)
Lefkowitz, Robert, 93–96
Levitan, Scott, 216–18
Liggett & Myers, 58, 71
light-emitting diode (LED) lighting, 109, 115, 191, 245–46. *See also* Cree (Wolfspeed)
Lindsey, Quentin, 81, 101–2. *See also* Board of Science and Technology
Linton, Richard, 161–62, 174. *See also* AgTech Initiative
Linux, 186–87. *See also* Red Hat
Little, William F., 28–29, 45, 53–54
Luger, Michael, 118–19. *See also* Goldstein, Harvey; research parks: *Technology in the Garden: Research Parks and Regional Economic Development*
Lumbee Tribe: Battle of Mills Pond, 51
Marcus, Joel, 164–65. *See also* Alexandria Real Estate (ARE)
Marks, Walter, 69–70. *See also* desegregation in public education
Martin, Jim, 87, 176–77
Maughan, William, 35
Mayefskie, Sean, 208. *See also* biomanufacturing: Holly Springs hub; Holly Springs
Meeker, Charles, 144–45, 151, 226. *See also* downtown revitalization
MEMS (microelectronic mechanical systems), 104–5. *See also* Microelectronics Center of North Carolina (MCNC)
Meta (Facebook), 191, 193
metformin, 113. *See also* Quintiles (IQVIA)
metropolitan statistical area (MSA), 146–47
Microelectronics Center of North Carolina (MCNC): collaboration with telecom companies, 106; establishment, 81–82, 101–3, 233; microelectronic mechanical systems (MEMS), 104–5; North Carolina Innovative Development for Economic Advancement (NC IDEA), 105; North Carolina Supercomputing Center, 103–4; quantum computing, 238; relationship with academia, 103–4; Rural Internet Access Authority, 105
Microsoft, 58, 101, 186, 188, 200
Mikhail, Sheila, 178–80, 182, 184, 240. *See also* AskBio
Mills, C. Wright: *White Collar: The American Middle Class*, 27
Mizelle, Jenny, 207–8. *See also* biomanufacturing: Holly Springs hub; Holly Springs
monogenetic disease (orphan disease), 179–80. *See also* AskBio
Monsanto, 164, 241
Moore, Dan, 62
Moretti, Enrico: *The New Geography of Jobs*, 4, 87–88
Morgridge, John, 106. *See also* Cisco
Mullen, Jim, 206–7. *See also* Biogen
Mumma, Mitch, 193. *See also* Intersouth Partners
Musacchia, Mary, 126. *See also* North Carolina Technology Development Authority (TDA)
Muscular Dystrophy Association (MDA), 180. *See also* AskBio

NAACP (National Association for the Advancement of Colored People), 51–52, 149
National Association for the Advancement of Colored People (NAACP), 51–52, 149
National Center for Health Statistics, 74
National Institute of Environmental Health Sciences (NIEHS), 57–58, 74
NCBiotech (North Carolina Biotechnology Center): AgTech, 160–62, 168, 174; biomanufacturing, 207–8; faculty recruitment, 96, 178; history, 82–87, 102, 176, 233; start-ups, 124, 155, 162, 168, 177, 204; workforce development, 173, 205, 211, 234
NCInnovation, 238
neighborhood schools, 150, 225–26. *See also* desegregation in public education: Wake County; Wake County public school system
Nello Teer Company, 39, 136–37
Newell, William, 13, 20
NIEHS (National Institute of Environmental Health Sciences), 57–58, 74
Nobel Prize: nominees, 45; predicted winners, 183–84; winners, 57, 76–78, 80–81, 84–85, 96, 124, 132, 164, 170, 206
Nortel (Northern Telecom), 98, 105–6, 119, 142, 188–89
North Carolina Beacon (Leader), 120, 137
North Carolina Biotechnology Center (NCBiotech): AgTech, 160–62, 168, 174; biomanufacturing, 207–8; faculty recruitment, 96, 178; history, 82–87, 102, 176, 233; start-ups, 124, 155, 162, 168, 177, 204; workforce development, 173, 205, 211, 234
North Carolina State University (NC State): AgTech, 162–63, 168; Gertude Cox, 32, 109; Research Triangle, 12; Research Triangle Institute (RTI), 32; role in Park formation, 19, 28; staff, 32, 85, 114–16, 191; start-ups, 109–11, 114–17; telecom, 106; Triangle University Computation Center (TUCC), 59, 101; workforce training, 162, 173–76
North Carolina Supercomputing Center, 104, 106–7. *See also* Microelectronics Center of North Carolina (MCNC); supercomputer
North Carolina Technology Development Authority (TDA), 123–26
Northern Telecom (Nortel), 98, 105–6, 119, 142, 188–89
Novartis (CSL Seqirus), 207–8
Novonesis (Novozymes), 161, 163, 172–74
Novo Nordisk, 171–75, 212; Foundation, 174
Novo Nordisk Foundation, 174. *See also* Novo Nordisk
Novozymes (Novonesis), 161, 163, 172–74

Oberlies, Nicholas, 43–45. *See also* Wani, Mansukh
O'Brien Atkins, 137. *See also* Atkins, John
Odom, Howard, 22–23
office park model, 129, 143, 151, 214–16
Ohman, Magnus, 210. *See also* Amgen (Kirin-Amgen)
Olson, Todd, 188. *See also* Pendo
orphan disease (monogenetic disease), 179–80. *See also* AskBio
Øvlisen, Mads, 171–72. *See also* Novo Nordisk
Oxaal, John, 239. *See also* Volumetrics Medical Imaging

Paclitaxel (Taxol), 34, 42–44, 248. *See also* Wall, Monroe E.; Wani Mansukh
Palmour, John, 246. *See also* Cree (Wolfspeed)
Pappas, Art, 122–23, 159; Pappas Capital, 122–23
Patterson, Jane Smith, 103. *See also* Microelectronics Center of North Carolina (MCNC)
Pearsall, Thomas, 50, 53. *See also* desegregation in public education
Pedersen, Harald, 171. *See also* Novo Nordisk
Pedersen, Thorvald, 171. *See also* Novo Nordisk
Peirce, Neal: citistate, 134.
Pendo, 188, 191
per capita income, 10, 23, 131, 143, 234–35
Phillips, Craig, 66. *See also* desegregation in public education
Pinelands Company, 35–39, 56
Pittsboro, 114, 229
Pritchett, Warren H., 17. *See also* Hodges, Luther Hartwell
public school system, 10, 50, 65–72; Wake County public school system, 70–71, 221
PyroMan, 247–48

quantum computing, 198–200, 238
qubits, 199
Quintiles (IQVIA), 32, 111–16

Raleigh Durham (RDU) International Airport, 35, 92, 127, 130, 133, 188, 218, 221, 224
Raleigh Durham Regional Association (RDRA), 130–32; Research Triangle Regional Partnership (RTRP), 164
Ralls, Scott, 234. *See also* workforce development
Rasor, Robin, 198–202. *See also* university commercialization programs
RDRA (Raleigh Durham Regional Association), 130–32; Research Triangle Regional Partnership (RTRP), 164
RDU International Airport, 35, 92, 127, 130, 133, 188, 218, 221, 224
Red Hat, 186–88, 193
regional amenities: activity centers, 136, 143, 148; arts, 111, 220; greenways, 129–30, 218, 221; quality of life, 27, 148; schools, 71, 149; talent, 106, 193; use in marketing Research Triangle Park, 27, 127, 220
regional growth, 139, 228; challenges, 135, 149, 221; patterns, 229; planning, 128, 134–35, 148; sprawl, 135, 143, 146, 148
regionalism, 127–34, 136–37
regional planning: outside of Research Triangle Park, 226–29; Research Triangle Regional Planning Commission, 48–49, 128–29, 229; *Research Triangle Region Development Guide*, 49, 128; scenario planning, 229; Triangle J Council of Governments (TJCOG), 129, 146, 223; Triangle Region Reality Check, 148; World Class Region Conference, 133–35, 148
regional transit: GoTriangle (Triangle Transit), 147, 218, 222–24, 228; highways, 48, 60, 62, 106, 147, 218, 222, 227; mass transit, 147, 215–16, 218, 221–25, 230; Special Transit Advisory Commission (STAC), 221–22; traffic, 62, 135, 143, 218, 238; Triangle Transit Authority (TTA), 133–34, 147, 221; World Class Region Conference, 133–34
remote work, 4, 168, 188, 191, 193, 215, 218
research parks: design, 29, 48, 219, 232; economic effect, 11, 23, 108, 118–19, 233–34; Levitan, Scott, 216; regional identity, 127, 131, 137; relationship with academia, 12, 23, 32, 35, 108; *Technology in the Garden: Research Parks and Regional Economic Development*, 118–19
Research Triangle Development Council, 21; Program and Plans Subcommittee, 21–22; Research Institute Committee, 31–33, 36; Working Committee, 21–22, 28, 31, 81
Research Triangle Foundation (RTF) 40; architecture, 48; attempted annexation, 71; Bob Geolas, 215–16; covenants, 61, 215; funding, 55–56, 215; Hub RTP, 48, 217; Jim Roberson, 130–31, 134; Park Center, 216–17; Raleigh Durham Regional Association (RDRA), 130–31; real estate, 41, 47–48, 54–57, 130, 215–16; regional planning, 47, 129, 148, 215–16, 218; reimagining RTP, 48, 215–16; Research Triangle Committee, 25–26, 31, 36, 39, 102; Rick Weddle, 148; RTP 3.0, 195, 217–19; Scott Levitan, 216–18
Research Triangle Institute (RTI): architecture, 29, 38, 45; founding, 2, 33–34; George Herbert, 33–34, 41–45, 102; Microelectronics Center of North Carolina (MCNC), 102–3; relationship with universities, 2, 38–40, 131; Research Institute Committee, 31–33, 36; talent acquisition, 41–45, 54, 116–17
Research Triangle Regional Partnership (RTRP), 132
Research Triangle Region Development Guide, 128
Rinde, Meir, 178. *See also* Gelsinger, Jesse
Robb, John, 78. *See also* Burroughs Wellcome & Company (BW)
Robbins, Karl, 35–36, 38, 56. *See also* Pinelands Company
Roberson, Jim, 130–31. *See also* Research Triangle Foundation (RTF)
Roberts, Patrick, 154–5. *See also* G1 Therapeutics (G-Zero Therapeutics)
Rooks, Liz, 216, 130. *See also* Research Triangle Foundation (RTF)
Ross, Deborah, 222. *See also* regional transit
Rothblatt, Martine, 125. *See also* United Therapeutics (UT)
Rowe, Roy, 17–18. *See also* Hodges, Luther Hartwell
Royall, Kenneth, 72, 100, 104, 134
Rudolph, Paul, 75–76. *See also* Burroughs Wellcome & Company (BW)
Ruvane, Joe, 121, 146. *See also* Glaxo

Sall, John, 109–10. *See also* SAS Institute
Samulski, Jude, 178–80, 240. *See also* AskBio
Sanford, Terry: 1960 election, 52–53; desegregation, 51–53; fundraising, 56; Jim

Hunt, 101; John F. Kennedy Jr., 53–54, 57; National Institute of Environmental Health Sciences (NIEHS), 57; North Carolina Biotechnology Center (NCBiotech), 87; public education, 47, 66
Sanofi-Aventis (Hoechst), 86, 112
SAS Institute, 32, 109–13, 115–16, 163
Saunders, William P., 35–36, 38, 56
Schmitt, Harvey, 71. *See also* Chamber of Commerce; desegregation in public education
semiconductor: Bob Davis, 114–15, 191–92; "Fairchild Eight," 98, 232–33; Microelectronics Center of North Carolina (MCNC), 81–82, 102–5, 109, 115, 192; Wolfspeed, 191–92, 246
Shaffer, Christy, 76–77, 79, 157
Sharp, Phillip Allen, 206. *See also* Nobel Prize
Sharpless, Ned, 152–56, 159. *See also* G1 Therapeutics (G-Zero Therapeutics)
Shope, Gary, 206–7. *See also* Biogen; Research Triangle Foundation (RTF)
silicon carbide, 115–16, 191, 245–46. *See also* Cree (Wolfspeed)
Simpson, George L., Jr.: background, 22–23, 25–26; on creation of new industries, 26, 28, 237; George Watts Hill, 32, 36; Gertrude Cox, 32–33; hiring, 22–23, 25; marketing Research Triangle Park, 26–28, 30, 36, 127, 220; Pearson Stewart, 29, 48
Sir Walter Hotel: January 9, 1959, address, 1, 38–39
Smith, Brian, 224. *See also* regional transit
Smith, David R., 200–201. *See also* Evolv; Kymeta
Smith, Stephen, 239–40. *See also* Volumetrics Medical Imaging
Smith, Wade, 68–69. *See also* desegregation in public education
Solid Biosciences, 182. *See also* AskBio
SonoVascular, 203
Sphinx Pharmaceuticals, 121–22, 156, 159
Stafford, Paula Brown, 112–14. *See also* Quintiles (IQVIA)
Stannett, Vivian, 41, 45. *See also under* Research Triangle Institute (RTI)
Starling, William, 203. See also SonoVascular
start-ups, 87, 238; AgTech, 165–66, 168; Council for Entrepreneurial Development (CED), 120–21, 123–24; culture, 108–9, 116–17, 119–20, 233; NCBIO (NCLifeSci), 177; North Carolina Innovative Development for Economic Advancement (NC IDEA), 105; North Carolina Technology Development Authority (TDA), 123–26; venture capital, 83, 119–20, 126, 193, 202–3
statistics, 26, 32–33, 41, 109, 112
Stein, Josh, 210
Stevens, Blake, 167, 204. *See also* Alexandria Real Estate (ARE); Avalo AI
Stevens, Richard, 222. *See also* regional transit
Stewart, Pearson, 29, 38, 48–49, 61, 127–30, 216, 218
Stone, Brad: *Amazon Unbound*, 190
Stranger Things, 214. *See also* Duffer brothers
Strum, Jay, 154–56, 159. *See also* G1 Therapeutics (G-Zero Therapeutics)
Sunbelt, 2, 13, 234
supercomputer, 103–5
Sussenguth, Ed, 105. *See also* IBM (International Business Machines Corporation)
Sykes, Richard, 78. *See also* Glaxo
Syngenta (Ciba-Geigy), 92–93, 161, 163, 246–47
Szulik, Matthew, 187. *See also* Red Hat

tax: base, 49, 72; incentives, 22, 37, 47, 172, 192; rates, 149, 226, 236; Research and Science Parks district, 130; transit, 147, 221–24; unitary, 100
Taxol (Paclitaxel), 34, 42–44, 248. *See also* Wall, Monroe E.; Wani, Mansukh
TDA (North Carolina Technology Development Authority), 123–26
technology centers, 4; commercialization, 162; comparison with Research Triangle Park, 2, 107–8, 119, 126, 162, 212, 236–37; information technology, 99, 102; life science, 165; lifestyle, 135, 143, 224; relationship with academia, 2, 11–12, 108, 232–33; start-ups, 108, 119; venture capital, 2, 115, 121
Teer, Robb, 137. *See also* Nello Teer Company
telecommunications industry: boom, 98, 142, 202; decline, 141–42, 185, 188; dot .com bubble, 142–43, 150–51, 185, 187; rise, 98–99, 105–7
Terman, Fred, 232
Textile Protection and Comfort Center (TPACC), 247
Thorp, Clay, 122–23, 155–58. *See also* Hatteras Venture Partners

Tolson, Norris, 161–62, 174. *See also* North Carolina Biotechnology Center (NCBiotech)
TPACC (Textile Protection and Comfort Center), 247
transgender legislation, 190–91
transgenic plants, 90–93, 246–47. *See also* Chilton, Mary-Dell
Triangle Universities Computation Center (TUCC), 59, 100–101, 104, 106–7, 124
TUCC (Triangle Universities Computation Center), 59, 100–101, 104, 106–7, 124

Ulanch, Paul, 164. *See also* North Carolina Biotechnology Center (NCBiotech)
Umstead, William B., 14, 17–19, 21, 49–50
United Therapeutics (UT), 76, 125–26, 243–44
Universal Product Code (UPC), 99–100
university commercialization programs, 197–204
University of North Carolina at Chapel Hill, (UNC): computer science department, 58–59, 100; Gene Therapy Center, 178, 184; Institute of Government, 50; Research Triangle, 12, 54; role in Park formation, 28; staff, 85, 118, 169, 184, 210; start-ups, 109; students, 15, 32, 37, 54; Triangle University Computing Center (TUCC), 59, 100–101
U.S. Sports Festival, 132–33
UT (United Therapeutics), 76, 135–26, 243–44

Vaden, Ted, 102
Vane, John, 124. *See also* epoprostanol; Nobel Prize: winners
Velleca, Mark, 157–58. *See also* G1 Therapeutics (G-Zero Therapeutics)
venture capital, 158–59, 187; firms, 121–23, 155–59, 193; presence in Research Triangle Park, 64, 121–23, 159, 193, 204, 238
Vincent, Jim, 206. *See also* Biogen
Volumetrics Medical Imaging: Model 1, 239–40
von Ramm, Olaf, 239–40. *See also* Volumetrics Medical Imaging
Voorhees, Walker, Smith, Smith & Haines, 48
Vouk, Mladen, 106

Wake County public school system, 149–51, 225–26. *See also* desegregation in public education
Wake Forest, 226–29
Walker, Jarrett, 222–23. *See also* regional transit
Wall, Monroe E., 43–45, 248. *See also* campthothecin; Taxol (Paclitaxel)
Wani, Mansukh, 43–45, 248. *See also* campthothecin; Taxol (Paclitaxel)
Watson, Tom, Jr., 58–61, 101. *See also* IBM (International Business Machines Corporation)
Weddle, Rick, 148. *See also* Research Triangle Foundation (RTF)
Wellcome, Henry, 73, 77, 79. *See also* Burroughs Wellcome & Company (BW)
White, Tom, 130. *See also* Chamber of Commerce
Williams, Joel Lawson, 42. *See also* Research Triangle Institute (RTI)
Wilson, NC, 211
Wolfspeed (Cree), 114–16, 191–92, 245–46. *See also* Cree (Wolfspeed)
Wong, Kwok-Kin, 153. *See also* G1 Therapeutics (G-Zero Therapeutics)
workforce development: 172, 189, 233–34; Biomanufacturing Training and Education Center (BTEC), 162, 173–74, 176, 206–7, 211; Biomedical Research Institute and Technical Enterprise (BRITE), 236–37; BioNetwork, 176; BioWork, 207, 211; Eli Lilly & Company, 211–12; Golden Leaf Foundation (GLF), 173, 176, 210–11; Industrial Education Centers, 24, 47; NCBioImpact, 211

xenotransplantation, 126, 243–44. *See also* United Therapeutics (UT)
Xiao, Xiao, 178–79, 240. *See also* AskBio

York, Smedes, 131, 216
York, Willie M., 47, 61, 99, 131
York Properties, 131. *See also* York, Smedes; York, Willie M.
Young, Bob, 186–87. *See also* Red Hat

zoning, 48, 61, 148, 206, 216